MAURIAC, Claude. The other de Gaulle; diaries, 1944-1954, tr. by M. Budberg and G. Latta. John Day, 1973. 378p il 73-7413. 12.95. ISBN 0-381-98253-X

The diaries of Claude Mauriac, son of Francois Mauriac, shed new light on the riddle of de Gaulle. From his vantage point as the head of de Gaulle's personal secretariat, beginning shortly after the liberation of Paris in 1944 and ending in 1948, we are given an intimate glimpse of the General's personality, problems, and policies that is frequently missing from other treatments of the man who considered himself to be France. The problems of establishing a provisional government and drafting a new constitution, the efforts at gaining an equal place in the Allied wartime and postwar councils, the anonymity of the years following his resignation are all illuminated. Additionally, however, the author provides tidy vignettes of postwar France that recapture the tenor of the times — the trials of Pétain and the Vichy collaborationists, the petty bickerings of Fourth Republic politicians, and the struggle to regain a role for France in the international community. Excellent illustrations; no index, which is especially regrettable for a book of this nature. Recommended for upper-level undergraduate and graduate libraries.

Diaries 1944-1954

The Other
de Gaulle

CLAUDE MAURIAC

DIARIES 1944-1954

The Other de Gaulle

*translated by Moura Budberg
and Gordon Latta*

The John Day Company/An Intext Publisher
New York

The publishers wish to thank the following people
for their co-operation in supplying the illustrations

AGENCE FRANCE PRESS 14, 58
ASSOCIATED PRESS 6, 12, 13
PRIVATE COLLECTION ARNO BREKER 17
CAMERAPRESS 1, 2, 3, 4, 5, 9, 23, 25, 27, 35, 43, 45
KEYSTONE 10, 11, 16, 18, 19, 20, 21, 22, 24, 28, 29,
    31, 32, 34, 44, 49, 51, 52, 54
COURTESY CLAUDE MAURIAC 14
POPPERFOTO 8, 30, 33, 36, 37, 38, 39, 40, 41, 46,
    48, 50, 53
RADIO TIMES HULTON PICTURE LIBRARY 15, 26, 42,
    47, 55, 56
UNITED PRESS INTERNATIONAL 7, 57

Illustrations 1–22 appear between pages 128–129
Illustrations 23–58 appear between pages 256–257

Diaries 1944-1954

The Other
de Gaulle

1944

On heady days like these, the Diary has to be put aside. I can, however, make a few brief notes.

11.00 *a.m.* Square Saint-German-des Prés, in a khaki shirt, with my F.F.I. armband, as some Allied tanks are halted alongside the boulevard, and others drive past cheered by the crowds.

In the Place de la Concorde this morning, a soldier in Leclerc's Division, his hands still black with smoke, stands in front of his burntout tank, describing yesterday's attack. Part of the motorized division are camping in the Tuileries Garden. It is sad to read the French 'Renault' trademark on a wrecked German tank. Some people, unaffected by the excitement, are carefully picking up souvenirs of the German retreat (feld-grau capes, etc.).

Go to the P.C. where the company has been given a rendezvous at 12.00. (There has already been a moving speech by Captain Morel followed by a fine Marseillaise.) Between 10.20 and 10.35 at the War Ministry, the sacred portals of which are thrown open to me, I pay a brief visit to my friend Claude Guy who told me on the telephone yesterday that he was A.D.C. to General de Gaulle. Both the place and its guardians most impressive. Lieutenant Guy's appointment obviously very important, but he still remains the Claude of the old days. He shows me the room where General de Gaulle spent the night – pyjamas on the unmade bed, butter and jam on the breakfast tray left untouched. Claude slept in the adjoining room. He talks to me of the General with deep respect. After giving me an enormous carton of American cigarettes and two tins of food, he says goodbye. We bump into a general whom at first I take to be de Gaulle, and to whom he introduces me. It is General Juin.*

Yesterday, at this time, at the Saint-André-des-Arts crossroads where the rues de l'Ancienne-Comédie, Buci and Mazarine meet, I watched the unexpected arrival and long marchpast of the Leclerc Division. And, only a few minutes before that, the barricade at the outposts of the

9

Senate was still in German hands. Unarmed but menaced from time to time by bursts of rifle-fire, I felt a pang at the idea of dying on such a day.

38 *Avenue Théophile Gautier*

Midnight. Marchpast with F.F.I. of our P.C. from the Pont-Neuf to the Gare St Lazare, then from there to the rue de Rivoli. I am exhausted, but I will just mention the drive of General de Gaulle down the rue de Rivoli in a fast-moving car. He is wildly cheered. Soon after I leave Jean Blanzat,* get into an American lorry.

There are simultaneous bursts of rifle-fire from all the roofs around us. Under the lorry, surrounded by death, on the very edge of death myself, remain very lucid. Behind me a man is spitting cascades of blood. The bullets whistle and hit. I take a chance during a lull to cross the road and slip under the arcades where an intense panic reigns which grips me. I finally reach a side-street . . . Shooting continues sporadically from one roof to another. (There were even some shots in Notre Dame, where de Gaulle was attending a Service of Thanksgiving.) Dinner with three soldiers from the Leclerc Division who already cease to make much impression on me. Got home at 11.00, dead-tired. And then there is a German bombardment. Jean and I go down to the shelter. We have only just come back. The night sky of this beflagged Paris is red from the light of burning houses. A telephone call from Claude Guy, very official, minimizing today's incidents, obviously according to instructions. Offers me a position with General de Gaulle. I reply that I do not deserve such an honour. Besides, I do not want it.

What a day! At the Pont-Neuf, people were dancing on the pavement between an American armoured vehicle and the barricade, while shooting went on in the adjacent streets. Saw a woman with a shaven head, roughly handled and booed by a vicious crowd. Whatever she may have done, such insults and outrages are despicable. All that deserves to be treated at length. But it is not the moment. Besides, I'm at the end of my tether. And, once again, this is only a notebook.

Sunday, 27 August, 1944

Go to the War Ministry at 8.30; Claude Guy, snowed under, begs me to help him out. I accept, unofficially and temporarily. A much too luxurious office where I have to reply to personal letters addressed to the General.

9.30 *a.m.* General de Gaulle comes into my office to find me alone in it. I introduce myself. He looks tired and greets me with a polite and casual weariness. The whole situation is so extraordinary that I am past being moved. The Allied Generals, Eisenhower, Montgomery and Bradley, are expected. They are coming incognito. Am very anxious about my father who is still in an area where the enemy have not been mopped up (Vémars) and has already had three articles in the Paris papers.

10.30 *a.m.* Still in the office adjoining that of General de Gaulle, who comes in from time to time. Claude Guy dictates in front of me the very confidential military and political report on the conversation which has just taken place between Eisenhower and de Gaulle in his presence. He was the only interpreter. I move to another office. The new premises are more discreet.

3.00 *p.m.* I have just had luncheon in a luxurious dining-room, its walls covered in armour. I was alone in the huge room with two head waiters to look after me. I had forgotten the existence of such delicious and copious meals.

Pierre Brisson* came here this morning on behalf of my father. Nothing can be done for him at the moment, as the area is still occupied. I'm living in a dream in which I do not recognize myself nor the life around me. Hardly slept at all last night because of a second air-raid. And there is so much work to be done.

Claude Guy talks to me about the General, about his character (which sounds as though it resembles my father's), his culture, nobility, etc.

A day of exhausting heat and hard work, summarizing the already large, though not yet voluminous, correspondence addressed to General de Gaulle. People lose no time asking for jobs, making the most of their activity or non-activity. An anonymous letter denouncing 'collaborating' officers; two lots of poems; and some very long-winded letters . . . Most of them likeable, all the same.

8.00 *p.m.* Am introduced to General Koenig, head of the F.F.I. and Military Governor of Paris. Mannerless but unaffected and relaxed. Some not very pleasant remarks about sons of great men who may or may not be capable of drafting letters better than other people. In fact he is referring to André Mauriac.

Yesterday there was still some shooting from the block opposite. But today the whole quarter is guarded and sealed-off by an imposing body of police.

At home, 1.20 a.m. I am noting for the Diary to come the following events of this memorable day. (I really feel I am dreaming.) Late dinner in the canteen with some black soldiers, some of Leclerc's men and

11

my two secretaries (one of them a splendid girl from the Resistance). The meal which seems to us and is Pantagruelian – composed entirely of tinned food. (The Algerians appear blasé.) Afterwards went back to the office. But the electricity goes off as it does all over Paris. And here, in the residence of the Head of State, nothing has been provided for. We are participating in the first hours of a new régime. Claude Guy takes the only existing oil lamp to General de Gaulle who, it appears, thanks him pleasantly and patiently – which he would not have done in the same circumstances at Algiers. Claude (the 'Lieutenant Guy' whose name is on every pair of lips in the house) jostles my little secretary who bursts into tears and has to be consoled by me in the darkness, as the gothic towers of Saint-Clothilde are silhouetted against the nocturnal sky.

"You must remember that we are working for General de Gaulle . . ."

"I've worked for him for four years but I shan't go on. It's not the same any more . . ."

Then Claude Guy, calming down and allowing himself his first relaxed moments of the day, tells us, beside the window of his office, the story of de Gaulle's epic journey from Cherbourg to Paris. As his A.D.C., he was in the General's car. He described the enthusiasm of the crowds, the moving speech in a certain town, liberated but destroyed, the General's rashness in ignoring the most elementary precautions, which might have got him killed twenty times over yesterday (a burst of rifle-fire met him just as he was entering the Ministry).

And suddenly the door opens – the door to the glamorous office – and there appears, lamp in hand, the figure of General de Gaulle, hero of the wonderful adventure which France is experiencing. He addresses a few kindly, unimportant words to us, then goes off to bed, so alone and forsaken, this man on whom the thoughts of all France are focused tonight (and whom by pure chance I am seeing in the flesh), so alone in this great dark palace, where only the shadows of the guards flit about . . .

While Claude Guy is busy in the courtyard trying to find a car to take me home, with an official badge to boot (nothing can surprise me now) and the young Keller (the name of the heroic secretary from the Resistance), is still overwhelmed by the spectacle of the General's sudden appearance, I wonder why I should have been chosen – I, together with this girl who really deserves this consecration of her activities – to represent the fervour of the French people before the saviour of France.

Knowing that the War Ministry is one of the primary objectives of the German bombers – and reflecting on the possibilities (now, admittedly reduced) of an attempt on his life, increases my pride. One may die after hours like these. But let us live, if possible, through the sequel to the dream.

Monday, 28 August, 1944

To the astonishment of the household the car with the official badges comes to fetch me at 8.30.

Details given me by Claude Guy of the General's journey from Rambouillet to Paris; the General refuses the armoured car recommended to him, under the pretext that it belonged to Pierre Laval*, and insists on an open car. He blows up at Claude Guy for having provided four motorized machine-gunners, who should have been on the spot as though by accident, and has them sent away. A woman in a sort of trance, with a child in her arms, stands in the middle of the road, gazing passionately at the General and compels the car to stop.

9.30 *a.m.* Saw, seated in an armchair waiting to be received by the General, Admiral d'Argenlieu*, whose appearance is far from ecclesiastic. Am introduced to him soon after.

Claude Guy has just handed me the dossier, marked *The Taking of Paris*, to be filed. Very moving documents. Letter of General Leclerc – written in his own hand – to General de Gaulle:

"23 *August*, 1944, 1.30 *p.m.*

"General,

Trévoux* has just got here and tells me that you are in Chartres. I am therefore sending you Captain Janney to liaise. I have just reached Rambouillet with a small advance detachment of a few cars. Unfortunately my divisional troops cannot get here before this evening.

"Guilleton, whom I sent ahead to achieve whatever he could, has come into contact with quite a number of Germans and lost a tank near Trappes. The F.F.I. may have liberated the centre of Paris by now, but the perimeter is still strongly held by tanks, anti-tank missiles, mines, etc.

"I shall therefore go into action tomorrow morning at dawn.

Respectfully,"

9.00 *p.m.* Still in the office and shall be for quite a time yet, without having dined, after a rather full day (relatively) – during which I only had one glimpse of General de Gaulle.

We decipher the General's illegible writing. He is growing impatient and already wants to read the typescript of what he has only just scribbled down. There are three of us dealing with it: Claude Guy, Colonel de Rancourt* and myself . . . And every now and then we have to appeal to M. Palewski* for help.

At home, midnight. Left the rue Saint-Dominique at 11 p.m., after having gone through, with Claude Guy, the hand-written comments which the General has put in the margin of my summary of letters received, which I had presented to him. I have to draft my replies in the light of these notes. The sirens go off while I am cycling back to Auteuil and there is the sound of gunfire. Telephone conversation with Pierre Brisson about my father's position, which is causing me considerable anxiety. Saw young Colonel de Chevigné* at the Ministry who played an active part in the taking of Paris. All these generals and colonels under forty . . .

The General seems to me to be in danger. He is not sufficiently guarded. The house opposite the Ministry has been ransacked and inquisitive faces have appeared at its windows throughout the day. Guard-mounting troops inside the Ministry. White gloves, plumes but no, or very few weapons. Outside, complete disappearance of all the troops posted there yesterday. The warning is still on. Nevertheless, I am going to bed. I have forgotten to mention my call on the President of the Consistory, rue de l'Oratoire, to whom I had to convey the General's apologies for having been unable to attend one of the ceremonies. American jeeps are bowling along through beflagged Paris. One has got almost beyond being surprised at anything.

Thursday, 29 August, 1944

Took down a long report from General Koenig's A.D.C. relating to this afternoon's march-past. Many points of friction with the Americans who have the cheek to invite the General, who is, after all, at home and Chief of State. From my office I see the General, accompanied by M. Cerat and Claude Guy, get into the car to go to the Concorde. Remain alone in the A.D.C.'s office. Electricians are busy in the adjoining office, the General's, with all the doors open. Anybody could hide anything in it. So much negligence makes one shudder. The General returns from the ceremony at the Concorde and shakes my hand. Meet a tall young naval lieutenant on the stairs. It is the General's son, Philippe de Gaulle, who has been in the fighting and is going back there (in a tank). Claude Guy a bundle of nerves. It is difficult to work with him. But our friendship compels him to be reasonably polite to me. "Nothing is of any importance. When one has understood that, one is saved," General Koenig said good-naturedly the other day when I was present.

Because I am taking Guy's place in his office, I have to introduce myself to a humble little man, M. Luizet, the new Chief Commissioner of Police, dropped by parachute a few days ago. Behind the office where Paul Reynaud* used to broadcast his radio talks (Palewski's, whom I am provisionally replacing) I have a serious telephone conversation concerning the destitution of a high functionary in the Ministry of Finance.

11.00 p.m. The General is going to record the speech which will be broadcast at midnight. The three of us have just finished going through it, Claude Guy dictating directly to the typist. "It is now four days since the Germans who held the capital capitulated to the French. It is now four days since Paris was liberated. An infinite joy, an immense pride has swept over the nation . . ."

One seems to hear already, so essentially his own is the rhythm of these sentences, the voice which has yet to give expression to them. The assonance of 'capital' and 'capitulated' struck Gorse* and myself as unfortunate. Claude Guy has just drawn the General's attention to it: after saying that it was unimportant he has changed 'capital' to Paris. And here comes M. Massigli*, who has arrived in Paris today. While I am introducing myself to him, I can hear the General's muffled voice reading his speech in the next room. Beneath my feet, the broadcasting cable; beneath my eyes, the General's manuscript which I read in time with the voice uttering it – all very moving. Then Guignebert, Secretary-General at the Ministry of Information, emerges from the General's study.

12.10 a.m. I am still at the Ministry. Claude Guy is waiting for the General to go to bed before following his example and he wants me to stay with him. Palewski is pacing up and down the office talking brilliantly. During one of his brief absences, Guy discloses the absorbing story of General Leclerc's insubordination: thrusting ahead to Paris contrary to the orders received from the High Command.

12.25 a.m. General de Gaulle has just seen Massigli to the threshold of his door. I am sleepy but dare not leave without having seen Claude, who is in with Palewski. The glance that the General has just given me . . . What an extraordinary adventure of mine this is. And my parents know nothing about it – not even that I was at the barricades during the insurrection. Le Bourget was only captured yesterday after hard fighting. Vémars seems likely to be right in the battle zone.

1.00 a.m. At home. General de Gaulle opened the door of his office once more and asked me to go and tell M. Palewski and M. Massigli

15

that he wanted to see them again. So I went to fetch them. And I pedalled along the wet asphalt through a silent, dark, deserted Paris. And then to bed . . . But, in the silence, one can hear the distant rumbling of guns.

Wednesday, 30 *August*, 1944

Met M. Coulet, Government High Commissioner for Normandy. A poor woman, who was collecting wood and ran away when a guard called her, was killed in the Ministry garden. A dull day: nothing of note to record and exhaustion resulting from lack of sleep and a crushing burden of work.

7.30 *p.m.* Great news brought by the hairdresser who lodges at my grandmother's. Vémars was liberated this morning. Fighting took place in the garden (unconfirmed). In the evening, towards midnight, had a long, very strained conversation with Claude Guy – owing to our tiredness and my pride.

Thursday, 31 *August*, 1944

The Presidential car comes to fetch my brother Jean and myself at 7.30. Traces of recent fighting at Le Bourget. We are slightly nervous lest the road may not have been completely mopped up. Arrived without incident at Vémars, where there were still a number of Germans yesterday morning. The fighting had come to a halt on the outskirts of the village. Emotion and delight. Father, Maman, Luce and Grandmama dragged out of bed. How much there was to talk about! By 11 a.m. my father is at home and I am at the rue Saint-Dominique. (On our return journey there were American soldiers all along the road, searching for mines with a kind of magnetic rake.) (My father's joy on seeing Paris free again) – (His astonishment concerning Claude Guy. "Everything happens as if we were dreaming . . . ")

General de Gaulle invites me to join his table. Six places – Captain Schumann (the 'spokesman of Fighting France' whom we have heard on the B.B.C. over the last four years), Captain Teyssot, Lt. Col. de Rancourt, Claude Guy and myself. The General's eyes and eye-lids – impassive but there is fire beneath the cold crust. It is a look that burns. Glacial, distant but with occasional sparks of corrosive irony. Schumann questions him a little too insistently. The General amused at first, finally lapses into silence. There are long pauses.

"When I think, General, that some Frenchmen – even intelligent ones, what is more Gaullists – still believe that you bought France at the price of her empire . . . "

De Gaulle replies: "Remember that they (the Americans and the British), remember that they will only leave when we chuck them out . . ."

Turning to the war, he says that the Germans, as far as can be seen, are no longer pursuing any coherent strategy. (Their obsessive determination to cling on to certain positions which are clearly indefensible and which it is pointless to defend, is proof of this.) However, he believes that Hitler still hopes to hold out until the winter and to profit from the relative lull during that season to perfect secret weapons which could alter the situation to a considerable extent if put into action. He says that their new fighter planes are superior to any other. (But then there is such a *material* superiority on the Allies' side.) When he feels called on to defend French sovereignty, the General is swiftly up in arms. I can see him, when merely quoting his answer to Roosevelt's invitation to come and see him, on his last visit to Algiers; I can see him draw himself up with an immense, pervading pride:

"I sent a reply saying that I was expecting him – but he never came . . ."

The last few words were uttered ironically. De Gaulle adds that Churchill and Roosevelt will certainly be coming to Paris in the near future and will no doubt invite him, as if they were not, in fact, his guests.

"I shall tell them that I shall be at home . . . all day . . ."

On the subject of America's complicity in the plot which Edouard Herriot's* refusal frustrated, which consisted of persuading the Assemblée Nationale to welcome the Allies instead of the Fighting French; and on the subject of the seven French divisions on the southern front against three Allied ones – with the Americans barely mentioning French participation – de Gaulle stresses the mistrust with which Anglo-Saxons inspire him. We also talk of Leclerc's recklessness. X says that this courage is physical in origin; that Leclerc does not know what it is to be afraid. De Gaulle stares fixedly at the speaker, shakes his head and says:

"That would be too easy. He dominates himself."

After a pause he adds with a smile: "In fact, he's a rabbit." (All this written down in a hurry, very tired, by the dim light of a candle at 12.40.)

This evening Claude Guy was able to leave the General at 10.00. He paid a visit to my father. A fascinating conversation about de Gaulle, whom he knows so intimately, about his courage (he, too, dominates himself, but he certainly risked being killed twenty times during the first two days after his arrival); about his political flair, etc. It would take up fifteen pages of my Diary to record it, but I am abominably tired. Arrival of several 'Algerian commissioners' today at the Ministry: Diethelm (War) and Pleven (Colonies).

Friday, 1 September, 1944

My father is invited to lunch with the General. Saw General Leclerc, sitting taciturn, with a stick in his hand in the A.D.C.'s office. Masses of work. Saw General de Larminat* and Jean Marin – who up till then had only been a voice on the B.B.C. Saw Admiral d'Argenlieu, M. Diethelm, etc., again.

My brother Jean, who has just joined the French Press Agency, wanders about the Ministry in search of news. Last night we faced the prospect of there still being a long war to come: now, we suddenly hear of a lightning attack by the Allies. They have almost reached Sedan and the Siegfried Line has been battered from the air (probably by the squadrons which flew over Paris this morning for more than two hours).

Am separated from a liberated Paris by this cloistered existence. I only see the city in the morning when I go to my office by bicycle or car, depending on the day. American tanks on the look-out at the corners of bridges; small jeeps flying the flags that still surprise us and gladden our eyes. Have dictated today about fifty thank-you telegrams in response to the congratulations which the General receives from the four corners of the earth with whom we are now in communication again; as many summaries of letters received; and a number of letters as well. All this amidst the noise and disarray of a small room where four typewriters are hammering away. Since yesterday I take my meals in the officers' mess, not in the staff canteen, from which Guy indignantly extricated me. The meals are excellent and copious. (Forgotten wonders: meat and coffee.) It compensates for the tiredness and lack of sleep. And I no longer even mention – one so quickly becomes accustomed – the tall body dressed in khaki, the figure of the General, of which I catch a glimpse several times a day between two doors.

9.30 *p.m.* The General, returning from dinner, passes through Claude Guy's office with Philippe de Gaulle, where I am alone, working. I get up. He shakes my hand, tells me that my father lunched with him.

"I found him full of fire," he adds, spreading out his arms in a wide gesture, and passes on his way, a cigar between his teeth.

Claude Guy says to me about François Mauriac this morning in front of de Gaulle: "He looked like someone who comes across the Lord God in flesh and blood."

11.15 *p.m.* Still here. Received from M. Cerat, Commissioner for the Occupied Territories, an important report which I dictated simultaneously to a typist. It concerns a revolutionary pamphlet from the Resistance groups which the General has decided to censure. The F.F.I. are already giving him a lot of trouble, and one can foresee serious political difficulties.

12.20 *p.m.* I have just been in to the General to have the correspondence signed. Stood behind him, on his left. He decides not to censure the questionable pamphlet.

"It's only a suggestion. People can suggest anything they like to me. For instance, that every man should be compelled to wear bowler hats . . ."

I remained half an hour with him in the huge office with its luxurious tapestries. He went through everything very carefully, added corrections in his own hand, explained and made brief comments while scribbling his unreadable footnotes. (Claude Guy has just told me that the General is pleased with my work and wishes to keep me with him.)

Yesterday at table, when I was present, the General said in a pessimistic tone:

"Hitler is supposed to have said to Antonescu* a few months ago: 'In a few weeks I shall have stabilized my Eastern front. Then I'll turn back to the West.' And he did in fact, stop the Soviet advance. And he is quite capable of holding on in the West until he has finally perfected his new weapons."

Guy tells me that the General made the same remarks this morning, quoting Hitler at Auboyneau*, but then suddenly exclaimed:

"My opinion on the war has entirely changed since this morning. Judging by the latest news, Germany is on the verge of collapse . . ."

1.00 *a.m.* I have just got home, tired but happy. Whatever it may cost me (the loss of all private life) I have decided to give all I have to General de Gaulle, my time, for a start. Who could have foreseen, only a fortnight ago . . .

Saturday, 2 September, 1944

This deeply-moved man, who emerges from General de Gaulle's office, leaning on Georges Bidault (President of the National Council of the Resistance), is one of the leaders of the Resistance, recently escaped from a Nazi prison, for whom the sight of his supreme chief has been too much.

The missing ministers have arrived from Algiers. I have just seen the General leave for the first Cabinet meeting; he walked through Lt. Guy's office, where I was standing in for him. Robert Victor*, who was also with de Gaulle – as we gathered from Philippe Henriot's* editorials during the Occupation – has arrived from Algiers and dines in mess (with Courcel*, Claude Guy, etc.). He too has a post in the Cabinet.

General de Gaulle wants to have Mass celebrated tomorrow at the Ministry. I have been told to find a priest and think of Father Danielou. He stammers with emotion and joy on the telephone.

Sunday, 3 September, 1944

A console-table, between the two windows opening on to the garden, serves as an altar. The blackened portrait of M. de Louvois presides at the celebration. Father Danielou officiates, assisted by Captain Gudin du Pavillion. The General has scorned the armchair which I had provided for him and taken a plain chair. He is alone in the front row. I stand behind him, with Gaston Palewski, Head of the Civil Cabinet on my right, and Lt. Col. de Rancourt, Head of the Military Cabinet, and the A.D.C. on my left. Add a captain and you have the whole congregation. De Gaulle, who has demanded this Mass, takes part in it, displaying no emotion other than mild boredom. Not a gesture, beyond the ritual sign of the Cross at the beginning and at the end. In the middle of the Mass he turns to me, makes a sign that he is about to speak and looks out of the window. I promptly imagine that he has spotted a sniper in a tree. But the General, in a voice well above a whisper, draws my attention to a squadron of Allied planes, shimmering in the blue sky.

During the lunch hour, I escape and eat in a restaurant with André Roussin*. Then spend a few minutes on the terrace of the Deux-Magots. It is my first outing in a week. Women forgotten . . . How wonderful! Back in the rue Saint-Dominique by 3.30. Have seen Jiri Mucha*, another friend snatched from the void; Jiri Mucha in R.A.F. uniform.

Have summoned a number of ministers by telephone on the General's behalf. The audiences went on and on last night, one after another, and I had to leave without getting the correspondence signed. This embryonic ministerial reshuffle is the main business of the day. The man next to me at table asks his neighbour "When did you leave Algiers?", and the answer is "This morning." I find it astounding, still unable to get used to being in communication once again with the rest of the world. Tired tonight, completely exhausted. Impossible to get home any earlier. But how desperately I need sleep!

Monday, 4 September, 1944

Gaston Palewski has entrusted me with the task of finding M. Billoux* (one of the only two communists in the present government) at all costs in order to hand him personally a letter from General de Gaulle. In the dining room at the Hotel Claridge, where I run him to ground, his face drops. Proof, no doubt, that he is not included in the new ministerial set-up . . . Altogether, this reshuffle does not seem to be going too well. I have just heard Claude Guy telling Courcel on the telephone that "It would be advisable to find a residence outside Paris in case the General should be compelled to retire tomorrow morning." I know that the Cabinet would like the news to get around. Telephone call from Paul Valéry*, the General's guest this evening, who asks me to send a car for him. A visit from Claude Gallimard*. His object – to find Malraux.

Yesterday, so I hear, there were a few V1s over Paris. Went to collect Paul Valéry at his house by car. Towards 11.00, after the General has gone to bed, Guy tells me that the political situation has been very dangerous during the day, de Gaulle finding himself without communist support and therefore without a conceivable government. Claude praises the General's political flair which enables him to extricate himself from this ugly corner. Actually, he has decided for the moment not to enlarge his Cabinet, which emerges from the crisis with hardly any changes.

Tuesday, 5 September, 1944

Numerous arrests. The purity of the first days is already besmirched. All this was to be foreseen. All this, in a sense, was even necessary. But I feel that my duties prevent me from disassociating myself from certain of the excesses. I should never have accepted the position.

Lunch with the General, Philippe de Gaulle and a colonel and lieutenant-colonel in counter-espionage, Passy and Manuel. Also Claude Guy. I am the only civilian. The General explains that the American armies are advancing and blocking the British on their left and the French on their right in order to enter Germany on their own. He believes that a secret German-American agreement exists, providing for American entry into Germany, which would save the Reich the initial shock of a Soviet occupation. This agreement would also make it possible for the Wehrmacht to return to Reich territory to determine the fate of Himmler and other Nazis.

On the day Hitler hanged a Marshal he alienated the Wehrmacht for good and from then on they did their best to sabotage his policies.

This from de Gaulle, his eyes bright and cheerful in that stern face. We often exchange understanding glances. He requires deep understanding and complicity from those around him but without flattery. The two officers of the B.C.R.A.* give some interesting details about the Information Services and the part played by the F.F.I. in the French campaign. De Gaulle returns to the Herriot affair, engineered by the Americans who, once again, tried to pull the wool over his eyes.

"It all came to nothing; as usual they went against the force of circumstances . . ."

To which one of the colonels replies quoting someone or other: "General de Gaulle has brought the Allies from Munich to Munich."

There is a gleam of satisfaction in the General's eye, but he says: "It is not me, it is the force of circumstances . . ."

The General also tells us the reason for the promotions within the F.F.I. army being so widely and immoderately awarded. Dessert arrives. A large cigar is planted between his pursed lips. Dark shadows lie under his eyes. And once more I wonder why it should be I who am here instead of one of these thousands of Frenchmen whose faith, devotion and courage would have so much more merited this reward and honour.

All this took place in one of the State rooms, full of draperies, gilding and armour.

Dinner at the Peignots, where I again find Col. Passey and Lt. Col. Manuel, with whom I lunched this morning at the General's table.

11.45 p.m. Have just left the General who signed the letters which I handed to him and indicated the replies I should make to those received since our last session. He broke off to comment on the families, family connections, fortunes and behaviour of the signatories during the Occupation. When we had finished, he turned to me and asked:

"Well, what do you think of it all?"

When I remained prudently evasive he exclaimed:

"The Allies! They are betraying us and they are betraying Europe, the bastards! But I'll make them pay for it!"

There was a silence and he repeated:

"I'll make them pay for it!"

After another silence:

"What's more, they've already begun to pay, particularly the British. They say 'It's all the Americans', but the cowards only had to do what

I did. Letting the Americans take Brussels . . .! A pretty business! They would have taken Paris if I hadn't been there! Now they can come and cry on my shoulder . . ."

This man gives out an impression of clear-headed strength, shrewdness and intelligent courage. Perhaps that is what genius consists of. To my delight, found Mother at home. She had come up from Vémars for a few days. Stayed for a long time with her, sitting on the edge of her bed, in spite of the late hour.

Wednesday, 6 September, 1944

The work becomes more organized. I am very busy ensuring that there shall be official enquiries into all the more or less arbitrary arrests reported to me.

Spent twenty minutes at the Café Flore where I had not been since it reopened. Saw X who shook my hand with effusive friendliness. I assess the new importance which circumstances have given me by other people's reactions. Left the office early (11 p.m.).

Thursday, 7 September, 1944
Hôtel de la Guerre

10.30 *p.m.* I was in the middle of dinner at the officers' (and officials') table when I was told that General de Gaulle had invited me to join him. Actually the arrival of Lieutenant Philippe de Gaulle, who had not been expected, necessitated this extra place. Thus I was privileged to be present at a meal that assembled around the General: M. Flouret, the new Prefect of the Seine (but who and what is not new in these days?), M. Soustelle (Director General of 'Special Services') and his wife and Georges Duhamel*, very moved by his first meeting with the General, and Captain Gudin Pavillon, the General's A.D.C.

Dinner began with a few strained sentences, punctuated by the General's muffled 'hhmmms'. He was addressing Duhamel as *'cher maître'*. The *cher maître* was saying nothing and this restraint, resembling that of an awed, well-behaved child, was so different from his usual behaviour that I was astonished. I was afraid, nevertheless, that he would not be able to keep silent long – for I know him well – as though I were responsible for him, and felt directly affected by the opinion de Gaulle would form of him. Suddenly, the General – who, I already know from experience, does not miss an occasion to display his hostility towards the Allies – began to speak of 'this coalition in which everyone wages the same war while remaining aloof'. When Duhamel replied timidly

23

that it would seem to have always been the same in the past, the General, in a manner that might have been considered slightly bombastic had he not been so passionately sincere, contrasted – only by implication – the attitude of France towards the Americans in 1917, the Serbs, the Poles and the Belgians (during the Great War) – with that of the Allies opposing this same France today.

"To a defeated Belgium, we recognized her full and complete sovereignty and asked nothing of her . . . To the Americans we gave arms, planes and tanks – and we asked nothing of them."

"I fully understand," Duhamel answered – thus showing that he had grasped the innuendo (which drew smiles from me, which I felt were hardly according to protocol) "I fully understand, but don't you think, General, that it is precisely to the glory of France that she alone possesses that quality: lack of self-interest?"

De Gaulle concurred.

The General then asked M. Flouret: "And how are things in Paris, Monsieur le Préfet?" Flouret replied that everything was completely under control. The Métro would soon be working again. There was no reason for the Leclerc Division to remain. They would be missed but they were no longer needed. (In fact, Philippe de Gaulle, who is in the division, is off tomorrow.)

The conversation turned to the behaviour of the town during the rising. And there again, there was a reference to that or rather, those, whom no one likes to name:

"They expected to be the only ones on the barricades (*i.e.* the communists), but the whole of Paris was there, which did not suit them at all. Nevertheless, the plot was close to exploding and it was time, high time, that you appeared on the scene, General."

And de Gaulle replied, smiling at the Prefect of the Seine: "I was well aware of it; and that's why I came!"

When he speaks like this, his eyes light up and that fervid glance, full of irony and implication, searches out yours and holds it.

Then we passed on to the Parisians' behaviour under Occupation. Georges Duhamel, dropping his reserve – and thereby causing me considerable anxiety – spoke of his own personal behaviour, his own personal relationship with the occupying forces, his resistance and his courage. I knew these stories from his book, which was pulped, his squabbles with the Germans and the superb reply he made to an offensive Nazi official:

"I would remind you, Mr. Bremer, that you are speaking to one of the greatest French writers." Duhamel repeats this same remark at the top of his shaking voice, suddenly full and vibrant, while the General

24

listens politely but without enthusiasm. "Then he stood to attention!" The General smiles. Duhamel, in his usual way, pushed his spectacles up on his forehead before giving us an account of a fable he had written for *Le Figaro* under the Occupation and the allusions to the Germans, which it contained.

After speaking of last Thursday's two exclusions from the Academy (Bonnard and Hermant), and the one that nearly occurred today (Maurras) – but there were only six votes in favour to five against – which seemed insufficient "even to your father", Duhamel said turning to me, "to bind the whole lot of them", we came to Pétain's case. Duhamel explained that the Academy was unanimous in hoping that, where he was concerned, there should be a veil of silence.

De Gaulle agreed, and, when asked what he intended to do about the Marshal, replied, in a calm, grave voice:

"What can I do? I'll provide him with a residence somewhere in the south, where he'll wait till Death comes to fetch him."

These last words, by their meaning and the actual sound of them, unleashed such unexpected emotion in me that, in the midst of this huge, lofty room, panelled, gilded and hung with arms and tapestries, where I had the privilege of being seated at General de Gaulle's table, I almost burst into tears.

Then de Gaulle and Duhamel exchanged reminiscences about the Marshal which were all the more moving for being recalled without hatred or passion, but on both sides with a careful objectivity that was unpremeditated but only natural for men of justice. Duhamel said that Pétain's successor should speak of him in the Academy as if he had died in 1918. To which de Gaulle replied:

"I saw Pétain die . . It was in 1925."

And he explained that through pride, ambition and a certain weakness in the face of his advisors, who were urging him to action, he abdicated as of that date, which led him 'in the thirties to be a part of the fifth column'.

De Gaulle told several stories, among them one concerning a dedication he had himself made to the Marshal in one of his books, in which he spoke, or seemed to speak, of Pétain's glory in the past tense. "But do you really believe," Pétain had asked, far from pleased, "that my glory is at an end?"

(In regard to this dedication I, or rather, the General, received a letter from Plon, in which the publisher, very embarrassed, asked timidly – because of a forthcoming new edition – whether the General did not wish to make a few amendments 'particularly to the dedication'. De Gaulle, to whom I passed on this request, smiled, looked me straight in the eye and said: "It was to the Marshal that I dedicated this book." And he scribbled on the summary of the letter I had handed him, 'Yes, but not the dedication.')

Later the General declared that Pétain, in the 1914-18 war was not a strategist (he lacked the audacity for that) but a tactician, perhaps the only great tactician. Afterwards, he made a profound study of German military literature and developed an immense admiration for the war-like qualities of the men beyond the Rhine – qualities which his experience in the Great War had not led him to underestimate.

So much so that our defeat in 1940 seemed to him deserved, seemed to be evidence of those qualities, and this contributed in no small measure to his adopting the attitude we all know towards the Conqueror.

An explanation more honourable for the man in question than the other one which de Gaulle had also given a few moments previously.

It was impossible for him to recover power in victory so he waited for defeat in order to triumph.

The General arose and we moved to the other end of the dining-room. The distressing problem of prisoners, whom the Americans are already expecting to arrive in great numbers, was broached by de Gaulle; then the problem of the government in the face of the alarming political inexperience of the nation's new leaders: they come to power with no knowledge of business just at a time when France needs administration more than anything else, and, in addition, they lack any sense of statesmanship.

And when Duhamel congratulates him on his escape from death the other day and quotes the unanimous sentiments of the crowd on the subject, he says:

"The main thing is to hold elections. Then France will no longer need anyone."

To the question: "When do you expect them to take place?" he answers:

"If I knew that the war would last another three years, I would not wait. But it may only be a matter of three months, in which case *it would be better for everyone to be there.*"

At table he had mentioned the frequent meetings that Hitler is calling at the present time.

"When, in a besieged town, the military leader summons a conference of the leading citizens – among them the least bellicose, such as the mayor and the doctor – it certainly means that things are going badly for him."

26

And he again refers to the probable sabotage of the Nazi Party plans by the Wehrmacht.

Georges Duhamel, bringing up the subject very adroitly from a considerable distance, prepared to leave:

"If I have the honour, General, to see you again in a year's time, we shall both recall this evening with emotion. There will then be, it's impossible that there won't be, a very elaborate and detailed protocol and I shall know, for instance, the exact moment when I should leave and let you sleep . . ."

De Gaulle smiled, and glanced at his watch, saying that this too would no longer be allowed and that we were, indeed, living in astonishing, unprecedented days without convention or tradition. And when Duhamel got up, it was the signal to depart. With a glance, de Gaulle instructed me to accompany his guests to the door and we left them alone, him and his son, in the great deserted hall . . .

A few minutes later, having said goodbye to Duhamel (when we assured one another that it had been particularly moving to live through such moments together) I had another glimpse of de Gaulle and his son (who is going back to the Front tomorrow), as they passed through Claude Guy's office where I was at the moment.

Despite my tiredness, I have forced myself to write this Diary. 11.45p.m.

Friday, 8 September
38 Avenue Théophile Gautier

10.30 *p.m.* I have seen liberated Paris today for the first time. By that I mean for the first time since peace descended on the city, I have been out at an hour other than the first or last of the day. It was at 7.00 this evening, at the end of an exhausting day's work at the office. I decided to walk and get a breath of fresh air. A downpour had cleared the sky, in which three French fighters were flying at low altitude – yes, French, with good and true tricolour markings – oh, what a miracle! And over those beautiful buildings by Gabriel, damaged but already in the process of being restored, floated our three colours. And all along the rue de Rivoli, only a few days ago still besmirched with Nazi swastikas, hung our own blue, white and red flags. I wanted to kneel down, right there, in the middle of this magnificent square, so small under an immense sky, and yet greater than the world. I would have done it had I been alone.

In the rue Royale, decorated with various Allied colours, I saw the first British soldiers and even more Americans – on leave, I mean walking, strolling along, out of their vehicles. Am struck by the free and easy carelessness of their attire; not actually untidy but so unmilitary. Their uniforms resemble civilian workmen's clothes, anyway. 'It's a war of garage-hands,' de Gaulle is supposed to have said, though he denied it hotly when my father reminded him of it the other day.

As the General was dining in town I was able to leave the Cabinet early (9 p.m.). I went to the Sphinx, certain of finding all the American expatriates there. There were so many soldiers and so many of them drunk that there were very few women in the noisy crowd. One or two, however, moved about, with naked breasts, from hand to hand and mouth to mouth. Under their inelegant helmets (possessing none of the tragic beauty of the German variety), in their mechanics' overalls, chewing gum and keeping their heavy jaws in motion, gay as children, the American soldiers shouted to each other in their half-incomprehensible and wondrous language. The Blacks outnumbered the Whites, who, in spite of everything, resembled our own men. I was naïvely surprised to find that under the different exterior America was like France and felt alone in a foreign world and laughed at my own impressive little 'head of General de Gaulle's secretariat'. I felt transported – not into an American film, for nothing would have astonished me there, and I would have found myself expatriated in complete safety – but into the world which the American cinema describes, transposes and photographs: and the surprise lay in not being surprised . . .

On my way home, pedalling in the dark night of the blacked-out city, I whistled – for the first time as a liberated man. But how deeply we are affected by becoming accustomed to slavery! I cannot get used to liberty. My first reaction is always one of suspicion, and, in the face of this world that is suddenly presented to me, I am like a bird whose cage has been opened and who remains huddled in a corner of his cell, unable to bring himself to leave. The simile can be taken literally because it is a fact that, after five years of total isolation, we are resuming contact with the world. But, spiritually it is even more valid. These days, so ardently longed for, so obviously desired, are here. We are living them. But in our dazed state, we are scarcely able to savour them. Yes, I ought to have gone on my knees . . . My gratitude is infinite. Life will never bring me again a joy as total and pure. One must offer up thanks for having known it.

A very fine article of my father's in *Le Figaro* on the delicate problem of justice. Mother has returned to Vémars. Still no news of my sister Claire, nor of my brother-in-law, Alain Le Ray.

Sunday, 10 *September,* 1944

Mass, like that of last Sunday, beneath Louvois' portrait. As I could not get in touch with Father Danielou, a priest from St. Honoré-d'Eylau officiated.

At 11.30 I took the letters in for the General to sign (for the third time). He declaims in a cavernous voice a poem of Mme. de Noailles's (on the passage of time).

Monday, 11 *September,* 1944
War Ministry

On Saturday I had a visit from Georges Izard* who has just returned from La Charité-sur-Loire, still under occupation. He tells me of the general anxiety about de Gaulle's domestic policies. He is afraid that his present isolation, following upon a long exile, may render him particularly vulnerable to the attacks and conspiracies of his enemies, who are legion. According to Izard, the General should create, without further delay, a political party which would unite all French people of good will around him. I reply that de Gaulle represents France and cannot revive that fusion of Party and State of which Hitler furnished such a deplorable example. Izard seems to be embarrassed by his membership of the S.F.I.O.* I recognize in him again the same warmth, intelligence and ambition that made such an impression on me almost ten years ago, when I used to call on the young deputy that he then was at the Palais Bourbon.

There is a new Ministry under Jeanneny, former President of the Senate, which is a useful link with the past. One must not forget that neither the United States nor Britain have yet recognized the General's government, which might seem lacking in weight if the country were not behind it.

But France is not all one could wish. The General is the knot that keeps temporary friends united, who had nothing more in common than their hatred of the Occupier. Without de Gaulle, they would split up immediately.

Even his presence does not prevent those whom my father called in one of his recent articles in *Le Figaro,* the 'irreducibles' (those who more or less openly remain faithful to Vichy ideology, and whose number appears to be still considerable) and, on the other hand, the extremists, particularly the communists, from fighting secretly against the new government which already seems to have lost (in the minds of an important section of public opinion) the goodwill which it enjoyed under the Occupation and during the first days of Liberation.

My father is shattered by the violence of the anonymous letters provoked by his articles. He begs me today not to betray signs of pessimism. "Let the General's entourage, at least, display confidence. Over
the last few days, the anxiety and uncertainty have been increasing, and
the rue Saint-Dominique is one of the sources of the rumours that little
by little drown our hopes."

He does not feel at ease within the 'little citadel of *Le Figaro*'
and turns to his comrades in arms; those on *Lettres Françaises*, of which
the first non-clandestine number appeared yesterday with an important
article of his, attacking Maurras.

Tuesday, 12 September, 1944

9.00 *a.m.* Read the speech which the General will deliver this afternoon
at the Palais de Chaillot.

Yesterday saw the reopening of the main Métro lines. But electricity
is still only available for twenty minutes each evening.

Reply by the General to A, who represents the Government in the
Marseilles zone, when, he declares that he is uncertain of being able
to maintain order (related by Claude Guy):

"You distress me, A. You represent the State. You owe it to yourself
to fulfil your mission."

This was at dinner, the evening before last. I saw them both pass by,
on their way to the General's office, from which his muffled voice
emerged through the closed door. "Just as I thought," says Claude Guy.
"He is hauling A over the coals."

4.00 *p.m.* Sat beside my father at the Palais de Chaillot. Overwhelming moments. The General enters through a slit contrived in the red
section of the vast tricolour hangings. The Marseillaise interrupts the
immense ovations. Georges Bidault pays tribute to the dead. The
General's restrained speech is cold and wholly devoid of demagogy
(not even what would be considered the indispensable minimum by anyone but him). On his right, the President of the C.N.R. (Minister of
Foreign Affairs for the past two or three days), and Georges Bidault.
To his left, President Jeanneney. Outside, planes and flags against the
blue sky: one cannot get used to such delight.

These were my first hurried notes to which I must now come back. I
had obtained tickets for Luce, Jean and my father, with the last of
whom I sat in the first row of stalls. The orderly officers of the F.F.I.;
at the back of the stage an immense tricolour drapery on which a gold
Cross of Lorraine stands out in relief; the crowds that one knows are
gathered on the principal Paris squares to hear the ceremony broadcast;
the blue sky humming with our own planes; the flags, the rejoicing, and

to crown all, in the very hall of the Palais de Chaillot, this fervent audience, composed solely of men and women of the Resistance, awaiting the imminent miracle – the appearance of General de Gaulle after years of oppression, danger, shame and blood. One's heart was already pounding before anything had happened.

And suddenly he appeared in his khaki uniform, very tall and pale, and the ovations were unleashed only to be halted by a thundering Marseillaise. The crowd, already on its feet, sprang to attention. Then the cheering broke out again and lasted till the General who was seated betwen President Jeanneney and Georges Bidault, stopped it with a gesture. Bidault rose – not in his capacity as Minister of Foreign Affairs (which has been his post for the past few days) but as President of the National Council of the Resistance, whose representatives were gathered on the stage to his right. He was brief and restrained, eloquent without being effusive, as he recalled the heroism of the living and the dead, punctuating his silences with small, sad gestures and nods of his head. A handkerchief swelled out – immodestly – from the breastpocket of this modest man, whose joy seemed still to be sorrowful and constrained. Too much blood and too many tears had been shed for this hour of triumph to be entirely without bitterness. I watched these men of the Resistance, finally rewarded for four years of heroism, and I called to mind the absent ones, all those whose last vision before death was that of a firing squad. And I felt shattered at experiencing a happiness denied to them. Among the living too, how many women and men deserved more than I to be there, face to face with de Gaulle, surrounded by the pomp of the official ceremonies?

Close to tears, I only dared to steal occasional glances at my father, whose pale face was tense with emotion. I watched the General who now and then applauded discreetly. Koenig was behind him, Debû-Bridel* among the members of the C.N.R. and in the auditorium a fascinated Jean Paulhan*, Edith Thomas, Robert Victor. I name haphazardly these various personalities, so diverse in talent and importance, but all basking in the same brotherly light.

Georges Bidault sat down (memories of Jacques Laval's first Mass before the war, where we first met). The orchestra played a military march, which began with the gay rhythm of circus music and ended on a graver note. Then de Gaulle stood up and spoke.

I had read his speech that same morning. He had been working on it for four days and when I took in the correspondence for signature the other evening (and he had broken off to recite in a deep voice that poem by Anna de Noailles on the passage of time), his desk seemed to be littered with pages of his unfinished manuscript. He did not read his

31

text; he had learnt the sequence of ideas by memorizing sentence by sentence. Following the speech from the written copy, I noted that he kept to the meaning of the sentences, while modifying their actual wording. The other night Georges Duhamel had mentioned that each of the Allies in turn had been hard-pressed before achieving victory and de Gaulle had stressed the importance of this state of affairs to our own country.

"That's what I'll tell them on Tuesday," he said.

And he did tell them, following up his praise of England, the U.S.A. and the U.S.S.R. with references to Dunkirk, Pearl Harbour and the Caucasus. Without appearing to dwell on them, he did not spare these proud nations a single one of their disasters thereby asserting in his own way France's right to be proud. After establishing our country's due demands and claiming for it one of the leading places in the world, he came to home affairs, addressing particular threats to vested interests and announcing that elections would be held as soon as possible to consecrate the new Republic, and put an end to the present provisional government.

A cold speech and one which remained restrained even at moments when he, himself, seemed to be moved. One felt him incapable of the slightest demagogic concession; severe, lucid and sparing his audience none of the reasons he had for displaying austerity.

A Marseillaise, the General loudly singing the words – with the whole crowd soon following suit – and the meeting is over.

I caught sight of Col. Corniglion-Molinier* at the exit – he fell into my father's arms and kissed him (ah, that huge Corniglion of my childhood!) – and M. Massigli, recently appointed Ambassador to London.

Then, once more, back to my work at the office.

It is 10.30. Claude Guy, who had just dined with the General – whom I see passing by as I do almost every evening – (and who says his usual goodnight to me as I stand to attention behind my desk) tells me that the Government has no control over certain insurgent groups of the F.F.I., in the Centre and the South. It seems that General de Gaulle has already been rejected by the moderates at Limoges, who, for want of anyone better, have appealed to Leclerc. He heard the news this evening from a cousin who has come back from there.

Tuesday, 13 September, 1944
Hôtel de la Guerre

10.30 *p.m.* Found time this afternoon to see the first newsreel of liberated France; pictures of the landings, of the General's visit to the

United States, the Paris Insurrection (to see these things and say to oneself – 'I was there!') and de Gaulle's march from the Etoile to the Concorde. I have deliberately left to the last, for greater emphasis, the General's arrival at the Town Hall on the day that the Leclerc Division took Paris. By now I know de Gaulle's expression well enough to understand the meaning of the one he wore in this hour of triumph – overwhelmed with pride and delight and radiating a pure and utter joy. Claude Guy told me that he had carefully prepared at Rambouillet the 'impromptu' words he spoke on that occasion, and that the only thing that had really interested him during the previous four days was what he should say on arrival in liberated Paris. It all took place in a room at the Town Hall open to the public. Claude Guy remembers a typist, her face distorted by *physical* love and a tall, wounded Negro; but on the screen, I only saw that man haloed with glory, that stupendous photograph of the very halo of glory. Claude maintains that it should be partly attributed to the fierce light of two projectors that were, at that moment, trained on the General, but I well know and so does he, that there was something else too – the miracle of a privileged moment in the life of the most privileged of men.

Glimpsing on the screen, at the General's side, the familiar figure of dear Claude Guy, witness and participant in these fantastic moments – seeing this reflection of my youth, this confidant of years ago, this best-loved of all my friends suddenly elevated, after a five-year silence, from the plane of everyday life to that of history – I was once again filled with astonishment. And I, myself, by the most unexpected stroke of luck had become the modest but close assistant of the hero, now being acclaimed by a crowd heady with affection and pride. It was impossible to explain. One could only accept with gratitude and keep silent . . .

The film also showed, to the accompaniment of boos from the audience, a number of German prisoners, and I thought of those I had seen on the previous morning in a lorry, pitiful in their soiled uniforms and seven-day beards. Such a short time before – barely three weeks – these soldiers had been strutting along the pavements, we had scarcely dared to hope to see the last of them and their atrocious Nazi swastikas floating from the tops of our monuments.

Admiral Thierry d'Argenlieu, whom Claude Guy told a short while ago in my presence that General de Gaulle credited him with the choice of the Cross of Lorraine as the emblem of Free France, was anxious to correct this historical error. "I was the first to discuss the matter with Admiral Muselier*, but it was he, and not I, who suggested opposing our Cross of Lorraine to the Nazi swastika. The General agreed with enthusiasm . . ."

O.G.—3

This evening Claude and I managed to escape from the office long enough to dine together in a restaurant near the Invalides.

He said: "What I'm about to tell you isn't to be repeated but I'm hoping that you may be able to do what I can't find time for: make notes . . ." (If he only knew what it costs me at the end of exhausting days!) And he went on to quote the contents of a personal letter from President Roosevelt to de Gaulle received yesterday, 'advising him' to include General Giraud* in his government, and the General's supremely impertinent reply.

"He has received innumerable insults from Roosevelt who, for instance, would call off a meeting at the last moment when his luggage was already packed . . . You saw on the newsreels what their meeting was like: on the one side, a beaming Roosevelt – a master of half the world – on the other a smiling de Gaulle, though only moderately so, and still maintaining a proud reserve; that of a France which, after all, has no reason to acknowledge herself a vassal – or even inferior in any way."

He also spoke of 'that type of courage that is born of serenity'; Leclerc's – and particularly the General's. And he described again the ceremony at Notre Dame: the faithful, face down on the floor but nonetheless yelling 'Vive de Gaulle!' Claude Guy himself, shouting 'Stand up!' and the bullets whistling past. Claude, expecting to see the General fall at any moment, pounced on a doctor whom he had spotted in the crowd (the one whom de Gaulle had consulted at Rambouillet about his sore throat – sore because of the speeches) and asked him to be prepared for any emergency. "When we came out, we really had the feeling that we were being shot at from behind. And I caught the slightest trace of a movement, quickly suppressed, around the General's shoulders, but one I recognized because I had shuddered in exactly the same way at the same moment."

The General – accompanied once again by his A.D.C., Lieutenant Guy – leaves tomorrow morning by plane; he will be away for several days, speaking in Lyons, Marseilles, Toulouse, Bordeaux.

"In peacetime it would have needed at least three weeks for the police to complete their arrangements for the ceremonies in Marseilles alone; but we're leaving just like that, without any measures being taken beforehand and fully aware of A's inefficiency. In addition, A has had to completely reorganize a ridiculously inadequate police force in a matter of days." Thus spoke Claude Guy. It was hardly reassuring.

Thursday, 14 September, 1944

10.15 *p.m.* I am at home, where I dined – as the General left Paris this morning and I am more or less on holiday for the next few days – by candle-light since the electricity is still cut off.

The death of Jean Prévost* has been confirmed. He was killed in battle, in the maquis of my brother-in-law, Alain le Ray, with whom he had been serving for a long time. I recall our last conversation at the Café Flore, on the dilemma separating thought and action. My Diary during the occupation will have mentioned it, but I forget what name I called him by. ('Théophile' was my father; 'Ludovic' was Alain. All this, in our naïvety, was to protect ourselves if there were investigations by the Gestapo. Poor Jean Prévost; dying less for France than for a certain conception of life.)

Indirectly, we have learned that Alain is safe; Jeanneney's son, who has just come back from there, told us that notices signed with his name ('Commander Le Ray') are stuck up everywhere on the walls at Grenoble. He is the head of all the Isère F.F.I.

Last night towards midnight, after the last audiences (d'Astier de la Vigerie* and André Philip*), de Gaulle had me in to deal with the mail.

"The old classmates showing up," he exclaimed ironically, while signing. "They all turn up now, but I never heard a word from them when I was in London!"

When the correspondence was finished he said, not to himself but addressing me directly – and it had nothing to do with the matter in hand – (It is his habit to think aloud in front of me, to profit by my presence to confide in me in a few brief sentences which spring from preoccupations of which I know nothing, but about which he pretends to believe me well-informed, and then to stop suddenly as though from shyness.)

"They're no longer ministers . . . So what?"

He is alluding to Philip and d'Astier.

"They may make a comeback," I say.

"Perhaps," says the General.

Fascinating visit from a fellow prisoner of Naval Lieutenant d'Etienne D'Orves, shot by the Germans in 1944.

Monday, 18 September, 1944
38 rue Théophile Gautier

We learnt from the papers that de Gaulle had spoken and been acclaimed in Lyons, Marseilles, Toulouse and Bordeaux, and for us in

35

the Cabinet this has virtually been a holiday. At least the evenings have been free and we have enjoyed a proper Sunday. I had forgotten how to employ my leisure; the new tempo of life to which I have grown accustomed made it difficult to adjust myself to any other. Only women retained their unapproachable glamour and it was to them that I mentally sacrificed all the joys of intelligence, heart and pride.

This afternoon I was left in charge of the Cabinet, as all those who had not accompanied him had gone to welcome the General and his entourage at Orly Airport. He came in, followed by Claude Guy, and replied to my greeting by saying that, all in all, he had had a good trip. Claude Guy (as soon as the door of de Gaulle's office had shut behind General Juin, soon followed by Diethelm, the Minister of War, who only remained for a moment) described the enthusiasm of the enormous crowds gathered around the General; and produced from his briefcase photographs, and provincial newspapers with unknown names, from which I derived a glimmer of those astonishing days when, for the first time, de Gaulle came into contact with the people of France. In the streets, in one photograph after another, in one town after another in much the same setting, the figure of Claude Guy – in his air-force cap and uniform – could be seen in the thick of the crowd immediately behind the General. He has become so familiar to me that I forget that less than a month ago I had no idea that he was still alive.

"Listen, Guy! I'm fed up with this security business. I don't want to hear it mentioned again."

This was the outcome of those days, in which de Gaulle's rashness was a constant source of anxiety to his staff. In Toulouse for example, when his attention was drawn to the danger he was running by getting out of his car, since the town was still full of armed members of the F.F.I., the General broke in:

"To avoid attempts on one's life, Monsier le Préfet, one only needs a little authority. And to acquire this authority, which I am not convinced you possess, it is advisable to exercise it."

And he stopped the car and walked the rest of the way.

The problem of the F.F.I. remains serious and the enthusiastic reception of the crowds does not prevent it arising in every town visited. De Gaulle met the leaders of the F.F.I. everywhere he went and explained to them that though they had fought heroically, the time had now come to form large combat units, which necessitated a uniform system of discipline and methodical training in camps (for both officers and men). The speech always had the effect of a cold shower but it was one which had to be made. These men are ready to go to war, but they reject its rules: the F.T.P.* in particular are determined to stress that they are not soldiers by addressing their colonel as 'monsieur' and not saluting him. The trial of strength between them and de Gaulle has not yet come to a head. The former, not feeling strong enough to smash certain of their opponents, come to terms with them; the latter obviously hesitate to come into headlong conflict with a man so powerfully supported by the nation. But sparks fly and a future explosion seems imminent. Claude Guy repeats this snatch of dialogue between de Gaulle and an F.F.I. colonel.

"How many men have you under your orders, Colonel?"

"Forty-one thousand, General, and not one of them prepared to accept orders from any officers but his own."

De Gaulle takes it. Elsewhere – in Bordeaux – it is decided to break an F.F.I. commander who turns up at the meeting surrounded by six men with machine guns. Diethelm furious at being treated as a civilian and a politician. De Gaulle is in the next room. Claude Guy and the other members of the Cabinet who are present have their hands on their revolvers. The commander ends by ordering his men to wait for him in the street, as Diethelm demands. And they obey reluctantly after having asked their leader, one by one: "Is it really an order that comes from you?"

In the passage they run into Lt. Col. de Rancourt, whom they address as 'monsieur'. Sparks fly and once again there is a risk of them setting off the powder keg.

But if de Gaulle gives in when the risk is too great, he knows how to make his authority felt when the moment is propitious, interrogating the F.F.I commanders brusquely enough when he is alone with them tête-à-tête, though showering them with compliments when they are in a group, and making them stand to attention. "He, who's much more of a history professor or economist than a military man," Claude Guy comments.

Today in the Charentes, having induced an F.F.I. colonel to admit that he had been requisitioning, arresting and carrying out executions, the General called these things by their real names in front of him and twenty other people: theft, pillage, abuse of authority and murder . . . And, after two prefects had confirmed the facts, he decided to appoint an officer to enquire into the colonel's administration. He even had the plane which was just taking off (from Cognac, I believe) stopped, so that Diethelm should warn the man in question of this decision.

The trial of strength has now started. It does not promise to be an easy one. The government, without radio contact or transport, is powerless outside the big cities, where the situation is returning to normal. It is reduced to sending commissioners, who run the risk of being arrested. As soon as one of the ports is back in shape (Bordeaux is the only one that can be used but the Germans are still in control there. 15,000 of them, in the vicinity of Soulac were expected to surrender to the General yesterday, but negotiations broke down during the night), as soon as the miners return to work and the government has some troops at its disposal ('Show its strength to avoid having to use it') the problem will be solved.

But Claude Guy quotes this remark of the General on seeing a poster proclaiming the glory of the F.F.I.:

"I never thought when I decided on the title in London, French Forces of the Interior – 'which will become F.F.I., we said' – that it would cause me so much trouble . . ."

I met the General again in the hall downstairs as he was leaving the dining-room. Then Claude Guy came home to spend the rest of the evening with us. Corniglion-Molinier, who had been dining, was still there. He shocked me by the offhandedness and lack of respect with which he spoke of de Gaulle, whom he knows well. Several of my friends, whom I have been able to meet owing to the General's absence, spoke of him in the same way. Such Frenchmen are incapable of taking anyone seriously. Even the glory of a de Gaulle does not impress them. Whatever happens, one must not be taken in. I, myself, belong too basically to that breed to be able to judge them severely.

If chance, in the name of Claude Guy, had not brought me, before I had time to appreciate fully what was happening, to the position which I now occupy – one in which I am bound to respect all the rules of the game (but the impetus is such that I do not have to strain myself) – if I had remained the determinedly objective man, which it has been both my weakness and my strength, my shame and my glory to be for such a long time, what reservations and pessimisim I might have harboured! How easily I might have gloated: does not disorder follow disorder and bloodshed, bloodshed? But such an attitude would have been less honest than it would have appeared to be (and than it would have appeared to myself). My wisdom would not have been without sophism, and my present folly appears to me to have a certain beauty.

Wednesday, 20 *September,* 1944

Georges Bidault, one of the three 'new ministers' from the Resistance – to whom my father only this morning devoted a fine article in *Le Figaro* – was telling me yesterday how moved he had been by the appointment.

I am overwhelmed with work. I have only nine secretaries when I need eighteen. My temples are throbbing, my mind is a block and the job is extremely tedious.

This morning de Gaulle had several members of his family – women and children – to lunch. And when one of them suggested that his staff needed weeding out, he explained (according to Claude Guy):

"I'm already in the middle of a desert! No one with me, no one to help me, and you want me to weed out!"

1.00 *a.m.* I have just come home. At the end of this exhausting day (the flood of letters has started again, which I found more and more difficult to cope with, since my only competent secretary has gone on holiday), I feel almost light-headed.

I saw the General at midnight. After the ritual "Let's get down to it," which he utters at the beginning of each session in a tone that is both determined and depressed, he said, with reference to General d'Astier, whom I had seen leave his office a few minutes previously:

"These d'Astiers, what a family! They're Florentines, as ready with a dagger as a speech!"

He always has this habit of making brief remarks to me on his latest preoccupations or occupations. Then he repeated his "Let's get down to it". And we got down to it.

He began by slipping the first batch of letters I handed to him into a drawer of his desk, one after the other: "They're from my family . . ." Then there were the usual instructions: "Answer it" – "I'll see him, but later" – "Answer it nicely" – "Put him off", etc., interrupted by the customary comment, "Isn't he dead yet?" or "I bet she's no beauty!" and allusions to people's behaviour in exile or under the Occupation – excellent, indifferent or reluctant.

The General answered in his own hand, while I waited, a very nice letter from Paul Claudel*.

The session lasted for over half an hour and I have only just got home. This evening I was struck by de Gaulle's youthfulness: he has such a clear, smooth skin. But the well-combed hair is thin on top, as I can see as I look down on it from my respectful position to the left of his armchair, while he reads his letters, a cigarette stuck in the middle of his mouth.

I should have a lot to write, if it were not so late and I had not so many hours of work behind me, about the sort of self-betrayal which acceptance of an official, governmental life involves; a life, which forces me, whether I like it or not, to participate in a political system that no qualities can save from the general contamination. But I shall have to leave it to another evening. Particularly as this wretched candle is ruining my eyes.

Since yesterday, the General no longer sleeps in the rue Saint-Dominique, but in a private house near the Château de Madrid, furnished for him in four days. A remarkable achievement, as he insisted that the national furniture repository should not be used. (It is this phobia of his about appearing to take advantage of the situation – as though he himself were not partly responsible for it – which causes him to refuse to move into the Elysée, when his staff already cannot find anywhere to live.)

A short while ago, I was still talking to Claude, when the General, his képi on his head, came into the office, shook my hand and muttered a "Let's go to bed" which intimated his immediate departure, accompanied by his faithful Lieutenant Guy. I waited for his car to drive off before I got into mine.

Thursday, 21 September, 1944
rue Saint-Dominique

11.45 *a.m.* Completely exhausted after a day of continual tension (struggling with the flood of letters with insufficient staff). Nonetheless, I must briefly note:

The visit of Bernard Duhamel, Medical Inspector of Prisons, who wanted to draw the General's attention, through me, to the conditions in camps and prisons. To persuade me, he took me to the Reception Centre at the Conciergerie. Stretched out on the floor of a dank, dark, vaulted hall where 209 women, who had still found a way, after a month's internment without any interrogation beyond that required to establish their identity, to apply make-up, and appear almost pretty (with two lavatories for the lot of them). But what weariness in their faces! The greater part of them no longer have the courage to talk or complain. But eager eyes are raised to Bernard Duhamel and me, messengers from outside. A cluster of women gathers around each of us uttering sad laments that are certainly justifiable. Even if all these prisoners were guilty, their distress would make me ignore it. But how many of them must be innocent, the victims of denunciations and jealousy? There are some who are pregnant, some ill, an octogenarian . . . Alice Cocéa is there and Germaine Lubin, both recently still fêted and admired. Bernard Duhamel recognizes them and I thank my stars not to have been caught by their eyes. There, too, is Mme. Bunau Varilla (wife of the editor of *Matin*), whose pretty, emaciated face is raised towards me beseechingly. Am too tired to describe it all. Or to mention the single cells crammed with as many as ten men, visible to me through the spy-holes; a sad negro, dejected youths, and men with hard, dead-pan faces. Or the rooms filled with former policemen, now prisoners. Or those taking the air (if one can call it that) in a narrow passage with one tiny aperture on to a leaden sky. Or the prison-bars. Or the smells. Or the guards. Or the poor, indifferent nuns. Or the men, who have grown accustomed to it all despite the squalor, and listlessly play cards . . .

Tea with uniformed ladies of the Resistance, some of whom act as my secretaries; after which, I return to the office where news-films are being shown for the General. Once again I see the uprising and the entry into Paris. Once again I see de Gaulle triumphantly acclaimed by a delirious crowd, and when the lights go on again, there he is, in person, a few feet away from me, between General Catroux* and M. Jeanneney.

Sunday, 24 September, 1944
38 Avenue Théophile-Gautier

11.45 *a.m.* Another trip for the General, to de Lattre de Tassigny's* headquarters and the Front, allow me the luxury of a free Sunday, and I find myself idle and lost. The last days have been calmer in a sense, in that my staff, thrown into confusion by the departure on holiday of the only secretary who was in touch with what was going on (more so than I, because she came from Algiers) has been reorganized through my efforts and is beginning to work well. I even had the satisfaction of having Georges Bidault ask me to give to his staff the text of seventeen standard letters which I evolved by rule of thumb and which are such a help in dealing with the less interesting but heaviest part of the mail. That the Minister for Foreign Affairs should have been reduced to such an expediency shows the state of disorganization of this very new government and its offices.

When I think that such an important department as that of private secretariat to the Head of State – even if the appointment is only a provisional one – has had to be improvised and by me – I, who have no qualifications for it in three small rooms, without staff and with makeshift resources, I can gauge the times we are living in. There were days when I was almost buried beneath the heap of letters and presents, both absurd and touching, received by the General. At the present moment, a packet of hideous socks, knitted by some old Australian women, and intended for the General's personal use (what huge feet they think he has!) encumbers my desk. There are no social services – there again a rough and ready solution has to be found.

This morning I was able to stay in my father's blue room – not just for five minutes as on other days when I am in a hurry – but for as long as I liked. I told him what I had learnt in the last few days about the

41

Americans' behaviour towards General de Gaulle. Their greatest desire is to see in power a malleable and 'understanding' man, in short, the very opposite of de Gaulle; someone prepared to give in and grant total economic control of the country to the U.S.A. At the same time, they are on the watch for the smallest lapse on the part of a government, for which they, themselves, make any form of government difficult, if not impossible (by refusing to recognize it; slowing down the supplies for its armies, etc.).

At the moment, F.F.I. forces, beyond the control of the central authority, are close to provoking a diplomatic incident on the Spanish frontier. Eisenhower did not miss the chance of writing to de Gaulle, who once again is made aware of what lies in store if he fails to maintain order or give the Americans the smallest pretext for intervention.

Therefore, the problem is not so much concerned with the General being held in check by one faction or another of the Resistance, but with this: the General must either obtain from France the discipline without which there is no conceivable government, or this discipline will be imposed by the Americans or their men of straw, which would mean the end of all effective French sovereignty.

My father who had listened with great attention, handed me *Le Figaro*, which had just been brought to him, saying:

"Read this and tell me if this article doesn't seem to you to have been written after our conversation." And I saw that he had, in fact, guessed where the real danger lay. With reference to the outcry made by the Parisian Press about censorship, to which certain newspapers are vehemently opposed, he had written: "We must, however, give this warning to our friends, our comrades:

'Beware of this transitional period, which has only just begun, and of which we have to face the dangers until the French people have recovered the right to free speech . . . A confused period during which the slightest sign of discord will be closely observed by Allies whose friendship canot be questioned, but who tax our patience by not talking to the Government of France as if they were talking to France itself. In the matter of a censorship incident, the newspapers flew to the aid of threatened liberty . . . And, in my mind's eye, I pictured a certain American colleague making a note of it. And we must show de Gaulle as a man who walks alone on the waters, observed by the whole world.' "

I shall not forget the short walk I took with Claude Guy after lunch two days ago, along the Seine embankment, during which he revealed to me the real explanation for what I was still calling 'the General's regrettable distrust of the Americans'.

At last some news from my sister Claire. An enormously long letter written from Béziers between 21st August and 9th September, in which she describes, with an often staggering simplicity, all that she has done and the thousands of dangers she has managed to avoid.

From this long letter, which in several places brought tears to my eyes, I shall not quote the passages about her visit to the maquis, or about the vicissitudes of the secret battle, later open, against the invader, but only these: "Once my wounded members of the maquis had left, we brought four badly wounded Germans back to Béziers. Before leaving, I spent about an hour in the hospital in a room filled with German wounded. They were in such pain that I was almost sick. I wanted to hate them but all I could feel was an infinite pity and a desire to help them. One of the ones we had brought back was a poor boy of eighteen with peritonitis so far gone that it was impossible to operate. His burning hand clutched mine and he gazed at me with such an imploring expression in his eyes that I was almost in tears. I thought of all those men who, like him, were dying far from their families. I even pictured Jean in a German ambulance and I did for that poor boy what I would have liked some young German girl to have done for him. This morning he was still alive."

And this: "I am sick to death now of my duties which consist in recovering the bodies of executed (militia) men. The grief of their families is almost unbearable. In the prison the men never stop howling. They are not the same as these others and they are traitors (though not always so) but nonetheless they are Frenchmen, men with wives and children . . ."

Friday, 29 September, 1944

What has there been of note during these last four days? My first visit to Mme. de Gaulle, recently arrived from Algiers at the unostentatious but very comfortable 'Villa de Neuilly' – "Rather better than what I wanted," says this simple, diffident woman. On the same day and at the same time, de Gaulle and his staff landed at Orly, after their visit to the front and to Nancy – which prevented me from going to meet them as had been arranged.

There was also the unexpected arrival of my brother-in-law, Alain le Ray, Luce being there. He told us stories of amazing heroism on the part of the Vercors maquis and about himself. The unfortunate Jean Prévost did not die in battle: he was shot.

Lastly, let me record the arrival of the proofs of my *Cocteau*.

In the rue Saint-Dominique, the work has at last become organized. But I am unable to get in to see the General, so that the correspondence piles up . . . He dines at home now and leaves the rue Saint-Dominique towards 9.30, which sets us free early.

Tomorrow he goes to Lille.

The war still goes on however, and while my father can write beautifully in his article this morning "about this liberated Paris, this France that has recaptured her youthful face of 1792", the leader writer of *Combat* (Camus?), always worth reading, is entitled to say: "We are emerging from our euphoria. The whole of France, in a burst of justifiable enthusiasm, had believed that the Liberation would immediately bring everything to an end and that Paris would find herself at peace again with her standards flying once more."

Saturday, 30 September, 1944

Last night. The end of dinner in the Armoured Hall where the General used to take his meals, but where we seldom go now. Claude Guy pointed to a corner of the room:

"It was over there this morning, after breakfast, that all the Republic's commissioners for the Northern Zone met. The General sat down on that sofa – and talked about France in such a moving way that I was deeply disturbed. He began by explaining to them that he had been faced with two alternatives; either to employ the divisions at his disposal to re-establish order in the interior, or to make them take part in the battle and thus gain the right for France to be present at the table where the peace treaty will be discussed and signed. He had chosen the latter, which was the only way of ensuring France's political and economic liberty."

He went on: "The Allies, or rather, those who pass under that title, went to war for reasons which are not only different but even divergent. So much so that the only thing that unites them is the struggle against the common enemy. And though some of the powers engaged in the war still have a number of views in common on the course of action to be pursued, France is allied to no one. She is entirely on her own.

"The United States (he actually said "a certain nation") seem to fear her recovery and are doing all they can to make it impossible. All the improvements (or almost all of them) that have taken place since the Liberation have been achieved in spite of her – without her assistance. We must not delude ourselves about the gravity of the situation: the alternatives which I mentioned mean that we have been unable to take any measures against the German forces that remain concentrated at various points of our territory, in particular on the Atlantic coast. For the same reason, certain regions are in open insurrection, especially

Limoges, where the communists systematically refuse to recognize envoys from the Central power. A total lack of communications (all the bridges are cut). No available ports, apart from Bordeaux, which cannot be used since the Germans still control it. (Marseilles is reduced to its eighteenth century potentiality. Cherbourg and Brest can no longer be mentioned.) It is therefore possible that we shall fall apart in the days ahead. Nevertheless, I believe we shall hold on . . . (After a silence) . . . Yes, we shall hold on . . ."

And the meeting was adjourned.

When we returned to his office, Claude Guy read me several letters exchanged between Eisenhower and de Gaulle. They all gave the same impression of systematic sabotage. At the moment, the General has abandoned the too inflexible decision he came to at first and is trying to compromise; so many divisions will remain as combat troops, so many will engage in restoring order and in mopping-up operations in France. But, up to now, the American High Command has not deigned to reply.

Yesterday, at the writers' screening Committee, there was a clumsy intervention from good old Duhamel (so my father tells me) who said, in regard to Pétain and referring to a private conversation on the subject which he had had with de Gaulle in my presence: "The General – I have it from his own lips – the General is in favour of silence." There was a sneering laugh, full of hatred . . . tragic. Someone said: "Ah, so the General is in favour of silence!"

It was Aragon.

A little later, when the question was raised as to whether having had faith in Pétain was sufficient to merit expulsion, the same Aragon had a note passed along to my father, who was presiding, and left the room. My father had to read out the contents of the note, in which Aragon said that if this point, already decided once and for all, were made open to discussion again, he would resign and refer the matter to public opinion.

In the evening, at a meeting of the National Front, attended by a huge crowd, at the Mutualité, my father sat beside Marcel Cachin*. When I came home at 11 p.m. he had only just come back himself, and I found him exhausted. Even more than by the overpowering arc-lamps, he had been worn down – and discouraged – by the sultry atmosphere of an impassioned crowd.

11.30 *p.m.* Approached my father on behalf of the General, displeased by his presence yesterday at the National Front demonstration. From midday to 4.00 waited for a plane to Brittany, where I have to go on a job with X. But the one I had ordered never turned up. Returned to rue Saint-Dominique.

Wednesday, 11 *October,* 1944
38 *Avenue Théophile Gautier*

11.00 *p.m.* The gravest accusation that can be made against a man was uttered in front of me about a Resistance general to whom I was introduced at Villacoublay airfield on Sunday, 1st October. In the fast American plane with French colours in which we were travelling, he sat beside me – a very young man with a tanned complexion; it was surprising to find him wearing two stars on his severe khaki uniform. His face was inscrutable, strong and pitiless. I was aware of his affiliations and his secret anti-governmental leanings; I knew that this courteous man would have sent me before a firing squad without turning a hair. In front of us, standing in the glazed turret, fascinated by the azure sky all around them, were two disquieting lieutenants in mufti; mackintoshes, fuzzy hair, spectacles. It was definitely a revolution – the first days of a revolution.

An hour after we had taken off from Villacoublay, we came down at Rennes to drop the General and his acolytes. The plane took off again at once, and X was able to come over and take the seat next to me. It was now our turn to stand up in the transparent turret and look down on the mysterious land below, where the pigeons skimming along the ground resembled fishes swimming in deep, limpid water. On the outskirts of towns, innumerable bomb craters showed up as round, light stains on the darker soil. We were flying low and the water was cloudy, but as we approached Morlaix, the sun appeared and then the sea – that miracle forgotten for the last five years.

X went on by plane next morning, and I went in a car filled with the possessions of General de Gaulle and his family. In Carantec (Finistère), the day before he left for England in June 1940, the General had entrusted all his things, at random, to a woman named Moncus. And now she had returned the dangerous consignment to us intact after keeping it safely hidden throughout the Occupation; not only silver, linen and furs, but also share certificates and a number of papers, of which X somewhat indiscreetly made an inventory in my presence, most notably the bitter letters of the Marshal about the book, *Towards a Professional Army,* written by de Gaulle, but on his, Pétain's behalf, the credit for which he suddenly found himself deprived. I remarked to X that it was none of our business to read these documents, and he broke off, looking embarrassed.

I spent that night at Mme. Moncus' home, after dining with her and her family, and left the next day by car, as I mentioned above. We passed by Mont Saint Michel, which I had never seen before, Arranches appallingly battered, and the small village of Saint-Barthèlemy completely destroyed. There were skeletons of tanks at the crossroads – and then, immediately after, the unmarred beauty of the countryside. At Morfain – not one house in fifty still standing. Desolate, bare walls above heaps of rubbish. We lunched at Le Teilleul; then passed through the forest of Andaine, victim of massive bombardments. A camp of German prisoners-of-war, with black soldiers guarding them. (I also saw prisoners in the harbour at Morlaix – also guarded by Blacks.) White soldiers are in a very small minority there. Landing-craft berth alongside the quays day and night. At dusk, the American vessels anchored offshore are lit up. Powerful spotlights illuminate the docks where work never stops. Many notices in English along the road: 'Mines are cleared to hedges.' At Joue-du-Bois, the cast-iron soldier from the destroyed war monument, stands guard among the ruins. The concluding stages of the journey proved extremely arduous, as the so-called 'red-disc' main roads were reserved for military traffic and we had to make long detours. At 9 p.m., however, my companion and I reached the 'Villa de Neuilly', where we unloaded our cargo – as well as two lobsters bought for Mme. de Gaulle at Roscoff's. There was a long discussion before we were allowed to enter the grounds. The password was 'Moscow', and by failing to know it we were in real danger. A shot rang out in the darkness of the gardens as we were transferring the General's belongings from the car to the villa.

Life in the private secretariat continues as usual; the work is so absorbing that the days pass quickly.

One day, my father received a warning that he and Georges Duhamel would be executed before the end of the year as a reprisal for the murder of Philippe Henriot. That same evening we learnt that the explosions which we had been surprised to hear during the afternoon had been caused by V1s or V2s. Claude Guy, who was dining with us, said that a systematic spraying of Paris was expected next day . . . And at dawn a terrific explosion woke us up. It looked as if, once again, we were on the threshold of dreadful days. But nothing further happened.

The General went to Lille one Sunday; on another to Havre, Caen and Rouen. Jean had the good luck to accompany him as a pressman. His articles in L'Aube were excellent.

There is a lot I could write too, about Claude Guy, who is creating a vacuum around the General. I had to get tough with him before I was at last allowed in to see de Gaulle, after a fortnight's interval; get him to sign his letters and broach the social service project, which is close to my heart.

Curious confidential information from Commander Charbonneaux ... Amidst all these intrigues, I float innocently on the surface.

Sunday, 12 October, 1944

Saw the General towards evening for more than half an hour while General de Larminat was kept waiting. I presented him for the first time with a brief report: *Trend of Opinion Drawn from General de Gaulle's Correspondence between 1 and 12 October, 1944* which set out, completely frankly, the various drifts of public opinion; suggestions and complaints relating to the political situation, etc.

The General ran over it rapidly but took it all in. He returned for some time to the paragraph on page 2 beginning: 'Sharp criticism of internment camps . . .' and picked up his red pencil.

The result: a letter signed by him, drafted by me, a very explicit letter to be sent tomorrow to the Ministry of the Interior. It is very different from the one I finally got from Z after a wait for three weeks, which he sent back to me every evening, more and more watered down, more and more conciliatory and indefinite. I have the feeling of working in very close contact with life and must profit by my luck in being one of the few people allowed in to see de Gaulle to keep him informed of what is going on. Public opinion accuses Palewski more and more (the initiated add Claude Guy), of isolating him. I do not wish to hang on to my job if I have to pay for it with the slightest compromise. De Gaulle proved to me tonight that he is prepared to hear the truth. But, in his circle, my initiative must already be beginning to cause anxiety. It is lucky for me that Claude is my friend. And, also, that he needs me. He has taken advantage of the exceptional conditions prevailing during the first days in Paris to place one of his own men in this important position – and one who is under his orders – whereas in Algiers, the head of the private secretariat was a senior officer who outranked the A.D.C. Already there has been a certain amount of friction, for I am not prepared to be a man of straw, but, up till now, he has made all the necessary concessions.

Wednesday, 18 October, 1944

I had written – and it was not one of my best turns of phrase by a long chalk: "All the bad memories of those cruel years are submerged by the promise that has already begun to be kept; that of a purified France, restored to honour and liberty . . ." De Gaulle, who had just signed the letter, jabbed the word 'purified' with his finger and, turning to me where I stood on his left, said:

"It's strange, Mauriac, don't you find, that people only have their eye on one thing: a change in their own situation or in that of France? And you too; you speak of liberty, honour and purification. And what about victory? What I have my eye on, first and foremost, is a victorious France."

And he added in his own hand: 'victorious' before 'purified', so that the sentence read: 'that of a victorious, purified France . . .'

Knowing that I was going to see the General this evening, my father sent a letter round to me by Claire at the last minute. Signed Francis Yvon Eccles, professor emeritus of French literature at London University, it could be summarized as follows on the slip I handed to de Gaulle: 'This note, in the name of the intellectual élite of the Allied countries, draws the General's attention to the grave repercussions which the death sentence on M. Charles Maurras would have on the international intellectual world, though it does not underestimate his culpability.'

I said, quite simply: "It is a serious matter which is troubling a lot of people just now." De Gaulle then said "Why?" inviting me to explain, which I did, while he listened to me attentively. I pointed out that all Maurras' errors had not sufficed to make him appear infamous in the eyes of his disciples.

"You know, General, the blind trust that Maurras' followers have in him: whatever crimes he may have committed, he is too closely identified with a certain type of Frenchman for them ever to regard him as a criminal. If Maurras were condemned to death and executed, an unbridgeable gap would be dug between you and a whole group of the French people . . ."

"But where is he?"

"In Lyons . . ."

"You can't imagine he's in danger of the guillotine there!"

(He said 'the guillotine'.)

"But in danger of the death-sentence, General. You know what goes on in the provinces these days, and the whole thing might be over and done with before you were aware of it."

The General rang the bell and Claude Guy came in.

"Ring up Monsieur de Menthon and put the call through here."

Two minutes later he had the Minister of Justice on the line. He started without preamble:

"I'm telephoning about Maurras . . . Where is he? It's important that he shouldn't be tried in some out-of-the-way place: the country wouldn't understand . . . No, no, it's a *political* trial. It's concerned with the instigator of the National Revolution. Lyons is out of the question!

He'd never be able to explain his actions in Lyons. *It's vital that he explain them.* The case should be transferred to the High Court, don't you agree? . . . Yes, no question about it, the High Court will try him. It'll be the trial of the National Revolution. So, it's agreed: (1) He mustn't be tried at Lyons whatever happens; (2) He must be brought up to Paris at a suitable time for him to appear before the High Court. I know I can count on you . . ."

I had stayed where I was, with my arms folded, apparently unconcerned but really very moved. This intervention by my father and me was so unforeseen. Had not Maurras, for years now, been the object of our enmity, of our hatred, if we had been capable of hating? What made us try to save his life tonight? Class solidarity, T said a short while ago in a fury, and his explanation was striking enough to give me food for thought. Much more, from a horror of bloodshed, from fear of the menacing terror which my father has been denouncing during the last few days in his courageous articles in *Le Figaro* which have already earned him the distrust of his friends before actually converting them into his enemies. And what can he fall back on then? There is nothing more apolitical than his sentimental attitude; but it is precisely because a certain purity of mind and heart is incompatible with politics. "I shoulder my responsibilities," he repeats these days – when he feels himself being drawn unwillingly into deep waters.

Watched with a deceptively neutral eye from abroad, France is fluctuating distractedly between the terror of the right-minded and the fury of the communists. There is no government to control this great, stricken country. The purge seems too severe to a part of the French people; but to many others, it seems absurdly mild. Already the people's courts, here and there, are carrying out the executions which the populace demands. The salvation of Maurras can prove as harmful as his downfall. On the one side there is T's fury at the idea that he might escape the death penalty; and, on the other de Gaulle saying to me:

"So, now, it'll be the High Court that tries him: and one can count on them not to do him any harm . . . High Courts are renowned for their leniency."

He said it with irony, in no spirit of self-congratulation: quite the contrary, as a self-evident statement. He had understood what was so apparent to me: that Maurras' death would deprive him for ever of the support of a large number of Frenchmen. But what about the main body? If it is not actually communist, it regards the communist party as the only revolutionary one, or one that, in any case, appears to be dynamic. Yes, Maurras' salvation might prove to be a menace.

And I begin to question my conscience, seized by scruples. I acted in good faith. The General paid more attention to what I had to say than I I could have hoped for. I was the means by which a vital decision was reached. While I retain my job, I shall go on serving as an intermediary between public opinion and de Gaulle. But I must beware of becoming anyone's catspaw. I must learn to remain a mirror and nothing else.

But how does one avoid taking sides? Involuntarily, I always give a certain slant to what I pass on. I suddenly wonder whether my personal intervention really should be objective. Neutrality is a treachery, too.

I have also been able to take steps, this evening – effective ones, I think – on behalf of Emile Roche*, still held in prison. Some personal letters to the General (and so passing through the hands of the private secretariat), but a number of them inspired, gave me an opportunity to intervene in a matter outside my province. It does not occur to the General to complain about these abuses of my position, for he is in no way concerned about the limits of my competence: he wants to be kept informed, and finds in me an assistant whom neither the desire to please nor the fear of being sacked reduce to an insipid correctness. I shall, perhaps, be got rid of before I can constitute any real threat. But, in any case, it will not have stopped me giving General de Gaulle all the information in my possession during the time I was still with him. I had a definite feeling today, what with my interventon on behalf of Roche, and even more so, with that on behalf of Maurras, of having burnt the candle of power at both ends.

But if I remain in this position of 'power' which I did not seek, where pure luck put me – where will it lead me? The future appears likely to hold even more bloodshed and violence than during the Occupation. The days of the Liberation have only been an ephemeral oasis. But not a mirage; we did really taste, we did really feel that unbelievable joy. This overwhelming happiness in a Paris restored to life again was no mere illusion. (Ah, the bells ringing out the news of our rescue during the night, Leclerc's first tanks reaching the barricades, the spectacle of the flags! . . .) Only, this promise of a new life has not been fulfilled . . . Or, at any rate, it has again been deferred: first comes the war, of which there are no signs of a speedy end; and then comes the revolution, which is not taking the form for which we had hoped but is becoming chaotic, unjust and violent.

It requires courage to keep up this Diary at the end of such days. (There is this journalist from Angoulême, whom I have been trying to save from the firing squad for the last two days, because death really seems too high a price to pay, but here again T is in violent opposition.)

I am a benevolent despot over a dozen charming secretaries, whom I have not time to look at.

Yesterday I saw General Leclerc. Today, General Giraud, who has just arrived from Algiers, and whose address is being kept secret for fear of his being killed by opponents of de Gaulle, who would then be accused of his murder.

The other night, everyone in liberated Paris who matters attended a reception for the heroes of the London broadcasts: — Maurice Schumann, Jean Oberlé, Jean Marin, Pierre Bourdan, all of them men who had been mere names, mere voices. All of them legends suddenly visible in the flesh! And I arrived in a car driven by a Republican guard, and was known to everyone as de Gaulle's private secretary. It was an astonishing episode, yet one that scarcely surprised me any more. But if anyone had predicted it three months ago! Life brings its own proofs and justifications.

Monday, 23 October, 1944
38 *Avenue de Théophile Gautier*

In a short speech broadcast a week ago, de Gaulle returned – only this time publicly and before the whole world – to subjects which I had often heard him discuss before, and with the same vehemence.

"The Allies are nations, each of which, while fighting the same common enemy as we are, pursues its own interests and its own policies. Many Frenchmen may well be surprised and saddened by the kind of minor role to which the other powers have relegated France in regard to everything affecting the conduct of the war and preparations for peace . . ."

And after developing this theme, he added:

"But for the moment, we have to take things as they are, realize that, in our present difficulties, we must rely primarily on ourselves and understand that our greatness will spring tomorrow as it sprang yesterday, not from the goodwill of others but from our own efforts."

The blunt frankness of his words astonished the world and wounded the British, whose *Daily Express* reminded its readers in an insulting article that everyone had always been aware of General de Gaulle's 'almost childish fits of temper, peculiar points of view and prickliness'. Career diplomats – in France as well as elsewhere – were almost in tears: this soldier was showing a complete disregard for the most elementary rules of the international game . . . He was ruining any chance of an understanding between the Allies and France . . .

And then suddenly we learnt this evening – what an unexpected conclusion to our many anxieties – that all the Allied Powers had officially recognized the Provisional Government of the French Republic. Full of joy I remembered the recent hours of distress and misgivings, when it was the future of France that seemed to be at stake in the person of de Gaulle. The political and military disorder in some of the Southern departments, not yet brought under control, a disquieting disturbance on the Spanish frontier, and the suspicious silence of the Americans gave one every reason to expect the worst. But suddenly everything was settled at a moment when it seemed least likely. Lieutenant Guyon de Pampelonne, rubbing his hands, rang the praises of de Gaulle's genius. "I remember, in Algiers, Massigli's look of consternation and his distressed gestures as he came out of the General's study . . . But it was always clear in the end that it was de Gaulle, against all opposition, who had known the right path to follow," and had been able to enforce his policy. That is what strikes one: the power of his personality.

Bidault, Minister of Foreign Affairs, for instance, comes to spend an hour with the General every two or three days and one suspects that, while he emerges enriched from the interview, he has contributed far less, himself.

This morning I was at Orly, with the official deputation to welcome the General when he landed after his visit to Dijon and the Eastern front. I saw him – tall and cold, with what, if one had not known him, would have appeared to be an annoyed expression on his face, but so attentive and alert and with such a military bearing – review the F.F.I. companies and the Republican guards who presented arms. Then, after Juin, Koenig, Diethelm, Tixier* and Palewski, I got back into my car, which was the sixth one in the procession. I could just glimpse the General's car with its pennant between a double hedge of helmeted motor cyclists. When my car passed, the arms raised to salute de Gaulle dropped, but the faces still retained their gleam of surprise and pleasure. (How moving it was, as we passed down the rue Monge to see, at the very spot where we had welcomed the Americans in the euphoria of a Paris intoxicated with happiness, the ruins caused by German bombs on the night of that same unforgettable day.)

I saw him again this evening, his face seemingly transfigured by ill-concealed satisfaction (at the 'recognition' finally won).

He was leaving the Ministry to go home, where a big dinner party awaited him. Catching sight of me standing behind the table, he turned suddenly and came over to me, with outstretched hand. I had never seen him so forthcoming . . . A few minutes later, as I was getting ready to leave, I had a glimpse of him in the semi-darkness of the courtyard at the window of his stationary car. He was waiting for his A.D.C. who had been delayed. He called me by my name, asking me to fetch

Lieutenant Guy. And even these few words were enough to fill me with pride and joy.

Maman was ill and had to miss the dinner at the Auteuil villa, at which the British Ambassador and his wife (the Duff Coopers), Mrs. Eden, General Juin and Georges Bidault were present. I was leading my father through the dark, wet wood, when I lost my way and saw to my horror the minutes fleeting by without being able to spot any landmark to help me. Finally, I found a Republican guard, who put us on the right path.

You can imagine my embarrassment, when the head of all the Gaullists, Courcel, asked me very seriously to show the General some documents which he considered important (does *he* have to go through *me* to see de Gaulle?). And when I pointed out the political nature of the matter, which should have prevented me from attending to it, he exclaimed that, unless I did, things would never get started . . . I had to sacrifice Emile Roche to X by telling him about my intervention in the former's favour, which served to make it useless, but I had to sacrifice someone, abandon this cause in order to pursue more important ones. To admit to Roche allowed me to keep silent about Maurras. I decided to take this slip deliberately, fully conscious of what I was doing, like a seasoned politician.

I have seen Georges Bidault several times during the last few days; once, crossing the main courtyard with a languid gait, on the day the Chinese representative presented his credentials. Telephoning him a few minutes earlier, to remind him of the ceremony, I had the genuine impression that I had dragged him out of bed. And he arrived too late, looking anything but ministerial, secretive and even quite alarming.

And, a short while ago, he said irritably in my presence,

"I can't understand the General agreeing to attend the meeting of the five Academies. Fifty per cent of them, at least, are traitors – not counting W, who has such an appalling record that I shall have to have him arrested."

11.30 *a.m.* My father has just come back. The General was radiant – but Palewski disgruntled: "We have been recognized, admittedly, but on what terms!" The British Ambassador declared that the war would be over in three months. The dinner was apparently cold, and on the whole, boring. The General seems keen on the meeting of the Institute. The five speeches that have been announced do not daunt him:

"I prefer listening to them than making them."

Monday, 30 October, 1944

12.45 *p.m.* The evening organized by my father at the Théâtre-Français last Friday in honour of the poets of the Resistance, was very moving. De Gaulle was there . . . It was I who handed him the invitation from Pierre Dux, the present administrator, and after a second's hesitation, he accepted. The Resistance played no part in his decision, only the prestige of the building where the ceremony was to take place.

"It will be an opportunity to go to the Comédie-Française . . . I must go once, at least, to the Comédie-Française."

"Where General de Gaulle is, there France breathes too," my father wrote in his introduction, read by Martinelli. And it was proved, too, by the enthusiasm of the audience when the General walked into his box and his tall, khaki-clad figure stood out between the gilt of the pillars. As he came on stage, each artist bowed to the General, whose profile I could just distinguish in the semi-darkness – and the mirror in his box dimly reflected Paul Valéry's face, rejuvenated by the shadows.

The grandeur of François Mauriac's text, the beauty of the poems recited (Aragon, Eluard, Supervielle) and the austerity of the décor (the simple tricolour drapery on which stood out the reflection of a luminous Cross of Lorraine), together with what they evoked – a France whom one had thought dead, and of whom we now had tangible proof that she had come back to life – but at the price of the anonymous courage of so many heroes, stabbed one to the heart. Once more I wondered why it should be me to whom the joy was given of hearing the Marseillaise welcoming General de Gaulle in the very heart of France. Those executed men, whose pathetic last letters were read out to us, had lived and died so that France should know this happiness, and I was there – and they were not.

Charles Morgan, come over from London for these few moments, appeared on stage and bowed before the dark box in which de Gaulle suddenly came into view. De Gaulle stood up, acknowledging the great English writer, and the audience instantly got to its feet as one man . . . Morgan read in English, his *Ode to France,* of which we were immediately given a translation.

I saw him again in the wings, where champagne was offered to him and a few guests by the Associates. And then I left, by myself, tearing myself away from History to resume my own little history, sadly neglected these last two months and to which I only return on rare and fleeting occasions . . .

For my personal life at the moment is France. France alone, and more precisely General de Gaulle, whom I love tenderly – according to Claude Guy's unexpected but true expression. ("I am sure that you love General de Gaulle tenderly and that you would not like to . . .") Two words from him or just one of his looks give me confidence and pleasure.

The newspapers announced yesterday morning his decision to dissolve the patriotic bands of armed militia which, on the pretext of keeping order, only perpetuate disorder, and immediately everyone becomes anxious (not to mention the minority which becomes indignant). But once more, I have confidence in the General's political acumen. If he has taken this step – which had to be taken – it means that he knows he can enforce it. Against all appearances . . . But why start questioning his ability when we have already had ample proof of it?

During this pathetic tribute to Resistance writers, I was haunted by the face of Georges Suarez, condemned to death a few days ago. Of course, he was a traitor, had been for years, beginning a new betrayal every day he awoke. There is no doubt about it . . . And Robert Brasillach too, whose trial is imminent and whose fate will be the same. But my aching heart feels disposed towards forgiveness. To save these men, whom I used to loathe, I would be ready to make considerable sacrifice. And I am in despair when I think that their death may be necessary, that de Gaulle may owe it to himself and perhaps to France to refuse them this reprieve. A few examples have to be made if a general amnesty is to be proclaimed. A little bloodshed will prevent a lot of bloodshed . . . But a little bloodshed is still far too much bloodshed. And twenty times a day, I am seized by a longing to run away, with my eyes closed, to leave the General, so as not to become a party, no matter how remotely or to what small degree, to these executions. Politics, more than ever before, offend something deep down in me. And I can see my father, as heartsick as I am, and also shuddering with disgust, as he, too, tries to save a man who has been one of his bitterest enemies: the Robert Brasillach who denounced him so often to the Germans in his paper, *Je Suis Partout*. How close I feel to my father, flesh of the same flesh, soul of the same soul.

10.35 *p.m.* I saw the General from 8.00 to 8.45. The session was so long because I had not seen him for more than a week and the correspondence had piled up. Nothing to record in the first forty minutes apart from his exclamation, both ironic and sad, about his classmates – there were at least five or six of them this evening appealing to him for help:

"They're all in jail!"

Or his recollection of Claudel's poem, recited the other evening at

56

the Comédie-Française, which he quoted from memory, his voice raised, and striking the table with his clenched fist.

As I was leaving him, he called me back to give me some papers (and a photograph dedicated to him in Chinese by Chiang-Kai-Shek), and suddenly said, point-blank, staring me straight in the face:

"They're finished – them and their militia!"

I scarcely had time to give a ghost of a smile, before he went on:

"Definitely! If they offer any resistance, we'll fire – in the air. But they won't resist. And, if some poor devil of a policeman is killed, I I shall be sorry for him, but it will at least have the advantage of attaching the police to the right side once and for all and making the others unpopular. I told them as much at the Cabinet meeting . . ."

His voice rose and became tremendous as he uttered the names of the two communists in his government and lifted a finger to point at them, as though they were there:

"In the middle of a Cabinet meeting, I said to them: 'Billoux! Tillon! This is what the government ought to do. This is what it *will* do . . . Now if you don't agree . . .' but they didn't flinch, they *stayed*, and once they'd stayed, once two communists had accepted joint responsibility for the decision, the game was won."

His face lit up with malicious pleasure. But what was even more impressive than his triumphant air and tall, erect figure, was his self-control and strength.

"You see, the communists aren't really dangerous. They're just reeds masquerading as cast-iron. You can't have a revolution without revolutionaries. And there's only one revolutionary in France – that's me."

And, on this declaration, he took himself off with long strides, for it was time for him to return to Neuilly for dinner.

After he had gone, Claude Guy told me about the General's meeting with the C.N.R.* representatives the day before at the house in Neuilly. When one of the delegates began by saying that he had come to inform the General that – the latter interrupted him in a tone of voice that knocked him back in his seat:

"But forgive me! It's I who summoned you here to tell you that there are only two alternatives: either there is one government in France, mine, and you submit to its decisions; or you think you can oppose it with your own, in which case we'll soon see who wins . . ."

Claude Guy added: "He treated them like errand boys. They were in a tight corner, despite their numbers. I heard one of them mutter, on their way out 'What a pity Saillant wasn't here', as if their president, who was out of town, could have held his own against de Gaulle. The result: in place of C.N.R.'s first motion – very inflexible and hostile –

there will be another one which you'll read in the papers tomorrow, and which is in very different terms. I can tell you, de Gaulle made up his mind in a flash. The other night, we learnt that despite the reprieves granted by the General in a case where the Maubeuge F.F.I. had tried to influence his decision, so much so that he had used his right of reprieve not because the accused deserved it, but because he wanted to show his authority, two of the three prisoners had been executed. But de Gaulle was not in the least disconcerted; next morning, there was the Cabinet meeting and the decision you know about."

I could not make out whether the Maubeuge affair had been the determining factor or whether it had just been a pretext having coincided with a number of other circumstances which made it possible to take action against the irregular forces. In any case, it seems that the two French divisions, so badly needed, have been released by Eisenhower.

Tuesday, 31 October, 1944

His face lit up and he smiled. This lasted for several seconds, and I wondered what it was that could have amused him so much among the papers he was looking through. Then he exclaimed – and it had no apparent connection with the matters we were dealing with:
"They're finished – them and their militia!"

He carefully read my report No. 2, *Trend of Opinion Drawn from General de Gaulle's Correspondence between 12 and 28 October, 1944.* The following passage struck him:

'With reference to the problems arising from the purge, the general impression remains one of dissatisfaction, with a *crushing majority of correspondents demanding more tolerance.* Which does not mean that the opposing minority view is lacking in importance, since those who hold it, have, for the most part, brilliant records of service with the Resistance.' It was the underlined words that caught his attention, and he said to me, looking extremely surprised:
"So they think we're too severe?"

I then ventured to draw his attention to the antinomy which seemed to exist between the extremist tone of the Parisian Press and the much calmer reaction of the bulk of opinion – at least as far as it is manifested in the letters he receives.

Claude Guy repeated to me the following words of the General about my father's membership of the Administrative Committee of the National Front:
"It's for him to judge, but he must know that he is supporting an organization that is working against France . . . It is not for me to

tell him what he should do. But he would be doing me a great service if he resigned and explained his reasons in an open letter. What's more, it would require less courage to make this gesture than to write the articles that are being published just now in *Le Figaro*."

On my advice, Claude will repeat de Gaulle's words directly to my father. My father and I spoke about it this evening. Fundamentally in agreement, we decided that it was a question of drafting the letter very carefully and then waiting for a propitious moment, which cannot be long in coming. But what a new experience for him, for both of us! (To alienate almost the whole of the Press.)

Among the letters he received today, my father found two entreating him to intervene in the imminent trial of Robert Brasillach. He alone, say his mother and Thierry Maulnier*, can save him from the firing squad; and my father is very perplexed, not knowing what line he should take in presenting this indefensible defence, which I feel, nonetheless, that he will undertake. He murmured:

"How much I long sometimes to shut my eyes, drop everything and escape . . . It makes my head spin when I estimate my supposed importance by the very different tone that ministers take with me. Besides all this is liable to end very badly."

"Yes, but your task isn't finished yet. Your voice is the only one that can say certain things nowadays."

"That's true . . ."

He will carry on.

Louis Salleron, who came to see me this afternoon, told me that the General has all the Gaullists behind him – and all the Pétainists. And it's a fact. The former *bona fide* defenders of the Marshal's policy have rallied round the General without reservation. (I indicated this in my report on the trend of public opinion which I gave him yesterday.) Very soon, after the first days of fluctuation, it was understood that he represented the only chance of any order for France. More than that – salvation. And here is de Gaulle dragging behind him the entire weight of the right wing – which in a way is not to be regretted, forming as it does an integral part of France, and indeed there would be no France without it. But the true revolutionaries fear that once again their revolution will be snatched from them. I have complete confidence, on this point, in the General's wisdom. Did he not tell me yesterday – and with what conviction! –

"There is only one revolutionary in France – it is I."

Monday, 13 November, 1944

I should have jotted down so many things; but I am completely exhausted and too distracted to react. On 11th November, opposite the Vincennes Prison, I saw de Gaulle speak to France.

The hedge where the executions took place, the devastated church, the horse guards ringing bells for 'the dead' . . . Then suddenly, the explosions which we first took to be salutes, then bombardment. (It was only during the day that we learnt the truth – which was exploited by the communists – an ammunition train had exploded.)

On 10th November I attended a luncheon which gathered around the British Ambassador, Duff Cooper, a veritable galaxy of writers: Aragon, Camus, Schlumberger, Siegfried, Duhamel, Wladimir d'Ormesson, Guéhenno (and I sat betwen Lacretelle and Eluard). My father and Paul Brisson had organized the lunch at the Ambassador's request and I was the fourteenth guest.

On 11th November I was present at the moving review and took my place beside my father who wept when the first soldiers appeared. Close to me were Churchill, Eden, de Gaulle. And what enthusiasm from the crowd when the General and the British Prime Minister, standing in their car, surrounded by mounted Republican Guards, went by at the head of the triumphant procession . . .

On the afternoon of the same day, following a conference in the General's office, I saw Churchill and Eden cross the staff officers' room where I happened to be. Churchill, just like his pictures, with an enormous cigar between his teeth. But I lack the courage to give more details to these memories. (I forgot to mention de Gaulle at the tribune of the Consultative Assembly at the Senate, 10th November.)

At this 11th November conference (at which were present beside the General, Bidault, Palewski, Duff Cooper, Massigli, Burin des Roziers*, Coulet), Churchill had promised:

1) reserve equipment ('of second zone') for the F.F.I. to constitute tactical units;

2) the same equipment for the troops who would eventually be entrusted with the Occupation;

3) a separate French zone of Occupation in Germany;

4) after the armistice, preparation of a common colonial plan giving France a more advantageous position in Syria. (Source: Claude Guy, directly after the conference; he had just been told this by Palewski.)

Guy, who was in their car this morning, told me he kept hearing them as they stood behind him, exchanging commonplaces while the crowd was cheering. A very enthusiastic de Gaulle, with a rather cool and blasé Churchill who, however, as the car crossed the Concorde Bridge, began to hum a tune that a military band had played before the statue of Clemenceau.

My brother Jean has just volunteered . . .

Sunday, 19 November, 1944

11.25 *p.m.* "It is so beautiful when he speaks with the voice of France . . ." Beside me, in the big office where we were alone, de Gaulle quoted from memory, while hammering the table with his fist, Claudel's poem which Jean Louis Barrault had recited at the Théâtre Français a few days ago. "It is so beautiful when he speaks with the voice of France." (Thundering voice of de Gaulle. The Voice of France!)

"I have suffered too much! They've hurt me too much! Twisted and twisted me. They've beaten my head against the wall. Trampled my naked belly. All this is only the body, after all. It is not that which hurts. I am old, many have been the blows I had to take. But I was not used to shame . . ."

The quotation was not quite right, nor in any way textual. But how exact was the repetition of that sentence which he accompanied by a more violent punch than the others: "I was not used to shame."

I have thought of those minutes this evening. It was at the end of a radio broadcast in which the General, in his own severe and beautiful style that permitted nothing of the second-rate, no ugly, yielding word, had just given tangible reality to our ever-present hope that a wounded but living France is beginning to rise, slowly but surely . . . (The invitation to Moscow, the success of the loan, the improved development of military operations, reconstructions begun in all fields – and above all the miracle of freedom and honour to which, so far as I am concerned, I cannot become accustomed, which grips me several times a day, this grateful joy, surprised, radiant, close to incredulity and nonetheless heavy with a cloudless certainty which is revealed in the colour of the sky, the aroma in the street, the transparent quality of the air, the walk of the passers-by, their faces . . .)

And my father said: "Never has France, who has never undergone such a terrible ordeal, known before such a wave of hope. Our luck is marvellous, but so, so threatened . . . May God grant that nothing happens to him, that no one tries to kill him or that he does not kill himself . . ." Words that tore at my heart and I heard again de Gaulle's magnificent voice when he rounded on Gaston Palewski who had come to present him with a few timid objections concerning the itinerary proposed for the General's Moscow trip.

"The pilots don't want to accept the responsibility? What pilots? But it isn't true . . . Listen to me, Palewski. Give me peace, once and for all; I don't want you bothering me with all these questions of security. Your plan would mean me losing three days on the way there and three days on the way back. And it is here, in Paris, that I must be – not travelling about."

And reminding Palewski that had he followed his advice and that of Rancourt (I don't remember on which occasion – Cherbourg?) 'he'd long ago have kicked the bucket'. I will always hear that prodigious voice, heavy with controlled anger, coarse in a popular way but without triviality:

"Leave me in peace, damn you, once and for all; I don't want to be messed about with these security details."

I saw him twice last week for quite a long time, the first time since the beginning of the month. I should say I have twice presented him with the mail. Rewards that compensate for so many harassing days, from 9.30 to 1.00 and from 3.00 to 8.30 – all devoted to the humble tasks of the private secretariat.

26 November, 1944

At 8.00 this evening, all the church bells in Paris pealed to celebrate the liberation of Strasburg and I remember that other night, so recent and yet so far away, when the arrival of the first Allied tanks (I did not yet know that they were French) was announced in the same way.

The glorious bells in the suddenly illuminated, rustling darkness, the first breath of fresh air after four stifling years! I had just fallen into bed, broken with exhaustion at the end of a sublime day in a Paris in revolt, and I was dragged out, intoxicated with joy and emotion, thrown hurriedly into the street on my crazy bicycle. The sounds of the Marseillaise broke through the night and the light from all the open windows (electric power had been miraculously restored), and the three-coloured flags already spread out on the balconies. A few minutes later I was pedalling up the odious boulevard de Grenelle, where there was not a murmur, or a light. Bursts of gunfire could be heard. Paris was again learning that Liberation was not achieved overnight – there was another morning, heavy with anxiety at our fresh barricade in the rue de l'Ancienne Comédie. The fortress at the Senate was there, quite near, out of sight because of the turnings of a few streets; there was the sound of detonations; an old man covered in blood was carried past on a stretcher; this threat of death was all the work of the Germans and I told myself that it would be a pity to die on such a day. From the Pont

Neuf I caught a glimpse of Allied tanks, on a bridge further away in the direction of Notre Dame (or perhaps on the Pont Saint-Michel). But for reasons of discipline and because my place had been marked out where it was and nowhere else, I gave up the idea of rushing off to see for myself. So that although these liberators were so close and I had *seen* them, I did not really believe in them. When the first French tanks passed just behind our barricade, the surprise was as violent as the joy. Such bliss, I doubt if I will ever live through anything like it again.

I don't know why I am telling all this. I had only taken down some brief notes during the insurrection days and there is much more to say about that. But there is still time, all the time in the world – these are not things one forgets.

So Metz and Strasburg are liberated. French divisions have played a decisive part in the liberation of Alsace. De Gaulle is on his way to Moscow. At the Consultative Assembly, two days before he left, and the day after the meeting when Bidault showed himself on the same tribune a sick, diminished man, I heard him announce new French victories and proclaim to the whole world that France will never ratify a decision, whatever it may be, on which she had not been previously consulted. That same evening, 22nd November, I was among those who came to his office to congratulate him on his birthday, and he said to us that it was not much fun to be fifty-four years old, but that his birthday once more coincided with the liberation of Alsace . . .

"I believe I can confirm to you that Saverne is taken . . ."

He had uttered the same grave words in the same grave voice at the Senate.

And in these days that are filled to overflowing with pride, joy and gratitude, in these days when we are witnessing the miracle of a France, dragged up out of nowhere, and in spite of the little liberty at my disposal, in spite of my tiredness at the end of a hard day's work, my little story continues.

The day before yesterday, repeat of *Asmodée,* after five years (and no doubt more than that). In spite of a new and questionable interpretation by Clarion, a forgotten joy, a pathetic rejuvenation.

I will not mention my move into a beautiful office (what a change after that cramped corner), my somewhat strained relationship with Claude Guy (the all-important Lieutenant Guy, today on his way to Moscow in the General's aeroplane), Jean's departure for Grenoble, Claire's for Belfort (only recently liberated) etc.

Sunday, 17 December, 1944

Yesterday at 2.25 p.m. at the Orly landing field, at the moment when I was saluting Mme. de Gaulle seated in the back of her car, a voice beside me signalled the General's aeroplane which I could indeed see soaring above us, preparing to land. What I felt then was the joy of meeting someone very close after a long absence.

A few minutes later the brass of a stirring Marseillaise made us stand to attention while General de Gaulle slowly and gravely reviewed the company which was greeting him. Then I saw one after the other, all those who had been with him in Moscow: Lt. Col. de Rancourt, Jouve*, Claude Guy.

And the house in the rue Saint-Dominique recaptured the atmosphere created by de Gaulle's invisible presence behind the door with red curtains.

I have never worked so hard as during these last three weeks when I entirely reorganized my office, considerably enlarged (now consisting of twenty-three people). Working for the General I no longer felt the encouragement of his close presence. He had once more become a kind of myth, without my actually realizing it. His return changed everything. And when at 8 p.m., leaving his office, he caught sight of me and came up with the gay and friendly smile of someone who sees a familiar face, whose existence he had forgotten during his absence, what I felt was, in its humility and modesty, a joy not experienced for a long time.

Sunday, 31 December, 1944

There could have been so many things to say but I had so little time; I have felt restrained; my freedom of spirit shackled. I hate only the German offensive (what a feat it is!) which seems under control but which sends a shudder down our backs and the threats, more and more definite, to kill my father.

1945

10.30 *p.m.* My first meetings with de Gaulle made such an impression upon me that when they took place the smallest detail seemed striking to me. I remember the time when I opened my Diary (the little note-book of the first days of the Liberation) every time the General went through the office. Habit, however, saw to it that I did not even mention the long moments that I spent standing beside him while he was signing and going through the correspondence. Even more serious events which I think deserved further commentary have passed by in silence because I lack the time to write them down. So much that had I wanted today to make good all my omissions I would not talk of de Gaulle but of myself.

If the 'audiences' granted me for the correspondence are rare (two since the return from Moscow, followed by a gap which lasted far longer than that long journey), my meetings with him have been brief but over-powering; there was the day when we congratulated him on his birth-day; several sittings of the Consultative Assembly where I heard him speak, either from the tribune or the government bench; there were the two Christmas trees of the Cabinet when he addressed the children with such charming shyness (and it surprised me to think of the self-assurance of the same man the day before, during an attack of Jeanneney, facing formidable opponents in the half-circle of the Senate and soon reducing them to respect).

Following this incident – during a debate on the domestic politics of the government – he was so angry that he refused to deliver the speech expected at the Assembly next day.

"I will go, but I will not speak . . . It no longer interests me . . ."

How disdainfully he uttered those few words in front of me, speaking to Brouillet* while the dazzled children around us were gazing at the Christmas tree.

There were the New Year greetings, once in the intimacy of the A.D.C.'s office, a second time in the presence of the whole staff. There was the very formal presentation of credentials of the new Nuncio, M. Roncali, to whom I was presented by the General along with the other members of the Cabinet. Above all there have been many encounters and hand-shakes between two doors (when he was passing by) or when I have found myself near him.

This courteous but distant man, particularly remote because of reputation, becomes more accessible when I am alone with him during our morning sessions. Not that he is more 'present' than usual: even if he is in front of thousands of people, he emits a radiance that puts everyone else in the shade. Neither is he any closer (for there is never a trace of familiarity in him, nor connivance, never!). But while signing or reading the letters I hand him, he comments on the contents, evoking very simply, olden days, dead friendships or the beauty of young girls in the past; relaxing into giving me interesting family gossip; now and then allowing a tinge of pride to peep through when talking about an ancestor whose name was given to a street (in Le Havre). And then suddenly, among these insignificant details, bursts out an unexpected, thrilling confession, a confidential bit of news concerning more serious State matters. Thus today he suddenly exclaimed – and his sentence sounded more like a question:

"Do you know that the Americans wanted to evacuate Strasburg?"

And showing my surprise, I said:

"What, have they gone as far as that?"

He replied:

"Yes, they've gone as far as that – in a complete panic. The question is going to be solved. Yesterday at Versailles, in the presence of Churchill, it needed a great effort on my part to convince Eisenhower, who was absolutely determined to evacuate Alsace, to economize on strength and manpower, he said. But I won my case . . ."

His calm was so great and his irony so peaceful that I did not feel as uneasy as this news should have made me. I would have liked to learn more but he was already on another subject – or rather remained silent and it was not the moment to ask questions.

A few minutes later when I confided in 'Lieutenant Guy' not so much the contents of the confidential talks as the spirit in which they were given (which had so surprised me) he said rather drily, as though he were afraid that I had exercised, or imagined myself to have exercised, some influence on de Gaulle.

"Don't delude yourself. He needs a mirror. Anybody else would have done just as well. In fact Palewski, whom everybody believes to be so powerful, plays no other role than that; listener to a man who thinks aloud but who pays no heed to the remarks of his interlocutor." (Words which I have no doubt are true, for that is also my impression.)

Thus the enemy, whose first offensive in Belgium had been slowed down with so much effort, has not given up the idea of conquering a

66

too-confident opponent who had allowed himself to consider the important successes which he had won as a definite victory. It would seem that the Germans grasped the chance which this weakness had given them and that they will attempt the impossible in order not to let it escape them. Not that they can discount the victory, but they hope perhaps to obtain an acceptable peace from an exhausted opponent. Whatever it may be, we experienced some appalling hours a few days before Christmas. The power of that offensive of which one could not believe the enemy capable, the obvious disarray of the Americans who did not expect such a thunderbolt, the panic of the commentators, the dramatic unreliability of news which was officially admitted to be forty-eight hours old, the fact that Allied lines had been broken and precisely in the direction of the eternal route of all the invasions, that gap of Sedan of such disastrous memory – all that froze the mind. Many were those who then imagined the seizure of Paris – Paris taken a second time, with all the tragedy that such an event would entail. I maintained an appearance of calm, though acutely anxious myself, and undertook to 'buck up' people around me, not only the family, of course, where the morale was very low, but even in the General's Cabinet.

My father wrote a fine article on the great fear of those days.

The situation was re-established. Calm returned to everyone's minds. But a new danger was in sight, and in the presence of all we still had to undergo, our weariness was overwhelming. (Jean is at a front which is comparatively tranquil, but my heart pounds several times a day at the thought of what might happen . . .) The other evening a few bombs fell on Paris, less than nothing, but enough to remind us of the presence of death.

Of death, in the familiar atmosphere of which a planet lives that has forgotten about happiness. Never has human life been reduced to such insignificance. One cannot help smiling (an ugly, contorted smile) when thinking of the emotion that would steal over crowds when only one human life was in danger. I am speaking of the happy periods in history . . . In France, in this France whose recaptured purity made us swoon with joy, an unjust Justice increases the number of death sentences. The prisoners reprieved by the General are often kidnapped and killed. (That new item in all the newspapers: Summary Executions.) Paul Chack* has been condemned to death. Béraud* has been condemned to death (in unacceptable conditions about which my father has written with great courage in this morning's article), Brasillach will be condemned to death. Suarez has been executed. And I know very well that all of them, in different degrees, have acted as traitors – that all of them, in different degrees, have behaved infamously. And I know well that

67

politics are politics. And that one must learn not to weaken when public safety is at stake. But these bits of paper that my father receives (a poem by Brasillach, a letter from Béraud, written in pencil and sent from the depth of the abyss where they are now) arouse a compassion which I know is not the worst in me. This evening my father, who had just received that letter of Béraud's thanking him for his article – and had learnt from me that the reprieve was by no means certain – was terribly upset. I, myself, could think of nothing but that man, *his feet fettered, wearing prison clothes, living through this agony.* That man, who did not believe he was a traitor. That man who is a man.

I am too tired to go on. I do not know how I have managed to write as much as I have after such a long, harassing day.

I only want to add that my father and I (and Mother, Claire and Luce) feel caught up in the toils of death. The longing one has to call a halt, turn one's head away . . . And yet, there is the radiant face of General de Gaulle's France. (12.15 a.m.)

Tuesday, 9 January, 1945

11.35 *p.m.* General de Gaulle looks worried these days. And there are certainly many reasons why he should. In the first place, there is the right of reprieve, which also entails a duty not to abuse it; a right, which his great conscientiousness will not allow him to delegate to anyone else, even partially. Claude Guy tells me that when he announces that Monsieur Patin, President of the Reprieve Committee, is waiting to see him, the General heaves a sigh – but not, as he does before other interviews, from boredom or fatigue. And, when he says "Ah yes, Patin again!" it is almost with fear and horror.

Paul Chack was executed this morning. Two documents in the voluminous file, which de Gaulle took home with him on Sunday and went through with great care, seem to have decided the issue; a violently anti-Allies pamphlet, signed by him and d'Hérold-Paquis, and an order issued to the members of the Anti-Bolshevik Action Committee to enrol in the Darnaud Militia, signed: Lieutenant-Commander Paul Chack.

Teitgen* told my father that de Gaulle had been heartbroken by Paul Chack's execution, and from my own knowledge, I have no reason to doubt it. But he has other reasons for anxiety: the enemy, who were thought to be on the point of capitulating have suddenly shown themselves to be much stronger than was anticipated. They are threatening our beloved Strasburg, recaptured with such pride, but perhaps too easily. The possibility of the enemy advancing again on Paris cannot be entirely ruled out.

The General is uneasy at seeing the facility with which Eisenhower, who was on the point of evacuating Alsace, changed his mind on the strength of a simple letter from himself, de Gaulle. (At the beginning of their interview, Eisenhower told de Gaulle that he had come over to his opinion, which was valid, from the angle of both prestige and sentiment.) But there were only two alternatives: either the evacuation was necessary for military reasons, in which case it was extraordinary to accept advice based on entirely different consideration; or his story of having to husband his resources had no real basis, in which case it was difficult to understand why he had put it forward. The truth, according to the General, was that the Allied Command was showing a disturbing lack of decision and vigour. To such a degree that one began to wonder what the Americans would do next if they came to the conclusion that the operation was not paying off . . . This little-recognized aspect of the situation, mentioned by Goebbels in one of his recent articles, had not escaped de Gaulle, who had put it into words two days earlier, in an angry outburst:

"And what am I supposed to do if the Americans leave us in the lurch: ally myself with Germany?"

I know this side of de Gaulle well enough myself now – the side which, according to Claude Guy, allows him to say what is in his mind really to anyone, even his driver, and use the office switchboard for highly confidential conversations – to believe that he actually did utter these scarcely credible words. The current belief that he is a man of Nordic passivity has surprised me for a long time. Cold he may be, but it is only on the surface, and he is unable to control his occasional explosions. Possibly, too, much less strong than he appears to be, but endowed with such grit, such an iron determination that he will always act like a strong man. To have refused a reprieve to Commander Paul Chack, he must have trampled on his heart. But he did not hesitate for a moment as soon as he saw where his duty lay.

His duty as a statesman. But while I understand the necessity for his decision and I can only admire him for submitting to it, there is something in me which rebels against it. The man in me, not the statesman – because I am only a man. And I well know that I could never accept the burden of power because it would face me with such decisions. No, I shall never be found in the governing ranks. I knew last night that Chack would be shot this morning. And all night, literally all night, I dreamt of the execution – and of Béraud and Maurras, over whom the same threat looms. And my heart was heavy all morning at the thought of what was to take place in the cheerless snow of the fort.

A short while ago, I was in the Montmartre cinema where they were showing the remarkable film, *Dr Jekyll and Mr Hyde* (which I went to see as one goes to see the performance of a classic, knowing that one will watch it with detachment, unmoved, and which, against all my expectations, quite overcame me: because that monster was me at certain moments and I recognized myself in it, and recognized the implacable upsurge of bestiality, the beast's inescapable capture of mind, heart and soul – body, too, perhaps; for I can imagine what my face looks like sometimes). And, watching the film, without my thoughts straying from it, I remembered de Gaulle responsible for Chack's death – I mean: but for whom, Chack would still be alive – and I shuddered with horror. How could I remain at that man's side and still be fond of him? I felt an urgent desire to get away, a long way from him, from the city, and from humanity . . .

Saturday, 13 January, 1945

I saw the General for about an hour and a half this morning, and it was fascinating. I began by giving him his military file, brought by M. Bayssas, Chief Clerk at Infantry Headquarters, who had kept it hidden away during the Occupation. He took it with obvious satisfaction, opened it unfortunately, at an uninteresting page, carefully read a long, hand-written note about himself (I do not know what it was), smiled and shut the file with an ironical: "What humbug!" But I had the impression that he would open it again later to read it more closely.

I then handed him the draft of the introduction, which I had prepared for his signature, . . . by X. He approved it and gave its contents the first compliments I have yet heard him utter:

"It's good. I'll make a few minor corrections, but it's good."

I had written: 'He understood that France could not decline from her secular greatness.' He read this aloud and said:

"Could not? Alas, it could . . ."

So the sentence became 'He understood that France should not decline from her secular greatness . . .' and then came this commentary, punctuated by gestures:

"You see, it's now that the question of France's greatness will be decided. It's easy enough to have the appearance of greatness during the euphoria of the Liberation. But it's in these days of trial, through which we're now living, that everything will be decided: it's from them that we shall learn whether or not we're a great people. Yes, everything will be decided" (here his fists drummed rhythmically on the table), "everything will be decided, while we suffer from lack of supplies, shortage of coal and the innumerable privations of the war . . ." And he repeated several times more:

"It's now that everything will be decided."

A little later we had this exchange, his first question being put point-blank, with no relation to the work on which we were engaged:

"What did your father say when he heard that I'd reprieved Béraud?"

"You know, he'd never envisaged the problem from the political angle, as you must have done, merely from a sentimental one."

I was wrong in saying this – which was well short of the truth, since my father had been motivated by feelings of charity and justice. (The subject of many discussions in the Press after one of his articles in *Le Figaro*) but I was taken unaware, and was nervous..

"As far as I was concerned, it was not a question of either sentiment or politics, but of justice . . . Collusion with the enemy? I study the files carefully and, in the case of Chack, who gave orders to Frenchmen to enlist in the Germany army, I say yes – but, in the case of Béraud, I search in vain for evidence of collusion or where it was supposed to have taken place."

Then he glanced at a newspaper, lying open beside him and added:

"They're not pleased with my ministers. But if I changed them it would be the same old story. The fact is that I took the best of what the Resistance had to offer."

And when, a little later, we were talking about the mediocrity of the Consultative Assembly as a whole, he murmured:

"France hasn't given me any real men."

To which I replied:

"It's because so many of them are missing, General."

He added nothing to this commonplace remark.

Claude Guy said unpleasantly, when I came out of the General's study an hour and a half after I had entered it:

"So you've exhausted the subject at last, have you?"

Some time after, running into André Roussin in the street, I found myself saying to him (and though my words were quite unrehearsed, they seemed to me so apt that I feel I ought to record them): 'You see, de Gaulle is so conscious of his superiority over everyone else, whatever their position or *nationality,* that I feel we can cherish the highest hopes . . .'

Another man who gives a striking impression of justifiable self-con-fidences, serenity and strength is General Juin, whose qualities have once more become apparent during the present crisis in the conflict. I saw him yesterday scrutinizing the war maps of the areas recently occupied by the Germans and, for some reason, felt reassured about the fate of our armies.

Sunday, 21 January, 1945

I saw General de Gaulle for about half an hour yesterday, but the arrival of General Juin and various ministers compelled me to break off before I had finished. It was an uneventful session, during which I stood beside my boss like any other employee. The General pulled me up on several standard courtesy phrases, which he considered incorrect, and explained why with meticulous care. (I had already discerned in him this pedagogical strain.) So three or four letters had to be retyped, because I had written to people of lower rank: 'I beg you to accept my expressions . . .' instead of 'Believe me to be . . .' I also had the painful duty of handing the General two photographs of his mother on her deathbed. (He did not have the happiness of seeing her alive when he returned to France.) He took them from me almost roughly, as though wishing to cloak his feelings, and put them on one side.

All these matters hold little interest and are not worth dwelling on. We both suddenly seemed to be divorced from current events.

But what appalling anxieties the man beside me, so distant, tense, and almost hostile, must have been facing! The domestic crisis is coming to a head and its immediate outcome seems likely to be the fall of the Ministry. A general uneasiness, becoming increasingly obvious, reveals the seriousness of the situation. After the first few months of euphoria (France's joy, her unalloyed confidence and her faith – from the miracle of the liberation up to those radiant days among which I single out those of 1st and 11th November), de Gaulle's France is rediscovering the imperfection and mediocrity of all earthly things. And I am rediscovering, unchanged, my everlasting convictions, now rendered even more painful by having been forgotten for a time.

An event has occurred which has brought it even more to a head: the death sentence on Robert Brasillach, who was so long destined for this fate that I never met him once during the Occupation without looking on him as a condemned man. A reasonable sentence, a necessary one, and so much in the natural order of things that one cannot see how it could have been avoided, nor by what subterfuge de Gaulle could have set it aside. But all these justifications, and many others, come to nothing when up against the repudiation of our hearts, the hearts of a number of people, who are by no means lacking in intelligence: my father (so much obsessed by the verdict that it gives him nightmares), myself, and so many young men, akin to the two students who, while not knowing Brasillach nor sharing his views, came to see my father yesterday, appalled and seeking some glimmer of hope that the sentence might not be carried out.

At home, my father, who only used to speak of Chack, and then Béraud, now only speaks of Brasillach. Some people find his compassion misplaced, and they are right. Politics is politics. Frenchmen, men who are completely guiltless, are killed every day by the thousand. All this is unquestionably true. But how these weighty words of my father find a responsive echo in me: "The idea of decapitating a head still capable of thought is unwarrantable." And he adds "It was this that was wholly unpardonable in the men of 1793."

The repercussions of these qualms become widespread when the man who experiences them has a platform. And what a loudspeaker *Le Figaro* provides for François Mauriac and what importance his least word takes on in its columns. His influence is such that he is rumoured to be a sort of behind-the-scenes Minister of Information whom de Gaulle uses to prime his various political moves. Yet my father has only seen the General twice – at two meals, and never alone. But the fact remains that he reacts with the sensitivity of a barometer and that his articles reflect accurately the fluctuation of public opinion – not that of extremists on one side or the other, but of the masses. His participation in the Resistance and the prestige that his reputation has conferred on him have given him an authority which has enabled him to do what no other Frenchmen could have achieved, without immediately becoming suspect: he was the first who dared to speak of clemency, charity and peace. And there he is, in this morning's article almost on the borderline of opposition, which is serious. (His two concluding sentences run: "Our future history will be shaped and determined for all time by the extent to which we pursue a domestic policy which my well-known charity prevents me from describing. But perhaps it is true that one should not be sorry for the dead.")

Now, I believe that it is precisely because he is in a tight corner that we should have trust in de Gaulle; that we owe it to him. That it behoves us to accept, for as long as possible, our disappointment in him. "France hasn't given me any real men . . ." he said to me the other day. And the mediocrity of his ministers confirms his words. But this man has been given to France and if she wants to survive she must put her trust in him without reservations.

But the fact still remains that while this man has to follow his present policy, even if it is the best one for France, I suffer from being one of those who, to however small a degree, collaborate with him. That is the

73

perpetual complaint of this Diary: the purity of a straight conscience at variance with the impurity of straight politics.

Monday, 22 January, 1945

When I got home last night, I was obliged to work out the details of a project that had been thrust on me during the day: an attempt to obtain Robert Brasillach's reprieve by drafting a petition, which would be signed by a number of intellectuals and then handed to General de Gaulle. Naturally, in view of my work in the General's secretariat, my name would not appear on it. And this is what I wrote between midnight and 2.00: –

"Monsieur le Président,

"The undersigned intellectuals, all, in different capacities, members of the French Resistance, and unanimous in condemning the evil political line pursued by Robert Brasillach, both before the Occupation and later in the very presence of the enemy, are nonetheless agreed in their belief that the carrying out of the sentence just passed on him would have serious repercussions on a wide body of public opinion both in France and abroad.

"They have come to this conclusion on the strength of their own reactions, which they were the first to find surprising, but which it is their duty to bring to your attention. The fact is that, wholly opposed as they are to Robert Brasillach and proof against accusations of connivance or leniency, they have all found themselves in a sense on his side once they learnt of his condemnation to death. The fact is that the thought of this sentence being carried out is intolerable to them.

"It is in no way a matter of complicity or even of more or less excusable sentimentality; nor is it a repudiation of justice, but merely the desire for a Justice transcending justice, the acceptance of a feeling of spiritual fellowship, the acknowledgement of the tragic collusion of all men endowed with the capacity to think and feel.

"There is, outside politics and above them, a human plane to which the best among us have recourse at the solemn moments of their lives. Now, faced with judging Robert Brasillach's case in our own hearts, we recognize the necessity of crossing from one plane to the other, while retaining a clear conscience in the process. All that we used to call, and quite rightly, this man's crimes, suddenly no longer seem to deserve the name once it is proposed to inflict on him crime's ultimate penalty. We recall to mind that aspect of himself, which he revealed in his best books. Behind the partisan, blinded by fanaticism, which betrayed him and led him into fatal mistakes, we remember the man whom, we were

74

surprised to find, not so long ago, loved, as they should be loved, all that was best in our French civilization and culture.

"We recognize that we all owe something to him. And without believing that it was permissible for him to follow any other political line than the one we have embraced in your wake, that of the eternal France in whose name Robert Brasillach was condemned, it seems to us that in following the line of surrender, the man possessing the understanding and sensitivity revealed in the non-political sector of his works, cannot truly be regarded in his own eyes (or in God's, add those among us who are believers) as a traitor.

"After so many ordeals, France rent in two and finding herself caught up, against her will, in the ghastly vortex into which the hated enemy thrust her, France rebels against this tragic destiny. She feels a pressing need to provide her own answers to the present happenings and no longer play the insane game that the enemy nations have imposed on the world, with such a force of persuasion that, on the very threshold of defeat, the hope of this ultimate victory still seems open to them, the contamination of the conqueror. France hopes that finally another answer may be given to bloodshed than further bloodshed.

"It is in her name that we believe ourselves to be speaking, Monsieur le Président, when we beg you to reprieve Robert Brasillach, who has accepted with dignity and courage the verdict of that Justice to which he confided himself. It is terrible to execute a thinking man, even if his thinking is wrong. For who can foretell the future of a poet? Far be it for us to reject the responsibility of intellectuals which, we are fully aware, is all the heavier because of their special gifts. On the contrary, we accept it fully. Only, we think as we contemplate this man, our enemy, facing the firing squad, in whom to our amazement we suddenly recognize a brother, that wrong causes have no need of martyrs and that pardon may sometimes prove the most effective as well as the wisest form of punishment."

Was not at all satisfied with this letter when I woke up. A judgement confirmed by my father, to whom I gave it to read. On the political plane, the only good argument (but one cannot produce it) lies in the existence of a government which has all the appearance of legality and officially collaborates with the enemy. (In my opinion, it was a vital mistake on de Gaulle's part not to have declared, once and for all, the validity of this extenuating circumstance and fixed the date up till which it was permissible, in good faith, to believe in the Marshal.) And what will de Gaulle, integrated in politics as he is, care about the arguments of an entirely different kind, which I bring up? In my father's view, my letter is far too complex and subtle, raises too many problems and will produce no unanimity on the subject matter. Yet how passionately he desires the reprieve of this man who used to be his mortal enemy!

I must admit that my admiration for my father grows all the time. Though his life is threatened, he never complains; he even has the strength to pretend not to mind. Only his silences from time to time and a perceptibly increased devotion to his religious life show that he is prepared for death. He betrays no vestige of fear. And only someone little acquainted with him could imagine that the threats, to which he has been subjected, could have influenced him to take up the cause of clemency. Only this morning he gave me an old copy of the *Bulletin des Ecoutes Radiophoniques* (6th January) which contained a talk broadcast in French from Germany by Jean-Antoine Cousteau. Entitled 'On the virtuous and tardy indignation, manifested by François Mauriac on the subject of Henri Béraud's conviction', it recalled with regret the period when my father was 'at their mercy' and ended with the words:

"For all this gives us food for thought. When you see so many men butchered simply because their views conflict with those of the provisional masters of France, you say to yourself, François Mauriac, that the day may well come when you, in your turn, become somebody's victim. And then you get a shiver down your spine, you are frightened, you want to call a halt. Too late, François Mauriac, too late, you are caught in the toils: you have to continue to the bitter end, suffer to the bitter end the infamous bestiality of your friends. Place no hope in your lamentations warding us off or melting our hearts now. You have done France too much harm. If your friends miss their mark, we, I promise you, will not."

My father did not turn a hair. But I, for my part, felt less enthusiastic about intervening on behalf of the Bérauds, Brasillachs and other Maurras, who were so ready to accept the monstrous reign of those militiamen.

At 2.30 I went to the Café Flore in the hope of finding Thierry Maulnier there, which I did. I then arranged a more discreet rendezvous, where we met shortly after. He approved of the spirit and even of the wording of my letter, which he will pass on to Robert Brasillach's lawyer. We arranged another meeting for the day after tomorrow.

Later. I had put on one side, taking it to be a family letter, one with a black border, neatly written, which began with 'My dear Charles', and ended with 'Well, I must finish now, my dear boy; I hope this letter finds you well and that, in spite of your multifarious duties you won't be too impatient with the gossip of your old aunt who kisses you with all her love, as well as your wife and children. Elisa.'

The General read this letter through carefully, with the deliberation and concentration which always surprise me in such a busy man. (All the more so, because the important papers which I hand him are never of great interest.) Then he said to me:

"Someone's making a fool of you. I don't know any Elisa."

"But, General . . ."

"I tell you, they've made a fool of you. They wanted the letter to reach me."

"I can't see what good it would do them . . ."

"It's obvious! Listen: 'This morning I queued for an hour at the butcher's to get 125 grammes of sausage for 1,250 kilos' worth of tickets. What do you think of that? Everyone was disgruntled and there was a lot of grumbling. I even heard someone say: "When the Germans were here, we were just as happy, if not more so. If they wanted to make us sorry that the Germans have left, they couldn't have gone better about it." Your Ramadier should be made to stand in a queue, then he'd know what's going on.' So there, it was just a trick to make certain I'd get the letter and read all that."

"It was quite clever."

"It certainly was . . ."

We laughed and passed on to other matters . . . Actually, we are crazy to worry about collaborators, when so many of our boys are dying every day and will go on dying . . . If Russia's lightning offensive inflicts another terrible blow on the Germans, the threat to Strasburg will become more acute. Jean is coming on leave; but I shudder to think that, when it is over, that that is where he may be sent.

23 *January*, 1945

I do find the French very difficult, and the task facing de Gaulle, even inside the country, where he is so constantly attacked, is a considerable one. As corroboration, I shall quote these words of Thorez* to the Communist Party's Central Committee, which would certainly have surprised us during the period when the patriotic militia was proving such a serious problem for France. (I must read what the General said about it again one evening):

"These armed groups served a purpose before and during the insurrection against the Hitlerite occupiers and their Vichy accomplices. But the situation is different now. Public safety should be preserved by regular police forces, formed for this purpose. The civil guards and, broadly speaking, all irregular armed groups, should not be maintained any longer . . ."

77

It was in pursuing his well-known foreign policy (which people accused him of making his sole interest, to the exclusion of domestic affairs) that de Gaulle brought off this splendid double result; not only neutralized the communists, but made them parties to his action.

"The Russians have covered half the distance between Warsaw and Berlin," we read in this evening's paper. And it is only a week since Warsaw fell. In spite of the many reasons for not congratulating ourselves once again too soon, what unexpected hope! And how much more vividly and poignantly I feel it ever since my young brother's life has seemed so closely threatened by the war.

The stream of letters, while not drying up completely, has greatly subsided. And my twenty secretaries look like losing their jobs in the near future.

24 January, 1945

In a supremely skilful or supremely clumsy article – who knows which? – appearing in *Le Figaro* this morning, my father returned to the theme of my recent letter. Or was it I who borrowed his in advance? The fact is that his:

"All that is best in France cannot find comfort after the destruction of a thinking mind," is certainly his own, but he has taken "even if what it thinks is wrong" from my draft. And I also recognize my property in "snatch from Germany a last victory; an inexpiable hatred among the French for each other." In this Brasillach affair, there has been an accord in our respective ways of *feeling* and we stand shoulder to shoulder. He did not believe that there was any hope left. I showed him that there was, and that, however small it might be, chance should not be neglected. Only an argument of a psychological kind persuaded me that it was worth making the attempt: the great importance that intellectuals, more precisely the most academic, the most scholarly, the most famous and the most highly-placed among them, might have in the eyes of this professor's son – and professor, himself – General de Gaulle.

I saw Thierry Maulnier at home, with my father, between 2.45 and 3.20. He told us that the lawyer had approved the text of my letter *in toto*. Nevertheless he proposed to draw up a second petition, much simpler and reduced to the bare essentials, for those unwilling to sign the first one. We made the final arrangements that should produce a rapid determination of the affair.

The Maurras trial has opened in Lyons (the Government having ended up by siding with those who refused to have it transferred to Paris).

The lightning Soviet advance continues. They have reached the Oder.

25 January, 1945

Copy of an express letter received yesterday.

Fresnes, 21 January, 1945

"Dear François Mauriac,

"I have very seldom met you, we have only corresponded two or three times and what I have written about you was never designed to win your friendship. Regardless of that, you wrote a letter to the lawyer for my defence which was read to the court and which, irrespective of the excessive praise it contained, went straight to my heart the moment I heard it because of its generosity and neglect of all that has separated us. I believe you were told this at the time; but now that I have passed beyond the bounds of convention and common decency, I should feel badly if I did not tell you so myself. Others, to whose talent I had constantly paid more wholehearted tribute than to yours, would not have had your courage. Today I have reached the moment of truth. Not only in the past have many things affronted me in your attitude, but, at the very beginning of the period through which we have been living now for five months, I was deeply hurt by what you said. Since then, the stand you have taken, which has led to so much criticism of you, has caused so many hopes to centre on you, that you may well be proud. The moment for which you were waiting, for which you were destined, when your output would become 'utterances' and no longer mere 'writing', has almost paradoxically arrived in the form of a counter-current to the stream which seemed to be yours. This inconsistency is only superficial. We must understand it and understand, too, that inconsistency is one of the greatest signs of Christianity.

"I am writing this to you this evening, under a powerful light which never goes out. Fifteen comrades left a short while ago for the police station at Poisy, to find, among thieves, eternal silence. The bed, on which I lie, was occupied three weeks ago by a man who carved up corpses. Like him, I wear a chain, attached to two heavy rings, around my ankles day and night. I still have Shakespeare's plays, the works of André Chénier and the Gospels on the small plank that serves me for a table. The ordinary prisoners, who bring us our food, are very polite and attentive to me, as are the warders; yesterday there was only a

Republican guard to stare at me through the grille and insult me, but he was the only one.

"The solitude, in which I find myself, no longer frightens me. Besides, I do not feel alone. Close to me are those whom I love, and those who think of me here and there, even in places where theoretically I should have no friends. Their presence has sustained me throughout the trial, during which I tried not to let them down; tried to explain my actions without repudiating any of the motives underlying them. I hope and believe I have not hurt any of my opponents.

"I wondered what chance – if it were chance – brought it about that you were seated in spirit on the side of the defence. When I was sixteen and read your books for the first time, both *Le Désert de l'Amour* and *Le Jeune Homme*, I could not foresee the strange paths that would lead the two of us to this invisible meeting. I, myself, would never have asked anything from you; it needed a mother's unpredictable, infallible instinct and the devotion of friends. They were not wrong in thinking that your heart would break down all the obstacles that your mind might erect. In all likelihood, we shall not now meet, except in the great unknown: if I were inclined to forget it, the chains I am wearing, which echo round my feet when I move from my chair to my bed, would constantly remind me. But, now, I really believe that we shall recognize each other in the unknown.

"That is why, dear François Mauriac, I send you, beyond these icy cells, my thoughts and my gratitude.

Robert Brasillach"

Up against a reserved Claude Guy, I won a difficult game – but hands down – during an after-lunch walk in the Saint-Dominique-Bac-Grenelle-Bourgogne quadrilateral. At the end, he was completely won over, which was a well worth while achievement in view of his position in the office. (In relation to Palewski and the General himself.) Robert Brasillach's letter, which I gave him to read, finally turned the scales; and as, in the General's empty office, I handed him drawing pins to pin up a map of the front, in preparation for the de Gaulle-Eisenhower meeting this afternoon, he was as keen as I was to find a favourable outcome. (The idea of the petition – the source of which I kept hidden from him – had his wholehearted approval.)

Press conference this morning. A cold, distant de Gaulle, almost insolent in his stiff correctness, gave disappointing answers to the questions diffidently put to him by the journalists present. No one brought up the vexed questions of domestic policy or of justice, which surprised me. De Gaulle reaffirmed his intention to see that France should safeguard her frontiers from one end of the Rhine to the other. He is much too contemptuous of the Press.

At 1.50, General Juin, loaded with maps, emerged from de Gaulle's office, simultaneously with the General, who came striding out, an unlit cigarette in his mouth.

Claude Guy declares that he is worried about the Russian advance which, in his opinion, is far too quick. He is merely echoing fears which, I strongly suspect, are not his own, fears that the Germans are deliberately retreating because they prefer to have their country occupied by the Russians. It is only too obvious that the *de facto* military occupation, when the cessation of hostilities occurs, will determine the post-war political positions of the Allies in Europe. And the Americans and the British are still held up on the Western frontiers. Guy considers this to be a matter of opinion. But the fact remains that, in theory, the Germans *should* be able to resist. We shall know the truth in the next few days. (But supposing the strength of the Russian offensive has disorganized them to such an extent that they really can do nothing more?) "One can't help feeling that the Russians are up to something," Claude Guy said.

Jacques Debû-Bridel, from the *Front National* newspaper, visibly irritated de Gaulle at this morning's Press conference by putting indiscreet questions about the 'brown maquis' (militiamen and Germans in France). He answered them with a regrettable airiness and levity. And this evening, as I entered his office to get him to sign his letters, he was saying to Gaston Palewski, who had told him that someone he wanted to see could not be found, 'No doubt he's in the brown maquis.' And he laughed with an irony tinged with contempt, possibly with an underlying bitterness, but candidly, without any kind of reserve.

At the Academy, this afternoon, my father obtained an imposing number of signatures to the shortened version of the petition. But, in certain cases, it was the preliminary reading of mine, which tipped the scales. Particularly in George Duhamel's, who, unjustly implicated by Brasillach during the trial (Brasillach claimed to have met him at the German Institute), began by vehemently refusing to sign; but after carefully reading my draft, asking who had written it, and being told in confidence that it was me, embraced my father and declared: "Well, in that case, I will sign!" (Dear Duhamel, so touching and so admirable, in every sense of the word.)

But, for all that, how can we blame General de Gaulle for refusing a reprieve? Before receiving the petition, he must have read the condemned man's appalling record and no doubt made up his mind. I overstated the case to Claude Guy this morning: our leniency, I must admit, passed all bounds and we could not reasonably call on anyone, particularly a Head of State, to share it. To Mother's questions this evening (dear Mother, rarely mentioned in these pages, but so close to me always): "But, when all's said and done, was it just from your own sense of decency or because you sincerely believed that his death will be detrimental to France that you wanted his reprieve?", I found it very difficult to reply.

These human considerations of mine have no other reasons than their own, which are unreasonable.

Saturday, 27 January, 1945

They have just come bursting noisily into my room – Mother, Father, Claire and Luce – blurting out words which I did not connect with Charles Maurras. "Solitary confinement!" General jubilation. I thought at once: "Now that de Gaulle does not have to reprieve Maurras, Brasillach has a chance . . ." But it was the thought of both Brasillach and Maurras that brought smiles to Mother's face: the threat which has been hanging over my father's life and haunting her for weeks, has receded. There is no longer any need for safety bolts on the door, or for the guardian angel, so much in the way that, in spite of everything, one refrained from calling on his services. Our neighbour, on the floor below us, will be able to remove the far-sighted placard pinned on his front door, bearing his name and profession in large capital letters, to prevent the assassins mistaking the floor or the victim. We learnt from kitchen gossip that rumours of reprisals, should Maurras be condemned to death, had reached his ears and he had thought it wise to take this precaution.

My father had to receive Brasillach's mother today. One can imagine how agonizing the visit must have been and the woman's ordeal, made even worse by a faint glimmer of hope. I cannot forget what this man is going through or what the future may hold for him. This revulsion in me, this revolt, deeper than any form of reasoning, has, I feel, a meaning. It is not merely the superficial side of me which is aroused.

All this reminds me that some good soul told me that I, too, was on the list of hostages. So now, I, too, am out of danger. Actually, I never took the threat seriously – and, in any case, nothing of that sort was capable of influencing my judgement. I think the strength of people like me (physical courage not being my strong point) is that we refuse to alter any course of action which we believe to be right under the pressure of outside events. Our type of honour lies in valuing our ideas beyond anything else – ourselves included – or rather, to identify ourselves so closely with our ideas that we cannot separate one from the other.

General de Gaulle's correspondence has been reduced by half since the first part of January. Is this a new sign of diminishing popularity, of which there are already perceptible indications? It seems likely.

It is certainly true that the General, after being attacked only through his ministers, has begun to be the target himself, though, admittedly, cautiously so far. When I see fit to say: "That is why we should do nothing to make his task more difficult, but rally round him all the more," my father agrees, but not without a reservation: "At the same time, you can't deny that he does remarkably little to encourage his supporters."

After consulting the correspondence registers next day, I realize that my estimate was completely wrong. In fact, there has been a considerable increase in the number of letters (see 31 January.)

Tuesday, 30 January, 1945

"It isn't possible! The German General-Staff have gone on strike," General de Gaulle is supposed to have said, almost reproachfully, as if the rapidity of the Russian advance went against all that one was still entitled to expect from the Nazi armies – and, primarily, against any proper application of the basic rules of military art. A German counter-threat still seems probable. But the facts speak for themselves: the gigantic and terrible exodus into the cold and snow of a starving, bombed-out population and the signs of panic and helplessness, perceptible despite the heroism of a people dying on their feet. This evening, German radio broadcast the martial songs, of which the choruses formerly reflected the terrific, loathsome *élan* of a triumphant invader. Now, at last, we could listen to them calmly, without pain or hatred. We could even indulge in a kind of nostalgia, which was by no means unpleasant. Laden with crimes, the German nation was paying and, unquestionably, the price could never be too high. However . . . my father summed up our feelings by saying: "We are like Tom Thumbs weeping over the death of the Ogre." And while the measured beat of the marches went on, he murmured: "Such a great people! . . . But what folly for a nation to get out on a path that has been mapped once and for all. Ideologies, all ideologies, are doomed to the same catastrophic failure! Napoleon, like Hitler. Politics might be described as the art of improvising, from day to day, of appearing, both with humans and things, to be as intransigent and unexacting as possible."

83

31 *January*, 1945

General de Gaulle was not in an expansive mood. Glum and distant – as though brooding over the article in this morning's *Combat,* in which the leader writer denounced the collusion between the government and the communists for the first time and had the audacity to write: "De Gaulle's silence and the inefficiency of his ministers dig an even deeper gap between us and the Provisional Government" – he did not even favour me with a smile.

I learnt this morning that the General has decided to put me in charge of all his contracts and, in a more general way, all his relations with publishers of books written by him or about him; a hard task in view of all the work for which I am already responsible at the moment and the disorder in which this new assignment has been left, but an interesting one, which I shall undertake with pleasure. De Gaulle confirmed the news without deigning to comment upon it. What he virtually said to me about it was:

"You or anyone else, as long as someone takes charge of it."

He ran rapidly through my third report on the trend of public opinion as revealed by his correspondence. The monotony of the incoming letters, their contents all much the same, made me give up these summaries a long time ago. But today I had a reason for resuming the lost habit. He read, first of all:

"General de Gaulle's personal correspondence is constantly increasing. The actual figures, since the correspondence department was opened on 17 November 1944, are as follows:

November	2,727
December	4,125
January	5,244

Total   12,097 letters

De Gaulle looked up and asked me in surprise:

"You mean, you really read four thousand letters a month?"

I briefly explained to him how my department functioned. Then he went back to his rapid reading, without so much as a flicker of an eyelid when he came to the passage, which was the underlying reason for the report:

"In general, few reactions to the death sentences and the pardons, granted or refused. Nevertheless, the Brasillach case has provoked an exceptional number of letters urging a reprieve. (About eighty to date, against less than ten for Henri Béraud, Paul Chack and Georges Suarez.)"

He passed on quickly, perhaps a shade too quickly, to speak about the following paragraph, concerning the organization of our social services . . . I had not flickered an eyelid either. But the whole thing was clear enough. He had understood me and knew that I knew that he had understood.

1 February, 1945

At the Academy, my father told me, the question of Maurras was raised immediately. Several members would have liked to dodge it, but this time there was no means of escape. My father said, as an aside, but loud enough to be heard, that if the matter were not settled that same day, 'he would be off'. Henry Bordeaux* rose and defended Maurras for more than five minutes, "not at all badly, I must admit". My father was fuming, but managed to control himself. The Duc de La Force* associated himself with Bordeaux's plea. Madelin* said: "As an historian, I should like to remind you that, in 1815, the Assembly regicides, who were members of the Institute, were expelled. Fifteen years later they were welcomed back again." Duhamel used an unfortunate phrase: "We are only obeying orders," which immediately brought an angry protest from my father. Actually, the Academy had no choice in the matter, as the penalty of national disgrace to which Maurras was sentenced automatically led to his being stripped of all honours. Duhamel drew attention to this, which enabled him to cut short the sweet/sour discussion that was on the point of breaking out.

In reference to the difficult situation in which Pierre Maurras, his brother, finds himself, which is causing us considerable anxiety (the latest news contained in a letter from him received this morning, is that he is liable to be brought to trial) my father said:

"That men so fundamentally honourable should undergo such experiences, or be threatened with them, is a sign of an unforgivable flaw in the present system." And I cannot help thinking once again: What a fuss about nothing! What fruitless discussions! How dare they all take themselves so seriously? What strange aberration makes them behave as though there were only one, solitary, absolute form of honour – their own? I know this may sound presumptuous on my part, but I must record it or suppress the truth: even in my moments of greatest excitement, emotion never clouds the most deep-seated sector of my intelligence. A mental reservation always remains, which prevents me from really condemning or hating: what relation does all this have to life, death and the essential history of the common man?

Having got that off my chest and while I play the game according to the rules like everyone else, I recognize as does my father, that the policy of the present government, of which we had such high hopes, is to some extent based on hypocrisy, deception and vengeance. Or rather, it is less the fault of the government than of the ideology from which it sprang and which has the upper hand today. I cannot help blaming de Gaulle for becoming an accessory, through his silence, to the pharisaic attitude of those who make use of his name. For it is a common characteristic of all forms of Gaullism: this deliberate hostility towards everything that did not originate with the Resistance and, more particularly, towards those Frenchmen who have sought to find outside it (against it, parallel with it, or on another plane) honour and good sense. That they were all more or less mistaken is by no means certain. In any case, I can safely say that there were innumerable degrees of error, and that the current official assessment of them lumps together the genuine traitors, those who strayed in good faith and men against whom no right-minded person should cast a stone. De Gaulle's great mistake unquestionably lay in failing to fix a *definite date* officially – for instance, the invasion of the free zone – after which no one any longer had the right to pursue the Marshal's policy without committing treason, but before which one could be regarded as loyal to France by staying loyal to him. How many Frenchmen of good will would then have been 'rehabilitated' whose services their country now so sadly lacks. I know that the 'first of the first' members of the Resistance would have had to do violence to their deepest feelings and would have gained no small merit in so doing. But France's welfare required them to sacrifice themselves on this issue, and be sacrificed, in return for which they would have been showered with decorations to make the surrender less bitter.

Admittedly, the choice of date would have had to be arbitrary in more senses than one, since any cut in the close-knit texture of events must be artificial. But to forgo isolating such a date, whichever it might have been, as the criterion for honesty and patriotism, was even more arbitrary and totally wrong. The results speak for themselves, and I do not believe that any right-minded man could consent with a clear conscience to the various expulsions and sentences which strike a blow at the integrity and honour of loyal, incorruptible Frenchmen.

In addition, there is the disturbing problem of communism which falsified and is still falsifying all the verdicts. (How can one really blame a man for having failed to realize *soon enough* that the communists were changing sides and that it was no longer they who were the traitors but those who condemned them?) And, as a result, we suffer from that feeling of uneasiness which, after slowly poisoning our initial euphoria, involves the most clear-minded among us in a dangerous, mental struggle.

And if I were to stop playing the game – thereby yielding to my innermost temptation – I should add: without taking into consideration the relativity of all this to the absolute, the force of arms which were not even ours, has decided, as an absolute, the 'national' worthiness or unworthiness of each of us.

Jean came home on leave yesterday from the peaceful Alpine front; magnificent in his *chasseur-alpin* uniform, with its red lanyards, and with a fringe of beard that makes his youthful face more vital and handsome.

2 February, 1945

Henry Bordeaux told my father the other day, with reference to his articles in *Le Figaro,* that he was "trying to extinguish the fires which he, himself, had lit". This offensive crack rankled in my father's mind and he grumbled that it was "extremely tiresome to be called a fireman by Henry Bordeaux".

At the Congress of the National Front, a delegate who opposed the re-election to the Administrative Committee of François Mauriac, advocate of a reconciliation regarded as disastrous, provoked – I am quoting *Le Monde* – "an incident which would arouse controversy at the conference and no doubt throughout France". Jacques Debû-Bridel "in a fiery extempore speech" declared: "Leniency towards traitors is a mistake, insomuch as it betrays our comrades on the battlefield and endangers the war effort. But the mistake is that of a Christian, whose every action and feeling springs from noble-mindedness. The men, whom he wants to save, sought to have him killed by the Gestapo. They attacked him continuously at a time when he was fighting side by side with us with the greatest courage. Don't forget what François Mauriac stands for throughout the world: he is the only member of the French Academy who secretly joined the Comité National des Ecrivains and gave active support to *Lettres Françaises.* He fought in all the National Front organizations and those of our Council. Such conduct was equivalent to signing his own death-warrant had he fallen into German hands, knowing himself to be easily recognized because of his fame. And he knew himself to be in particular danger because of the hatred surrounding him. To vote him off our Council because he asks forgiveness for his enemies would be an act of appalling injustice towards a great artist, who does us honour by taking part in our open discussions, in which his sentiments have as much right to be represented as any other. It would be an injustice towards a man who did not wait for the invasion to defend the cause of law and order as, for instance, during the Spanish civil war. And, finally, it would jeopardize the ideal of French unity at which we aim."

A vote was taken amidst great enthusiasm. Debû-Bridel's motion was carried by 1,809 delegates in favour, three against and one abstention. It amounted to a plebiscite for my father. (When he went back to the Congress in the afternoon, he was acclaimed.)

This plea of Debû-Bridel's moved me, but a feeling of uneasiness prevented me from taking unqualified pride in it; the same feeling that prevented me from approving of my father joining the National Front during the Occupation. Can nothing other than this new form of illusion and bondage really be found to slake our craving for liberty and integrity? With what readiness and servility all these fine gentlemen obey Master Stalin's words of command! A purge? No longer mentioned. Nor the war, unity and everything else for which we fought for so long. In return – silence on the subject of a revolution. Before his journey to Moscow, General de Gaulle's name appeared very rarely and never to his advantage in L'Humanité, which, at the time of the apotheosis of 11th November, even contrived to speak of entirely extraneous matters: But since then – just the opposite. However, what good does it do to dwell on it? One only wonders how there can still be people simple enough to be fooled by a confidence trick performed so openly.

It thus becomes clear that the whole art of politics in troubled times lies in the ability to acclaim, at the right moment, those whom we would have condemned to the firing squad a short while earlier. ('We', only in a manner of speaking, since, I, myself, would never condemn anyone to death.) We must not forget either that in the absolute there are no traitors – and that the communists' game, should they win it, will appear an admirable one on numerous grounds. Only, on this level, those who believed in a European France (or, at least, in what they so called) and who are now being shot, are not traitors, either. In short, the present political conformity is just as stifling to a man of integrity as that of Vichy. And the fact that I find it more attractive does not convince the other part of me, now continually wary, of its legitimacy.

My father, who was invited this evening to the U.S.S.R. Embassy and expected a large reception, was very surprised, on arrival, to find no signs of festivity in the ill-lit building. In fact, he dined alone with Bogomolov and Bidault. He was compelled to drink a great deal of vodka, since the ambassador seized on the least word – for example, 'Unity', though that can hardly be numbered among the least – as a pretext for proposing a toast. On the way out, even before they had left the building, the Foreign Minister expressed some reservations about Bogomolov's 'culture'. "You're undoubtedly right," agreed my father, who took exception to his speaking of Fuslange de Coutel (unless it was Debû-Bridel.)

Sunday, 4 February, 1945

Having seen my father waiting rather nervously in the A.D.C.'s office yesterday morning, I was curious to learn the results of the conference to which de Gaulle had summoned him out of the blue, and the first time they had been alone together. So, as soon as I got home in the evening, I rushed to the little blue room.

"Proust wrote somewhere," he said, "that there are no places or circumstances where one is less oneself than in 'society'. A very true remark but even truer if applied to an interview like the one I had this morning. I had left my own body and was floating somewhere far away from the tense, concentrated being who was there ... The General must certainly have found me half-witted. And I, on my side, formed an alarming impression of him. What struck me most was his enormous capacity for contempt, the 'noble officer' side of him – the attribute I gave my hero in the *Mal Aimés*. Very courteous, of course, and polite, but in a manner belonging to men of another race. He comes from the *nobility* and the *army*, and that in itself is enough to make him a being apart. But, above all, one feels him so full of pride and the consciousness of his superiority that the real difference between him and other people lies there. He is playing a dangerous game, because we are, after all, a democracy in systematically renouncing the popularity that might so easily be his. You can imagine what an effect it would have had if he had put in a brief appearance at the M.L.N.* Congress or the National Front's. For they were his followers there, the ones he could have most readily won over. Ten minutes, face to face with them, a short speech and all these good people would have gone home, warmhearted and re-assured. Instead of that, he does not let a day pass without giving his staunch supporters fresh grounds for dissatisfaction. And I repeat, this can have serious repercussions in a democracy. But there are, of course, other paths to success than through popularity. De Gaulle no doubt knows himself to be irreplaceable. No doubt, too, he can see much further ahead than we can, and it may be in accordance with a 'well thought-out and judicious' plan that he deliberately does the exact opposite of what we should have done in his place. So, while I did not draw much encouragement from the interview, it would be a mistake

89

to jump to pessimistic conclusions. My overriding impression, nonetheless, was that France had at last found her Master."

A master, not in the totalitarian sense of the word: that went without saying. But a master devoid of good nature or weakness, and of a breed not wholly to our liking. My father found an amusingly apt simile, with which to illustrate the uneasy effect that General de Gaulle has on him:

"I had the unpleasant sensation of being shut in for half an hour with a cormorant, who spoke in cormorant . . ."

The first part of the comparison tallies very correctly with the physical side of the man. The second gives an idea of his characteristic oddness.

"And as the alleged reason for the interview was your articles in *Le Figaro,* did you feel that he was trying to take you in hand again and issue a few directives?"

"Not at all. There were no complaints . . ."

"Any compliments?"

"None of them, either."

Compliments are not in his line. My poor father found this out when playing the fond parent. After the General had remarked 'that he was pleased to have his son working with him,' my father replied – expecting to elicit a kind word – that he hoped I was coping all right, and received no reply whatever.

"Isn't he a little deaf?" my father asked me, somewhat ingenuously, I should think.

"What did you talk about?"

"The National Front, to start with. De Gaulle asked me 'What, basically, is the National Front?', listened – or possibly didn't listen – to my reply, and then said: 'You know, all that is of no consequence, once we can be certain that the communists and socialists will never get together.' Some time later when I brought up the subject of private trusts, he sneered: 'Trust – there's no such thing,' which took me aback (and was also rather disturbing). He did not listen when I tried to explain to him why Vichy, for a time, had had the appearance of legality – a fact which explained, without entirely excusing them, many of the acts of treason. He answered me 'indirectly', and I saw that it would be pointless to pursue the matter. He seemed extremely surprised when I told him that there existed 'to a very small extent, admittedly, but it did exist,' a Pétain myth. 'You really think so?' he said, looking profoundly sceptical. All the same he was least reserved when he spoke about the Marshal: 'He is our great problem. And it is distressingly difficult to find a way to solve it.' He denied that the Marshal was the godfather of his son, Philippe, and added 'It's just a tall story. Like the one that claims I'm the Marshal's illegitimate son . . .' Seeing my surprise, he went on: 'Haven't you ever heard it? It keeps cropping up.' "

After that the General spoke about Chack. Then the conversation turned naturally enough to the case of Brasillach, which my father ventured to bring up. He got the impression that the General was favourably disposed:

"Brasillach . . . it's a matter of opinion . . . I don't think he'll be shot . . ." But he admitted that he had not yet studied his file. The precedent of Chack therefore warns us not to rejoice too soon. However, this one important factor has been established: the favourable approach to the matter by the judge of final appeal.

"I got the distinct impression," my father said, "that the *political* angle would not influence him one way or the other when he came to decide whether to grant or refuse a reprieve. Joxe*, whom I saw at luncheon, agreed with him – though he, too, regretted it. But it is a quality that contradicts de Gaulle's apparent inhumanity. I must add that he spoke to me about the purge with great tact and compassion . . . 'I always reprieve minors. Militiamen or not, I reprieve them.' About Maurras he made the following remark: 'Through being right, he's where he is now.' And the irony was not, essentially malicious. One feels that he is a man in the Maurras mould."

6 *February*, 1945

Against all expectations, the reprieve has been refused and Robert Brasillach was shot this morning.

8 *February*, 1945

While waiting to go into the General's office, for the first time since the Liberation, I saw Yves Farge, the erstwhile 'Bonaventure' and 'Grégoire', now the Republic's Commissioner at Lyon. He seemed pleased to run into me again and recalled "the days when we used to hug the walls together," in the Boulevard Saint-Germain and at Auteuil.

Never before had the General been so relaxed, so smiling and so approachable. Never, too, had I felt so much at my ease with him: for the first time, completely thawed, freed from hero-worship and saying whatever came into my head, as though talking to an equal.

I began with the latest job to come within my sphere of operations – publishing – and submitted a number of projects to him, among them the dummy of a book of extracts from his speeches. On the page facing short selections from de Gaulle were quotations from Marshal Pétain.

The General criticized this presentation and the spirit underlying it.

"A dialogue of this kind is out of date. More than that, it's inopportune. The time for reconciliation has come and it's no moment to highlight the reasons which the French have for failing to agree. Pétain is not a personal enemy and I want to unite the French again, without going as far as Pétain, but almost, peripherally."

He objected, too, to the omission of certain of his speeches, which he regarded as important – those at Brazzaville and in the Levant – from the clandestine editions issued by the same publishers (Le Groupe de la rue de Lille) under the same title: *Pages of History.*

I then set out, briefly, the unacceptable terms proposed to him in relation to the publication of an illustrated volume of *La France et Son Armée.* I had taken it upon myself to reject them and insist on another contract. De Gaulle smiled, as though these financial matters were scarcely worth bothering about – but I felt that, underneath, he was glad to have his interests protected.

Then the General approved Hachette's plan to issue a short study of himself, the text of which would be entrusted to me. Then he signed the sixteen letters I handed him, without making corrections in any of them. Referring to one written to Pierre Bourdan about his book, *Carnet de Retour,* he said with a smile:

"You know, that one has always been putting spokes in my wheels."

Then he read the summaries I had made of letters which might interest him. One, from Mme. Lemaigre-Dubreui, made him put a call there and then to the War Minister, Diethelm, about her husband.

The following note raised a smile: "Request to General de Gaulle for the ashes of General Frère*, executed by the Germans as the leader of the secret Army in France, which have been discovered near La Rochelle, to be laid to rest at the Invalides."

"It is difficult for me to transfer to the Invalides a general who condemned me to death. For it was he who presided at the Court Martial which condemned me to death . . . And it was he who was executed, poor chap."

He wrote: "You. Answer politely," and added:

"I want to keep my relations with that family down to a minimum. For, after all, he did condemn me to death. And one never knows what may happen . . ."

All this with a serene, deep irony.

As I left, M. Teitgen, Minister of Information, who had been waiting, took my place alongside the General.

The General has invited me to the Villa de Neuilly this evening for the first time. An ultra-official dinner. Poor Jean, who returned from leave tonight, as a humble rifleman to the Alsatian front, is a little sad and dazzled at the same time to see my father and me in the limelight, so closely associated, if not with affairs of state, at least with those responsible for them. Georges Bidault, the Foreign Minister, has invited me to a small, intimate dinner on Monday. My father leaves with the General on his next trip, which is still being kept secret.

Friday, 9 February, 1945

So last night I dined at the villa. The conversation never rose above the utmost banality – to which an extremely odd lady added an individual touch. ('But of course, Monsieur! Certainly, Monsieur!' she kept on saying to General de Gaulle.)

The General maintained an absentminded courteousness.

General Koenig, President Cassin, Laloy (who acted as interpreter during the visit to Moscow), Commander Patou and Lt. Col. Spillmann were the principal guests at this dull reception. Nevertheless, it was thrilling to be there and to dwell on the two young, unpretentious men, who were exchanging polite remarks with the ladies: de Gaulle and Koenig.

The General mentioned, incidentally, in the middle of dinner that the Americans had apparently launched that same morning the strong offensive so eagerly awaited because the synchronization of two thrusts East and West might well lead to speedy victory.

Monday, 12 February, 1945

11.00 *p.m.* Am exhausted, at the end of a day taken up with petty routine matters. Georges Bidault, our host, arrived even later than we did: he led us, Claude Guy and myself and young Alain Cordier ('a comrade in the difficult times') past the huge staircases, across the gilt salons and the pompous halls. Briand's* private dining-room, the one common to all Foreign Ministers and his own; a small blue room, very unpretentious, made even more intimate by a log fire. I was drunk with work, Claude Guy was drunk with work, Georges Bidault was drunk with work: our words seemed to come from a long way off. Bidault at once alluded to some matter, which was causing him great anxiety. At that moment, de Gaulle was having a decisive interview, and in a short while he, Bidault, would be sent for. Claude Guy knew what he was talking about and Cordier may have known, too, but I was completely in the dark. All I was aware of was that Bidault was trying hard to speak about something else, forget about it – but could not help returning to the source of his worry. What mood was the General in? How had he slept the night before? How long was the interview we all knew about likely to last? – It was already over. It had been very short. "Twelve minutes," answered Claude Guy, who had just been told so in an enigmatic message.

"I'm really very worried" – Georges Bidault repeated. "I'm particularly afraid that the General may have adopted a position before seeing me. He is playing a very dangerous game . . . The whole situation is very, very serious . . ." Finally I gathered what he was talking about: the Big Three conference, which is being held just now somewhere beside the Black Sea, and to which de Gaulle had not been invited, even *in fine*, as he had been led to believe he would be by a false Press report in the past forty-eight hours.

Bidault, after a brave effort to talk of other matters (of 'Max', of 'Bonaventure' and all the treasured memories of the underground), returned to his worries and muttered:

"With all that those three are hatching up, they're liable to get a terrific rocket from the General . . ." After a pause he added:

"De Gaulle seems to have right on his side in the circumstances, but I'm still dead against it." And he quoted the General's riposte when Caffery, the United States Ambassador told him that, at the conference-site, Stalin was staying ashore while the representatives of the Western Powers were on board ship at sea, with messengers flying to and fro between them. The General had retorted:

"It reminds me of the meeting at Tilsit, on an island in the Niemen, during the first of the Franco-Russian talks and that declaration of Alexander's to Napoleon. Do you know it?"

"I knew it," Bidault said, "and I shuddered, for it wasn't just a joke. In short, what he said was 'I hate the English as much as you do.' "

Without knowing anything definite, I could, little by little, reconstruct the whole situation. One of Bidault's first sentences before we sat down to dinner came back to me and gave me the final clues:

"There are two things, which exasperate de Gaulle; two things he can't stand . . ." And I remembered how he had spoken of the Americans with hostility and prejudice, a few evenings before, at his house when he gave as an example the fantastic amount of litres of scent which France had handed over to them, without receiving anything in return – or so he said at first – but later admitted casually, as though it were not worth taking into consideration: "In payment for which they released rations and weapons for our army."

I shall not readily forget Georges Bidault's exhausted expression, his lassitude, and his puckered face . . . He scarcely drank at all and did not touch any of the delicious dishes served to us.

Referring to a cartoon of Claude Garnier's 'de Gaulle's Tanks', which portrays the Foreign Office's victorious tank, driven by Bidault but with de Gaulle in the turret, at the head of a line of more or less bogged-down tanks (the convoy ends with the Service Corps' donkey-cart) Bidault, who was nonetheless flattered, remained clear-headed enough to remark: "There are a lot of people in that tank, far too many of them" – the complaint of a minister who is not master in his own house and has lost control of its policies. He spoke of General de Gaulle without bitterness but with a certain disenchantment.

"That's where ambition leads one: to despair. Or rather – for despair is not quite the right word – to desolation, and despondency. Ambition or a sense of duty. For it is not necessarily a question of ambition . . ."

He was thinking of General de Gaulle's loneliness.

Bidault had to be at the Villa de Neuilly by 10.00 for the conference that seemed to be making him so acutely apprehensive. So he left us and we spent the rest of the evening alone, surrounded by his official papers, in the empty Foreign Ministry, all left entirely at our mercy.

When I got home I forced myself to write these pages in my Diary despite my fatigue. My father returned this morning after an exhausting but wonderful trip, with the General: Colmar, Metz, Strasburg. The Strasburg, the Metz and the Colmar of the Liberation.

13 *February*, 1945

This morning's papers published the text of the Big Three's declaration at the end of the Yalta Conference. It puts little value on France – which finally cleared up last night's episode for me . . .

20 *February*, 1945

It is hardly worthwhile being in the President's office if I have to learn state secrets from the newspapers. The explanation of Georges Bidault's odd behaviour on the evening of 12th February was given me by a morning paper, *Combat*: "We were greatly surprised to read in the Paris edition of *The New York Herald Tribune*, on Sunday morning, a story alleging that President Roosevelt invited General de Gaulle to meet him somewhere outside France to discuss the results of the Yalta conference, and that General de Gaulle declined the invitation . . . That President Roosevelt's invitation was received on Monday the 12th at 9.00 p.m. and a reply requested by 6.00 p.m. on the following day, which would have given General de Gaulle less than twenty-four hours to prepare such an important brief . . . That the General's decision was approved by a large majority at a Cabinet Meeting on Tuesday the 13th. *The Times* claims to know, however, that M. Bidault and several other Ministers were against rejecting the United States President's invitation.

"By refusing to come to France and inviting the Head of the French Government to territory which has been French for more than a century, the United States President has struck a double blow at national pride." And this evening there was a Reuter despatch: "The general opinion is that de Gaulle was tactless in refusing the invitation, but, on the other hand, the French point of view is well understood."

I spent half an hour this afternoon with an unapproachable, cold and distant de Gaulle, on whom, whatever one did for him, no matter how well-intentioned, made no impression. He rang up Palewski while I was there and asked to be kept in close touch with the way the debate in the Consultative Assembly, in which Menthon* would be attacked, was going.

"If it becomes messy, I'll go round there to lance the abscess and make that lot see reason."

As I left, General Leclerc went in, thin and slender as a young man.

Then, I went along to the Senate: a gutless speech by François de Menthon, heard or rather not listened to, in an atmosphere of cold hostility. Then a violent, interminable speech by the communist, Gillot* – the first name on the list of seventeen speakers due to take part in this debate on justice. Donnedieu de Vabres went out from time to time to telephone Palewski. There seemed to be no need for the General to intervene. By the end of the day, as I left the Chamber, a second speaker was approaching the rostrum. It will go on for several days.

21 February, 1945

When I went into the General's office yesterday, he rang for Guy who had just left him, and said sharply:

"On the other hand, there's one man, just one, whom I have to see: Couve de Murville* . . . Of all the riff-raff you've jotted down on that list, there's not one who's of any interest to me; they'll just waste my time . . . But Couve de Murville, whom I do want to see, is not on it . . ."

Guy respectfully drew the General's attention to the fact that this gentleman's interview had already been arranged – which evoked a very military:

"Then it's 'as you were' for me. Forget I said it!"

For the record, I should like to copy down the list of the riff-raff: General Leclerc, M. Ruch, Jacques Soustelle, and General Juin. (Possibly this last name was not on the slip of paper that de Gaulle was looking at when I was there.)

I handed the General a letter from M. Albert Kammerer, the French Ambassador, which accompanied his lengthy *The Truth About the Armistice*. Its most notable passage was:

"I venture to draw your attention to page 129 and the following ones, which deal with the origins of the plans for a Franco-Britannic Union. Some inaccuracies may have slipped in . . ."

De Gaulle made me turn up the appropriate passages in the book, which he read with the cursory attention so typical of him. He jabbed the following sentence at the bottom of page 129 with his finger and gave it his approval, with a definite "All that's quite correct: 'One can accept, until there is any proof to the contrary, that the plan was conceived by Monnet*, and General de Gaulle, though the wording of it, as published, was entirely British . . .' " The following page received the same approval: "Tell him that it's all perfectly correct."

Tuesday, 6 March, 1945

On Friday, the long-awaited speech on domestic policies was delivered to the Consultative Assembly. The General, whose body seemed to emerge from the rostrum from the knees upward, spoke with his usual moderation, but without making any concessions, and once again raised the level of the debate to the only one he accepts for France: that of greatness. I had been one of the fortunate few, even among the General's personal staff, to be given a seat. Bustled by the last arrivals into the narrow gallery reserved for the Presidency, I found myself only a few feet away from Lieutenant Philippe de Gaulle, his sister Elisabeth, and Mme. de Gaulle.

"Immediately I arrived in Paris, on the 25th of August, 1944, I was handed a communication from a representative of Marshal Pétain. This representative had, by virtue of a written order dated 11th August, full powers to join with me in seeking 'such a solution as would avoid a civil war'. I showed the representative out: Gentlemen, where is the civil war?"

Applause crackled out in the Assembly, so detached and inattentive a short while before, but which had not stirred, once the General had reached the rostrum.

A little later, the silence became even more marked when de Gaulle came to the hoped-for declarations:

O.G.—7

"Yes, tomorrow, it will be the State's task itself to ensure the development of the great sources of energy – coal, electricity and petrol – as well as the principal means of transport, rail, shipping and airlines, and the means of transportation, on which all the rest depends. It will be its task to raise the main metallurgical industries to their essential production level . . . It will be its task to provide credit . . ."

He was interrupted by thunderous applause. But a moment later, a wave of disappointment ran through the assembly. De Gaulle went on to postpone the implementation of his splendid promises:

"But the timing and the drawing-up of the provisional terms for transfers and nationalizations are matters of opportunity, preparation and resources . . ."

There was a stifled backlash and some derisive laughter. A voice from somewhere was raised in an ironical: "So that's that!" I was struck by the sceptical and disillusioned expression on Georges Izard's face, when I happened to look his way.

"Ladies and gentlemen, in setting out the plan, which it has followed in step with the Liberation, which it wishes to continue to follow and which it recommends to the nation as something worth striving for in the long days to come, the government seeks less than ever to conceal the immensity of the task. But, if we should ever come to be daunted by it, we should only have to harken to the profound voice of our people, as one listens to the distant murmur of the sea to be strengthened in our determination. For, between the sickly shadows of decline and the clear, harsh light of renascence, we know what the choice of France would be."

On this peroration, warmly applauded, the session was suspended.

When it was resumed, the platform was almost empty; after the star had done his 'number', everybody had left. But I had suspected that this was not the end. André Hauriou* was the first to speak, and both his compliments and criticisms were fair. His speech gave the General an opportunity to define his ideas, more clearly on one important point, in a few striking sentences, which his tone made even more telling. Daniel Mayer, General Secretary of the Socialist Party, then went to the rostrum and was much more incisive and bitter:

"I shall confine myself, General, to reminding you here of some of the matters which I have already raised in the privacy of your office. The purge is unsatisfactory: it is proceeding too slowly, and it creates an impression of injustice. The injustice of verdicts, disparity between one region and another and sometimes, when the sentences pronounced unquestionably correspond with the country's expectations, its anxieties or, in any case, its sense of justice . . ."

98

(At this point, I saw the General shift in his seat, the whole length of his body bristling with impatience.)

". . . the exercise of a right of reprieve, against the principle of which, all the same, I must solemnly stress, we are in no way opposed." ('That would be the last straw,' seemed to be passing through the General's mind. He was becoming increasingly restless, his irritation exasperated by the applause with which all these circumlocutions were greeted.)

". . . all tend to confirm the regrettable impression that there are two kinds of justice." The speaker took advantage of the applause to make a pregnant pause. Then – with de Gaulle wriggling more and more in his seat – he added:

"General, in reply more perhaps to your smile than to your speech – I shall cite only one example, dispassionately, straightforwardly and loyally, as you must well know. The country has not understood the reprieve granted to Henri Béraud."

More applause and the beginning of a new sentence, but de Gaulle (who could stand no more) interrupted the speaker, and there was the following exchange, which I take from the *Journal Officiel,* though the words were so weighty that I shall never forget them.

The President of the Provisional Government: You know that I cannot reply to you on this subject. Perhaps it would be better if you did not raise it.

M. Daniel Mayer: Then I will not pursue this part of my speech, in order to save you from not answering me. (*Smiles*)

The President of the Provisional Government: You are aware of the responsibilities and the nature of the right of reprieve, you are aware of whence it springs. And I repeat that it is impossible for whoever acts provisionally as Chief of State to give explanations of the way in which he exercises this right of reprieve in accordance with his conscience.

M. Daniel Mayer: General, I had no intention of embarrassing you . . .

President of the Provisional Government: You do not embarrass me at all. I merely wish to repeat that the right of reprieve being what it is you might have spared us this dialogue on a subject which I cannot be discussing.

What the official shorthand report does not convey is the feeling of weariness and reluctance in the phrase 'whoever acts as Chief of State', moderated by the relief of the adverb 'provisionally', (fortunately, though only implied, was nonetheless expressed). What it does not convey is the pathos of the sentence in which he referred to his conscience. And, finally, the impatience of his: "You do not embarrass me at all."

There followed a much less honest speech from the communist Jacques Duclos* – with a rather comical digression on the subject of Marshal Pétain's representative:

"I hope he was arrested?"

His tone was full of scepticism, a scepticism that raised a laugh in the Assembly. Then the General replied, too low for us to catch what he said from the gallery. The *Journal Officiel* reports it as:

"You need have no doubts about that . . ." All I myself, heard was the 'Monsieur Duclos' – but it was clearly filled with contempt.

When Monsieur Albert Gazier, representing the C.G.T.* followed Duclos on the rostrum, the General slipped away – and I did the same.

7 March, 1945

When I was talking to the General about the 'war of 1940', he pulled me up sharply. It was still one and the same war, he pointed out. One can sense the importance he attaches to this point – which, of course, no one would think of disputing.

Otherwise, he was pleasanter than I have ever seen him. My session with him was in two parts, as we were interrupted in the middle of what we were doing by a delegation. He spoke a lot – and I a little – of one thing and another, not very interesting in themselves, but acquiring importance coming from his lips, and it occurred to me that, if I did not participate in the inner life of his office (not being among those who attend the Palewskian morning conference), I nevertheless had the incredible good fortune, rare even among more important members of his staff, of seeing him, de Gaulle, in person.

Having been given an autographed letter of Gambetta's, by 'the widow Ranc', he read carefully through the typewritten copy of it, which I had attached. His finger stabbed at the third line, which he read out loud to me:

"But, take it from me, socialism and the Motherland will always be two different things." His tone of voice, expressing full approval, became increasingly emphatic. He picked out another sentence to read to me: "The oriental war ethic assumes a religious form," and added the comment, "That's not far off the mark," which he repeated about various other passages.

When he had finished it, he asked me to whom the letter had been written and, when I told him, wrote neatly in blue pencil, on the third page, 'written to Ranc'.

Then – he had no engagements that evening and was not in any hurry – he lingered over the copy of the *Journal Officiel* of the Commune, which the 'widow Ranc' had also given him (No. 92 – Monday, 2 April, 1871). He read aloud:

"The Paris commune enacts: 1) The title and the functions of the Commander in Chief are abolished. 2) Citizen Brunel is relieved from his duties . . . etc." and pointing to the signatures of the members of the 'Executive Commission', he said, ironically:

"Eudes . . . Bergeret . . . Ed. Vaillant . . . All members of the F.F.I., eh?"

And he was still smiling when he read me the following sentences, which bear a close resemblance to those we are constantly reading in today's papers:

"An outrage has just occurred. A public service, directly answerable to the citizens, which can only justify its receipt of a licence by the integrity with which it carries out its commercial duties, has been shamefully sacrificed to purely political interests. In the last few days, the postal service has been systematically disorganized by those who accepted the mandate to run it . . . etc."

The General was surprised a moment later, to find in this copy of the *J.O.* of the Commune a report on the Versailles Assembly – 'presided over by M. Grévy' – and read me the first few lines. It was obvious that his contempt for all the pettinesses inseparable from politics, which impede his progress towards the noble goals at which he aims, found fresh fodder in these proceedings.

General de Gaulle picked out this sentence from a report by my social assistant Cécile Idrac: – 'In spite of their morale, it was clear that the old Free French troops were hoping to receive special treatment' – and commented, slightly ironically but affectionately:

"Those old Free French troops were always a bit touchy!"

When one is with this man, so peaceful and serene, it is difficult to think of what his preoccupation must be in these days of tension with the Allies. France has refused to be a power 'playing away from home' at the San Francisco Conference. While the bulk of the American Press deplores this new snub of de Gaulle's to the Big Three; one of their papers, *The Baltimore Sun*, considers that France's refusal to patronize the conference is part of a 'clever and complicated game of de Gaulle's, who thinks that the only way to preserve the present equilibrium is to keep national pride near its boiling point.' The paper expresses the hope that the French people will stop de Gaulle should he show signs of going too far . . .

It was not that great equilibrist by the world's exalted standards who received me this evening. With reference to a remote relation's request to see him, General de Gaulle said to me:

"They're extraordinary, all these people, who haven't a moment's hesitation in pestering the Head of the State with their petty affairs . . ."

And when Charles de Gaulle utters the word 'Head of State', damn it, one knows just how much they mean to him.

A telephone call from Luizet, the Prefect of Police. Very amiable. The second of the day. It concerns the 'transfer of the body' requested by my father. I don't know anything about it. Never mind; everything has been arranged. I learned this evening, when I delivered the message, that it concerned Robert Brasillach who was still in a common grave and whose family had appealed – naturally – to my father. Poor Brasillach whom I used to watch with such hatred sneaking down the street. That poor Brasillach, in whose face I had read a long time ago the execution to come. A weak face – deceptively so – for his courage was magnificent. He is already becoming a legend. But this evening my father was quite content to have retrieved his body. The irremediable makes one less demanding. And I knew, before having heard him express them, the General's views on the exercise of the right of reprieve. So, in spite of my disappointment, you might even say my revolt, there was never a moment when I could really hold it against him.

Full dress-rehearsal and first night of the *Mal Aimés*. It was very good and seems to be an enormous success.

Wednesday, 14 March, 1945

Shall I make another attempt to recall General de Gaulle's words last night, during dinner at the Villa de Neuilly? Their importance does not seem to me to warrant such an effort. Frankly, what gave these moments their particular value was not so much their actual content as the fact of having been present during them. Those conversations between de Gaulle and Vincent Auriol*, the President of the Provisional Government's monologue on Oradour, the information he gave on the powers of resistance of a Germany defeated on all fronts, but still continuing to fight on all of them, and on the astonishing offer from the Reich to return us all our deported women, old men and children – his outbursts, his innuendos, his silences; all these counted for little, in short, compared with the amazing fact, to which I cannot get accustomed; my presence alongside this man, whom I had regarded for so long as the most glamorous and, equally, the least credible of myths, whom nothing had led me to believe I should one day have access or suppose that the liberation of my country would ever render this miracle possible: to meet, see, touch and hear Charles de Gaulle. Now it had come about that he had become Head of State and had invited me into his own home. It had come about that he was aware of my existence, *since he knew my name.* It was, in fact, this small detail, that helped me to measure the immeasurable character of this astonishing adventure. He presented me to Vincent Auriol, he presented me to Mme. Monick, wife of the governor of the Banque de France and it was really my name, all the syllables of my Christian name and surname that issued from his lips. Even more, in the course of conversation, he happened to ask me a question and called me Claude. This last point, if one knows de Gaulle, is virtually inconceivable: his inhabitual graciousness, which in his behaviour towards me almost amounted to familiarity (in so far as he is capable of it . . .)

"Nothing makes me more conscious of the complete lack of able men from which France is suffering than the importance I have acquired," writes my father, simply, modestly, after becoming the most noted journalist of France, and his article gets off to a brilliant start.

6.45 *p.m.* Claude Guy who had just been present at the recording of the speech, which de Gaulle is delivering this evening on the occasion of the Japanese aggression in Indochina, told me that the General said to him: "I am going to build up the incident." In fact, he seems to have magnified the French resistance and particularly, its effectiveness.

"Had there been only two Frenchmen, who had taken refuge in the northern sector of the country when fighting broke out, it would have been necessary to build up the incident in view of the Americans and their possible claims."

When I got here about 3.00 for some odd reason not one of the A.D.C.s was around. It fell to me to welcome the General when he arrived. This boiled down to opening and then shutting the two doors to his office.

When I anxiously asked Claude Guy, a few moments later, whether I had committed a breach of protocol in failing to help the General off with his coat, he answered:

"My God, no! He hates it. Lighting his own cigar and taking off his own coat are the only gestures which still give him a certain illusion of independence . . ."

15 *March,* 1945

With the arrival of Spring, some forgotten joys are open to me, of which I avail myself all the more readily because an unaccustomed physical euphoria has succeeded the exhaustion of the last few months. At the wheel of my delightful convertible, I get tipsy on fresh air. My republican guard rides in the dickey. I take some of my friends along with me. After lunch, Jean Duché and I drive to the Bois to get some exercise.

Today my father came with us. We discovered, in one of the most charming corners of the Bois, near Longchamp, a small monument commemorating the dozens of young men shot there by the Germans in August. One of the trees still carries horrible scars, at the height of a man's heart. The sunlight never seemed so dazzling to us as it did at this spot, nor so moving the slight green haze enveloping the branches of the trees. We thought with heavy hearts of this insane world: those luckless young men might well have been spared man's inhumanity to man.

This morning I had a very long session with General de Gaulle. In reference to a petition, he told me that within the next few months, all militiamen, whether tried or not, who had not committed crimes, would enjoy an amnesty, allowing them to make good in, for example, Indochina. I was struck by the humanity with which he announced the decision, coming as it did, so unexpectedly from a Head of State. He had just read very carefully the summary I had made of a letter from Mme. Lorquil d'Estienne d'Orves, the adoptive mother of an executed resistant. "Wants to have an interview to explain the position of two young men, to whom she is greatly attached, who have served in the militia. These two brothers, whose family include three French marshals, were misled as to the real role of the militia; she vouches for their loyalty to France. The elder, who was studying for his entrance to Saint-Cyr, wants to enlist, but cannot do so because an arrest warrant has been issued against him. His class has been called up and he will be listed as a deserter. She wants to know what can be done to help him." The General murmured:

"So the poor boy's lying low . . ."

After considerable reflection, he went on:

"He must be told to be patient. All those wretched men won't be kept in prison indefinitely. Sooner or later, in a few months, when things have calmed down . . . They must be patient."

Then de Gaulle wrote on the summary of the letter:

"Reply that I've read her letter and advise patience."

On another extract, relating to a summary execution carried out in the neighbourhood of Limoges during the insurrection, he wrote in his own hand: "Admiral Ortoli. (He is the new head of the War Office, having replaced Rancourt.) Take up this matter personally with Diethelm. If a *crime* has been committed, I consider it vital that it should be *punished*."

I have not yet spoken here of the inconceivable naïvety of those who send in reports concerning the importance of their work. Earnest gentlemen, smothered in diplomas, who have no hesitation in writing to me a dozen times about some plan for national restoration, scarcely less trite and utopian than the current projects. One of them, a Professor at the School of Political Science, handed me, with the utmost seriousness, a hackneyed rehash of Balzac and Courteline on employees and bureaucrats . . . "You may read it if you like," he told me condescendingly as he gave me the letter addressed to the General (as if I were not obliged to read everything and make a selection).

This morning, I handed his letter to de Gaulle, who began to read it with his usual attention, conscientious as he always is, even about minor matters. But he was brought up short by the following passage: "Today, instead of rejoicing in victories, I am in mourning for the eager flower of youth, more victims of the blunders of their friends than from the blows of their enemies. And my influence is insufficient to snatch from the general confusion the few men of goodwill left us, who are dazed by the incoherence of the crew from which with a colossal attempt for humanity, you have formed a government."

The General laughed and closed the file, saying:

"I'm certainly not going to reply to a gentleman, who speaks like that about men in whom I've placed my confidence . . ."

21 March, 1945

For quite a while, numberless people who, sincerely or otherwise, unbiased or otherwise, have taken an unfavourable view of the government's policies, have not included General de Gaulle in their harsh criticisms. But this restraint on their part has not lasted for more than a few months. Today, it would be an understatement to say that General de Gaulle has come in for some criticism: he has, in fact, become the target for the greater part of it—still obliquely in the Press, but quite openly in general conversation. Very few people, no matter to which party they belong, have escaped the contagion: it is fashionable now to denigrate Charles de Gaulle, to spread it about that he is not a man you can trust, that he has given ample proof of his incompetence in dealing with Government business, and other such charming remarks. In political circles, things have even reached the stage where the attitude towards him is faintly ironical, as though it would be absurd to take a soldier seriously.

Only yesterday there I was watching these independent-minded people in the Consultative Assembly at the moment when the debate on

the colonial budget was coming to an end and de Gaulle stood up . . .
His speech was awaited with a curiosity, in no way compatible, I must
record, with the assumed indifference exhibited towards the General.
All the delegates were there, an unusual thing in itself; even more unusual, they kept quiet and refrained from reading their newspapers.
There was total silence, heavy with suspense, when General de Gaulle
rose from his seat and began to speak, almost in a conversational tone of
voice:

"It is remarkable, during a debate on the present issue, that a common
idea, though with subtle differences in concept, should have emerged in
these surroundings in relation to something for which we have found a
beautiful word; one which henceforward we must retain not only in our
speeches, but in our institutions: French community."

There was applause, but the attentive silence was quickly re-established as everyone eagerly waited for him to go on. De Gaulle then
alluded to another danger threatening our empire – not one coming
from our enemies but from our friends. He did so in measured, un-
emphatic, but explicit terms:

"Gentlemen," (I am again quoting from the *J.O.*, but I can still hear
his weighty words) "no more than the Minister for the Colonies does the
President of the Government attach greater importance than they may
deserve to suggestions from newspapers or conferences abroad. Nevertheless, there are many reasons why we should keep our ears open. And
I should add that the events taking place in Indochina at this very
moment, events steeped in bloodshed for us and equally for our friends,
give us much food for thought."

Then de Gaulle read out a telegram to the Assembly, which the
government had received that same morning from the heroic defenders
of Monkay. This direct contact between the Assembly and the army in
Indochina, which was what the General intended, was established
immediately, and, for the first time, one had the feeling that these delegates, as a body, represented something other than their various
mediocrities, something infinitely greater: France.

"Lieutenant-Colonel Lecoq" (the officer commanding our troops in
Monkay, de Gaulle explained) "has been killed in action during the
attack at Hakoi." At this first sentence of the telegram, the whole
Assembly and the public in the galleries stood up. The General went on
reading:

"I am insisting that the parachuting of arms and ammunition shall
be carried out." On this de Gaulle commented:

"You are aware, gentlemen, from whom these drops are expected and
still awaited today."

Then followed the last words of the telegram, which brought the hard, far-off fighting so close, as well as the sentiment so underlying them:

"As long as we have arms and ammunition we shall hold out. Help us in every way you can. Morale is excellent. Long live France!"

"Long live France!", Georges Bidault echoed, in a choked but audible voice, and, amidst the applause, other delegates took up the cry. The emotion that seized us then was truly historic; by which I mean that it did not relate to anything that we experience in everyday life. And it was as if a hand were gripping my heart when General de Gaulle exclaimed, before resuming his seat:

"Gentlemen, I conclude by appealing to you all to join with me in establishing that, when vital matters are at stake – and for some months to come there are likely to be none other – we are, all of us, completely *united*."

This last word, which he stressed in his powerful voice, unleashed unanimous applause even from those who, in general, seek to escape from the union thus proclaimed and acclaimed. Willy-nilly, they found themselves compelled to recognize it in principle, and to recognize the very man of whom they were so anxious to rid themselves, but who, they could not fail to remember, had served their country, the country which no one knew better than he how to defend, since he was the incarnation of it in the eyes of the world.

Naturally, these great gusts of history swept away the trivial political alignments. Neither the R. P. Philipp* nor Jacques Debû-Bridel, with whom my father dined last night, made any allusion to this memorable session, at which, however, they had been present. No doubt, they have already recovered from it. No doubt they were already regretting their momentary enthusiasm. But it was too late, gentlemen: General de Gaulle had shown you clearly, once again, that when the voice of France speaks through his lips, you can do nothing but silence those of your petty ambitions. (I am assuming here, quite gratuitously, that the R.P. Philipp and Monsieur Jacques Debû-Bridel represent a state of mind which may not be theirs at all but which is the very widely-spread one I was denouncing earlier on.)

. . . . .

My cousin, Bernard Brousse, was killed in Germany, in battle, on 21st April. He was twenty-two.

. . . . .

Tuesday, 15 *May,* 1945

Midnight. Perhaps I only fully realized that peace had been restored to us this evening, as I walked down the Avenue Marceau and passed the lighted windows of a private house, opening on music and the shadowy figures of dancers at a ball. The abandon of the crowds in the transfigured Paris of the V days had filled me with wonder without entirely awakening me to the reality, I now suddenly discovered. But here I am, aghast, after an exhausting day, faced with having to write this Diary after a silence of nearly two months. If I decide to take it up again (a task which has become more difficult each day because of the accumulation of things left unmentioned) it must be without any thought of returning, for the time being anyway, to those days which have passed by without my having jotted down any notes on them. So I shall keep silent about the tears I shed, when I heard that, by a miracle, my brother had escaped death in battle; I shall keep silent about my writing – which partly and quite truthfully explains the neglect of my Diary – in particular, the compiling of *Aimer Balzac,* already in the publisher's hands and evolved from some previous notes, considerably improved; I shall keep silent about the hours spent over the possible adaptation of *Asmodée* for the screen; the publication, at last! of my *Cocteau* and the disillusioning days at the office; I shall keep silent about the emotions aroused by victory and the Nazi capitulation, the marvel of an untouched Paris, scoured in every direction in the car, day and night, amid the overwhelming joy of the crowd, with its flags, its dances, its shouting, and its wonderful monuments, rescued from the dark for the first time for five years, I shall keep silent about my youth, more prolific than ever, richer than ever, in promise and plans . . . But keeping silent about all that, in the way I am doing it, amounts to telling it – and, alas, telling it badly!

This afternoon de Gaulle addressed the Consultative Assembly on the victory: he spoke with restraint, wasting no time on appearing triumphant, since his victory was patent to everyone. It wrung one's heart to think of all the sacrifices it took to make this speech possible. There was a particularly moving moment when the General recalled France's entry into the war in 1939, alone with England, alone, weak and short of resources, in the avant garde of other countries – and when he declared that, despite all that her chosen path had cost her – France had no regrets. The entire Assembly rose to its feet enthusiastically, all except the communists, who could not disassociate themselves from their present programme policy, and remained rooted to their seats, pale and assuming indifference. A Marseillaise, this time joined in by everyone, followed the General's speech, a Marseillaise which the R.P. Carrière*, more purple in the face than usual, invigorated with his powerful voice and prevented from coming to a premature end. Then to shouts of "Vive la France!" came those of "Vive la République!" which seemed designed to oppose the former rather than mingle with them – an ill-timed demonstration of the communists, whose president Felix Gouin, clumsily stressed the indecency of the performance by shouting: "That's right, gentlemen: Long live France and long live the Republic. The session is adjourned . . ."

An hour later, I was in the General's office. I have passed over many work-sessions we had together by failing to keep up my Diary! His windows were open on to the summer garden, where blackbirds were chattering. The white flakes of the poplars snowed gently down. This man, whose khaki sleeve, with its two glittering stars, held my eye, was the very same man whom I had seen at the Arc de Triomphe, on Victory day, surrounded by a crowd wildly cheering him, his face lit up by a joy he could not restrain; the very same man, who, a short while before, had addressed a victorious France from the Senate rostrum. And there he was now, adding a postscript to a letter I had handed to him for signature, thanking Mme. Mante-Rostand, for a beautiful copy of *L'Aiglon* which she had given him on Victory Day:

"I have often repeated, during the last five years, these lines of Edmond Rostand:

'All I want to see is victory!
Do not ask me: after that?
After that – I am ready for the dark night
And the sun beneath the cypresses.' "

Then he read, one after the other, all the pro-Pétain letters, which I had given him. (Now I come to think of it, it is since I stopped writing my Diary that the Marshal gave himself up.) He had not spared a glance or a thought for the much more voluminous file of 'anti' letters, but he paused for a moment over the others, saying "It must have taken courage to sign . . ." (I had not shown him the anonymous ones) and then remarking: "There are still men and women who have faith in him, there's no doubt about that." He added, as if in confidence (but I had heard him say much the same thing a short time before at a dinner in the Salle des Armures):

"I don't believe either, that he imagined he would go as far as he did, or wanted to . . . He was a great man, who was ruined by ambition and by age . . . I saw this great man that he was die in 1925 . . . And I must say that he did not assume power in 1940 with any good intent."

He said this to me, the humblest member of his staff, who did not venture to reply.

"What do you think of the elections?" he had asked me point-blank, during one of our preceding meetings. But then, seeing that it was a direct question, I did reply as best I could, saying that I had not expected the communists to be so successful.

"No? Why not?" When I gave my reasons, he pointed out that the success was more apparent than real, since it was obtained by falsifying the electoral rolls and through the good offices of a 'number of idiots'.

"Besides, I've worked it out: in the aggregate, they haven't made any headway: they haven't gained a single seat in Paris and, if anything, they've lost in the provinces."

Another time, referring to two books by Jacques Maritain, which I had brought him, he said:

"Those lucky dogs who can afford the luxury of speculation . . ."

"It's finished now, General, as far as he's concerned, thanks to you." (An allusion to Jacques Maritain's appointment as Ambassador to the Holy See.)

"Oh, not for long . . . "

On yet another day, a letter from Vice-Admiral Hall in connection with Lady Baden-Powell led to some remarkable disclosures about the Intelligence Service.

When I left him, this evening, he was still murmuring some of Rostand's verses.

Now, I can go to sleep, almost with a clear conscience. But, naturally, a great deal has been left unsaid: about this peace which is just beginning and which is in danger almost before it is born; about my personal life, at the heart of these great events, of which I know practically nothing, but which cast me alternatively into the depths and heights; about the exhaustion of my overtaxed mind, and about the great hopes of my unencumbered heart. But, the fact is, I no longer have time to write a worthwhile Diary.

25 June, 1945

The shape which the Constituent Assembly will take when it next meets is still the subject of long discussions among us. The ultra-reasonable Brouillet argued with increasing determination against Palewski, who wholeheartedly embraces the General's point of view. Brouillet, with a shade of irony, declared himself surprised by the favourable impressions which the Republican commissioners, who all collected in Paris yesterday and the day before, carried away with them, according to Palewski, after their various interviews with de Gaulle. He pointed out that the General has a particularly convincing manner, when face to face, of exposing and imposing his ideas, and that the Republican commissioners, who, for the most part, are young and comparatively diffident, cannot fail to be momentarily impressed by him. The fact remained that they very well knew what they want and, even more, what they did not want. With one or two exceptions, they were, according to him, dismayed by the General's desire to establish not one Assembly but two. Brouillet, whose slow, quiet, judicious way of talking, made the underlying vehemence all the more apparent (no doubt he is less haughty when with the General and just as diffident as the Republican commission) declared that it was all wrong for de Gaulle to go against the solemn promises he made to the country during the Occupation, when he announced the establishment of one Constituent Assembly.

Louis Vallon* again supported Brouillet's view, saying that the only wise and just policy was one which inspired confidence. To originate a duel Constituent Assembly would denote a fatal distrust of universal suffrage. If the intentions and goodwill of the Assembly were called in question even before it met, the majority of its members were bound to be alienated, even though the greater part of them were disposed to serve the General. It would be far better if the Assembly, which would be fully occupied with its constitutional tasks, were itself to entrust the executive power to the General rather than that he should claim it in advance.

The upshot of all this is that the General's intentions – though it is not yet possible to say in what form or when they will be disclosed – are clearly to ask the French people for a vote of confidence: either they acknowledge his right to govern and grant him full powers – or he goes. Brouillet saw this as blackmail and open to the strongest criticism.

However this may be, I have a growing impression that the General's real intentions – or, more precisely, his aspirations – remain unknown, or anyway unfathomable even to his closest associates. In my opinion de Gaulle is determined to save France along the lines he has chosen because they seem to him the only effective ones. But it is France which is always uppermost in his mind, and not himself. So much so that it would surprise me if he showed any stubbornness should she deliberately refuse to be saved. My father said to me, sadly, a short while ago, that he was afraid that de Gaulle is too big for France.

Admiral Barjot, Juin's right-hand man, declared in the cold, measured tones that always arouse my admiration (Brouillet is incapable of such detachment) that the third world war had already virtually begun, though there was still hope that at least it would not break out in Europe. Actually, while Soviet ambitions on the continent disquiet the British and prompt them to take steps which could lead to war at any time, they cause little concern to the Americans, whose interests do not clash in any way with those of the Russians in this particular sphere. According to several staff officers, to whom he had spoken, the Americans are determined to avert any armed conflict between the Russians and the British (in this connection Barjot said that the real interpretation of the present occurences in Syria is to be found in the lack of confidence which the British have in France's ability to resist the imperialistic aims of her Russian allies; namely the securing of strategic bases on the edge of the Asiatic continent, at France's expense.)

On the other hand, American and Russian interests are likely to conflict in Manchuria and it is certain that, even if the third world war can be averted, there will be localized clashes in this area. Barjot believes that the war against Japan is bound to last for another year and a half at the minimum. By taking Okinawa, which involves them in enormous losses, the Americans have now acquired the stronghold that will enable them to undertake operations designed to cut off Japan from her armies fighting in China, either by further landings to establish a bridgehead in the southern islands of the Japanese archipelago, or by obtaining a foothold in China.

My resignation, delivered to Palewski and refused by him, has at last enabled me to occupy the place in the office which he should have given me of his own accord a long time ago, but which only the threat of my departure and of the explanations I would give for it in front of General de Gaulle have driven him to grant me. In spite of this, the very limited but, at the same time, individual duties which fall to me give me a special position of my own in the office, with which I am well satisfied, since my ambitions lie less and less in the political field. The publcation, some time ago, of my *Cocteau*, which was very well received and the imminent publication of my *Balzac* have aroused in me a taste for more private activities.

26 June, 1945

Gaston Palewski's faith in General de Gaulle's infallibility continues to astonish me. His confidence is such that he cannot conceive that it may not be shared by every Frenchman. When Brouillet said, this morning, that if the socialists and the communists were to leave the government, the General would be compelled either to retire or to face the elections with no other support than the right, Palewski declared that the socialist party would certainly be split when the question arose of its being responsible for the General leaving. Brouillet seemed sceptical but on this point I think Palewski has not misjudged the situation and that my father was right yesterday in saying that when the crisis arises, as it must do sooner or later, de Gaulle will discover that he has numerous true friends in all the parties. It is clear that the General's position will never be stronger than when he has been led to retire from an office, to which he will be recalled with little delay. A fact which, in parentheses, and applied to my own modest part in the affair, does not give me much hope of a long holiday.

Brouillet told me that he had a long conversation with the General yesterday on the subject of the Constituent Assembly. He stated his own point of view without reservation, but found the General impregnably entrenched in each of his positions, which he defended by employing a dialectic so closely woven that no critic could have penetrated its texture.

"Nevertheless," Brouillet added, "I did score on one point, just one, when I said, in reply to his arguments: 'The parties which you keep on mentioning no longer represent a living soul in France.' By adopting the system of proportional representation, he was, in effect, making these parties the framework of the political institutions in process of formation. My line of argument seemed to strike him; it was obvious that it had not occurred to him before."

Whether or not this is so, and despite Palewski's claim that he has taken up a position from which he will not budge, the General, starting this evening, is going in for widespread consultations. Saillant, Blum, Reynaud and other seigneurs are on tonight's list.

I have not made much progress, myself, in getting to know the General. He is always extremely amiable towards me. When I saw fit to hand in my resignation to Palewski once again, he refused it and told me "that I was greatly appreciated in the firm and particularly by the General". The character of the matters which I have to handle, does not put me in a position to participate even in the smallest degree in the conduct of serious matters and I draw little profit from my interviews with de Gaulle. I did not think I was wrong, however, when I sensed at the very start, not that he despises his fellow-men, as some people claim, but that he attaches no importance to them as individuals. All that concerns him is what they represent, and one could say of him what Alain said of Balzac, namely that he envisages them in sets. In a preface by Nachin to a collection of the General's old articles, of which I have just read the proofs, there is a similar remark. But Bénouville, Director of the Ministry of Information, whom I saw in his office on Saturday, told me that during a mission which took him to Algiers, under the Occupation, as representative of the Resistance, the General flew into a violent temper when told that he did not like his fellow-men. I believe, actually, that he is capable of friendship, even affection, based on respect. But it is certain that, from his earliest youth, he has been at great pains to conceal it. The comments which he makes when I inform him of the death of one of his comrades-in-arms reveal a human interest even if only expressed in monosyllables.

27 June, 1945

My father lunched yesterday with Léon Blum, who was to have an interview that same evening with General de Gaulle. Blum seemed very unhappy about the General's obstinacy in insisting that all his ministers approve his decision to establish two Chambers, according to the spirit and letter of the Constitution of 1875. The result is that the socialist ministers will be forced to resign and, so, in principle, will the communist ministers: "though one never knows, with them," said Blum, who, according to my father, felt that de Gaulle was seeking to retire from office.

Palewski, to whom I repeated this conversation, told me that he saw Blum, last night, when he left the General's office: "Mr. President," I said to him, "are you going to take the responsibility of removing the support of the left from the General?" He answered in that soft, plaintive voice of his: "I don't see how I can possibly do otherwise."

This evening the General is seeing Maurice Thorez, who obviously holds the key to the situation. If the communist ministers resign from the government, the crisis will be overt. Anyway, for the first time for several months one feels able to breathe freely. I prefer a clear-cut situation like the one looming ahead to the heavy atmosphere of suspicion, uncertainty, deceit, petty plots and mediocre ambitions in which we have been suffocating.

Extract from today's *La Nation*: '*Killed in error*'.

"A few days ago, a pianist named Delerue, better known under the name of Peter, was kidnapped by some men in a car and killed. Investigations have disclosed that it was a case of mistaken identity. The murderers, in fact, had believed that they were dealing with a militiaman, named Peter, also a musician, who had acted as a Gestapo agent. This latter had already been executed by the maquis in July 1944."

The collective aberration has reached such a point nowadays that such news items can be published in this form without it occurring to anyone to be surprised.

Marshal Montgomery has declared in all seriousness – according to this report in *Le Monde* of 23 June: –

"British troops do their best to obey the ban on fraternization," said the British Commander-in-Chief, "but young German girls, in their scanty clothes, may well have formed an organized plan to induce them to disobey the order. After consultation with General Eisenhower, it has been agreed that soldiers may say: 'Good morning, how are you?' to young German girls, but it is to be feared that things will not stop there."

Thursday, 28 June, 1945

Following Maurice Thorez's visit the outlook, on the whole, is optimistic. It is too early to say with any certainty that the General has won the battle, since the communists seem still to have reserved their decision, pending a reply from Stalin, whom they have no doubt consulted on such an important question. But in the morning's *Le Populaire*, Blum seems disposed towards making certain concessions, which is a definite clue. We shall know in a few days where we stand.

Not a single day passes, however, without a new *casus belli* dividing the 'Allies'. Today, it is the new arbitrary Soviet claim to the Straits. The Turks appear to have rejected their demand, which explains the presence of those British troops, who, surprisingly, were seen taking up positions in large numbers the other day on the borders of Yugoslavia and Greece.

Last night, I dined with my father, Michel Brousse and Henri Guillemin at the Maison des Alliés. The conversation we had during dinner enabled me to pinpoint once again one of my most continual sources of uneasiness since the Liberation, namely—the qualms of conscience I experience at finding myself, in no matter how small a degree, an accessory to the injustices of the present Justice. In my view, one of General de Gaulle's mistakes lay in failing to have his government in Algiers prepare the case against the Marshal, so that it could have been heard, in his absence, as soon as the Liberation occurred. This would have allowed the degrees of guilt of those who, at one time or another, had adhered to the Vichy Government, to be precisely determined. Smiting the leader would have made it possible to show leniency towards those who had been genuinely deluded by him. By failing to do this the General has put justice up to auction between parties and passions. It is shocking to see sometimes death and hard labour dealt out to the small fry while those really guilty get away with minor penalties. In this connection, it is noticeable that, due to the fact that there are a number of soldiers and lawyers in the government, the accused who belong to these professions get off with minimum sentences. No lawyer or judge has been executed; true, General Dentz* was condemned to capital punishment, but it does not look as though it will be carried out. On the other hand the intellectuals have nobody to protect them and Suarez, Chack and Brasillach have been shot. In any case, Robert Brasillach's trial should have been postponed until the other members of the staff of *Je Suis Partout* had been arrested, and as he was the only one with sufficient courage to stay in France and surrender to justice, and, besides, had left *Je Suis Partout* more than a year before, a plea of extenuating circumstances would have saved him from the firing squad.

Wednesday, 4 July, 1945

Last night at the Comédie-Française, where the Old Vic was playing *Richard III,* I caught a glimpse of François Valéry. He is very anxious about his father's health. It is only thanks to penicillin that he is still alive. François told me that Paul Valéry talks a great deal, as though that vast intellect, on the brink of its annihilation, were functioning with increased vigour. A touching detail: Paul Valéry had Balzac's death in Victor Hugo's *Choses Vues* read to him the other day. François is not optimistic: despite encouraging words from the doctors, he is by no means sure himself that the stomach ulcer is not cancerous.

At the end of the performance, superb at times, the audience displayed an enthusiasm which, transcending that due to Shakespeare and his interpreters, was probably meant for the British people. Laurence Olivier expressed his thanks in French with charming ease. But the presidential box was empty and the national anthems were rather heart-rending, because their fraternal union rendered the present dissension between the two nations even more painful. Never has our outward attitude towards England been more false and these public manifestations of friendship—though spontanious and sincere—can have no effect on the profound disagreement, which recent events in Syria have disclosed.

As we went home in the car, thinking of the imminent trial *in absentia* of Abel Bonnard—one of the familiar faces missing from the little changed Paris of today—who will no doubt be sentenced to death, I said to my father, fully aware of it being a commonplace, that we were living in a Shakespearian era. He replied with restrained vehemence, that our times were worse, far worse, for what Shakespeare put on the stage were, dynastically, no more than family dramas, in which few people were directly concerned. Today, the whole world was, itself, the very substance of a unique drama, from the outcome of which few people could escape. When Marshal Tito suppressed public worship in the Catholic Church in Yugoslavia, where, it was said, there would no longer be a single priest left; when Marshal Stalin deported the Estonian population; when beyond the Elbe, there began what General Catroux apparently called the other day 'the reindeer age', Shakespearian dramas seemed quite tame. In this connection, I must quote the *mot* which the Swiss Minister, Burckhardt, attributed the other day (at a luncheon at the home of the Duchesse d'Harcourt, at which I was present) to Stalin, as he emerged from long contemplation of a map of the world and covered our continent with his large hand: "How small Europe is!"

This morning's Press is even more disquieting about the consequences of General de Gaulle's uncompromising attitude towards the establishment of two chambers and not one. *Le Pays,* a pro-government paper, declares: "We must view with the greatest disgust the various rumours, which keep harping on the word 'resignation'.

"No one wants to envisage as possible a departure which would be the most sensational but, at the same time, the most heartbreaking of all: nothing could justify it, not even a bitter conflict on the two opposing proposals." A deep anxiety is perceptible beneath the superficial optimism of those lines.

L' Aurore suggests that on the eve of the debates on the constitutional proposal "General de Gaulle should ask for a vote of confidence". Whatever happens, whether the General should be defeated, which appears to me unlikely in the immediate future, on a matter of domestic policy, or should he be led to resign as a result of external events, it does not seem possible that he should remain in office. The reason is that France does not measure up to this man, who is, perhaps, the last incarnation of the secular grandeur, denied her today by events. That being so, with the name of General de Gaulle forever a symbol, it is not impossible to conceive, assuming the best, that France, as a result of worldwide disorder, shall once more manage to emerge from the abyss by appealing again to de Gaulle, her only resort, the representative of her pride, her unalienable greatness and that side of herself the best one, which will always repudiate degradation and slavery. But who knows if it would not once again, alas, be a question of the last gasps of her death struggle? Today I feel pessimistic, for the world outlook is not very reassuring, nor is what a talented songwriter has called, the 'peace of Damocles' very secure.

The vivid lights of civilization that is admirable but in process of decomposition, do not obscure the smouldering furnace lit in the East by History which rises from the ashes of a millenary culture. And how contaminated we are already! And how admirable and staggeringly distant, in these years when a man's life counts for nothing are the times when a single act of injustice was sufficient to unleash a storm of honest anger over France!

Friday, 6 July, 1945

In all this morning's papers, from ten different angles, the poor shaven skull and the bewildered eyes of Jean Luchaire*, brought back yesterday to Paris, leapt out at one. And though, of course, I would not dream of casting doubt on his guilt, which is a serious matter, any man, however grave his crimes, is purged in a way of his sins once he falls into the hands of his enemies. Moreover, he will not escape the punishment, which pays once and for all, according to the well-known cliché, a debt worked out in advance. And Jean Luchaire, with his air of a cornered beast is pitiable because of his total solitude and defeat. The cries of vengeance, the sneers and abuse hurled at him are painful to hear. Despicable journalists dare to write that he 'struts' and 'swaggers', and, much he appears to, the poor devil, who has nothing ahead of him before the inevitable firing squad but a calvary of taunts and abandonment.

In connection with this, I must mention the shamelessness of those photographs which affront our instinctive good taste. I am not referring to the German charnel houses since, perhaps, it is necessary for us to have an exact knowledge of the appalling lengths to which that nation was prepared to go. I was thinking much more of photographs like those which showed us the fascist Starace as he received his sentence. Surrounded by a dozen faces, radiating a small malignant joy, his own face, the detachment of which seems to mark the only human being among all those puppets, has an out-of-this-world serenity. I imagine that the public, like the journalists, did not realize what was appalling about that contrast between the hatred and the serenity; that the serenity had nothing serene or happy about it, but was born of despair so deep that the man experiencing it was unable to display anything but a sad irony. But if it was shameful that the publication of such a photograph (in *Action*) could pass unnoticed, the abomination of the one published by *Le Monde Illustré* is so flagrant that it has been openly discussed. It shows the same Starace not facing death as, like traitors, he is compelled to turn his back to the firing squad, but he is on the very brink of death. And from among the thousand shades of expression, which an evil and curious joy plants on the faces of the spectators, emerges his own face, about which I prefer to say nothing. I believe the crimes of this man to have been many and his death to have been justifiable. But, once again, that is not the point. There is, in all that, the absence of that elementary pity, which the sight of death demands, if we are not to compromise our dignity and, in a certain sense too, just as important, our security. To sum up, no one who has seen those faces of which I have written, will ever be able to feel quite at ease again anywhere on this planet, or elsewhere.

After Bogomolov, the Soviet Ambassador, said to him, in a sanctimonious voice, the other day, that he did not see why this question of the two Chambers was so important, Palewski immediately guessed what the communists' reaction would be. And, sure enough, this morning, they displayed an attitude that could not have been more conciliatory, which settles the question for the moment. So the General has won the battle, but it was the communist decision which turned the scales, and it is to them that the General owes his victory. Palewski, quoting with sad irony a famous *mot,* said that the communists were supporting the government in the same way as the rope supported the hanged man, but solidly. However that may be, if we are not careful, many electors voting in favour of two Chambers, as the General wishes, will believe that they are voting communist and they may not be far wrong. Such, at the moment, is the strength of this party (though very much exaggerated according to Vallon) that it can afford to yield on all points in the confident certainty that they can still control the situation. This is why the communists insistently urging a merger on the socialists, are prepared to sacrifice many outward appearances, including the name they bear, if it will enable them to achieve their project. After all, what does it matter to them what the thing is called as long as it is their thing?

Sunday, 8 July, 1945

The General returned yesterday to the rue Saint-Dominique, after spending three days in his villa. An unusual rest period. But, no doubt, his main object was to put the finishing touches, in peace and quiet, to the subtle scheme which he disclosed at today's Cabinet meeting and which will shortly be announced to us officially. His obstinacy in regard to the principle of two Chambers seems to have been a bluff. I must confess that I have difficulty in grasping his motives, despite Palewski's explanations. In the evening, after a lapse of several days, I managed to get the General to sign my letters. I have never found him more serene, nor has he ever given me such an impression of authority. He was very agreeable but not very talkative. His finger stabbed down on the name of Mme. Halna du Fretay, at the bottom of a letter I handed to him – and his nail left a mark on the paper:

"It was at her house, in 191-, in Arras, that I first met Pétain!"

Friday, 13 July, 1945

The morning papers on 11th July came out violently against General de Gaulle's projects, as announced in a communiqué issued at the close of the Cabinet meeting. They spoke of 'All Fools Day', of 'dictatorship', of 'personal power' and even of 'the three-card trick'. It was highly improper, they said, to leave the elector with only two alternatives: the re-establishment, pure and simple, of the Constitution of 1875, or the establishment of an Assembly with no real powers outside its constituent role.

Yesterday morning, Brouillet, Vallon, Burin des Roziers and I convinced Palewski that there were legitimate grounds for the general dissatisfaction. As de Gaulle was not to speak till the evening (at that moment he was engaged in drafting his speech at the villa) there was still time, perhaps, to persuade him to reconsider his position. Faced by a caustic and vehement Brouillet, supported vigorously by Vallon and from time to time by Burin des Roziers and myself, Palewski did not try to conceal his confusion, and, though he began by defending the General's position, he did so less and less confidently as he went along, and ended up by agreeing with his opponents.

Our arguments ran as follows: General de Gaulle's great strength in the country sprang initially from the essential integrity of his position since 1940, and it was precisely this integrity that his present projects called in question for the first time. The French people had the impression, and they were not entirely wrong, that the General mistrusted them and that he was engaged in a battle of wits with universal suffrage. By his present actions, he was discouraging and confusing his friends, so much in the majority that they should have inspired him with confidence, and was giving his enemies, the communists in particular, a splendid opportunity to launch an effective attack on him. All the accusations of personal power, which it was part of their game to formulate, seemed, in fact, to be well-founded, and was a point round which the dissatisfaction could be crystallized. It was obvious that the communists and possibly other parties as well, would advise the electors who belonged to them to leave their ballot papers blank; thus many Frenchmen would believe they were not voting against the General, whereas in reality, the total of the abstainers and the 'no's' might well reach an imposing figure, which even if the General got a majority, would damage his prestige and his authority.

Brouillet and Vallon disclosed that the General had everything to gain by propounding the problem quite frankly, which would give him a clear picture of the number of his supporters, while causing those who felt it their duty to vote against this proposal, which meant against him, to reconsider their decision. Palewski took pen in hand and we all set to work to frame the two questions in a new and franker form. After various fumbling attempts, we arrived at the following, which, could, of course, be better worded, but would not change in its essentials (it relates to the two questions to be put to the voters):

1) Do you approve the first clause in the ordinance of the . . . directed to the election of a Constituent National Assembly? (If the majority of electors vote 'no', this Assembly will be the Chamber of Deputies in accordance with the Constitution of 1875, and steps for the election of a Senate will be taken.)

2) Do you approve article 3 of the ordinance of the . . . establishing, during the term of its mandate, the respective prerogatives of the Constituent Assembly and the Government? (If the majority of electors vote 'no', this Assembly will be endowed with extended powers.)

It was understood that the General, in his speech that evening as well as in all those he would deliver before the elections, would clearly voice his own preference, that of a Constituent Assembly with limited powers. The disadvantage lay in the possibility of him finding himself in the minority; but, apart from this being highly improbable, it seemed better that he should put the question of confidence quite plainly to the French people.

"I'll go and see him about midday, when he'll have finished his speech," Palewski said. "That'll be the best moment to try and persuade him."

At 6.00 the General recorded his speech. The ringing of the inter-ministerial telephone and then a technical error compelled him to restart reading the last part of his text twice. A few moments later, I went to see Palewski on a matter connected with my job.

"The General agreed," he told me. "His speech doesn't give anything away, but his decision will soon be made public. I must admit I feel very uneasy about it all now. What do you think?"

I answered that it was obviously a very serious choice to make, but that it seemed to me better than any of the others; as a result, the country would be able to vote with a full knowledge of the situation, the General would preserve the integrity of his moral position, and the country would still have a resource if it took the responsibility of depriving him of executive powers. Palewski listened attentively, nodding his head in agreement, anxious to be reassured.

"Yes, yes," he murmured, "all the same, I shan't sleep a wink till the elections."

What astonishes me is that so grave a decision should have been taken at the last minute, and that a step which might well have changed the course of History should have been checked, without any proper time being given to weighing up the consequences. Everything was staked within a matter of hours. I wonder, with considerable curiosity, whether our cogitations this morning in Palewski's office played a decisive role or whether the General, warned from other sources and already convinced from reading the Press, would not have altered his decision in any case.

Monday, 16 July, 1945

Went to enquire after Paul Valéry on behalf of the General. His son Claude brought me his answer:

"Ask him to tell the General that he knows how to win hearts as well as minds. I'm too tired to thank him as I should, but I know he'll understand how grateful I am." François told me: "When I came back from London the other day, I found him horribly changed. Then, suddenly, the next day, he was his old self again. Instead of monosyllables, simple reflections of physiological conditions, he began talking again in quite his old manner. When the doctor told him that, just as he had called his milk *flat,* he must also find an adjective for water, he replied: 'No, water is not at all flat; water is fullness, water is full.' "

From *Le Figaro*: "General de Gaulle made no reference in his broadcast to the possibility of a second question being put to the electorate on 14th October. The communiqué issued yesterday at the end of the Cabinet meeting told us that the first proposal for the Constitutional law has been modified in this sense. As well as having to decide whether the Assembly shall or shall not be constituent, the citizens will have to say, in the event of their answer being in the affirmative, whether the Constituent Assembly shall be sovereign. But the question will not be put to them in so simple a form. It will run as follows: 'Do you approve of the Government's bill to continue exercising civil powers until the Constitution comes into force?' "

At the end of our letter-signing session this evening, General de Gaulle asked me 'what I thought of it all'. I told him, awkwardly and clumsily, for he still intimidates me, and he replied with astonishing confidence and serenity:

"There's no doubt about the response 'yes' to both questions. They can't do otherwise."

Then he referred to the setback of the communist demonstration in the streets on 14th July with quiet cheerfulness:

"All that is of no importance. You can forget it. There's nothing behind it. Just a lot of windbags."

Vallon accuses us of overestimating the communist strength. Does not de Gaulle underestimate it?

After 11th November, 2nd April and 18th June, there was another review on 14th July, and once more I was close to de Gaulle on the tribune of honour; de Gaulle whom I could not see a short while ago without being overwhelmed, de Gaulle whom I could not take my eyes off. But one gets used to everything, even to miracles. Even alone with him in his office, I hardly give a thought to where I am; I hardly give a conscious glance at this man, as I look down on his balding head, on which, this evening, I noticed a few white hairs.

In the part of Paris where I had been during the insurrection, I experience for the first time on this 14th July of liberty, the emotion engendered by dancing in the street, accordions and a joyful crowd. A firework exploded over the Pont-Neuf, where I had experienced more violent joys.

Sunday, 22 July, 1945
Vémars.

The radio gave us the speech that de Gaulle delivered yesterday in Brest, the broadcast of which, because of its political importance (it was the first time that he had put forward his views on the elections) demanded perfect reception. But a technical hitch made the end inaudible.

After talking to my grandmother, my uncle and my aunt Gay-Lussac, I realized that the General's concepts are not very comprehensible nor indeed, very clear. He will have to go on dotting his 'i's to the very end, as he began to do in yesterday's speech. The two questions in the referendum do not automatically seem to evoke the almost unanimous responses anticipated. Neither the right – which supports the Constitution of 1875 – nor the left – which seeks a sovereign Constituent Assembly – will feel spontaneously disposed to vote, in the case of the former: 'yes' to the first question, and in the case of the latter, 'yes' to the second, I myself admit that I have not yet understood the reason for the General's *volte-face* from the Constitution of 1875, of which he had, at first, openly declared himself in favour and which he repudiated overnight, to the amusement of the initiated (Palewski and Pompidou in particular). I am definitely not cut out for politics.

1 August, 1945

The last time the General asked me in his customary turn of phrase "what people thought of all that", I was, as usual, taken aback and displayed, in the first words of my reply, a spontaneity, of which the frankness seemed to me clumsy, even as I spoke. With reference to the proposed Constituent Assembly, I said: "People are slightly confused: there have been so many changes." And the General without showing any signs of ill-temper, replied:

"There won't be any further changes. And the response is certain: 'yes' on both questions."

Today he seemed to me less self-assured. And I, on the contrary, found myself, for the first time, meeting his ritual "So what are people saying?" at the end of our session, without panic or timidity. I spoke freely, and it was he who replied to me, for quite a long time. An unprecedented event.

He was less sure of himself about the result of the elections and the support he could expect from the country (the Consultative Assembly at the end of long debates, some of which I attended, showed itself hostile, by a large majority, to the constitutional projects which are his own and which he declared himself ready to amend.) But not, it seemed to me, unsure about the legitimacy and strength of his position. Finding him so calm and clear-sighted, and seeing his sarcastic smile and the unostentatious casualness of his expression, coupled with the indefinable strength, serenity and determination which illuminate his face, I realized how ridiculous all the rumours were, that reported him discouraged and pushed to the point of resignation. When, in answer to his question, I told him how disgusted I was – and many other Frenchmen, too – by the hypocrisy and the dishonesty of the delegates – ("For, after all, what have they got to fear: the choice of President is left to the electorate; it is given the chance to promulgate the Constitution it prefers; it is only for a period of seven months that it is asked to leave control of public affairs, and that under considerable limitations, to the Head of the Government!") he said to me:

"What strikes me, is that there wasn't one man, not a single one, to see the matter from the point of view of the State . . . Their stupidity dismays me and astounds one. I'm not speaking of those whited sepulchres, the radicals, but of the moderates – set on the Constitution of 1875, without being able to get it into their heads that nobody wants it. Once again they are playing into the hands of the extremists who only want disorder, anarchy and street demonstrations, with processions, flags . . . "

Then I ventured to say: "General, you're too kind to them, you pay them too much respect," and went on to speak of his good intentions and his scrupulous regard for republicanism, which they rewarded disgracefully by branding him as a dictator when they themselves sought the worst form of dictatorship of all. He waved this away with a faint smile.

No doubt, at that moment, we were both dwelling in our own way on the France dragged back from the brink of the abyss, and possibly close to safety, but whose forgetful children were already straying away from her. For who is thinking of France's welfare in all this business, if not General de Gaulle, who, having saved her from death, sees himself already suspected, already spurned by a nation without memory or loyalty?

"I must admit, General, that I am beginning to feel uneasy about the result of the referendum."

He asked me again, insistently:

"What are people saying?"

"It's difficult to judge about the country's reaction from the few people one talks to," I replied. "But I'm certain that the disgust I spoke of is felt by the large majority. All the same, I'm not much reassured, because those parties and party members whose dishonesty, duplicity and strength we can already assess, lie between you and the electorate. We can expect the worst."

He did not deny. I even think he agreed. But it was then that his face radiated its serene confidence.

I was fairly launched. I began speaking of the Pétain trial, which had got off to such a bad start ("for, so far, they've only spoken about the armistice, a question on which, rightly or wrongly, the French will never be unanimous. What matters far more than the armistice is what came of it, the uses to which it was put"); and of the pitifulness of those witnesses' depositions which only testify for themselves – the Reynauds and the Weygands.

"Blum's has been by far the most notable, for the dignity of its tone."

The General nodded, smiling, and said: "That's because he was the only one who wasn't in office at the time!"

I added that it was vital to prevent the trial becoming bogged down. Above all it was important for it to be concluded before the Constituent Assembly met again; otherwise, we were liable to see an Assembly, without judgement or restraint, taking the matter into their own hands. He agreed, declaring that everything would be finished in time. But he also agreed that the return of Laval, who was handed over to us yesterday, would not facilitate a speedy conclusion.

I then went on to describe to a mocking and patently amused General, Pétain's trial as I had seen it yesterday on the newsreels: a marmoreal Marshal, more imposing than ever, amid the ineffectual excitement of spectral judges and lawyers, whose ridiculous beards, emphatic gestures and laughable demeanour showed up Justice in its worst light. The film being a silent one, the silence made the disorder of the spectacle even more hallucinatory.

An hour later, I was in the Palais de Justice for the ninth sitting of the High Court. I saw Marshal Pétain in his silence, his military bearing, his solitude and his great age, crushed, but having lost none of his dignity, in a large armchair, beside a young, pink republican guard. On his uniform, the ceremonial military medal; in his hands, a pair of expensive gloves; in front of him, his glowing red képi; just as he was in the time of his legendary glory, and at the time, too, of the Vichy comedy. A face of white marble, sometimes attentive but more often far away and indifferent to a degree that already seemed beyond this life. General Weygand, brought from prison, but dressed with the elegance of someone returning from the races, dry, dignified and haughty; and a few feet away, Paul Reynaud, nervous, tense, bitter, his face continually twitching. The dialogue between these two men consisted entirely of an exchange of blows – and the ones below the belt were the more numerous on both sides and rendered even more hurtful by the polite terms with which they were couched. I shall only have to reread the proceedings later, to see this scene again: Weygand sitting down and turning his back on Reynaud whom he pretends not to hear, truly regal with the stick on which his right hand leans; then, suddenly, on his feet again, facing his opponent, whom he lashes with a few words and then turns away from him again, with a sardonic smile on his worn face.

To the meticulous eloquence of Paul Reynaud, who continued his defence *pro domo* with a fresh supply of more or less plausible arguments, he retorted with sentences, the cruel brevity of which scored a bullseye. Reynaud (who had taken the blow with a false air of detachment) was anxious to defend himself and not make such a poor exit from the public stage, but was not allowed to do so. Moreover this futile quarrel threatened to go on for ever, and History does not require so many explanations to reach a verdict. A verdict on Reynaud and Weygand, of course. For in these proceedings, there was a lot of concentration on Reynaud, a lot of concentration on Weygand, too, but very little on Pétain.

General Héring*, called for the defence, referred to the Marshal's dilemma, but at a level on which there was no point in discussing it. For who has ever doubted Pétain's genius at Verdun or the admiration in which the French people held him, de Gaulle as much as anyone? After the interpolation of a passionate statement which, for that reason, was of little significance – though it did raise some vital questions, (notably, the question of the Marshal's responsibility for the repression of the Resistance) – General George made a long speech about the armistice, which he defended with the sole purpose of defending himself – and achieved the remarkable feat of avoiding any mention – anyway, spontaneously – of the Marshal's name. . . . All this was unreal, futile and useless; the judges covered in ermine seemed to me to belong to another world; and neither the barking of leading counsel Payen nor the warm voice of Isorni made the defence any less ridiculous. Pétain's impenetrable silence; the stupidity of certain questions asked by the jury; the disgust, whatever his crimes may have been, at seeing a Marshal of France arraigned by such individuals; the sadness, too, of seeing – and hearing – the men who had governed France at the gravest hour of her destiny – seeing them, in their weakness, the like of other men – hearing them disclose in public what had been State secrets, but such petty secrets, suited to the petty creatures they were: it needs leisure to comment properly on these 'impressions of the hearing'.

I must come back to the forty-five minutes I spent in the General's office this morning, and note down:

– his thanks for my *Aimer Balzac,* which I sent round to him at the villa (last night), and which will only appear officially in a month;

– his remark, following the protest I passed on to him about a woman condemned to death, whom he had reprieved: "One doesn't shoot women!" A sentence which he repeated twice again, adding: "Giraudoux said it in *Les Anges du Péché* and we mustn't forget it: Women, no matter what women, are capable of the best and the worst . . ."

– these lines which he wrote at the bottom of a letter I had given him to sign: "The battlefield has broadened out. But the struggle remains hard."

Friday, 2 August, 1945

There are several ways of being pessimistic and critical about the present situation in France, that of insincere men; and that of some honest men, humanists by tendency, who, incapable of being anything but disappointed and offended by all politics, are inevitably so by the current ones. Spontaneously, of course, I belong to the latter school of thought, and only my veneration for General de Gaulle tempers the effect for the time being. Louis Salleron, who came to see me today, is of the honest species, with a clear-sightedness deflected by old convictions which he will never bring himself to revise. Perhaps on the whole he is right, since, error being inevitable, it may be better to hold on to those of which we have proved the qualities and the partial truth. And there were some constructive ideas in his viewpoint, bearing in mind the bitterness, very natural for a sincere non-resistant (in the official sense of the word).

"What the country finds hard to forgive in de Gaulle is his sticking so assiduously and rigorously to the rules of a game, in which everybody feels deep down he does not believe, and by doing so, since it no longer has any relation to reality, may well ruin France. For democracy is now only a myth and a dangerous one, if it allows itself to be deceived by its deadliest enemies, whose main objective is to prevent France from choosing the leader of her choice, the one who can save *her*, not them."

I replied that the General has always considered himself as the provisional director of the State, and he is extremely scrupulous about his status (refusing for example, to live in the Elysée or even borrow from the National Furniture Repository what he might need to make his house habitable). But, speaking for myself (for he has never told me anything of the sort), I added:

"Once the elections have taken place, we shall, no doubt, see a change in his attitude. If he is retained in office, he will no longer hesitate to govern; if he is defeated, he will be in a position to speak as an individual and rally round him those of the French people who support his actions and his policies."

4 *August*, 1945

I expected to experience some excitement at the Pétain-Laval confrontation yesterday in the High Court, but there was none. The arrival in the court-room of the accused, Pierre Laval, repatriated the day before from Germany, where Franco's government had returned him after mature consideration, a black, puny, little man with a humble expression, his hat in his hand, his briefcase under his arm; a man tracked down and doomed to the firing squad, could not, however, fail to be poignant. He stated his name to the judge in a toneless voice: "Laval, Pierre . . ." The words emerged with difficulty from his

*1. Normandy, 14 June 1944, the beginning
of the return to Paris.*

2. (Above) *Bayeux, mid-June 1944, and first contact with the liberated citizens.*

3. (Right) *Paris at last, 26 August 1944, being greeted by General Leclerc outside the Gare Montparnasse.*

4. (Above right) *Being briefed with Leclerc and General Juin, and making plans for the liberation march.*

5. *Leaving the Cathedral after the service of thanksgiving for the liberation of Paris, and yet minutes before the ceremony German snipers were unsuccessful in an attempt on de Gaulle's life.*

6. *Day of triumph, 29 August 1944.*

7. (Below) *The allied Anglo-French leaders, August 1944.*

8. (Above) *In the offices of the Rue Saint Dominique.*

9. (Left) *With victory assured, the General makes his first political address to the Consultative Assembly.*

10. 26 July 1945, the Pétain trial: Lebrun,
last President of the Third Republic.

11. 3 August 1945, the Pétain trial: Laval.

12. (Left) *6 November 1945, having resigned as Chief of the Provisional Government, de Gaulle makes his first formal appearance in mufti to address the General Assembly.*

13. (Above) *Later that month, the first Cabinet.*
(Front row left to right) *Georges Bidault,* FOREIGN AFFAIRS; *Maurice Thorez,* MINISTER WITHOUT PORTFOLIO; *Vincent Auriol,* MINISTER WITHOUT PORTFOLIO; *General de Gaulle; Francisque Gay,* MINISTER WITHOUT PORTFOLIO; *André Tixier,* MINISTER OF INTERIOR; *Louis Jacquinot,* MINISTER WITHOUT PORTFOLIO; *Ambroise Thomas.*

(Second row left to right) *Jules Moch,* PUBLIC WORKS AND TRANSPORT; *Raoul Dautry,* RECONSTRUCTION; *Paul Jacobbi; Tanguy-Prigent,* FOOD AND AGRICULTURE; *Pierre Teitgen,* JUSTICE; *François Billoux,* NATIONAL ECONOMY; *André Malraux,* INFORMATION; *J. Soustelle,* COLONIES; *Robert Prigent,* POPULATION (NEW MINISTRY).

(Third row left to right) *Edmond Michelet; René Pleven,* FINANCE; *Eugène Thomas,* POSTS AND TELEGRAPHS; *Charles Tillon; Marcel Paul,* INDUSTRIAL POPULATION.

14. (Top left) *The author and the General about this time.*

15. (Bottom left) *Paris, just beginning to regain confidence after the liberation.*

16. (Above) *The first Armistice celebration since the beginning of the War.*

17. (Above) THE TRAITORS: *Robert Brasillach (right) with the notorious Nazi, Otto Abetz, during the Occupation.*

18. (Below) *April 1945: General Dentz who, upon orders from Vichy, led French troops against the Allies in Syria.*

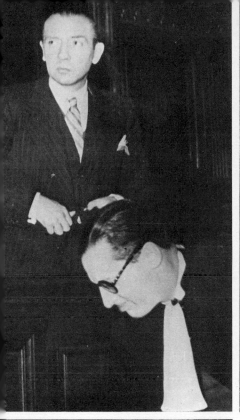

19. THE TRAITORS: (top left) *Jean Luchaire, sentenced to death, January 1946.*

20. (Top right) *Georges Suarez, another journalist, also sentenced to death.*

21. (Left) *Yves Bouthillier, Vichy Minister of Finance, whose hair turned white while imprisoned, July 1948.*

22. General Noguès, who had fled to
Lisbon in 1943, returned to France in
1945. But it was eleven years before his
health permitted him to come to trial.

constricted throat. But he soon recovered his self-assurance, defending his politics with his old parliamentary eloquence, dealing tactfully with the Marshal in so far as it suited him to use him as a cover for his actions, but cunningly piling on the accusations at the very moment when he appeared to be defending him. Pétain, in his armchair, where I no longer sought him out (it required a mental effort to be surprised any more at seeing him in these surroundings and to believe in the historical importance of the hour) – one becomes so quickly accustomed to things that this second contact with the illustrious defendant already seemed quite normal and uninteresting – Pétain listened, without expression, to the statement of this man, by whose side he had lived the gravest days of his life. So persuasive was Laval's voice, so consummate his art; so inadequate were the presiding judge and prosecutor shown to be up against this old fox; so easy was it to be won over by the force of persuasion of someone appearing in person to explain his actions; so great is our (or anyway, my) tendency to trust any man, whoever he is, put myself in his place and believe in his good motives in advance, that I felt myself – despite the weight of the charges crushing him down (or, rather, because of them) – favourably disposed towards the witness. I must admit it: I was spontaneously *for* him (and against the judge, who was devious and inept, into the bargain); as pleased with the numerous points he made as I was annoyed by his indiscretions, I am speaking of my reaction of the moment, of a reflex that could not have been less reasonable and even went against all good sense. It is fruitless for me to be surprised at myself. For that is how we are made; incredibly vulnerable and weak when it comes to facing life, once we are dispassionate and sincere. A consistent attitude, that is never betrayed by a contradiction is only possible if we are deliberately or passionately self-controlled, basing our life on certain principles – arrived at through reason or through the heart – from which, it is accepted, we shall never turn aside. But with tiredness (ours and his) Laval's defence became less convincing and also less assured. On his pre-war politics, on the National Assembly of 10th July, 1940, on Montoire and on 13th December, he was impassioned and thrilling – so much so that I was naïvely surprised that this able politician, who had chosen to play the most difficult of games, was on a capital charge. But certain words of his, whether uttered because they were essential to his argument (Anti-Bolshevik Legion, Sigmaringen) or let slip by mistake, as when he said 'aggression' for 'landing', destroyed in a flash the fruits of his eloquence and our credulity. I suddenly recalled what the hated name of Pierre Laval had stood for under the Occupation and exactly what he had done. I suddenly recalled that the expression 'traitor' had a meaning which in all justice (national justice) could not but be applied to him . . . (But was I so certain of it, at that very moment?)

He finally gave a by no means unskilful explanation of his famous sentence: "I hope to see Germany victorious." I remember the impact it made on me on the evening I heard it on the radio in some room which I can no longer place. Then two warders came to fetch him, and he picked up his hat and briefcase and went off back to his prison. The Marshal was then invited to tell the court what he was saying at that moment to his lawyer. After a short hesitation and in spite of his wish to remain silent, he declared that Laval had lied in saying that he had given his consent to the use of that sentence: "When I heard it repeated on the radio, I was astounded . . . I understood that it had been eliminated . . . I am distressed . . . greatly distressed that it was left in . . ." The quavering voice of those terrible years was back with us again, but even more pitiful and broken than before. One felt that this man, whose intervention proved that he could still hear and understand, was, nevertheless, elsewhere despite his feigned presence, like those dead friends whom we see alive in our dreams; alive but – since we know them to be dead – bearing a stamp of unreality.

And in this same day when I had seen a Marshal of France rise opposite an old, ridiculous prosecutor, his accuser, and pull the small table in front of him slightly aside to clear the way for him (he had made exactly the same gesture the first time I had come, at once humble and courteous, but with a proud humility and a haughty courtesy, on this same day too, when I had seen one of the men who had represented France before the world (now, while he was not yet before his judges, he was already before Justice), take advantage of a pause in the proceedings to seek an approving, or at least encouraging, glance from the journalists closest to him, (he managed to smile and exchange a few words) – while the wretched Paul Reynaud, sitting as erect in his seat as he could, listened eagerly, the reporters, Jean Schlumberger and Albert Camus, looked like judges, and the judges and jury resembled puppets – on this same day, a few hours later, I saw our beloved, great de Gaulle, accompanied by his ministers, enter the Hall of the Senate, where, amidst an uproar of the lowest order, the Consultative Assembly was ending its last session. The few conventional official words, which the General uttered, gave no indication of the contempt in which he holds these men, who lack any 'sense of state' . . .

"I have never believed in human justice," my father said to me yesterday. But I myself had believed in it. I was suddenly aware that I had believed in it, to my distress and disgust.

Wednesday, 8 August, 1945

Yesterday, for the third time, I attended a hearing of Pétain's trial. I saw there, specially brought from their prison in Fresnes, a crestfallen, hesitant and discreet Peyrouton*; a self-confident, brilliant and casual Jacques Chevalier*; a precise, methodical and concentrated Bouthillier* – and some people of lesser importance. Admiral Fernet, the former prefect François Martin, and State Counsellor M. Roussel, who had had the rare courage to defend the old Marshal publicly. The old Marshal, who in his present abasement still preserves all his old haughtiness, responded in a chary and distant manner to the bows of those who had come to testify on his behalf. As though it were in the natural course of things that they should bow with respect in front of him. As though there were nothing unusual in this devotion of his loyal servants, but only in the sternness of so many ungrateful Frenchmen. And I must say whatever the basis of the trial is, such an attitude is not without dignity – and when the Marshal rises politely to let prosecutor Mornet pass without the latter even granting him a glance, it is not the Marshal who emerges diminished from the confrontation.

As far as the basis of the trial is concerned, it seems difficult to judge fairly and get into proper prospective the guilt, the innocence, the senility, the impotence, the mistakes and the crimes. Was there ever any deliberate crime, any concerted treason? Frankly, I do not think so. In any case, the problem is initially badly set, because it has been done with passion. It is partisans, not patriots, who are accusing Pétain, and they have condemned him without hearing him. They have condemned him, not because he betrayed France, but because he betrayed the Republic. And it is true that the Marshal who triumphed in Vichy was often a partisan, and not a patriot. He had cheerfully profited from a defeat which, in his eyes, much more than that of France had been the defeat of hateful democratic ideas. On this question the trial could well be based, a trial for treason, if you like, but for treason committed in the midst of a civil war. Where the trickery begins, in my opinion, is when we are led to believe that Marshal Pétain betrayed by connivance with the enemy. I mean to say: betrayed at his own will, in a deliberate and concerted way.

Despite this mockery, for the first time yesterday, I had the feeling that Justice might still be possible – and present. It was a fact, in any case, that the trial was being held in public, that everything was taking place in the light of day and that the accused had at his disposal adequate means of defence. It was a fact that the trial was developing in a way that offended the authorities and especially the active part of public opinion in authority. So much so, that I suddenly wondered whether the dissatisfaction of the public and its disappointment, did not entirely spring from the direction the affair was taking. Supposing the sole reason why so many people – and myself on occasion – felt so disillusioned with Justice during the Pétain trial was that the Justice was not the one that they wanted?

For many Frenchmen talk as though the matter had been determined in advance. And that being so, why go through the comedy of a trial? Of a trial which, in the present state of affairs, can be criticized on various grounds, but which, up till now, does not seem to have betrayed the serene and intangible Justice.

A little more than a month ago, André George, Louis de Broglie's collaborator, drew up a report for General de Gaulle, which I passed on to him, on the progress so far made in the disintegration of matter, and, in particular, the military use – if one may mention it – to which the experiment can be put. Now, the news has been made public of the construction of an atomic bomb by the Americans, who have already dropped one on a Japanese town, which, we are told, was sixty per cent destroyed. I have no comment to make. But we really seem to have embarked on a new era.

From a correspondent of the Associated Press – without comment: "There is reason to believe that the town, which numbered 340,000 inhabitants before this event, has been completely wiped out. Colonel Tidde, after completing his successful mission, was welcomed on his return to base by General Spantz, who presented him with the *Distinguished Service Cross*, one of the highest American decorations."

9 *August*, 1945

Yesterday, in the early afternoon, in the basement of the rue Saint-Dominique, where we had gone to see the newsreels with a view to possible censorship, we were unexpectedly joined by André Malraux, who will now be attached to General de Gaulle's staff. I had only met him once before, during a private showing of his film *Espoir*, just before the war. I was surprised by his youthfulness and by his looking 'like anyone else'. Naïvely, I had expected his prestige and his latent genius to be reflected in his face. I avoided being introduced to him, from timidity, modesty, and pride.

Monday, 20 August, 1945

"What a galaxy of generals!" André Malraux said to me with slightly embarrassed irony, after General Juin had just shaken him warmly by the hand. We were in the A.D.C.'s office, waiting for General de Gaulle to come out of his own in order to preside over the lunch, to which most of the office staff had been invited, including us, to commemorate the completion of this first year's work together. "I must confess that I can't get used to seeing you in these official surroundings," I said to him. He growled: "But it's to the General, to him, personally, that I'm attached . . ." He is a curious character, from whom I cannot take my eyes, on those days when I am writing up the notes made on him during the last months of the Occupation, and which already compose three-quarters of a book. Today he spoke to me for a long time about his work, with that surprising eloquence and remarkable fertility in original and weighty ideas.

Tuesday, 8 September, 1945

I saw the General yesterday for the first time (I mean in a working session) since my return from my holidays. I was prepared for his final ritual "So, what are people saying?", a question which Charles-Henri de Levis-Mirepoix told me, the other day, he never put to a member of his staff in uniform.

When I replied by referring to the European role which the public seemed to be beginning to understand and appreciate his adopting, he interrupted me with a "My European role!", spoken with sad irony. He went on to tell me that America and England wanted an independent Libya which was madness – for one knew what kind of independence was intended – and extremely dangerous for the whole of our Northern Africa.

"No! Libya *must* remain Italian. In this whole business we fully support Italy."

Then he asked me about the referendum, concluding the discussion with a very categorical:

"France *must* vote *oui-oui*. She must. Otherwise, I . . ." and as he raised his hand in a gesture of farewell, I was once again impressed by his calm, smiling face, radiating self-confidence.

Friday, 21 September, 1945

What strikes me about nations' governments (in as much as, a modest spectator, I can observe that of France; in as much as Palewski, to some small degree governs France; not that, in governing, he does not go to great pains to avoid letting anyone know what is going on – anyway, not me – nor General de Gaulle, himself, either!) – what strikes me is the powerlessness of those who claim to be in power. The march of events drags along with it, like everybody else, those who attempt to direct it. Those, in Europe, who are among the best informed on European affairs, only have an incomplete and distorted view of them. Possibly the leaders at the various internationals do, in fact, play a directing or indeed a motive part, but their number is infinitesimal, and I am certain that none of General de Gaulle's ministers, nor, doubtless, de Gaulle, himself, are privy to their secrets. So History goes on its way, pulverizing bodies and souls, indifferent and inhuman; and only a few initiates momentarily return to account – or direct – its inevitable course. Here, in the rue Saint-Dominique, in that holy of holies, Gaston Palewski's office, rumours filter through from the boundless stream, which become lost in the backwaters of a dark, shallow morass. Burin des Roziers informs us of "the conclusions that seem to emerge" from this or that conference or from this or that foreign crisis – ("From the way things are going, it looks as if . . ." – "It seems probable . . .") without any – I will not even say certainty, but *precision* issuing from these meticulous and well-phrased lectures. And in the sphere of domestic politics, too, which, after all, should be easier to handle, the same urgent problems are brought up again, week after week, considered from all angles and carefully assessed and weighed, without any of the proposed solutions ever being adopted, or very nearly so. Yet I know there are countries where a road, that has been deemed necessary, has been laid across virgin forest within a month; where this or that weakness in the social system (army, family, etc.) has been effectively remedied. New, dynamic and optimistic countries, whose example France, alas! seems far from being able to follow. But it is certain that even in those States, immense spheres of national life evade all attempts to control them, and that governing there, too, often consists of pretending to exercise, in practice, the powers recognized in law.

27 October, 1945

Letter of the General's to Lebrun* – the first draft of which was written one evening while I was there and recopied later. Its deference, significant of his character and his politics, his displeasure because I had not given him Albert Lebrun's book sooner. (One of the first times that he has ticked me off, but not excessively.) His irony, when he read me this letter and commented: "He hasn't been brilliant, but . . ."

A little earlier, Georges Bidault had gone into the General's office and came out again after about twenty minutes, obviously furious. Turned the pages of the engagement book; "No, Tuesday . . . that'll be quite early enough, in view of *his* state of mind." Sarcastic at the announcement of an official dinner, which he considered pointless: "And one refuses things that make sense!" On Tuesday, as compensation, Bidault insisted on a long appointment: "There'll be squalls. A good hour won't be too much . . ." He was speaking his thoughts aloud. I thought his: "You've been playing some nice tricks on the Institute" referred to Palewski's absurd idea of sending me to represent General de Gaulle the other day at the ceremony commemorating its one hundred and fiftieth anniversary. But, in fact, he was alluding to the impropriety of M. Germain Martin, who, it appears, had been 'branded' during the Occupation, being present on this solemn occasion.

6 November, 1945

If I knew André Malraux was in the building, I never sought to see him. Our only meeting was the one I mentioned at an official luncheon.

And it was he who summoned me today to his office, which was formerly occupied by my staff and is now newly furnished and painted, and resembles the white, luxurious room of a young girl. He asked me to forgive him for his reserve at our first meeting – and for his apparent indifference, saying that "he didn't know then that it was me"; actually he only knew me then in my most commonplace capacity, which might well have aroused his suspicion. But, since then, he has found out more about me; has read me; knows that I am writing about his work and, as he says, "there aren't so many serious critics about". I was surprised to find him attaching some importance to the critical study I am devoting to him. He promised, without being asked, to let me have the proofs of a novel which I had not heard of. And he went on at once to speak of his *Psychologie de l'Art,* which, to tell the truth, did not greatly interest me, since as yet it is only mapped out.

135

Apart from a few notes, on his own admission, dictated and more or less improvised, which appeared in *Verve*, nothing remains of the work: as happened to the final chapters of his last novel, "the Gestapo made curling-papers out of it".

He regarded his findings to be of such consequence that he immediately began to enlighten me as to their general lines, since, he said, what was valid for Art was also valid for Mankind. I gave this example in *Verve*: "If it was God who made the artichoke, it was Mankind who made the acanthus leaf. It is a matter of an improvement to a pre-existing element. The real question is to discover how, from the acanthus, we can proceed to, say, Goya. Mankind changes the order of affinities, he recreates the world according to his capacities and this is what constitutes artistic creation."

I asked him whether I was wrong in taking God, in his analysis, as merely a convenient word and nothing more; he answered in the affirmative. 'Chaos' seems wrong to him, since creation is not chaotic; he thought 'the individual being' a dangerous phrase because of the use to which it has been put by philosophers. God is preferable.

He was interrupted and had to go out just as he had begun to speak of my *Aimer Balzac* in terms that I found fascinating. When he returned he brought up the subject of the Constituent Assembly's first session, which he had just heard about. I, who had attended it a few hours before, could corroborate the gloom experienced by all those present, who had nonetheless arrived full of hope and expectations.

Five years of bloodshed and ordeals, heroism and sacrifice, only to be faced with demagogy of that old radical-socialist, president for the day because of his age, who was not even capable of raising the level of debate on such a momentous occasion as this. Yes, it was really lamentable. . . My father, as we walked to the meeting together, along the glorious Seine, reminded me that it was almost five years ago, to the day – on 28th October, 1940 – that Rosenberg was glorifying national socialism on the same platform from which one of the constituents was today about to address those elected by the people, and we genuinely felt light-hearted, hopeful and delighted. General de Gaulle, who was making his first public appearance in civilian clothes, was welcomed with sustained applause, but one felt that, for the majority of the Assembly, it was no more than a polite gesture, the pretence was so obvious that one could hardly call it deceitful.

André Malraux, in his abrupt style, then made the following comments on the political situation:

"The communists, according to the last estimate, have sixteen per cent of the country for them and thirty-two per cent violently against

136

them. It is the result of their propaganda, which, like all propaganda, has in the end to present a balance-sheet, the people won over set against those who are lost; it is due to their excessive use of propaganda that the communists have now turned a considerable part of the country violently against them, which otherwise would have remained neutral. The situation in France is exactly the same as that in Germany before Hitler, but without Hitler."

He added:

"The fear of all those cowards, by whom we are surrounded, a fear which seems to be shared by the Assembly, is ridiculous: one must have the courage to stand up to the communists; it is not so difficult, nor so fruitless. And, of course, one must be prepared for mud-slinging. In my opinion, it requires less courage to attack de Gaulle in the *Lettres Françaises* than to defend him here. Here, where things will get tough in the days ahead. We'll see some fun, I promise you. It's my only excuse, my only justification for being in this office."

He went on to talk about the General, whom he very seldom sees, but for at least an hour whenever he does:

"You know what he is like: a terrific thinker, whose whole strength lies in being as firm and unshakeable as a rock. He asks you a question or two, lets you make a 'blob', then interrupts you and does the talking himself, developing the point that interests him, but without letting you get a word in. In fact, *Le Fil de l'Epée* portrays him perfectly. That the whole man should emerge from this book, is not at all surprising: the majority of great men foreshadow their destinies before having lived through them; a strange phenomenon which all biographies confirm. There are various possible explanations for it."

He mentioned *Marion Delorme*, written two years before the meeting with Juliette Drouet and launched into a brilliant improvisation which I had some difficulty in following:

"You know him better than I do; you know what an astonishing man he is. Fascinated by principles and consequently invulnerable in a world without principles, with all that entails of positive and negative – what I call his seventeenth century side. Positive: the extraordinary pains he takes to restore the framework of the state, an experiment which will only bear fruit in twenty years. Negative: his obsession with the Rhine, which goes beyond all bounds. And his ignorance, in his position, of the people, unless it is an awareness of his abstraction, alive, admittedly, which he owes to Michelet. But what a mistake: never to have had a meal with a workman!"

A confusing (to me) improvisation on human destiny and the way in which unforeseeable events which occur are nonetheless foreshadowed, in the personality of the subject, and by the characteristics which manifest it (writing, horoscope, yes, he did invoke the horoscope). All the same, I understood enough to remind him of the Bergsons' pages on this subject, in, I believe, *La Pensée et Le Moment.*

On this we parted.

Friday, 16 November, 1945

The possibility of General de Gaulle's departure has become a probability. This afternoon, late, on my way to the office, (with everything going on without any assistance from me, and feeling myself to be useless and dispensable, for the first time since the Liberation, I had gone to the cinema in the afternoon). I learnt from the headlines in the newspapers that the delivery of de Gaulle's letter of resignation was imminent. An amorphous crowd in the underground. In the rue Saint-Dominique I was told that Palewski and Guy had been looking for me during the afternoon to tell me of a decision of the General's that concerned me. I telephoned Guy at the Villa and arranged a meeting for 10.00 that night at Corniglion-Molinier's (which was called off during the evening). Burin des Roziers told me that the decision was connected with the possible removal of the archives. I waited feverishly in Brouillet's office where an extraordinary ballet of comings and goings was taking place, while the telephone and the new arrivals kept us in touch, minute by minute, with the movements and actions of Palewski, who was holding the General's letter of resignation; however, he remained for the time being at the Villa, the delivery having been deferred; then left Neuilly; reached the President of the Assembly's house; handed the letter to Jouin. . . But we learnt that its publication had been put off. Assembled round Brouillet were Police Prefect Luizet, Joxe, the Governmental Secretary-General, Géraud Jouve, from the French Press Agency and Herpin from the Cabinet's press service. Suddenly Gaston Palewski arrived and we all followed him into the next room. Standing around his desk were those above-mentioned and almost the whole of the staff (Colonels Allegret and Tochon, Burin des Roziers, Elisabeth de Miribel, etc.). Palewski was seated, lit by a lamp against a shadowy background, with a wall of curious faces surrounding him. Would the letter be made public? No doubt about that. (In fact, it was made public during the evening.) The General was giving up because the communists were demanding one of the three key ministries which he could not see his way to grant them: Interior, Foreign Affairs, War.

(This is how things developed: interview between de Gaulle and Thorez. Letter from Thorez disclosing publicly the difficulty that had arisen. Reply from the General, also published. Another letter from Thorez revealing a hardening in the communist party's attitude.)

Personal position: a great longing for rest and freedom. But France. . . France. . .

Saturday, 17 November, 1945

Gaston Palewski suggests that there are two theories which might explain the position taken up by the communist party; an electoral manoeuvre, designed to show the country that the party is prepared to shoulder its responsibilities and, if it proves impossible to form a government, the blame does not lie with them: or, direct intervention by Moscow, as a result of the present tension, between the U.S.S.R. and the U.S.A., arising from the Americans' refusal to share the secret of the atom bomb with Russia. If this were the right one – and it appears the more probable – the French domestic crisis is merely one of the consequences of the international crisis, a point scored by the Russians, a preliminary move towards establishing a Soviet bridgehead in France and one of the first hostile acts in the war to come. However that may be, the new element – which no one had foreseen – is the determination of the French communists – whether acting under orders or not – to assert their right to office.

A messenger from Felix Gouin, President of the Chamber, having been announced, we left Gaston Palewski. A long wait and interminable discussions in Brouillet's office. Palewski had told us that the General was wondering whether he should broadcast a message to the country, to which Brouillet was strongly opposed, declaring that by thus overriding the vote in the Chamber, de Gaulle would be breaking with a parliamentary tradition that had always been observed, an act all the more to be deplored because up till now he had always shown unfailing respect for Republican practices. In his office, where we waited in vain for Palewski, we argued fiercely on the subject. Towards 6.00, in the A.D.C.'s office, Commandant de Bonneval, Captain Gudin and I heard the General deliver his appeal in the next room. I was to learn later that, though the microphone was plugged in at the time, the recording did not actually take place. A vigorous speech, despite the underlying restraint, which placed the crisis in its proper perspective; in referring to the possibility of war, it denounced discreetly but with precision, the collusion between the communists and Moscow. So the bridges have been burnt.

Then the ballet continued; Palewski passed through the room separating the General's from his own (coming from the General), exchanged two or three words with Dupraz and myself, and dashed back again, jostling a furious Quilici. Comments bubble up on all sides. Everyone was anxious and at a loose end. The same people kept on bumping into each other as they came and went from the various offices. We learn that the communists were trying to stop the speech, giving in and proposing compromises. A copy of the speech, taken from the recording-van stationed in the yard, was already circulating in the Palais-Bourbon, where people were talking loudly of Bonaparte. Gouin, however, came to see de Gaulle and stayed a long time with him in his office (I think it was shortly after the recording of the speech of which I caught snatches from my office – it, too, separated from the General's by a double door). I met Louis Vallon on the back stairs. He said: "Gouin told the General that the whole affair could be settled, and that he must put off the broadcast (arranged for 8.00). To which the General is supposed to have replied:

"Then it must be settled by 7.45." It was then past 7.00. At 8.00 the broadcast took place and I heard it in Elisabeth de Miribel's office. In the meantime, we tripped over the radio lines. Gaston Palewski executed some *entrechats* in Guy's office, threw in three less recognizable steps and went out again. General Juin arrived and Colonel Laporte and Brouillet. They all had appointments with General de Gaulle.

All through the day I was arranging with Colonel Allegret and Mlle. Milliez, who share with me the responsibility for the secret operation, the eventual removal of the archives, which was to be carried out with all possible speed and discretion. The General wanted everything to be ready by Sunday evening. An order may be issued during the night. X, happy to live through the glorious hours of France Libre again recalled them, and spoke of loyal comrades, weapons and forged papers, while, in the adjoining room, staff officers were engaged in drawing up some remarkable plans. Early in the afternoon, my father dictated his article to me: *Le Champ Clos*. With remarkable prescience, he adopted de Gaulle's position before de Gaulle. This often happens. That is why people think he often sees de Gaulle and receives orders from him.

I can still hear Brouillet mutter, just before entering the General's room: "Now, it's all a matter of chance . . ."

Sunday, 18 November, 1945

I was at the rue Saint-Dominique from 10.30 to 1.00 and then from 5.45 to 7.30, getting the archives ready. Gouin's candidature is backed

140

by the communists. Roger Stéphane has come into the picture. Maurice Schumann and Francisque Gay, high up in the M.R.P.* (which seems the only party to have remained loyal to de Gaulle) arrive in answer to a summons from Palewski, who had a message to give them from the General. But Palewski had returned to Neuilly. Schumann was irritable: "We're living through a time when every minute counts . . ." He is no longer the dashing young man – but still humble in spite of his celebrity – whom I first met in August 1944 lunching with the General. He has acquired an air of importance. Even physically he has filled out. He is referred to as 'Monsieur le Président'. He referred, not without complacency, to the five million voters he has behind him. "A fat lot of good that'll do you in prison!" said Quilici who had come in with him (all this took place in the A.D.C.'s office). Schumann retorted, "It'll help to make the experience more tolerable!" But Francisque Gay was shaking his goatee: "Like a rock, the M.R.P., like a rock . . ." Quilici appeared to be getting increasingly agitated. A call was put through to the villa. Palewski was still there. "That's fine!" Schumann muttered. "Just when it's all a matter of minutes." Guy arrived, in mufti. With an authority that I cannot help admiring, he took charge of the whole situation and decided that Gay and Schumann should go to the villa. At that moment, a telephone message announced that Palewski was on the way. A few minutes later I met him with Vallon just behind, on the back staircase, where he was giving Mlle. Milliez a manuscript of the General's which had to be typed urgently: a few moments later, he was on his way back to Neuilly. It was another letter to Gouin, in which de Gaulle confirmed that he intended to stand. It was made public towards 11.00.

Monday, 19 November, 1945

For the first time, the General's behaviour lacks its usual appearance of rectitude. For the first time, he seems to have changed horses in midstream. For, on Friday, he was certainly resigning. But as the word had fortunately not been actually mentioned, the General was able to give, after the event, in his speech – and more particularly in yesterday's letter – another interpretation. And now he is standing for election when one party in the Assembly (the communists) no longer want him, though he refused to stand when all the parties were unanimously for him.

Enormous optimism seems to reign over the rue Saint-Dominique. Yesterday's letter is considered as a master-stroke which has retrieved the whole situation, just when it seemed to be lost. A small majority (relatively) is anticipated, which will enable the General to form a Cabinet of technicians (with some socialists, if possible). At the present moment, it is anticipated that the communists will vote against him and that the S.F.I.O. will abstain; thus, the General may win with the votes of the M.R.P. and the right (plus the U.D.S.R.)*. But it is all very much in the balance and anything can happen by 3.00, when the Constituent Assembly meets for a session which promises to be thrilling.

The General saw Léon Blum during the night who, according to Claude Guy, went in to the General with all the appearance of a man deaf to any persuasion, ("It's a matter of a parliamentary crisis – not an international one") and left it shaken, possibly even convinced. Palewski declared that the General's arguments made a considerable impact on Blum. As I am writing (12.25) de Gaulle is receiving Le Troquer in the next room. He has already seen Vincent Auriol and Gouin this morning. The last minute problems still, as always, are bound up with the socialists. He will be seeing Georges Bidault, too, in a few moments. From the adjoining office, come snatches of a well-known voice: the voice of General de Gaulle. His companion is also talking a little more loudly than is necessary.

The session was disappointing, in spite of Duclos' efforts to enliven it. Through André Philip as their spokesman, the socialists are preparing the path towards betrayal. And it all ended up with a peremptory mandate being given to the General by the Assembly, to form a tripartite government with a 'fair' distribution of seats. I was appalled as I heard it announced, and it may well bring us closer to the abyss.

Tuesday, 20 November, 1945

12.45 p.m. The destiny of France is being decided in the room adjoining that in which I am writing. There are snatches of conversation, cynical laughter and moments of silence, which are even more disturbing: and then the calm, even voice of General de Gaulle . . . In there, summoned by him, following yesterday's vote, in a last attempt to come to an understanding are: Duclos, Thorez, Bonte (all the communist big guns), the M.R.P. delegates (Schumann, Gay, Collin) and those of the S.F.I.O. (Mayer, Auriol, Philip).

A heavy silence. Then, once again, the General's voice.

1.00 p.m. They have just left. I saw the three scoundrels in the courtyard, posing for the photographers. Next door, however, the General continues to speak in a loud, strong voice . . . to whom?

1.05 p.m. I have returned to the A.D.C.'s office. I saw Schumann in the courtyard in the middle of a large group of reporters. All the delegates, so I am told, refused to say anything: "We have promised not to make a statement." But Schumann added: "It is up to you to interpret our faces." At the time he was radiating optimism and Gudin du Pavillon drew favourable conclusions from changes in Thorez's expression, before the interview and after (his surly, inscrutable look becoming relaxed). And the General is still talking. His voice grows louder: I can hear him say: "I am sick of it!" quite fiercely. I learn that it is Philip who is in with him.

3.45 p.m. Maurice Thorez is in the General's office.

The consultations were interrupted, late in the evening, because fog made it impossible for the people concerned to find their way to the villa in Neuilly.

Wednesday, 21 November, 1945

At 3.00, the General had not yet lunched. I saw Malraux emerge from his office at that time. He went out of his way to shake my hand, since recently he has begun to take notice of me. A quarter of an hour ago, the Cabinet was formed (with André Malraux as Minister of Information). The General, adopting an idea of Burin des Roziers, will supervise the War Ministry which has been split into several departments. In this way, the communists will be satisfied, without the General losing face.

Saturday, 1 December, 1945

Two new ministers, Vincent Auriol and Jules Moch*, were the stars of this evening's reception, at which the General in his customary fashion did most of the talking. After dinner, he isolated himself as usual, at the other end of the sitting-room with the more important guests – while I remained with the small fry, making polite conversation to the ladies. Again, according to ritual, the General joined us for the last few minutes of the evening. Everybody crowded round him, seeking information, and he talked to them without, this time, asking insipid questions as he had done at the beginning of the reception while waiting for the last guests to arrive when the languished conversation had only been kept alive by his meritorious efforts ("And you, Madame, what is the longest journey you've ever made?") Nor did he confine himself to brief sentences, as he had during dinner ("In the Nuremberg Trial, it is always Goering who has the most human expression.")

143

("I must admit that, in defeat, the Japanese are good losers.") No, now he was genuinely confidential: about the letter sent him by Himmler in January of this year proposing a plan for Franco-German resistance to Anglo-Saxon and Russian imperialism. ("But it was high treason on his part!" exclaimed one of the guests, to whom de Gaulle replied very calmly: "It was his policy.") About his conversations with Stalin. What had struck him most was that Stalin had never spoken of the U.S.S.R. but always of *Russia,* without prefacing it with 'Soviet', "just as the Tsar would have done . . ." (And I understood that he was thinking: "Just as I, myself, speak of France") which provoked an indignant comment from Vincent Auriol: "And here we're regarded as belonging to the fifth column if we accidentally speak of 'Russia'!" About the probable reasons for Stalin's current disappearance, declaring that his withdrawal was probably strategic: to let the purges and necessary reforms be carried out by someone else – and then to return as peacemaker. He spoke of all this with his usual ability and as if it had not come at the end of an exhausting day's work. Vincent Auriol was the first to leave, at about 11.00. He was going to the Chamber where a committee was in the course of discussing the plan for the nationalization of credits.

1946

Thursday, 3 January, 1946

The day before yesterday, during the debate in the Constituent Assembly, arising from the scrutiny of the budget for Armaments and the Armed Forces, General de Gaulle was nearly defeated. In fact, he would have been defeated, if only it had been possible to envisage a replacement for him. And, indeed, he is entitled to declare "that it does not look as though any of his actions can be found to conflict with national sovereignty," since every representative of that sovereignty always ends up by conforming his acts to the only sovereignty that exists, the factual sovereignty, not the legal one: his own. In as much as he is irreplaceable, the General can take no credit for sticking to the rules of the game, when there is no risk in doing so. One had proof of it again in the Assembly on 1st January, when he insistently adumbrated his imminent departure, thereby compelling the deputies to give way once more, barely keeping up appearances. This is all very well, but General de Gaulle's influence and his reputation seem to have fallen considerably since the elections. France's diplomatic isolation, the increase of restrictions (heavy electricity cuts and the reintroduction of ration cards giving a lower standard of living than existed at the time of their discontinuation) and blunders and mistakes of a government whose incompetence is only too evident, make people forget the external and internal problems, which de Gaulle has to face. Soon, he may well be so far discredited that the deputies will venture to take him at his word when he speaks of leaving. And what will happen? His ambition, like his indifference, may lead to the gravest consequences. In either case, the outcome is unpredictable.

It is with profound gloom that I record the nation's growing lassitude. They have no more hope, courage or willpower. Our people are close to that stage of apathy, when every form of disloyalty becomes a possibility. Admittedly, the whole world has lost hope and war is lurking at the threshold of this new peace in which no one has any faith. Once again, the representatives of the three Great Powers are meeting in Moscow. But will France, not admitted to their discussions, accept decisions made in her absence? Once more de Gaulle has elected to be

O.G.—10

145

intransigent, and compelled his ministers, willingly or otherwise, to pursue the same course.

I was with him in his office yesterday morning, when Palewski, with an eye on the approaching Cabinet meeting, tried to persuade him to adopt a less categorical attitude. The General received his suggestions with almost savage rudeness, answering with a peremptory negative each argument that Palewski put forward in his expressionless, patient manner. De Gaulle's repetitive "I don't give a damn!" and "So the U.S.S.R. will treat us as they did after Yalta – what do you think we care about that?", his unpleasant, rasping, nervous tone of voice and his obvious exasperation did not stop Gaston Palewski from propounding one by one the points he had decided to raise. But I felt that, defeated from the start and conscious of it, he was only speaking from a sense of duty. Faced by the monolithic intransigence of this man, who incarnated to us in the solitude of the office, as he did to the world outside, an incorruptible France claiming its due rights, and who was prepared to overlook her current frailty for the sake of her eternal greatness, (for such is de Gaulle and, if through his actions, France should go astray, there is nothing to be done about it; for France today is *he*, this man and no other, with all his qualities, of course, but also his defects, his nobility, but perhaps, too, his weaknesses) – faced by this massive block of arrogance, Palewski's tenacious humility held a certain beauty. Instinctively, I am always for the underdog. May not France also play such a role confronted by her ferocious Allies?

Some weeks ago in connection with the strike of civil servants, about which he had abruptly asked my opinion at the end of a working session, de Gaulle referred to journalists, deputies and even his ministers in a voice in which the anger was mingled with contempt: "They are cowards, utter cowards!" – and I was reminded of what Bidault had said to my father: "If only you knew the way he treats us; us, his ministers!"

Monday, 21 January, 1946

Asked by the General's Cabinet to accompany a mission to Brazil (Paris, Casablanca, Dakar, Natal, Rio de Janeiro and back, all within a fortnight, with about a week in Rio) I have had nothing else in mind during the last few days but the wonderful trip due to start on Thursday. But today all this has evaporated into thin air. "General de Gaulle has resigned . . ." Without any intention of returning, according to him. What is certain is that the decision is irrevocable at the moment . . . At the end of an exhausting day, I am writing this in my office from which most of my things have already been moved. What a lot there is to record! But I shall soon have the time to do it.

Saturday, 9 February, 1946
38 *Avenue Théophile Gautier, Paris*

Since the events of 21st January, an acute attack of influenza has kept me in bed and the disorientation caused by the illness has prevented me from fully appreciating the other, much deeper-seated one, due to the abrupt departure of General de Gaulle. I shared the surprise of everyone else, not so much at his resignation, which had seemed inevitable for several weeks, as at the form or rather, lack of form, in which it was cloaked. I was also hurt to see the Liberator go, even if provisionally, on a defeat that affected his prestige, and abandon the France he had saved, with his aims still a long way from being achieved. The artificial optimism of his letter to President Gouin had shocked me, while the indifference of the country, which seemed already to have forgotten the man whom they had once loved so much, distressed me less than it should have done: by that, I mean that it struck me as normal and, in some degree, deserved. Meanwhile, in his retreat in Marly and then in Mèzieres, de Gaulle was acquiring prestige of a new kind, strictly historical, and already as inaccessible and mysterious as that of a dead hero.

I received a message from the deceased in the shape of a photograph with this exaggerated inscription: *To Claude Mauriac, my friend! faithfully C. de Gaulle.*

I was happy to be summoned by the General yesterday to his old home in Marly, and be invited to continue acting as his secretary.

It was still daylight when the car, which had been sent to take me to the house, entered an avenue in the Parc de Marly. The regal perspectives were already making me anticipate a princely retreat when, on my left, I caught sight of a modest lodge, which appeared even smaller because of the tall, leafless trees surrounding it. Three or four policemen. A light: maybe his. I was moved. My driver drew up in a small yard and I walked in by the back door and found myself in the servants' hall. In the adjoining room, General de Gaulle's dinner was cooking on a low fire in copper pans. This intimate scene, on which I had come unexpectedly, also moved me. I should have found the same intimacy had I entered by the front door. The cook told Claude Guy of my arrival, and he came to fetch me, wearing his new captain's bands. He took me to his bedroom, a sort of cabin, with no window other than a glazed bay, which, I had just learned, looked on the well of a staircase, when I caught sight of the truncated figure of Charles de Gaulle in mufti, coming down with a guest whom I could not see. Claude Guy – who rushed out to see him to his car – told me that it was Vincent Auriol, President of the Constituent Assembly since Felix Gouin replaced the General as President of the Provisional Government.

A few minutes later, Claude showed me into the study, where the General welcomed me with a warm smile that, too, was in keeping with the new intimacy of the surroundings. He offered me a cigarette and told me to sit down. I ventured to tell him that I was glad to see the thick layer of dry mud covering the broad soles of his shoes, for I knew how much he had suffered from being confined. He mentioned the good walk he had taken that afternoon (during which, Claude Guy told me later, he had burst into cheerful song) and immediately turned to my present employment: "Do you want to stay with me?" When I replied in the affirmative, he explained that I should have to: 1) reply to his correspondence as I had done in the past, and draft letters for his signature, 2) help him to go through and, eventually, put in order all his historical archives since June 1940, 3) "as you read a lot", keep him in touch with articles and books which seemed to me worthy of his attention, particularly those concerning himself.

"I don't mean the daily Press . . ." he added, giving the sentence a contemptuous inflection.

He handed me a briefcase stuffed with letters (to which Claude Guy was to add three large, thick envelopes containing the rest of the correspondence received after 21st January). Then, after we had dealt with a few last essential details, he asked me "what people were saying . . ." I discreetly fell back on my fortnight in bed and referred him to the newspapers, which he had no doubt read, as I had. And then, he took over the conversation, radiating a wholly unexpected satisfaction, but one so open and serene that I soon found nothing abnormal in the optimism that, to begin with, had been so disconcerting.

"How right I was to go, eh! And to go *without saying a word*. They were expecting explanations . . . but *pouf* . . . Suddenly I'd vanished. Everything's already been forgotten about any considerations that might have left the resignation open to criticism."

And he laughed, his eyes more ironical than ever, and his face reflecting calm arrogance and complete self-confidence. Once again, I began to feel uneasy. He gave the impression of being out of touch with reality. But, at once, his force of personality changed my anxiety into admiration. It was impossible to resist him – and, having yielded, impossible to have doubts about him. All the same, I ventured to say that, with things getting worse and worse for France, people were becoming more and more apprehensive: "Well, all the better, it'll do them good . . ." Once again, I was shocked. I understood what he meant, but was shocked that he seemed to be thinking more of himself than of France. He was forgetting that he identifies himself with France, to the extent that he believes himself to be her last and only hope.

He saw me to the door. In the next room Mme. de Gaulle was glancing through magazines, waiting for me to go before she came in. The feeling of intimacy was again acute. A few seconds later the General closed the door of his study on himself and his wife.

In the evening, in my bedroom, I began to go through the voluminous correspondence which the General had read without arranging it in any sort of order. Very secret letters were next to one from a madman. And there were such touching letters from unknown members of the public: "We have been weeping for ten days now! For the love of God and the good people of France, come back, we beg you! You probably knew you were loved, but you could not have known how much you were loved. Legions of little, humble people, those who are never heard of, looked up to you, full of faith and hope" etc. – "I am an old woman of seventy-three, but I do not want to die without having expressed to you my great admiration . . ." – "I cannot bear it any longer. I must write what so many French people have in their minds . . ." – "I must write and tell you that we still love you. Why did you leave us? Now we feel like orphans . . ."

Tuesday, 12 February, 1946

I went to Marly in the evening. The trees, overlooking the lodge, are not so high as I thought: merely standing on a mound. There was a smell of cooking as I went in – by the front door this time, as the cook had complained of my involuntary indiscretion of the other night. Outside, a nightbird was launching its plaintive cry into the dusk. The General who, it appears, has been sleeping badly, looked nervous and tired. I handed him some thirty letters to sign: "Don't give the impression that I'm retiring for good. Give non-committal answers," he said, with the first flourish of his pen. I told him that I had been careful to do so – and he signed the lot. As I left, I saw a lighted window from the yard. The nocturnal bird was still screeching. It was close to nightfall with its good country smells. What solitude! No longer any police, at least, no visible signs of them.

Thursday, 14 February, 1946

My father, who is going to Marly tomorrow, reappeared in *Le Figaro* with an excellent article on de Gaulle. I will quote the opening sentences, which express so well from what heights we have fallen, naturally, without laying any blame (at this stage) on the Liberator: "It would have been too easy, if what we had dreamt of in the darkness had come true in the light. General de Gaulle's departure has dispersed the last traces of grace and of the miraculous still floating over a resuscitated France. The charm of the Liberation is vanishing, before we had completely ceased to be under its spell."

I spent the day typing, myself, twenty letters for the General, as there is no secretary; which reveals the lowly nature of my job. But de Gaulle has too great a reputation for me to consider it anything but an honour to serve him – and, after all, it is not my real profession.

Saturday, 16 February, 1946

Yesterday evening, I went down with my father to Marly. As night fell, we ran into fog, which made the forest resemble all the forests of my memories. My father reminded me how the courtesans used to whisper – according to Saint-Simon – "Marly! Marly!" in order to get picked up by the King on one of his journeys. Impressed by past associations, as we entered the park, he said: "Obviously such a setting makes one more inclined towards Maurras' ideologies than republican ones." Claude Guy, who was in the orchard, on which the lodge looks out, (three or four gnarled old pear trees) welcomed us, and there was a smell of moist earth and mist, which made one long for country life. We were moved by the beauty of the valley. We walked in. My father was shown into the General's study at once, and Guy, Commandant Bonneval and I stayed in the adjoining dining-room – rustling the newspapers that we were reading ostentatiously, so as not to hear – or look as though we were listening to – what was being said in the next room. As far as I was concerned, I did my honest (and perhaps stupid) best not to pay any attention to that well-known voice of Charles de Gaulle, of which the even delivery and familiar tones touched me. Now and again, but rarely, my father's tired voice broke in: all the same, I did catch snatches of the General's long monologue – and, for a few moments, abandoning all discretion, I lent an ear:

". . . I left, because they were lying in wait for me at every turn. Besides, I had always said that I would leave as soon as the elections

150

were over . . . There were two very different types of Resistance. So what? France is the only country in Europe which is independent. No one's dying of hunger. There aren't even any more tramps . . . You can't imagine, but I'll speak out one day, I'll speak out . . ."

The rest of the sentence was lost, but I heard my father say: "I'm well aware of all you must know about that . . ." Then Giraud's name was mentioned several times by both of them before de Gaulle resumed his monologue. My father's voice broke in, more loudly: "I only wanted to say, General . . ." but it was at once drowned by the other one, regular and rhythmical as ever and occasionally raised several degrees. I glanced through a book on 'The Marlys' of Louis XIV: then got up and looked out on the misty valley, settling down to sleep in the twilight. And I was suddenly conscious that in these surroundings, which had almost reverted to their wild state, but where victorious nature still bore the deep imprints of one of Mankind's greatest centuries, History was still being made and that I was present at one of the important moments in its unfolding.

The conversation went on for about an hour before the two men came out. De Gaulle caught sight of me and shook my hand. He was worried about keeping my father waiting, for I had several letters for him to sign, but they only took him a couple of minutes. I was not struck by his youthfulness, as my father was (so he told me a few minutes later): I do not look at him, I do not see him . . . The only thing I noticed, while he was signing the letters I handed to him, was a scratch on his left hand. I joined the others: on the coat-rack, our things were hanging up next to the General's, and I admired his elegant grey hat. One of the trifling details that attract me by their domesticity – so far removed from the pomp that reigned so recently in the rue Saint-Dominique. In the same way, I was touched a short while ago to see Mme. de Gaulle, through the glass door of the kitchen, talking to the cook. While he was putting on his coat, my father took advantage of a moment when Guy and Bonneval were out of earshot to say to me: "It was a fascinating evening . . . And it's quite true: he farts fire . . ."

I can now reconstruct what was sandwiched between the few sentences that I overheard. My father has summarized the main points of their conversation. De Gaulle told him that he had been compelled to go, as the various parties made it impossible to govern. He had realized it and had come to his decision a long while ago. The choice of moment was unimportant, within a week or so.

"The fact is that it's impossible to govern under the party system. It's also true that no Assembly, however constituted, has ever governed in France – that no Parliament, of any kind, has ever succeeded in acquiring executive powers. It's a leader that the country needs."

My father then remarked: "He gave me his views on the form the Constitution should take, and I can assure you that if he had his way, the President would certainly possess powers!"

De Gaulle had said: "There are three institutions, which should never be a subject for debate: the Army, Diplomacy and Justice." According to him, the general outlook for France was not as bad as it seemed. The U.S.S.R. and the U.S.A. had innumerable problems. England was less independent than France, the only European power to remain entirely independent – at least, he had left it so when he resigned. Just as he had left her Empire united and intact.

"Of course Bidault has already begun to make concessions . . . It needed a far different man than a poor little popular-democrat to stand up to the Foreign Office. But there is no reason to despair: when all's said and done, it's not the men who matter but the institutions – and the fact remains that France has been put back on her feet again."

Men. His contempt for them struck my father. Roosevelt and Churchill were two great men whose like would not be seen again. He had come up against them often enough to do them this justice: "One can justifiably say that this is not the era of giants!" In France, for instance, there was no one: "I know old Gouin's ministers; they are the same as mine . . ." Gouin, Philip, the communists, he treated them all with the same contempt, convinced that he was right and the only man in France of any outstanding qualities, which is impressive. "When one's with him," my father went on, "one feels oneself becoming half-witted. He does not see you. He does not look on you as an individual. He judges what you say to him *in abstracto,* without relating it to what you are or what you know." According to him, there were three possibilities in the days ahead: "Either all the existing mess and mediocrity will continue for a long time; or the communists will seize power – which means the certainty of a foreign war, since the Russians will move into France, which the Americans and the English will never agree to under any circumstances; or I return . . ." The third possibility has been stated with exactly this calm simplicity.

De Gaulle had also explained to my father that there had been two kinds of Resistance – between which, after the Liberation, there had been no possibility of any agreement. "Mine – yours – which was resistance to the enemy – and then the politicians' resistance – which was anti-nazi and anti-fascist, but in no way national." (I suddenly remembered his voice reaching me from the study: "They all wanted

152

to make use of me, to take advantage of me . . .") As for England, he would one day reveal the extent to which she had intrigued against us from the very beginning of June 1940:

"Through Churchill – yes, in those very first days . . . But he altered his attitude almost at once, demoralizing the Béthouard troops, whom I had won over and taking the action you know at Mers-el Kebir, which resulted in my being met with gunfire at Dakar . . ." (I could see him again, during the last session of the Assembly at which I was present, replying proudly to Edouard Herriot that, between Vichy and himself, there had been not only an exchange of letters, but also of gunfire.) "And Churchill went so far as to threaten to put Giraud over me! Giraud, who was entirely in the hands of the English . . ."

(Other snatches of the long monologue overheard through the door, come back to me: "But France had no further use for the Senate which, in her eyes, was completely discredited . . . Do you know what would have happened if there had been two Chambers – by a majority of the first, with eighty votes against, the Senate would have been . . ." the end was inaudible.)

According to my father, de Gaulle maintained that the outlook had not been particularly serious at the time of his resignation, that there was nothing abnormal in the inflation and that the monetary problem did not exist. "But in three days those idiots jeopardized everything by undermining confidence, and losing, in one full sweep, the credit that France had in America." My father went on:

"Last night, I thought over what de Gaulle had told me and I came to the conclusion that he had been replying point by point to my article in *Figaro,* though he made no direct reference to it. It was to show me that he had well and truly untied the triple Gordian Knot, which I had said that no one would succeed in doing: 1) There was no monetary crisis, or rather there had been none up till his resignation. 'What did it matter, printing a few notes? . . . There was full confidence . . .' Now that they make public what should have been kept secret, disaster is certain. 2) France was independent, perhaps the most independent of all European countries. 3) An understanding with the Resistance was impossible, due to its internal corruption."

Thus spoke my father this morning.

"That unfortunate Bidault," "That wretched Philip." A perjorative adjective always precedes the name of the person he is talking about. "That good old Gouin." It is impossible not to regard it as a weak spot in this great man's mental make-up.

Tuesday, 26 February, 1946
Marly

The tall trees in the valley are haloed with a sort of red glow from the rising of the sap. I came down with General Chomel – the last head of the Army Council in the ex-Cabinet: he had just come back from London, where he had been a member of the French delegation to U.N.O., and had not seen de Gaulle since 21st January.

When we had finished working (for the first time in a friendly, relaxed way) the General asked:

"Well, what are people saying?"

"The rumour is, General – and it's widespread – that you're under house arrest."

"And they aren't surprised?"

"Hardly. As my father remarked, one longs to say to them: 'What, you believe it, and yet you do nothing about it, you just accept it?' "

"There you are! There's cowardice everywhere – incredible cowardice . . ."

After a pause, he added:

"What's needed is for the parties to break up. And it can be left to them: they'll break up on their own."

"But I can't see how those, which are getting financial and moral support from abroad, will break up."

"You mean the communist party? It'll survive, of course."

"Then, if all the other parties have disappeared, except that one, I don't see . . ."

"But that one's vulnerable, by being a party *on friendly terms with a foreign power*. The national interest will demand its suppression. It'll be simple enough."

"It won't be all that simple. We shan't avoid sabotage and we shan't escape a civil war."

"But, my dear friend, what can I do about it?"

He asked this with malicious irony; then went on:

"There is nothing one can do about the parties. Just look at them! They're on the verge of breaking with Franco. And what does that invite? That Russia says: 'I'm breaking with him, too, and I'm coming to help you.' Then what happens, I ask you?"

I remembered something that Georges Bidault had said to my father, a few days before: "The General is convinced there'll be war." I give the General Koestler's excellent *Zero and the Infinite,* and the last number of Sartre's review. In the straight avenue leading to the main road, we pass Palewski's car approaching the lodge.

From cowardice, or a desire to be on the winning side, or merely in the hope of surviving, no matter what happens, and surviving in comfort, how many people at the present time, are flirting with the communists! I do not mean those who are communists by conviction – those who, rightly or wrongly, really believe in it – but all those poor, ambitious, timid, weak creatures. Though I am attracted by what I see to be sincere in the communists and should not mind at all to be converted (it would be marvellous to find some grounds for hope!), I cannot fly in the face of a conviction which seems more warrantable every day: that communism is the reverse of everything I believe in, not only as a Frenchman, but even more as a man. Whether it will win the day or not is a different matter. I should be more inclined to bet on its victory than on that of General de Gaulle. (I mean: on that of a humanist democracy.) But I willingly accept any risk that may exist in remaining with de Gaulle. On condition, naturally, that he does not assume the role of dictator.

I have been told that Malraux is engaged in mysterious activities. It would cause little surprise if he were adding a new chapter to his biography. Otherwise, it is the same old story: wherever we are heading, it is not towards peace . . . As for Malraux, it was certainly mere gossip.

De Gaulle has entrusted me with the proofs of a new edition of his speeches between 1940 - 41, corrected in his own hand. It is interesting to see what he has deleted. He was surprised at not finding, in the typescripts returned to him, the text of his intervention about Syria in the Assembly, in June 1945.

"I am anxious that it should appear in the collection of my speeches, to brand England with the infamy, of which she should bear the scars for ever."

Monday, 4 March, 1946

The car went by way of Neuilly, to pick up Colonel de Wavrin (the famous Passy of the D.G.E.R.*) who, if I am to believe the questions he asked me, was going to Marly for the first time. The snow, which has been falling for more than forty-eight hours, compelled us to take another route, which was considerably longer. Pink and fresh-complexioned, wearing a pair of light-coloured gloves, a leg recently broken at winter sports stretched out in front of him, Passy spoke of "those French people who only think of eating and drinking and with whom there's nothing to be done." I remembered his legend and doubted if men of his kind were the ones to induce de Gaulle to take the right road. But we embarked on a conversation, during which I made an effort (which taxed me more and more) to speak, and to speak well. And if I feel more disposed towards Wavrin it is perhaps only because I have become so towards myself. When he said that the way in which the General had resigned from office had shown an exceptional nobility, displayed by few other statesmen, I had a few reservations, redeemed immediately by these reflections, all of which I did not pass on to him, but which I should like to set down in full here:

"The letter of resignation only hurt the French (and me, Colonel) by coming two months too late, an infinitesimal margin of time, which will have disappeared when History looks back on it. In his actions, de Gaulle always has due regard for the historical perspective. It is less considerations of domestic politics that weigh with him than the study of international contingencies. He foresees a conflict and plays the game accordingly, convinced that, one day, his presence will almost certainly be needed. For there are only two hypotheses: and if one of them proves right, his return to office is inevitable."

Passy agrees and reminds me of Hamlet's words, quoted in the *Fil de l'Epée* "To be great is greatly to find quarrel." The landscape consists of small snow-covered cottages. This man with pink cheeks who has been something of a Fouché says: "All those dirty little tricks in politics . . . De Gaulle is made for a great quarrel, not for picking through dustbins . . ."

We reached the long, low lodge by an unfamiliar road. Claude welcomed us, looking mysterious: Baron Guillaume, the Belgian Ambassador, was with the General, whose study opened on the only room where we could wait; and the visitor must not know that Wavrin was there. The General's luxurious Cadillac was parked in a sort of converted stable open on all sides. It was there, in the front seat, with his injured leg stretched out on the running-board, that I found Passy a few moments later. The straw was shining, as in Verlaine's poem. The General's driver was doing odd jobs, having exchanged his uniform for country clothes. Agricultural implements were side by side with the most modern and powerful of cars, a present from General Eisenhower. The Belgian driver was joking with the General's. At last the coast was clear and Guy came to fetch us.

While Passy was in with the General, Claude told me that, on the first evening of his retirement there, in Marly, de Gaulle had read fifty pages of my father's *Marguerite de Cortone* and my *Trahison d'un Clerc*. A fine way of getting used to one's new surroundings!

156

The working session was uneventful. We spoke a little about Koestler, whom he had read. When we had finished, I kept on running into Mme. de Gaulle, loaded with blankets and other household articles – and came across Elisabeth de Boissieu. A tiny house, where Claude Guy told me in the car taking us back to Paris through the snowy night, "the cancer of boredom was beginning to gnaw at the General".

Before leaving, Claude Guy had made him sign his lease; three months: 15,000 francs. He hopes that his house in the Haute-Marne will be ready by the first week of May.

Daniel Guérin, a Trotskyist, interrogated by the bourgeois that I am – and on his guard – told me that his comrades would not step up at all their struggle against communism. "It isn't the right moment," he said. "I'm doing my best to convince them that, in the event of a conflict between the U.S.S.R. and the Anglo-Saxon powers, they must unhesitatingly range themselves with the U.S.S.R. For, in spite of everything, it is she and she alone who is 'progressive'."

Am very shaken by Koestler's 'provocative' book (it is the communists who call it that) – but which seems to me in a certain sense, a provocation to admiration (of communism). However, one must not let oneself be influenced by it – and I have pulled myself together. But I must not forget that I am only anti-communist because communism is totalitarian. As a result of hating what is odious in the things it stands for, I was beginning to regard as suspect the truths it defends. I must not forget, either, my reasoned, as much as instinctive, aversion for the so detestable, pre-war, right-wing parties.

Thursday, 14 March, 1946

Because of a lack of available cars, it took me two hours yesterday evening to get to Marly. First of all, I had to pick up Mlle. Potel – the family's housekeeper – somewhere behind the Place de la Bastille – and take her to the 'Petit Clamart', a greengrocer patronized by my hosts at Marly: turnips, cauliflowers, salsify, potatoes and salad ingredients were loaded in impressive quantities into the Citröen – and I noted, with admiration, that all these modest but rare vegetables were sold at the official prices which was a miracle in these days of widespread black-marketing.

When I reached Marly – by way of Villacoublay still displaying extensive bomb damage, and Versailles – it was after 7.00 and the General was impatient at having such a long wait. He gave me the proofs of his second volume of *Speeches*, overburdened with extremely interesting corrections. That same afternoon I had seen Repessé, the head of Berger-Levrault, to settle the final details of the new edition. I told the General of the decision we had reached, finding myself for the first time completely at ease with him. I mentioned the famous interview which appeared yesterday in the (disguised communist) newspaper, *Liberation*. Under the heading: 'I shall come back if' the author, who had obviously spoken to one of the visitors to Marly – put into de Gaulle's mouth words best calculated to do him harm. The most annoying thing was that the General does, in fact, make such observations: "The conflict between the U.S.S.R. and the U.S.A. is inevitable . . . The M.R.P. will not preponderate in Paradise." The author went on: "de Gaulle always regards the greater part of mankind with a supreme contempt, from which parliamentarians are a long way from being exempt . . ." and other charming remarks, with a nod of approval to the communists in passing. De Gaulle asked me what I thought of it, with an expression simultaneously indifferent and attentive (his own particular way of listening interestedly, a glint of irony mingling with the light of an acute curiosity). I spoke of gross breaches of confidences and reported, on the testimony of my sister, Luce, who had been in Lyons on the previous evening, that a local paper was announcing on a four-column spread 'Sensational Revelations by the General'. It was referring, of course, to *Liberation*. I insisted on the necessity for a denial, in spite of the difficulty of finding the form it should take. De Gaulle was convinced, took a sheet of paper, and began writing. But after a few seconds he gave up, deferring it till later, and said:

"Obviously, they win either way. If I publish a denial, I'm merely giving the matter more importance. And if I don't, I seem to be admitting the words attributed to me."

And suddenly, with that serenity of his, rather disturbing by its self-confidence, he added:

"After all, perhaps it's better to let them stew in their own juice and say nothing, do nothing; just let them be till they . . ."

He did not finish the sentence – and I ventured to say that, in the present circumstances, I did not share his opinion. And I gave my reasons.

When we had finished our work and I was leaving, so loaded with official papers that the General called Bonneval in to help me, Mme. de Gaulle and the young Boissieus were in the dining-room, waiting for me to go. We exchanged a few polite words. Alain de Boissieu, who at the moment is on the same staff-college course as my brother-in-law, Le Ray, referred to their joint captivity. I took advantage of the opportunity to relate a generous gesture of his: Boissieu, having learnt that

Le Ray was further forward than he was in his plans to escape, promptly offered him all the marks he had managed to collect, and which he badly needed. Here General de Gaulle spoilt all the effect, for the second part of the story was just as admirable as the first, by bursting out laughing and asking:

"And he never gave them back?"

I protested. And Boissieu answered for me: "No, he'd refused to accept them."

The rumours of war, exploited by the anti-communist Press, which would have set our nerves on edge if ten years' experience had not toughened us, are greatly exaggerated. But it is only fair to say that they are not without foundation, and seem to become more detailed every day. On the threshold of the atomic age, the world totters on the brink of its annihilation, and our intelligence can no longer keep up with all this folly and science. My father, a journalist with a good nose, who sniffs the wind and predicts events before anyone else, sent an article to Pierre Brisson three days ago of such an alarmist character that the latter did not dare to publish it to the author's great resentment. A few hours after what had appeared to be an attack of cold feet was justified by the facts – which the newspapers did not hesitate to embellish. (Iran, Turkey, etc.) The article, re-drafted and played down, will appear tomorrow.

Tuesday, 19 March, 1946

André Malraux received me yesterday evening in one of the only as yet habitable rooms – his sister-in-law's bedroom – in the house in Boulogne, which he is in the process of converting. I found the rhythm of his speech disconcerting at first, so much so that I had difficulty in listening to him. Soon, however, I heard nothing but his extraordinarily fertile eloquence, spurting like an unruly flame from a hidden furnace. We begin at once to speak of de Gaulle, or, rather, it was he who spoke of him in a long monologue which only became a dialogue at the very end.

"I have known a relatively large number of statesmen, but none – by a long chalk – his equal in stature. To understand his actions, we must never forget that he is a *man of destiny*, perhaps tragic, in any case, dramatic. Those ludicrous creatures who call him to account, make me laugh. We have not followed him in order to be paid for it. He owes nothing to anyone. The price may perhaps be the firing squad. And then what? We have embarked on a tragic adventure. We must accept the risks, stick to the rules of the game and, if necessary, lose with serenity. De Gaulle does not want to be bound by those rules on a level which is beneath him, parliaments! That is why he has transferred the battle elsewhere – or at least, his battle strength. It was not his resignation that was upsetting, but the letter in which he announced it, or, anyway, the unfortunate words: *All is well*. There was a first draft in which he told the French people quite openly the real reason for his resignation: 'I promised to give democracy back to you,' he said in it, 'and I kept my word. Now it is my duty to tell you that, in a country which has lost the place in the foremost ranks that was hers up till a few years ago, the party system of government is a dangerous anachronism.' But he was afraid that, by uniting them against him, he might be giving an appearance of life to the parties he was denouncing, so he decided on the second letter – which is defensible – or, rather, would be without that deplorable sentence."

Malraux added:

"I ventured to say to him that the man of 18th June could not resign with nothing more than a letter to President Gouin. He agreed, but nothing followed. However, I believe that he will speak out one day when the occasion presents itself. And then the French people will have to choose. The fact is that we are witnessing the end of Europe. People of my generation and even of yours will not suffer too much because of the momentum with which it is happening. The influence of Athens, you know . . . But people are insufficiently aware of the extent to which this very influence became weaker over the centuries. Michelangelo was, after all, better than Picasso. From the way things are going, it looks as though civilization were deteriorating in quality, as though the grandeur of Mankind were diminishing a little more with every passing century. One can no longer predict where or how this downward course of civilization, which took it, without much loss from Athens to Rome, from Rome to Byzantium and so on, will end up in the general mediocrity that has set in. General de Gaulle, to whom I mentioned this, seemed very much struck by it. But all that concerns human civilization. If we turn to politics – what do we see? Europe's only hope – a Western block centred around France and England – no longer exists. We are nothing more than a country with forty million inhabitants (for our colonies are no longer ours) up against colossal empires. So vassalage is inevitable – and any policy, which does not take this new state of affairs into consideration, is absurd. France absurdly continues to think of herself and make a semblance of acting as a great nation. But she is already no more than a pawn in a game that is none of her concern.

"I am afraid that, in the war which seems imminent – and which, in our case, will be accompanied by a civil war, we shall be compelled to fight against those who, in spite of everything, represent what is best in France. I mean that General de Gaulle is liable to have the whole of the left-wing supporters against him, who, despite the communist taint do represent an élite."

"Put another way it's certainly a great pity that de Gaulle should have united against him all the forces of the left. All this might not have happened if I had met him earlier. The great weakness of that great mind lies in the fact that he has never sat down to a meal with a workman."

"I'm wondering whether one shouldn't go even further and say that de Gaulle has never treated *any man*, no matter to what class he belonged, with proper respect and attention."

"They do say that he despises mankind, but I've never noticed it. It's true that he *crushes* most of them, and he's quite aware of it. He lorded it over Cabinet Meetings brilliantly – only allowing some small say to Maurice Thorez, whose contributions, very restrained and almost ecclesiastic, were the only ones to carry some small measure of weight. The tiresome lot were the socialists. If de Gaulle despised the communist ministers it was because they *lied*. It was their lies that he despised. For instance Marcel Paul, presenting a report on the nationalization of electricity, put forward a plan, of which the sole object was to place control of electricity in this country, in the event of war, in the hands of the communists. This did not escape de Gaulle, who attacked the plan indirectly, without openly showing he had not been taken in. His contempt was directed then at Marcel Paul's duplicity, not at his insignificance – at duplicity, moreover of which he did not realize the full import. That is why I don't agree with you when you say that he is even further away from mankind in general, than he is from the workman. For between him and a member of the middle-classes, there is the bridge of a common vocabulary. I know that de Gaulle uses in their original and best sense words that the middle-classes debase, but in the end a common tradition makes each of them comprehensible to the other. Whereas he cannot understand and, what's more, cannot make himself understood by a proletarian from Saint-Denis, to whom Thorez, knows very well how to talk. This is a grave flaw, but one which it may be possible to cure. For he's only too anxious to understand. But naturally, neither M. Pleven nor M. Philip are the ones to do the explaining. I tried, myself, and I don't think it was a total failure. He has – and you know to what degree – a sense of grandeur. As a result of his education and breeding, he has a precise, limited conception of this grandeur. But he is prepared to admit that it may take other forms. I believe I managed to make him accept the idea that Saint-Just had just as much as Thiers, a sense of French grandeur. But having said that, it is vital that we shouldn't support the proletariat when it pursues a wrong course. Though I'm sure that the proletarian party exists in Russia and nowhere else, I'm equally aware that the U.S.S.R. is not the place to find the *values* which give the proletariat its real meaning."

"This does not alter the fact that, in a civil war, we shall have to fight against the best elements."

"Perhaps we shall be able to win them over before fighting them. Indeed, the course of events seems likely to ensure it. For, no doubt, we shall have to face here what happened in Vienna, for instance. If war breaks out, three thousand Soviet parachutists will drop on Saint-Denis. Well, suppose they do: an occupier is always an occupier, and the French, proletarian or not, will resist."

"In that case, de Gaulle's only course would be to return to his microphone in London."

"No question about that. And no question about the Americans winning."

"You know the Trotskyist policy: support the U.S.S.R. against the capitalist powers (in the event of war). So if the U.S.A. wins, shan't we have to begin all over again?"

"Everything always has to be begun all over again."

We continued for a long time along those lines in that luxurious room, furnished in a lovely, golden baroque. Malraux was wearing an elegant grey flannel suit on which a tiny green ribbon – the cross of the Liberation – recalled his heroism, which one was liable to forget when seeing him in his present surroundings. But the tone of his voice, his expression and his whole manner belie this apparent indulgence. When he spoke (in connection with Koestler) of the condemned cell, they were not just empty words, nor were they when he censured his *Temps du Mépris* for being the work of a man who had not been in prison. "Anyhow, not yet," he added. No doubt, he has never before been so wholehearted about anything; never accepted so calmly the risks involved in a venture. Does the merit of the cause, which he has taken up, seem less important to him (as to Garine) than the fight it entails? He will accept the issue of the struggle philosophically. Condemned to death, he will not clamour of injustice.

Having made his decision, he does not join in plots and has no intention of doing so. "Since de Gaulle has kept silent, it is the duty of his followers – and particularly of his former ministers – to keep silent, too." After talking to me for a long time about his lost manuscripts:

his *T.E. Lawrence*, the second volume of his *La Lutte avec l'Ange*, and his *La Psychologie de l'Art*, destroyed by the Gestapo, he told me that it would certainly be this last work that he would embark on again. "For, after all, I've been in the midst of bloodshed since 1936, and I need a rest. I want to find out why I like Masaccio." From somewhere in the house, came the sound of Chopin's music. He explained "She plays the piano – my sister-in-law, you know, my brother's wife."

After tea (served to us by the young woman in question – charming in a pretty bright dress) Malraux sketched the broad outlines of the humanism which he thinks it may be possible to instil, as may be evidenced in one of his works in ten years' time. Mankind, without God, achieving through creation a dignity equivalent to that of a saint. But I would do better to use our fascinating conversation to enrich my study of him, which I have taken up again in the last few days and have nearly finished. However, I will record the following:

"Hasn't the invention of the atom bomb made this desperate quest for an inaccessible hope still more difficult?"

"No, for Homer's posterity is just as relative as ours will be, assuming the worst happens. The miracle is that man can survive himself, even for an hour."

"And also that, thanks to the work he has launched in the world, he can live in places beyond where he actually is, and possibly even more intensely."

He thought this over for a moment, agreed and went on to stress this new opportunity open to mankind. I said:

"However, the fact remains that between the Christian and ourselves lies that abyss of eternity, which is at his disposal but denied to us. He eternally *preserves his chance*."

"Yes, but in a sense, that is too facile a solution. Besides, the saint plays his game without this in view. That is his greatness, which is of the same character as that to which we can aspire."

Outside, it was the first spring evening and the blackbirds were whistling. I was rather tired, for we had spent an hour and a half, striding up and down the room without sitting down.

Wednesday, 20 March, 1946

Yesterday, at 6.30 I was in General de Gaulle's study, after General Billotte* had emerged – a study which I was seeing for the first time in daylight. When we had finished work, there was the ritual question, followed by a long conversation, during which I confined myself to briefly tossing back the ball, so that this rare and fascinating tête-à-tête

163

should not end too soon. What a new lack of reserve, and what evidence of confidence on the part of de Gaulle!

"Well, General, they're saying that in the Spanish affair, the snub was not long in coming – and was painful." (An allusion to the exception taken by the Anglo-Saxons to the French memoranda levelled against Franco – when, as a piece of vote-catching, we had already initiated breaking off relations with him – which puts us in a difficult situation.)

"And you're surprised? Did you expect anything else from the incompetent government? Perhaps the French people will get wise to it one day. In any case, I could not go on indefinitely lending my name to those absurd party politics. I could only try to achieve something as long as I wasn't handicapped by them. For you know how useless a minister, who represents his party, is to the government from a national point of view. He is never concerned with France's interests but only with those of his own party, to whom he is answerable."

"Couldn't you state your opinion on this subject publicly, one day, General? Because I don't think that the French people, as a whole, have grasped the real reasons for your resignation."

"They'll understand once they're in danger –"

"But that may be too late. I mean: once war's broken out."

"It certainly will break out . . ."

"Don't you think, General, that recent events have been orchestrated, even created, by the Americans, to prepare public opinion in their country and that it was Truman who told Churchill to make that alarmist speech."

"Oh, Churchill isn't a man to obey orders. However, I agree that Truman no doubt gave his consent, leaving himself free to repudiate it later. That war must come is certain. And France, from the very first, will be a dead loss to the Anglo-Saxons. If the Americans had so wished, if they had agreed to assist in the restoration of a morally and materially strong France (for they go together) I could have held the bridgehead. But they weren't willing to do anything. They obstructed me on the Rhine, in Indochina, everywhere; they took no steps whatever to build up the country's vital supplies. I could not stand by and let the French swallow these insults, indefinitely. The truth is that the Americans have their own individual conception of the war: they concentrate on securing bases for future operations."

"In Morocco . . ."

"Yes, accessorily . . but mainly in the Far East."

"So, strictly from a strategic point of view, France . . ."

"Since they can't be everywhere, they've no doubt decided to sacrifice France. In any case, I couldn't hope to hold the bridgehead on my own. The only hope would have been a solid *bloc* of Western powers . . ." (I noticed that he named all our neighbours except England) "But that, too, has turned out to be impossible. So what could I do? A *coup d'état*? But one can't carry out a *coup d'état* without having public opinion on one's side. No one would have backed me up. Had there been no Bonaparte, Hoche would have brought about the 18 Brumaire – what, he was dead? Then Jourdan, anyone . . . In the same way, Louis Napoléon was sent for, with the almost unanimous assent of the nation. But I should have been on my own. So what else was there to do, but resign? Play M. Philip's little games? Most certainly not!"

"I don't think the country will stand for occupation by the Russians."

"No, that's certain. But the communist fifth column will govern with the support of the Soviet Army, as the other one did. And the communist ministers will be just as effectual as Pétain's. Not a pleasant prospect."

"It's easy enough to understand the discouragement and weariness of our wretched people."

"They're tired, yes, and discouraged, but not deeply affected. Patriotism does exist. Look at the M.R.P. And the morale of the troops is good. It's only the leaders . . ."

"You really think they . . ."

"Of course! They're third-class Briands, Sangnier-type internationalists, with a perpetual squint to the left like Bidault. (When did you ever see him attacked by the communists?) and they've completely forgotten what France stands for."

There, I didn't agree with him (any more than I did about the *coup d'état* – but no doubt he only brought that in as a retort to the right-wing half-wits, who were expecting him to carry it out). There I detected certain limitations in the great mind. I merely said:

"But what a tragic destiny for France. Whichever way the struggle goes. Will the smallest particle of her independence and greatness survive? I know, of course, that our culture will remain . . ."

"Not even that: history proves that there has been no great civilization that was not supported by immense material resources. However, we shall see, we shall see . . . One thing's certain: if things get much worse I shall emerge from my retirement."

What elation I felt at being in such close contact with a great man! What pride in being one of his chosen men! How willingly I accept all the risks! How easy to decide not to let what disappoints me in

165

him keep me on the sidelines! Too easy a solution. But a terrible sadness fell on me, on my way home, as I passed the Arc de Triomphe, looming up gigantically out of the golden mist of this spring evening – and as I passed the Invalides. France, poor France, threatened with annihilation in a struggle which is no longer hers. I ponder, too, on de Gaulle's serenity. Malraux once told me that when anyone tries to prove to him that some point or other of his policy was a mistake, he replies:

"They said that to me in 1940, in 1941, and in 1942 . . . And certainly, Vichy seemed to hold all the cards. But I myself, decided on a different policy and I've stuck to it."

Monday, 25 March, 1946

"Well, General what they're saying is that the elections are drawing near and they haven't received any kind of guidance."

"They must vote *against* the Constitution naturally! Against this scheming by the parties, this 'business deal' which is what the idiotic Constitution they have cooked up represents to them. It would be an appreciable step forward if the country were to show that it wants nothing to do with it. People say to me: 'But what a catastrophe, if that happens, to have a Chamber elected for seven months!' But what's it matter? The important thing is that the country should realize that party government is impossible. The rest is trivial."

"But as the parties will tell their members to vote for the Constitution . . ."

"Not all of them. The M.R.P. won't be so much in favour of the Constitution; far from it. The radicals and the right will vote against it. And it wouldn't be at all a bad thing if the communist and socialist parties were repudiated by the country. The M.R.P.'s stupidity made them miss a wonderful opportunity. If their ministers had resigned from the Government at the same time as I did, the M.R.P.'s success at the elections would have been *shattering!*"

"I get the impression, General, that most French people think that it was you who dissuaded them."

"That's completely wrong! Naturally, they want people to believe it, but nothing could be further from the truth! And, fundamentally, everyone knows it."

"The difficulty will lie in getting those Frenchmen who take part in politics – a small minority but, in this field, it speaks for everyone – to recognize that the party system, to which they have been accustomed for so long, is in need of revision."

"That's the abscess which will have to be lanced, sooner or later."

I was less and less in agreement and I had less and less confidence in General de Gaulle's political judgement. "Those are the Frenchmen we'll have to beat." He did not quite say that, but his sentence about the *abscess*, the actual words of which I cannot recall, had precisely that meaning.

When I arrived, I found him engaged in writing his *Mémoires*. He told me so, himself, pointing, not without pride, to the sheets of manuscript strewn about his desk.

Tuesday, 2 April, 1946
Back from Marly.

7.30 p.m. The General started right away to talk about my letter of 26th March, which I had dismissed from my mind after Guy had told me that it had met with no reaction. He told me that, since 1940, journalists – French ones as much as Anglo-Saxon – had systematically misrepresented what he had said and saddled him with statements which he had never made. It had no importance, he declared: the only thing to do was to let them go ahead – and wait.

We talked for a long time this evening – or rather, he talked to me for a long time: about twenty minutes before sitting down to work and as much afterwards. I found him looking rested, he has a good colour, is plump-cheeked and more relaxed than I had ever seen him – and very optimistic beneath his superficial pessimism. By this, I mean that he had great hopes for the future (of France) though he remained despondent about the present. He went to a cinema in the Champs-Elysées yesterday with a small party, and told me how sad he had felt when they showed the newsreel: Gouin in Strasburg, a nonentity wrapped in silence (and it is he who represents France!) – Blum in America where he had gone to solicit loans which he would not obtain, and France made ridiculous and degraded by the personality of this man of goodwill, lacking willpower and 'national guts'. He again expressed his disgust with the M.R.P. ministers, their cowardice and their desertion, and spoke contemptuously of the Resistance exploits of X and Z (though he acknowledged that they had run risks: but these were more at the hands of Vichy than of the Germans – and Monsieur Z admits quite calmly, without causing any surprise to himself or anyone else: "Well, yes, I did write to the Gestapo." "Of course he wrote to the Gestapo, the poor, dear man, it's only natural!")

The sheets of his *Mémoires* were scattered about the desk in front of him – the *Mémoires* that tell of his great adventure, France's great adventure – and as he brought his fist down on them, he said:

"The French are a discouraging lot; they really are! After the disaster that France suffered, I led the Gauls back to the Rhine and re-established them. Do you suppose a single Frenchman marvels at it or rejoices? Far from it. All they see – and immediately raise cries of indignation – are an A.F.A.T.* in uniform or a colonel too many. I give them back Hanoi – and that was no easy matter. But all they take any notice of is that one has kicked a socialist Pressman's bottom. I hold on to Syria for them, where France has shone for a thousand years. But that's of no interest to anyone. And, scarcely is my back turned, before the French government gives up the Rhine, Indochina and Syria. Not a single newspaper has mentioned that, not one; *Le Figaro* no more than the others."

The barb went home. It was only some minutes later that I responded – and badly, pleading the editorial staff's own lack of information.

"What? *Le Figaro* knows what went on on the Rhine, doesn't it? What went on in Indochina and Syria? So what do they do? They choose the moment when the English are more than ever undermining our attempts to rehabilitate ourselves – by sabotaging Blum's mission, by preventing the Ruhr coal being handed over to us and by taking over Transjordania – to present them as desirable allies. I certainly don't want to see them treated as enemies. And I know what an alliance with England means; I even made one all by myself at one time. But one doesn't base one's foreign policy on sentiment. In that sphere, one only unites *against* another Power – and provisionally – and without any of the allies ever abandoning between them an everlasting struggle.

Timidly, I interposed: "France feels so alone," to which he replied in ringing tones:

"But one is always alone. The U.S.S.R. is alone, the U.S.A. is alone . . ."

I had no time to observe that their economic resources made their solitude less tragic, before he added:

"England doesn't want France to become powerful again on any terms."

And went on to deliver a number of variations on this theme. Then I ventured to say a few words and the following exchange took place:

"But, General, surely it would be to their own interest to help us?"

"Of course! If there's a war, they'll be only too glad to have the French on their side, getting killed like themselves, with themselves once again. But this time, their hopes are liable to be disappointed. The

French don't want the army I gave back to them any more. So there we are . . ."

A hint of sadness clouded his expression and he repeated "There we are" two or three times in a discouraged, absentminded tone of voice, then went on:

"The French will no doubt realize in the end. Realize that it's impossible to have a government controlled by the parties."

"Yet France was governed in that way, General, and not so badly, at the end of the last century and at the beginning of this one."

"Wait a moment! The circumstances were not the same. First of all, France was living then on a large capital. She still had considerable resources in the way of prestige, power and money. What's more, the Jules Ferrys, the Clemenceaus and the Poincarés were not party men."

"They had all been party members."

"But they had separated from them. It was France, whom they were representing, not this or that party: you should have seen with what contempt Clemenceau treated the radical party. Today the parties 'govern' – that's to say they just let things slide. Responsibility is watered down; France is forgotten. It is only the communists who reap the benefit of the others' cowardice and weakness."

"But if party government is done away with, what's left?"

"Look at the U.S.A. An assembly should be legislative and nothing else. In such an assembly, it is quite right that the various political schools of thought should be represented. But the Government should enjoy the complete confidence of the country *over a given term*. When that term is up, if the Government has failed to prove satisfactory it is replaced."

As my eyes strayed through the open window, to the lawn sprinkled with multicoloured primulas, General de Gaulle pointed out to me that the political face of France had not changed since Vercingetorix; which was clearly his way of saying: for many centuries.

"One fifth takes no interest in public affairs and never votes – a fifth of the French people has always been like that; another fifth consists of revolutionaries who, today, are called communists – there have always been French revolutionaries; a third fifth is made up of all the envious, the cuckolds and the failures – they are today's socialists and yesterday's radicals, and then, of course, there are the propertied classes – "

He did not complete his enumeration and ended with:

"But the proportion, taken by and large, never alters."

"All the same, I said, there's no denying that, decade by decade, we're seeing the country slide towards the left."

"Much more, the parties slide towards the right, allowing naturally, for the modifications brought about by changes in the economic field."

I switched the conversation to the prestige which communism is now enjoying among the intellectuals. I was not referring to the petty intriguers and the other self-seekers, but to men of integrity: "French intellectuals have always betrayed France," General de Gaulle answered, and quoted to me two extraordinary texts of Voltaire, addressed to Frederic II after Rosbach, in which the French bottom ('cul') is made to rhyme with defeated (vaincu) and the incompetence of the same French in battle contrasted with their skill in pillaging. He quoted all this impeccably, enunciating every word, and delivering it like a slap in the face.

"If you think back, you'll find that the intellectuals have always sided against France."

I mentioned the Maurras of old, during the period when *L'Action Française* gathered all the intellectuals round it, even those belonging to opposing parties, and to my great surprise, de Gaulle said:

"But Maurras was against France, too. Against the France of his time."

This was exactly my own opinion, and I was delighted to find him so unexpectedly sharing it. I could not help thinking that, in his violent opposition to the parties, he, himself, was not far off siding against the France of his time. But I merely said:

"That's where the whole problem lies. France's worst enemies often believed they were serving her. They loved a France of their own conception: and it was to this entity alone that they accorded the name of France, experiencing no sense of betrayal in fighting against the other, the true one."

"What surprises me about the attraction that communism has for the intellectuals," de Gaulle broke in, "is that anarchists can come to terms with a party advocating totalitarian dictatorship."

"I imagine that they become anarchists through their failure to achieve the order at which they are aiming. But that they do earnestly want such a system."

"There's obviously an element of despair in that sort of alliance. The intellectual, Maurras, was not a mere nobody, nor was Suarez, or Brasillach, or Béraud. (Moreover, Béraud had no contact with the Germans. But he was against me.)"

I did not like him placing writers of such different quality on the same level, but I was pleased when he repeated:

"That Brasillach was not a mere nobody."

He finished up more hopefully:

"I'm confident the parties will furnish their own proof of their helplessness. Things can't go on like that much longer. The moment will come when events take charge, when it'll become impossible to govern without a feeling that one's boat is being carried along on a strong wave. And that wave is what they lack. It isn't there. A financial crisis, an international crisis: the event is unpredictable, but it will certainly come. Where were the parties in June 1940?"

He was also more reassuring about the chance of peace, talking of Soviet bluff and of the Russians' reluctance to embark on a war, which they would inevitably lose, etc.

"Without the West, they were letting themselves get beaten by a country of seventy million inhabitants – which was scarcely to their credit."

While we were working, he told me that he had decided that I should never pass on requests from his correspondents to the appropriate ministers:

"If they follow them up, I shall be indebted to them – or, anyway, they'll think I am, which I don't want: and if they ignore them, it'll be equally disagreeable."

Wednesday, 3 April, 1946

"In the present circumstances, one must view things as a whole and forget about the details." These words of the General reminded me of what my father said to me one day on this precise subject: namely, that great politicians operate in pursuit of a few very simple general ideas, and while I took pleasure in the coincidence – which resembled the pleasure I take as a critic when I come across a particularly happy quotation – I absentmindedly contemplated the primulas on the fresh lawn and stopped listening to de Gaulle.

Yesterday I finished my *Malraux*, which gave me more of a headache than any of my other essays. All it needs now is a little polishing up here and there. And now I have a sudden sense of freedom, a wonderful feeling of leisure.

Saturday, 6 April, 1946

My mother and brother came with me to Marly, where I went in *Le Figaro* car to take some azaleas to the General and Mme. de Gaulle who are celebrating their silver wedding anniversary tomorrow. While Maurice, the driver, carried the flower-pot into the lodge, from which I had discreetly stopped the car some distance away, we glanced, with some emotion at the little house, with smoke coming out of one of its chimneys. In my case, the fact of coming there outside my usual working hours and for private reasons, made me view Marly with a kind of detachment: I could already see the modest lodge in the perspective of History, and was assailed by recollections of the memorable times I had spent there, as though they were all in the past; as though I were not coming back there on Monday and again later to work with Charles de Gaulle.

Monday, 8 April, 1946

While reading a letter to an ex-Commissioner of the Republic, in which I had written in his name: ". . . during the period when I was President of the Government," the General struck out the sentence and said:

"Be careful to avoid saying anything which might give the impression that there is no difference between the two governments, between myself and Gouin. The truth is that something immense had been and has ceased to exist, and can never be replaced, and that now there's what you very well know, what bears no comparison to what preceded it."

These superb words were uttered with the grandiose serenity of God the Father contemplating his work on the seventh day.

The General thanked me for my flowers, congratulated me on my article on Koestler in *La Nef,* spoke again about Georges Bidault, made another allusion to the time when the French people would drop their present political system like a hot brick and expressed his relative satisfaction at Thursday's elections to the Academy (Paul Claudel – Jules Romains*). I was tired, far away, almost absent in spirit and our conversation did not last long.

"Everything seems to be continuing as it is at present because nothing has happened. But let an emergency arise and you'll see whether the French people do not display their lack of confidence in the parties in a decisive fashion!"

Outside it was a spring evening in the valley. The evening sun gilded the young, transparent greenery, the shapes and colours of which were superimposed without obliterating each other. The goat was grazing nearby, and Mme. de Gaulle told me that the General brings it grass every day towards dusk.

On my way home, the Invalides and Montmartre emerged above the forest trees in the warm, luminous mist of a Mediterranean night.

Tuesday, 9 April, 1946

Seated on Paul Claudel's left at a luncheon arranged by Pierre Brisson at the Ritz, I felt compelled to defend the Stendhal of the *Rouge et Noir* and *La Chartreuse de Parme* and the Flaubert of *L'Education Sentimentale* whom he arrogantly declared to be half-witted and worthless. He was only softened by the plight of Japan, when James de Coquet, who has just returned from there, described the appalling destruction. He was less deaf than I had been led to expect, with an old peasant's face, which even the contortions and rictuses of his powerful jaws did not make ill-natured. When he launched into a criticism of introspection – with reference to Stendhal – maintaining that man is what he does, not what he thinks, I could not help saying: "That's what Sartre says, too," an interruption that sent the whole table (especially my father and Mondor) into fits of laughter and made him visibly furious.

"One can judge the importance of the Academy, which is so much disparaged, from the delight of those elected to it," my father said to me, later.

Mondor's elation, in fact, was only surpassed by that of Claudel. Yet, Claudel . . .

Monday, 15 April, 1946

Just as I was entering the lodge, I collided with the General, who was seeing Diethelm to the door. He was even more courteous and attentive than usual, taking his time – or, rather, minc – which I was only too happy to give (one feels that he is finding the days long and is in no hurry) – but he did not break much new ground in his appreciation of the situation. He patiently stresses a number of simple points, all very much alike: the impossibility of governing under control by the parties and the long-standing division of France into five distinct categories. If I racked my brains, I could recall one or two other themes.

Referring to the predictable breakaway from tripartite government by the M.R.P. (on the Constitutional question) I ventured to say that he had misjudged that party.

"It's time that it pulled itself together," he said to me, "high time. But don't get the wrong idea: it's the militants who have imposed this step on the leaders; who have remained as they always were: pledged to every kind of concession."

I said that this break would fortunately clarify the situation on the eve of the elections.

"Yes, but by splitting France in two," de Gaulle retorted with a note of genuine regret in his voice.

"Since it was bound to happen, anyway . . ."

He made a sweeping gesture, signifying: "You don't have to tell me that!" Then, after expressing his satisfaction with the M.R.P. developments, he said:

"I only hope that all this takes place with the least possible disruption and damage to France."

During the rest of our conversation, it emerged that he considers the socialist-communist government cannot survive because, in the present circumstances, it is vital really to govern, not to drift with the current. Various crises will occur in the near future (he was most insistent about this), which will sweep away all the half-heartedness and weakness. He foresees, principally, a monetary disaster rapidly approaching.

Sunday, 28 April, 1946

Having reached Marly yesterday a little earlier than usual, I had tea with the General, his daughter, Boissieu and Claude Guy. The conversation, which began by touching in some detail on rainy and fine weather, later moved on to politics, but without anyone displaying much enthusiasm. So the General felt compelled to bring the few important points up again during the private conversation which followed our working session.

I stayed with him for a long time after we had got through our business. We both stood in front of the fire, which scarcely seemed necessary at this time of year, and discussed the political matters, to which I give little thought when I am away from Marly, but which completely engross this man, whose presence alone is enough to remind me of the gravity of the problems, which I am inclined to regard as minor in the course of daily life.

De Gaulle seemed to me radiantly optimistic about home affairs. He predicted a majority of 'no's in the referendum next Sunday, but he appeared to find the possible victory of those in favour (which I consider probable) scarcely less welcome, since the issue will then be clearly defined and a strong, coherent opposition already in existance.

"I've put them properly in the soup with the referendum," he told me with the delighted air of a man, who sees his cunning, carefully constructed plan working out just as he expected.

"The Consultative Assembly, instinctively following the right course, rejected the scheme. But as it was never able to reach an agreement on any other practical scheme, I was free to go ahead with mine. Through the referendum, I have finally managed to get the French to concentrate on the communist problem. Before it, I had failed. But now, at last, the question will be put to them in its proper form. Just as the preceding referendum boiled down to voting for or against me, so Sunday's will lead to a decision for or against communism. And whichever way the vote goes, it will have a vital effect on our future. So you can see how right I was to take myself off: if I had remained in office, they would, first of all, have produced a constitution even worse than this one just *to do me down*; and then, again, some of the parties – the radicals, for instance, who now will vote 'no', would then have voted 'yes' for the same reason. I can't understand why the communists have put themselves so much in the forefront and made a personal issue of this constitution. It seems to me that they've chosen the wrong tactics."

I, myself, think that they, too, have understood the real issue and are prepared to face it: a 'yes' or 'no' for communism.

Answering a question I put to him on the possibility of a majority of 'no's and, nevertheless, a marxist majority in the next Assembly, the General said:

"It's a possible outcome. Are you suggesting that the Chamber will then restore such an anti-democratic constitution? If it does, the marxists will have to shoulder the responsibility for the whole mess before a country which is waking up and will accuse them of making any practical way out of it impossible."

His optimism is so great, from whichever angle he looks at things, that he occasionally has to pull himself up and moderate his expression of it. And I have an acute impression that this man, who is no longer a topic of conversation, whom many people (among the masses) have almost forgotten, and many people (party members) pretend to have forgotten, is still controlling France's destiny from his solitary retreat. Having set his plans in motion before he left, he is waiting for the force of circumstances to produce the desired result. Not that he is unaware of how often political achievement eludes man's grasp, however exceptional his qualities; how complex and unaccountable are the elements that separate him from it. But, today, the game has not yet started, everything is possible, his success above all. No, he never envisages failure, this man who, in looking forward to his victory, regards it primarily as a victory for France, a democratic France, but one armed for the perilous life which nations face in the world of today.

For his pessimism about the international outlook is profound. When I asked him if things were going well at the conference now being held in Paris (Byrnes-Bevin-Molotov-Bidault)*, he said, with a bitterly ironic smile:

"How do you expect them to get anywhere when the war has already begun? There won't be any peace conference. How could there be *when the war has already begun?* It began in Berlin with the problem of the central German government, in Rome with the Trieste problem, in Paris with our referendum. And it can only end up, at one time or another, by resort to arms. Walter Lippmann, the American journalist, whom I received here the other day, told me, naïvely: 'I read Stalin's speech and I'm really beginning to think that the U.S.S.R. is expansionist.'

"How could she be otherwise when no one *stands up* to her. You people in America," I said to him, "you're restricted by oceans and you've practically conquered all that was open to you to conquer, South America included. This does not prevent you having economic and political interests elsewhere, naturally, but that's another matter. Whereas the man who, at the moment is the most powerful in Europe is driven on by the desire to acquire the whole of Europe. Charlemagne, Napoleon, Hitler and now Stalin – it's a law of nature. Eastern Europe is not restricted by oceans. So Russia will continue to advance until it comes up against a categorical *no*. Hitler's story is starting all over again. And there is nothing to be done. History is moved by forces, which, for the most part, are beyond the control of politicians, however great they may be."

De Gaulle well knows how his own plans may be upset or destroyed.

"But now," he went on, "where are the great men? The whole world is governed by little father Gouins, the U.S.S.R. excepted."

I mentioned the crushing superiority that the U.S.A. still enjoyed, thanks to their possession of the secret of the atomic bomb, and evoked the shade of Roosevelt. De Gaulle said:

"Yes, with Roosevelt, everything would have been different. He was capable of shouldering such a crushing responsibility."

And I sensed that he felt that he, too, belonged to that breed. He repeated:

"But what can you expect from the little father Gouins? Democracies never attack; they never react to imminent mortal danger."

He paused, enormously tall in his civilian suit. Then, looking me straight in the eye, he went on:

"If, in my small way, I'm to play a part in this great drama, I must be left unfettered. Completely free. Uncompromised. That's why I had to go, had to leave the mediocre scheming."

"But don't you think, General, as I do, that, in that case, your resignation would have been even more effective if it had come a little earlier; after the elections, for instance?"

"I agree," he answered slowly, stressing two words, "I agree, and that was what I intended to do. Unfortunately, I allowed myself to get entangled."

"From the point of view of sentiment, it had fatal consequences. I'm speaking of the French people's affection for you. And then, the week chosen in advance for your resignation turned out to be particularly unlucky. It was a week of stricter rationing and new discomforts."

"That's so, but hasn't it all been more or less forgotten by now? Those things have to be judged with detachment (detachment before the event) and as a whole. And the French wouldn't have understood, either, if I'd left them just as they had begun to trust me."

There was an inconsistency in this, which was not resolved, as we parted at that moment.

General de Gaulle, as the result of an anonymous letter, blaming him for not having re-established the Constitution of 1875, gave me his reasons:

1) The Chamber would have deliberately ignored the Senate.

2) It would have necessitated the acceptance *de jure* of the eighty parliamentarians who had voted against Pétain.

3) It would have necessitated the restoration of Albert Lebrun – since, as he, himself, told the General: "I never resigned, I'm not making an issue of it, but I never resigned."

4) A large number of other insurmountable difficulties.

Saturday, 4 May, 1946

The eve of the referendum. France is going to say 'yes' or 'no' to the Constitution, and probably 'yes' by a small majority. But General de Gaulle, who welcomed me with a bantering: "Well, things are hotting up, eh?" is still by no means convinced of that and even hopes that the 'no's may carry the day:

"Anyway, the majority will be so small in the event of a 'yes' that the Constitution won't be viable."

And he repeated (having no doubt forgotten that he had said it to me before):

"At last, France has taken sides, has been compelled to take sides on the communist question. When I returned to France, they were everywhere, mixed up in everything and I should have been booed if I had even attempted to state the problem straightforwardly."

In spells of ten, fifteen or twenty days, de Gaulle returns to and elaborates the same very simple themes, no doubt in the same words, for each of his visitors. The notes which the regular visitors to Marly make of their conversations with the General must be very similar.

In reference to an anonymous letter, full of bitter reproaches, which he had received, he said:

"Vichyites cannot forgive me for refusing to play their game. I'm certainly not a fellow traveller with the communists and the old scores between us will have to be paid off sooner or later – I shall see to that. But as to being a supporter of the Vichyites – they shouldn't count on that."

When I asked him whether he would be voting tomorrow, he replied that, his polling station being the sixteenth precinct Town Hall, he was too much afraid of the crowds he would run into there to go. I tried to persuade him to vote very early or very late and he did not give me a definite no, but I felt that he did not want, at any price, to run the risk of becoming the centre of some kind of demonstration.

"I am a shy man," he told me, in a manner which, at first, made me think he was serious, to my great surprise. But the glint of irony in his eye reassured me and, even more so, the news he imparted to me immediately afterwards, without any relation to what had gone on before, his face illuminated with the malicious pleasure of a schoolboy about to play a practical joke on a master.

"Old father Gouin has written to me, inviting me to be present at the Victory celebration. Naturally, I didn't accept. You can see at once the position it would have put him in and how embarrassing it would have been for him . . . and for me. No, I don't want to subject him to such an ordeal. No, on that day, I shall just go – keeping, moreover, a promise I made to myself in London – I shall just go . . . to Clemenceau's grave."

He stopped and watched me, waiting delightedly for the effect this would have on me. And the effect was considerable.

"What a splendid idea, General! It has a touch of genius."

I repeated it, while he nodded in agreement, without saying anything, but still wearing the same expression of cheerful irony and satisfaction.

"And would you speak?"

"I may say a few words, yes, but you mustn't tell anybody."

"It really is a wonderful idea."

"It is, isn't it? I'll go with Clemenceau's son. It'll be just the right thing to do."

I do not think I have seen a man so pleased with himself, nor such striking evidence of bliss enjoyed so deliberately and minutely beforehand. What a character he is!

On the way back, Bonneval told me that the day before, the General had been greatly struck by the similarity of a large number of letters, which revealed the confusion in which many honest Frenchmen found themselves and begged him to let the country know what his attitude was towards the Constitution. ("It was a fat lot of use explaining it to them at great length at Brest," he had said to me the other day.) "He thought about it for a long time, frowning and looking very worried," Bonneval went on. "Then he asked me: 'In your opinion, seriously, do you think I ought to speak out?' Really, he seemed very shaken."

Sunday, or rather Monday, 6 May

2.00 a.m. My parents have just come back from *Le Figaro* office. They tell me that the 'no's have certainly won. At midnight, in front of the ex-*Paris Soir* and *L'Aube* offices, I had got the impression that the 'yes's had just brought it off. So de Gaulle was right after all.

Wednesday, 8 May, 1946

A Passy-D.G.E.R. scandal was launched during the night of the referendum: perhaps at the moment when the victory of the 'yes's seemed certain? It was a direct blow at de Gaulle, but if the battle has started, he will find a way to win it. Claude Guy called in this morning and told me that the General had decided to return to the fray.

His proposed visit to Clemenceau's grave has become known. But he does not intend to make his *big speech* on that occasion. Actually, he sent Claude Guy to ask me to look through the recent invitations and see if there was one which might be suitable for his return to politics.

10 May, 1946
Marly.

We talked about a trip to the Vendée and another one to Bayeux (in June). The General, wiser than I expected, has decided not to do anything before the elections. His speech on Sunday will be the only one, and as unpolitical as possible.

"No party. Just France. I shall never let them hear anything but the voice of France – and at the exact moment when the voice of France needs to be heard . . ."

Guy, who is organizing the trip to the Vendée, telephoned while I was there. I could hear Gaston de Bonneval outside in the passage. Then he came in to submit a programme: reception at the Town Hall and dinner with an important member of the local Resistance. This was turned down at first but finally accepted as it stood. The General, whom I informed that Albert Ollivier, from *Combat* would be in the party (I had met him the day before at the Henri Mullers')* insisted on the journalists accompanying him being properly looked after and on a reception being arranged for them, too. He mentioned to me again the trick that he intends to play on Gouin:

"I must say, it was a lousy letter of his," he remarked. Then, gloating modestly (his own proud brand of modesty) he added:

"You saw the referendum, eh? I told you so."

And he again brought up the 'soup', saying that they would never get rid of it: "Because I've reintroduced the referendum into the political field."

Saturday

Travelled in the car provided by the Agence France-Presse, for which by brother is reporting the trip. La Feté-Bernard (lunch). Angers, Cholet, spent the night at Essarts.

Sunday

The 'Croix de Feu' side of the ceremony embarrassed me and the enthusiasm of the crowd with its shouts of 'Back to power!' did not arouse any enthusiasm in me. The 'evil geniuses' turned up again, self-important, loud, tiresome and clumsy. The top French and Anglo-Saxon journalists were there and treated abominably. De Gaulle was very pale when he reached the 'Tiger's' grave, and visibly moved. It was a wonderful moment.

Jean is first-rate at his job, despite having to contend with the apathy of his colleague and the aggressive ill-will of X who snatched out of his hand the copy of the speech which the General had just given him. He recovered it in the end and telephoned to Paris in record time from the Château de l'Aubraie, with some help from me, as we caught a glimpse of de Gaulle through the open door and, out in the courtyard, Elisabeth de Miribel was giving the official account of the day to the English and American journalists.

Monday, 20 May, 1946,
Paris

At Marly, the day before yesterday, General de Gaulle was particularly pleasant to me – I would almost say affectionate. I had not seen him since that Sunday in the Vendée, where, as in former days, he was a distant figure amid the pomp of an official ceremony, kept apart from me by the guests of honour, the enthusiasm of the crowd, the glamour of his legend and the jealous care of his two watchdogs. But on Saturday, he was again the private figure, wearing an almost rustic civilian suit, close by and accessible. He had just had his tea and had a cup brought for me; then poured out, himself – and I slowly and absentmindedly took the sugar he was offering me, as though he were a young well-brought-up daughter of the house.

Before settling down to work, he spoke to me for a long time about communism – with an almost lyrical zest, a forcefulness that was meant to be, and was, persuasive and a dynamic quality that I had never seen in him before. And I was surprised once again that he made such an effort for me.

"Listen to me carefully: the communists have missed their chance and they won't recover from it. You can see that they're already on the defensive, and being dropped – or just about to be – by a lot of little scheming skunks! They had two chances, roughly speaking, and bungled them both. The first was at the time of the Liberation when their presence in all the branches of the Resistance and in all the vital posts would have made it easy for them to have seized power. But France crystallized round me instead. The second – and here again I intervened in time – was in the parliamentary field, where they could have assumed power by legal means. And they certainly would have done so, if I had re-established the Constitution of 1875 (for, in campaigning against it, that is to say, against me, they would have gained a crushing majority throughout the country) – or if I had set up a Constituent Assembly for an unlimited term and without its actions having to be sanctioned by a referendum. But to achieve my plan, I had to resign when I did. Had I done otherwise, a mass of little cowards would have voted for the Constitution in order to vote against personal power, represented by me. Whereas, if I were no longer there, the dictatorship to be feared was no longer mine, since I had chosen that moment to disappear from the scene, but that of the communists! Now, believe me, Mauriac, they've left it too late."

(It was one of the few times when he called me by my surname and I was far more touched than I had been on the two or three occasions when he had familiarly called me Claude at his villa in Neuilly, or at the French Embassy in Brussels.)

"Unless there's a Russo-Allies war," I answered.

"Of course, if that broke out, I shouldn't be able to prevent the Russians from occupying Paris . . . But whichever Thorez plays Pétain's part then will be, willingly or unwillingly, like Pétain, a tool of the enemy. And as victory, in the end, will fall to the West, France will be saved.

The millions of dead who would lie between France and her salvation (if things were to happen in that way) obviously counted for nothing in the eyes of that man, who always views everything in its relation to History. The blood that has not yet been shed has already dried up for him, the scars of the wounds to come are already healed.

"But, you see, for all this to become possible, France had to remain firm on the question of her independence, whenever it arose. A country that makes the smallest concession on this point is lost. That is why, much as it has cost us and distressing as it was to do, I have always answered in kind the slaps in the face that Roosevelt or Churchill gave me."

He pointed to the thick manuscript of his *Mémoires,* on the desk in front of him, with the satisfaction of an author pleased with what he has written.

"I shan't go further than 1941. When will I publish it? I've got to finish it first. And it's got to be *very good.* I mean: as good as possible."

Mme. de Gaulle's thimble was lying on a nearby table. She came in for a moment to borrow the evening papers.

Saturday, 25 May, 1946
Last day at Marly.

"No, I shan't go on the 18th of June at their invitation," de Gaulle said to me. Lying open on his desk was a letter from President Gouin, which the General described as stammering and lyrical – and in direct contrast to the dry invitation to Victory day.

"I said so this morning to Zerbini" (head of Gouin's departmental staff) "when he came to see me. It would create an awkward situation for the Government. And, besides, I don't want at any cost to appear beside him."

"Still, it would be *your celebration,* General."

"Exactly."

A pause. Then:

"No, on the 18th of June, I may perhaps go to the tomb of the Unknown Soldier in the evening – but alone. And those Parisians who want to come will come."

I did not approve. I mean that my first mental reaction was one of disapproval. But I have not had sufficient time to think about it properly, to come to any definite conclusion. So I kept silent. De Gaulle said:

"You see, we've got to achieve a 2nd December without the same means as 2nd December. But the result must be the same. You know what I mean and the analogy I have in mind. I spoke in the Vendée. And I shall speak whenever it is important for France to raise her voice. On 16th June, for instance, the anniversary of my landing again in this country. The parties are disintegrating more and more, and what still remains for ever and ever? The same unshakeable rock, the same solitary, secure rock."

He was referring to himself. I have ceased to be astonished by the extraordinary faculty this man has for identifying himself with France and speaking in her name, without any kind of vaingloriousness entering into it – and making it impossible for one to harbour the slightest doubt, the smallest twinge of irony or scepticism.

Claude Guy told me a little later that the General had said to him, the other day: "You know, there was never a time in my life when I was not completely convinced that one day I should become the head of France." And he had appealed to his wife to bear him out. "Only, things did not turn out as I had expected. I always believed I should first be War Minister and that everything would start from there . . ." When Guy had pointed out that, in actual fact, Reynaud had offered him a very similar post, he had said: "Yes, but it wasn't the same thing. I hadn't foreseen it that way."

De Gaulle went on, with that radiant self-assurance and serenity of his, to give me his reasons for being optimistic about France's chances of emerging victorious from her eternal difficulties – that is to say, of emerging victorious, himself.

All I said was:

"And what about men, General? You'll need men – a team of really competent ministers."

He was sitting down, with a waxen face, thick-set, almost motionless, his ponderous chin buried in wrinkles, in a relaxed, easy attitude that was wholly unlike him; looking older, too, than I had ever seen him before.

"It's always the same thing: having to do everything with nothing."

And on this, he brought the subject to a close.

"So this is the last time I shall be seeing you here at Marly, General."

"It's also the last time I shall be here, myself."

"It's sad to think that I shan't see you at Marly again."

"You never know . . . You may see me back here again."

Outside, in the small orchard in front of the lodge, I picked a daisy and put it in my button-hole, happily breathing in the summer country air and casting a last backward look at the peaceful valley and the

183

small house, which de Gaulle will leave tomorrow evening for his property in the Haute-Marne. In the car taking us back to Paris, Guy told me that the General was certain that, sooner or later, the parties would ask him to decide between them, and that he would refuse to form a government, once, twice, as many times as necessary, until he secured an "unconditional surrender".

5 June, 1946

Owing to a series of mishaps, Claude Guy and I only reached Colombey last Saturday about 8.00 in the evening, which compelled the de Gaulles to give me dinner and put me up for the night. At the outset, the General was in a bad humour and none too gracious about showing us over the property. The rain had only just stopped after coming down all day. We followed him in Indian file along narrow, sodden paths, across a garden smothered in damp foliage. De Gaulle asked a number of questions and uttered a few curt sentences in a manner that was somehow both absentminded and attentive, in the clouds yet curiously present. And quite out of keeping with the confined, uncultivated garden.

He foretold, with a confidence that surprised me by its precision, the outcome of next day's elections: the communists would lose seven seats; the M.R.P. thirty-three; the socialists the same; and so on. I do not remember the exact figures - only that he announced the gains and losses he expected almost down to a single unit. And while I am not surprised to have seen his forecasts belied by the facts, I find it disturbing that he could formulate them, on the very eve of their being put to the test, with such an appearance of quiet certainty.

When we got to the top of the slopes, he invited us, but not insistently, to admire the view over the austere woods and barren, lonely country-side. A heavy farm-wagon was moving along the road below and the old man nonchantly astride the lead-horse looked up at the General without acknowledging him. On the way back, he spoke to Guy about the rally at Bayeux on 16 June: "I shall express my views on the constitutional question in detail . . ."

Shortly before, in reply to Guy's announcement that the Government intended to relight the flame on the evening of 18 June, he had declared offhandedly but nastily, "Then, I shan't go . . ."

And the bleak house came into view again, with its tiled roof, too-new walls and the ground ravaged with quarry-stones and clay all round it. (Our tour of the rooms, almost all of them unfinished, had taken place before the short walk.)

During the brief wait before dinner was served, I had a moment alone with the General, who embarked, with a lyrical quality that surprised me, on a criticism of the traditional conception of France as a mild, equable country. He denigrated the climate, raised the mountains and inflated the rivers with a sort of dogged persistence, as though there could be no greatness in mildness and equability and he wanted to prove that, geographically, France had the harsh configuration that breeds a great people. He contrasted it with the easy division of Germany into three very simple geological zones and with England "with its little cottages by the side of little roads in little countrysides beneath the little rain".

I did not dare to tell him that, for possibly analogous reasons, (for those anti-resisters had their own way of 'resisting') Drieu La Rochelle had sketched an identical portrait of France in one of the first numbers of the collaborating *Nouvelle Revue Française*.

Dinner was simple and uneventful. Bonneval went back to Paris by car very early on in the evening; Guy, who had come to relieve him, went off to the small room reserved for A.D.C.s in an old maid's house in the village; and Mme. de Gaulle retired to bed. However, they were all still there when the General took exception to my view that there had been a very favourable but recent change of public opinion in his favour. According to him, the people's confidence in him had never wavered. They had not reacted to his retirement because they had known unconsciously that it was not a real retirement.

"But you judge by the reactions of the scum surrounding authority. You aren't in the middle of the swell of the masses, you've no knowledge of its depths . . . The scum also backed Giraud against me. But I, myself, knew that the vast majority of the French people were still faithful to me, and events proved me right."

No one dared to contradict him. Yet what disaffection there had been from him in February, when his disappearance had caused no other emotion – amidst general indifference – than that of surly satisfaction.

"But the people are difficult to get to know and difficult to handle. They want to be guided but they don't want to support whoever wants to guide them. They want to be captured but they refuse to give themselves up. They hate weakness but they can't bear the idea of yielding to strength."

"Just like women," I thought but, as Mme. de Gaulle was still present, I held my peace.

Still earlier, in reply to Bonneval, who had mentioned some decision or other of the government's, the General had asked aggressively, ironically and maliciously, "What Government?", and we had all laughed, in a rather servile fashion.

Referring to Marly, he had said:

"It was only a provisional expedient . . . Like Darlan . . . Like Colombey . . ."

And again, indicating the soaking grounds of his property:

"I shall wait here till the situation clarifies . . ."

It was also before the others had left that he said, in connection with Madelin's latest book, "If Napoleon could only have taken a year's rest, his whole destiny would have been different."

Later, when we were alone together and had a long conversation about Hitler – incidentally, about Mussolini and Roosevelt, too – I was struck by the frequency with which he spoke of Napoleon as of an equal.

What an amazing person he is, a block without a cleft, a mind rid of its doubts, a heart without repentance! Unquestionably a superman, but it remains to be seen whether he can respond to his destiny or rather whether his destiny can respond in full to his expectations.

When we were left alone in the newly-decorated dining-room, his first question, once again, was a triumphant, "Well, wasn't I right to leave?" Then:

"On the 16th of June at Bayeux, I shall confront the French with my conception of what the Constitution ought to be. I shall confront the electors with their responsibilities. And they will do as I tell them. They can't not do as I tell them . . . Because they've already come too close to the whiff of the cannon-ball. And because public opinion will crystallize round simple, wise ideas which, from then on, they will know to be mine . . ."

And he added:

"In any case, tomorrow's elections are unimportant. Believe me: the dice are thrown . . ."

It was with reference to the P.R.L.* and the danger from the right, which I told him existed, that we talked about Hitler. I explained the psychological reasons that lead me to believe that Hitler was still alive – and though he tried to demolish my arguments one by one, de Gaulle struck me as slightly shaken in the end.

Owing to lack of time, I can only refer briefly to the surprising portrait he drew of Hitler and his romanticism (which, for example, caused him to sacrifice his Stalingrad army, a mistake that Napoleon would never have made) and to his rather naïf declaration, spoken with great conviction: "What I don't forgive him for are the atrocities. Atrocities are unforgivable . . ."

I replied that every dictatorship is led willy-nilly into committing crimes. And, to a lesser extent, no government can escape this fate. I quoted Montaigne's dictum: 'The public welfare requires one to betray, to lie and to massacre.'

De Gaulle answered me in a few monosyllables and reflected on what I had said for a long time – with a suddenly grieved, gloomy expression on his face. And he cut the discussion short by summoning me to work.

It was close on midnight when we finished. Then he conducted me to my room (the guest-room, which I was the first to occupy) and, with all the graciousness and kindness of an accomplished host, showed me the lavatory and bathroom.

After a good night, I wrote my next article, 'Grippe-Soleil', looking out at the broad, austere horizons on which my window opened. I was paying a visit on Claude Guy in the village when the chauffeur rushed in to fetch me. In the presence of a gloomy, silent and morose de Gaulle, I lunched quickly with Mme. de Gaulle. Then we all went to mass. I was next to the General who, as usual, was extremely bored and turned in every direction to inspect the congregation with meticulous attention: they, on their part, were discreet enough, in these holy surroundings, to conceal their curiosity. Only the young children turned their backs on the altar and stared intently at the tall, awesome figure. The curate seized with panic, broke off his sermon abruptly in the middle of a sentence. Immediately after mass, I left Colombey by car, accompanied by Mme. de Gaulle, who was also going to Paris to vote. Which the General was not. The journey took three hours and twenty minutes. We were in Paris by 4.00.

That evening, the whole family went to Le Figaro office to find out the latest news and join Pierre Brisson and the Georges Duhamels.

The wholly unexpected success of the M.R.P., of which we only got confirmation on the following morning, gave us new confidence in France's future. "If I had to choose between one man – however great – and a body of opinion like that, I wouldn't hesitate for a moment," my father said. Nor would I.

The day before yesterday, there was a big tea-party at home in honour of Claire and her fiancé, Ivan Wiazemsky.

An appalling amount of work. (The General, my two weekly columns, and the last chapter of my Malraux.) Impossible, alas, to keep up my Diary. Yet there are a number of important matters that I ought to go into in detail. The fruitfulness of my present encounter with surrealism, for one. But I shall no doubt write a book on that particular subject.

Wednesday, 12 June, 1946

I spent last Friday at Colombey. Leaving Paris by the 8.15 train, I reached Bar-sur-Aube at 1.00, where I was met by Claude Guy. We got to Colombey at 1.30 and sat down to lunch immediately with the General and Mme. de Gaulle. At 3.30. I worked with the General for an hour. Then we went for a drive (I, beside him, in the back of the narrow Citroën; Guy in front with the chauffeur) till 6.15, when they dropped me back at Bar-sur-Aube station. In short, a whole day spent with General de Gaulle, which means an exhausting one, since he does not merely expect you to toss the ball back to him: he expects you to provide creative, informative conversation. And this persistent political obsession of his struck me as particularly tiresome on a day when my mind was taken up with matters of an entirely different kind – no doubt because André Breton's *L'Amour Fou*, which I had read coming down in the train, ran parallel with certain past discoveries of mine and endorsed them.

In the car, for instance, beside this man, to whom no passer-by thought of paying any attention, but who was General de Gaulle; beside this great man, who did me the honour of talking to me and listening to me (though I felt appallingly barren of ideas) – what warmed the cockles of my heart was not his presence but the glimpse of a pretty, young cyclist, her skirt lifted by the wind.

Yet de Gaulle was speaking to me about matters of great importance: the future of France, whom political parties were leading to her doom, and how it was time, high time, that she pulled herself together; and the future of the world, driven towards an inevitable war, divided as it was into two isolated zones. But I was preoccupied by a much more urgent drama, which lay outside the field of History: nothing less than that of Man and his Destiny. So when General de Gaulle favoured me with his prognoses on the outcome of the political crisis, his constitutional concepts (the President to be elected by a broadly-based assembly comprising, over and above the deputies and general councillors, all the French mayors) and his optimism, in spite of everything, towards France's future and his own ("the elections seem to show that the country has at last decided to take the right road"), you can imagine how little interest I took in it all and what a painful effort it required to pay proper attention during a four-hour tête-à-tête! And he can scarcely have failed to notice my lack of constructive ideas and the indifferent assistance I was likely to provide.

All the same, I was greatly struck now and then by the originality and creative quality of his views. As when he replied to a remark of mine about the final disappearance of monarchies (in reference to the proclamation of the Republic in Italy):

"Not at all! It's quite the other way round: monarchies are becoming increasingly popular all over the world. Tito in Yugoslavia, Peron in the Argentine . . . China, too . . . Not to mention Stalin . . . As for the U.S.A., they lost their monarch when Roosevelt died, but they bitterly regret it."

Or when he described the winning party in the election as reluctant to assume power which it knew to be illusory but which still left them responsible for all the setbacks. (Inflation being inevitable as a result of the agreed rise in salaries.)

"There can be no way out as long as people go on playing the party game. At the moment, there are three main problems in France, and there isn't one of them on which the parties who will be governing together (or, rather, be giving the appearance of governing) are capable of seeing eye to eye: foreign policy, financial policy and education."

Occasionally, I ventured to express my anxieties and doubts: "But if we abandon the party system, we have to rely entirely on one man, and what security does that give us?" I added politely, "Assuming, of course, that the man in power isn't you."

But my interventions were clumsy and what I had believed to be my soundest arguments suddenly seemed without validity, easily demolished by the weakest and least convincing replies. Nevertheless, for a couple of minutes or so, there was human contact and a productive discussion, during which I did not have to think over what I was going to say but could say uninhibitedly what was on my mind. IIe was signing his letters at the time and, as we had come to a number of stock replies, all of them roughly the same, he was signing them mechanically. Suddenly – while continuing to sign – he asked me, point-blank:

"What are they saying in Paris?"

The question was so direct that I did not immediately realize that it was the one to which he confined himself when he had little time to spare and consequently chose the most urgent. Equally directly and simply, I replied that people were still in a state of euphoria after the elections, which, on the whole, they found encouraging; that few people outside political circles had any idea of the difficulties that would be encountered in forming a government; and that the French would find it hard to understand if he were not beside the government on 18th June.

On this last point, he answered me at considerable length, and I found him more set than ever on his proud refusal. When I asked him, later on, whether he would accept membership of the Academy some time in the future, he answered:

"It's impossible after having represented France, after having been France, to join one particular section of the community: the king of France did not belong to the Academy, nor did Napoleon."

From the modest car in which we were driving, it was indeed the royal glance of a man in whom the whole land of France is incarnated, that he cast on the forests, meadows and heaths. And it was as their owner, with the anxious pride of their owner, that he spoke to me about them. Yes, perhaps in France, too, we are heading towards a monarchy. But the prospect gives me little pleasure.

Tuesday, 25 June, 1946

The speech at Bayeux, which I heard from a position close to the platform from which de Gaulle spoke, is now in the past; so, too, is the Mont-Valérien ceremony, which I did not attend at all. The principal result of these events has been a crystallization of the two separate political realities which coexist in France today: the one consisting of the sum total of traditional party members, the other personified by the lone figure of General de Gaulle. And I shall not be surprised if, in the end, this extraordinary man carries more weight than Parliament, the trade unions and the combined House committees.

Last Saturday, I found that work on the house at Colombey had almost been completed. Now, the dining-room is only used for meals, as the drawing-room has been suitably arranged for conversations and the office for work.

Once again, I was astonished that the man, who is commonly supposed to be walled up alive in his solitary grandeur, should prove to be so straightforward, so simple, so accessible and so confiding. It is only natural that he speaks of himself with the calm objectivity of someone who knows himself to be a part of History and in its foreground.

"It's essential that the Mont-Valérien ceremony should be carried on every year, that every year the tomb of the Unknown Warrior and the plot commemorating the victims of the firing squad should be united in the same symbolic ceremony, so that the French become accustomed to thinking of this Thirty Years' War as a single entity, in which, admittedly, there were ups and downs, but which ended nonetheless in a victory for France. Foch, Clemenceau, de Gaulle are one and the same, and it is important that the French people realize it."

In answer to my question: "Do you think that the M.R.P. will go as far as to defend in the Assembly the right of dissolution that, in your speech at Bayeux, you declared to be one of the President's essential prerogatives?" he replied haughtily:

"In any case, I can't see them opposing, in front of their electors, what de Gaulle has said."

He spoke of himself in the third person like that, radiating self-confidence and certainty. One of the first things he said to me (Bidault had not yet formed his Cabinet) was:

"I'm not asking for anything. Let them straighten everything out themselves. Nobody's stopping them . . . But I'm not worrying: sooner or later, they'll have to acknowledge their helplessness. I want an unconditional surrender."

And when I said that it looked as though the three-party alliance, whether led by the M.R.P. or another, would manage to limp along till the next referendum, he replied that he was not as certain of this as I was:

"The twenty-five per cent rise in salaries which has just been agreed will produce a thirty per cent rise in the cost of living – and then a financial crisis is inevitable."

Several times, in terms that were often the same, word for word, as those I had heard him use before, he resumed his indictment of party government, ending up by exclaiming:

"They're always throwing the 18 Brumaire and the 2nd of December in my face! But they're forgetting that the two Napoleons weren't causes but effects; that they were called on by a crushing majority to make a decision that would never have occurred to them otherwise."

He told me that, during the scrimmage at Mont-Valérien on 18 June, he had been very much afraid that the demonstrators would seize him and carry him in triumph to the Elysée. He said with the merest shade of irony:

"That was why I didn't want to take part in the day's official demonstrations alongside the Government. God only knows what would have happened and what the crowd would have done to me. All the half-wits who begged me to accept Gouin's invitation have had to admit it now."

He dwelt at considerable length on his conception of what the constitution should be – both at table and after lunch in the drawing-room in front of a silent Bonneval and Mme. de Gaulle, who was writing letters.

"I have already managed to insist on two things: the 'no' to this crazy scheme for a constitution – thanks to my idea of a referendum; and the necessity of having a Senate, the principle of which is no longer opposed by anyone, even the communists."

When I remarked that the power of dissolution would be a bitter pill to swallow, he replied that an election campaign would bring him victory on this point. I then went on to say that, as an election issue, this offered considerable opportunities to the opposition, who could avail themselves of facile but effective historical arguments, since French political consciousness has been awakened over a long period to the dangers of Presidential power. De Gaulle listened to me attentively and even seemed to concede me certain points, but I felt that his conviction was quite unshaken. It appeared, in any case, that a dictatorship was not what he wanted – since the Presidential term of office is of limited duration – and because the electorate is always free, when it comes to an end, to withdraw its support. What he did regard as indispensable was that the man responsible for the nation's destiny – and whose responsibility had been solemnly acknowledged – should be able to work for the country's good without being constantly supervised, spied on and thwarted by political parties more attached to the further-ance of their own ideas than to France. He will certainly pay due attention to the political slant of the majority of the electorate, but it must be open to him to take the helm and act on his own for the country's good – even though he may appear to be acting against it:

"If Lebrun had been a different type of man, and if he had possessed the powers I have outlined, he would never have recalled Pétain in 1940."

There was obviously the unavowed sophism in all that of a man who seeks, cost what it may, to avoid the eternal dilemma, expressed by Valéry: "If the State is strong, it crushes us, and if it is weak, we perish."

I heard him murmur, with a sincerity that could not be suspect (I mean that one felt that there could be no question of his trying to brush aside the historical axiom): "Experience proves that dictator-ships nearly always end badly."

He touched on many other matters. From 12.30 to 5.30, he talked almost without stopping, apart from the hour and a half we spent working in his newly-appointed office . . . He mentioned the young men whom he had undertaken to turn into ministers – 'little Teitgen' and Frenay* – "but now they won't learn anything: being around a Gouin or a Bidault isn't the way to acquire the right training!"

He told me, during a short walk we took alone together in the garden, of his confidence and optimism in the destinies of France, which had finally and decisively embarked on the right road.

I took more than a thousand letters back to Paris, among them a number of fascinating documents of unquestionable historical value, and all of them relating to the present crisis.

With reference to d'Argenlieu, who came down to Colombey on his recent return from Indochina, Bonneval told me of an amusing slip he made when he said, "Yes, monseigneur," in reply to a question from the General.

Yesterday, as Molotov and then Bevin drove past us in their luxurious cars, Antonin Artaud ceremoniously saluted Breton, who was sitting on the terrace of the Deux-Magots, surrounded by his imposing circle of disciples. And passed on his spectral way.

Wednesday, 3 July, 1946

At the end of our work session on Monday at Colombey, we remained alone together for nearly an hour, sitting opposite each other in his office – and he confided in me unreservedly. The man, whom I had so often seen reflecting on France's destiny, reflected on the world's destiny in front of me, with the seriousness of one who really believes himself to be among those responsible for our planet's future. It was the day immediately after the Bikini test (which took place just as I was watching, from the foot of the Montmartre basilica, an absurdly small, charming firework spread its pale flowers over Vincennes). The General remarked that, from the first reports, the results of the tests did not seem very convincing – and I was struck by his ability to form a coherent, colourful picture of the whole set-up from the meagre information available. He described the Bikini atoll to me and the 'guinea-pig' fleet standing off it, as though he had seen them with his own eyes after the bomb had been exploded, and added a number of precise, even picturesque details.

"This problem of the atom bomb is the only one now of vital importance, the only one which must be solved at any price, since the future of the world depends on it. I intend to make a public statement on the subject soon. I shall certainly support the American proposal formulated by Mr. Baruch*. At the moment, all I know of it are the broad outlines published in the newspapers, which is why I shall ask you to obtain the full text of it for me (together with Gromyko's Russian counter-proposal), but, at first sight, the offer seems effective and straightforward. There is even a certain nobility in the American attitude that I find admirable. For a nation in a position to annihilate its opponents – including Russia – and the sole possessor of the secret of the atom bomb to propose the destruction of the devices that it already has in stock and submission to international control of atomic energy argues a surprising disinterestedness and generosity. Naturally, in order to gain time and make the U.S.A. lose their lead, the Russians reply: 'First destroy your bombs under international supervision and then we'll see about instituting international control of atomic energy in every country – and at home.' But the U.S.A. insist – and rightly so – that from now on every nation, including the U.S.S.R., should open up their frontiers and their factories, giving a right of inspection that the Soviet régime might well not survive. So what we have to find out is whether the world is prepared to run the appalling risk of total destruction in order to allow the Soviet régime to continue."

Thinking aloud, I said: "It's true that the very foundations of humanity are overthrown, every historical perspective changed by the atomic secret, and henceforward nothing seems worth struggling or hoping for . . ."

And de Gaulle, thinking aloud, too, seemed to me for the first time to find something *too much* for him, to become a frail, anonymous man amidst the anonymous, frail throng of men:

"The whole situation is certainly appalling . . ."

But, after a brief silence, he adds, in the manner of a man emerging from the common herd to engineer its protection:

"So appalling that we must, at any cost, institute this international control and bring to heel any nation that tries to wreck the organization."

It is equally in relation to the rest of the world that he goes on to speak on the scale of France's future ("France recovers a little more day by day but, day by day, the State becomes more nebulous"), and it is in relation to the rest of the world that he calls to mind the French past, still so close to us, in which he played so vital a role. With reference to Italy's violent reaction after France's acquisition of Tende and Brigue, he said:

"They're a disheartening lot! I really thought we could make something out of them, but I'm beginning to doubt it after seeing their determination to insult us. And God knows I warned them that they'd lose that insignificant part of their territories; genuinely insignificant alongside what we had every right to demand from them . . . What I wanted to do but was prevented from doing by the obtuseness of the British . . . Their stupidity and malice are past belief . . ."

Here, he began to speak as though he were daydreaming, his eyes staring into the distance, as he sketched the broad outlines of the scheme he had conceived but been unable to carry out:

"What I wanted to do was to form a Western federation which would have grouped round France and England all the small nations in the

194

West: Belgium, Holland and Italy, naturally. This *bloc* would have proved a powerful attraction to all the western German provinces – since, in any case, they would have found themselves separated from Russianized Prussia – the Palatinate, Saxony, Thuringia, Bavaria and Wurtemberg – and, of course, Austria. . . From then on, between the Soviet and American formations, there would have been a powerful *bloc,* capable of safeguarding the independence of the West and, when it came to atomic control, in a position to tip the scales. But Churchill would never support me on this issue – even though he knew I was in the right. All our disagreement sprang from that. He told me: 'If I had to choose between Roosevelt and you, I should never hesitate to choose Roosevelt.' And I'm quite aware of the reasons which prompted him to make that choice. But, in doing so, he sacrificed his country's independence and turned it into an American dominion. When the Battle of the Atlantic was at its height and he sent out his S.O.S., asking the U.S.A. for the fifty destroyers for which they had no further use and Roosevelt answered: 'All right, but give me the Antillas for ninety-nine years', and Churchill agreed, he gave clear evidence of his irremediable defeat. If he had immediately spoken on the radio and explained the whole situation – 'At this moment, as I speak to you, our convoys of supply ships are being destroyed one after the other and the U.S.A., which has fifty ships doing nothing, demands the Antillas in return for them; a demand to which I cannot concede with a clear conscience' – well, then, the weight of public opinion, even in America, would have forced Roosevelt to give way. . . Did I give away Dakar or Casablanca or Saint-Pierre-et-Miquelon despite the constant pressure from America? I did not part with a single French possession, and God knows I had none of Churchill's resources."

De Gaulle went on to tell me how he had barred American ships from French waters off Saint-Pierre-et-Miquelon, which he reinforced under their noses, and had threatened to fire on them if they entered our territorial waters:

"And what happened? Roosevelt put his claims back in his pocket – with his handkerchief on top of them – and never mentioned the matter again."

De Gaulle constantly repeated the words 'stupid' and 'malicious', which seemed summary and almost childish when applied to such complex problems; but one felt that he was sickened by so much obtuseness and misguided selfishness:

"From then on, the English let us down the whole time. What's more, they let down the Cross in the Near East. And there, they let down the West and themselves at the same time. I told Churchill as much.

195

I said to him: 'In the end, it's against your own interests that you're acting.' "

Earlier, when he had finished signing his letters and we were looking at the proposed jacket for the new edition of his speeches, which he had completely recast, he drew my attention to the Press conference, at which he had made his final appeal for Anglo-Saxon understanding (Washington, July 1944) – and to the speech, 'which will remain like a brand on England's forehead' (Consultative Assembly, 21 December 1944) – and read me in a vengeful voice the sentences in which he openly accused Churchill of having, on a certain occasion, refused to allow him to speak on the radio, and Roosevelt of having printed artificial French currency (a euphemism for what it really was: counterfeit notes):

"I said to Churchill: 'By agreeing to the U.S.A. imposing on a nation like France a man selected by themselves (Darlan), you are not only betraying France, you are ruining yourselves.' But he couldn't forgive France for June 1940 or the French for having, almost to a man, disowned them at the time – for that's what they did, though I have always officially denied it," (he said this with a bleak smile). "That's what they did and he knew it. And he couldn't forgive us, either, for having fired on them, forgetting that it was they who fired first."

What struck me was the extent to which de Gaulle identified himself with a France which, at that time, was Vichy France, and how he envisages no break in her historical continuity, believing that she cannot err in her instinctive, national feelings, even when they lead her to appoint a Pétain government. The response to the ultimatum at Mers el-Kébir is a national reaction, to which the whole of France is committed. The Montoire meeting does not commit her in any way, since it is unconnected with any national sentiment. Naturally, de Gaulle said nothing of this, but it was implicit in what he did say.

I asked him, later, whether he approved of the movement recently initiated by Capitant* at a meeting on 29 June, at which I was present – one which seemed to me dangerously compromising in the use it made of de Gaulle's name. The organization, which declared itself to be 'above all political parties', had adopted the title of 'Gaullist Union for the Fourth Republic'. He burst out laughing: "Compromise me!" The idea plainly struck him as farcical. But I insisted: "Everyone knows that M. Capitant is one of your closest friends. No one will believe that you didn't give him permission to use your name." And, in fact, he did give it, without giving it in so many words, but still giving it. His reply was ambiguous – neither a yes nor a no.

"It's embarrassing," I still went on, "that two defeated candidates

in the last election, Capitant and Soustelle" – "Capitant wasn't
defeated: he withdrew," de Gaulle broke in, with a flash of annoyance
– "In any case, he isn't a member of the Constituent Assembly, and
here he is laying down in principle, before the Assembly elected by
the country has even begun working, that it's incapable of carrying out
its duties properly and that those sharing your constitutional views
should be on their guard. The least one can say is that it is ill-timed:
don't you agree?" Again, he would not say yes or no. He took it all
in, but did not say where he stood.

"All the same," I said, "the answer to those who ask whether you're
involved in this business must be: *No, certainly not; in no way
whatever.*" He agreed, but not, I strongly suspected, without mental
reservations.

In regard to home affairs, I found him less optimistic than he had
been at our last meeting. He blamed Bidault for having given a larger
number of ministerial posts to the communists and at a moment when
there are fewer of them in the Assembly:

"When they were the majority party, I only gave them five ministerial posts – and five to each of the other parties, but balanced by a
large number of ministers without party connections."

He thinks that the new Constitution will certainly be an improvement on the last one, but still unsatisfactory, since it will not provide
for the separation of powers, without which there is no security.

"But it doesn't matter, because events, sooner or later, will sweep
away a Constitution, for which the country will have no great respect,
in which it has lost interest even before it has come into being and
which no one will be disposed to defend when it is attacked, just as
has already happened to the one of 1875."

He ended up by reading me the text of what he had said on the
occasions of his two interventions in the Assembly on 31 December
and 1 January last, stressing each of the sentences which announced
quite clearly his imminent resignation (and sometimes very amusingly),
and, even more so, the ones giving reasons for it, which people, at the
time, had some difficulty in realizing the importance.

4 *July*, 1946

I had a visit from Claude Guy yesterday, very much worried by the
business of the Gaullist Union. Judging it to be liable to compromise
de Gaulle, he had taken it upon himself to tell Capitant that the
General formally disapproved of the word 'Gaullist'. The fact that the
ex-minister only put up a feeble resistance shows that de Gaulle has

not given him the go-ahead that I was afraid of, but, soundly, is still in a position to repudiate him should things go wrong – or the need arise. In any case, impressed by the General's calmness, I reassured Guy, telling him that all these epiphenomena, glowing above or, rather, below a man of destiny had no real importance, and that, in fact, de Gaulle was someone *who could not be compromised* (other than by himself).

In *Le Figaro* this morning, there was an article by my father, inspired by a certain vision of himself that de Gaulle imposed upon me, and which I had passed on to him. The truth is that the better I get to know that man, the greater my confidence in him and the deeper my admiration for him.

My sister Claire is getting married civilly today and in church tomorrow.

Sunday, 14 July, 1946

Yesterday at Colombey, General de Gaulle suddenly stopped signing his letters. He looked up at me without any attempt to hide his feelings and asked me with the utmost simplicity:

"What do you think is going to happen? Do you really imagine that things can go on much longer as they are? What's to be done about it all?"

Then he immediately added, in a discouraged tone of voice:

"There are times when I'm so . . . disgusted . . . yes, that's the word: disgusted."

And he went on to describe France's tragic situation, with the State no longer in existence, her currency threatened and her Empire breaking up:

"It's frightening, you know, the extent to which the Empire has disintegrated since I left . . ."

Then he repeated the same questions, plainly revealing his perplexity and distress. That he should confide in me in this way, put me at my ease and I answered his questions quite frankly, since, after all, it was to me that he had chosen to put them and not anyone else. Reverting to Capitant's movement, about which I had been questioning him a few minutes earlier, forcing him by my persistence to make his attitude clear – when he had gone on repudiating it without repudiating it – I said:

"In my opinion, the vital thing is to stick to the rules with the idea, once your position is established, of asserting yourself, which should be quite possible. Don't you think it would be better, with this in view, to

198

moderate your constitutional aims, accept the new Constitution, however unsatisfactory it may appear to you, and, at the same time, avail yourself of a party, of which the vast majority supports you even if its leaders are disloyal: the M.R.P.? For your party, General, is not M. Capitant's indefinite movement: it's the M.R.P."

"I can't belong to any one party. France wouldn't understand it, France wouldn't like it. The French people look on me as belonging to the nation."

"Yes, of course, but it wouldn't be a question of joining the M.R.P., but of relying on their support. It would also be a question of rallying the French around you, outside the limitations of parties, but without compelling them to abandon their parties, to which they've become attached; of introducing them to a higher level of loyalty; that of the State."

"But that's exactly what Capitant wants to do!"

"Yes, but clumsily, by making use of your name."

"I haven't encouraged him to use the term 'Gaullist', which I've never used, myself. 'But you can't forbid me,' he told me, and as a matter of fact . . ."

"But you *do* have the right to forbid him: that's what gives rise to the ambiguity. A movement supported by your friend M. Capitant and bearing your name inevitably appears to have your approval."

"But I can't discourage well-meaning men, who are prepared to conduct a campaign throughout the country, advocating my own constitutional ideas . . ."

"Very well. But I still say, you must stick to the rules."

"Particularly as Capitant has very sound ideas about the Constitution."

"The only trouble is that he's not a member of the Constituent Assembly. But, even so, there'd be nothing against the movement if it did not bear your name. 'Gaullist' makes it factious, and you won't succeed unless you play cards that are recognized to be good ones by the mass of the country, which is firmly attached to its republican traditions. If M. Capitant's organization were called, for example, *The Movement for the Restoration of the State*, you could lend your support to it much more openly and no one would object: it would achieve the vital task of restoring to the French, who have lost it, a conception of the State, without doing any violence to their republican principles. A movement of this kind, which would undoubtedly have a wide following, would rally the French, above mere party loyalties, to the cause of France and around yourself."

"But there's nothing I should like more – for Capitant to give his movement that name. It would be much better. As far as my possible return to office is concerned, the parties are certainly in favour of it – but only to get a tighter stranglehold on me. It makes me bitter when I think of that forsaken Republic, which I put on its feet again at the same time as France, and gave back to them – to those who cared so little about her in her hour of peril – and whose only aim now is to get rid of the man who saved them . . . And you really want me to accept the Presidency of the Republic? But I'd be powerless, gagged and deceiving France, who would believe me to be at the helm when I should really be a mere figurehead, compelled to ratify all the decisions of a ministerial council, over which I should preside without having the slightest authority over it . . . At least, before, I was the boss: if a minister refused to carry out my policies, I sacked him."

"But, at least, you'd be there, General; you'd be there . . ."

"So you want me to submit to the Constitution in order to overthrow it immediately by a *coup d'état*? Don't forget that, *coup d'état* or not, one would have to ensure the restoration of a strong executive. Conditions, outside or inside the country, would necessitate it, alas, sooner or later. Perhaps too late . . . France's unhappy situation today would be less serious if the country had any time to spare: then there would be some hope of recovery. But we're living at a period when war is imminent, an inevitable war. And it's appalling to think that we shall lose our independence as a result, whoever proves the victor – the U.S.S.R. or the U.S.A. – that, in either event, Europe will be the loser, due to the unforgivable crime of the English in failing to appreciate what was going on. It's also appalling to think that we're heading towards a dictatorship, that we shall be unable to avoid it and that it's the worst thing that could happen to France at the present moment."

He said all this with great sadness, tormented by his feeling of impotence and the conviction, rightly or wrongly, that he alone is capable of saving a France which, while not rejecting him, nonetheless remains beyond his reach – without there seeming any way (always excepting the possibility of a national disaster) by which she can return to him, when he has abandoned her to her fate, more in love than anger (unless he accepts the Presidency of the Republic).

My arguments in favour of his returning to office in the very near future, whatever it may cost him, (since it offered him an opportunity to elbow his way to power later), clearly impressed him. But he always reverted to the lack of executive power that would be his in the immediate present:

"What else could I have done, for instance, in the present circumstances, other than ask Bidault to form a government? And he'd have appointed the same ministers and pursued the same policy . . . You're surely not suggesting that I should endorse Bidault's policy when I ask forgiveness from God and man every day for having installed him at the Quai d'Orsay?"

And the conversation went on in this way, with him signing three or four letters, then stopping, putting down his pen, talking, signing a few more papers and picking up the subject again where he left off.

Wednesday, 31 *July,* 1946

As the General wanted to prepare his Bar-le-Duc speech in peace, I only saw him for the first time yesterday since 12 July. Michel Debré* came with me, going down by train and returning by car. We sat down to lunch as soon as we arrived. The conversation, trivial at first, very soon turned to the threat of war hovering over a world only just emerging from the abyss. De Gaulle, referring to the Peace Conference, which had called a meeting in Paris that same day, for the first time, between the 'smaller nations' and the 'Big Four', spoke of the indifference and scepticism of the general public, convinced that there could be no real prospect of peace:

"War is inevitable, a war that no one wants – neither the U.S.A. nor the U.S.S.R. – any more than Hitler or anyone else wanted the last one. The doctrine of free will seems to have received its **death-blow**. Despite the fact that no nation wants war, war is, nevertheless, drawing ineluctably closer – without there being any way to ward it off. Indefinable forces, beyond the power of mankind to control, are threatening the world."

His words, trite enough in themselves, acquired a new importance, as much due to the personality of the man uttering them as to the serious, humble, reflective tone of his voice. After lunch, the conversation was almost entirely carried on by de Gaulle and Debré – a nervous Debré, though confident enough at heart if not in appearance, who struggled to say what he had to say in spite of continual interruptions from the General. When he did leave him free to develop his arguments, he conveyed the impression of having lost all interest in the subject. But it was only an impression because, when he came to reply, it was clear that he had been listening attentively.

After de Gaulle had delivered his customary criticism of the régime ('party government') in the now familiar terms, Michel Debré tried, very soundly, to persuade him (as I had done a fortnight before) that he must play the cards available to him; adding that there were signs of a new attitude in the M.R.P., a party as lacking in men of ministerial quality as the others, but richer in men of intelligence and goodwill. In short, the leaders of the M.R.P. were now prepared to accept the idea of taking part in a government without representing their party in it. "All they want is to become ministers, everyone knows that!" the General broke in, ironically – which compelled Debré to agree that there was no one left in public life with any 'sense of State'. And suddenly, in a burst of emotion, the General took charge:

"Whatever folly is it, I ask you, that leads us to place the country's welfare in the hands of parties, which disappear completely the moment she's in danger? That's what happened in 1940 and we shall see it happen again. When a crisis arises, there's nothing and nobody – no parties, at any rate, as you'll admit. The whole question – and the vital one for France – is to decide whether we must really wait once more till the last moment before we take steps. For if the war comes before we have regained some sort of stability, we are lost. We shall count for nothing, everything will happen without our having any say in it, any participation in it, except, of course, by our deaths. Your M.R.P., involuntarily, I agree, but through its congenital impotence, has systematically betrayed the State since it came to power. It was only because I threatened to appeal to the country and they were afraid that the electorate might turn against them, that they decided, at the last moment, to campaign against the Auriol Constitution. But what are your leaders of the M.R.P. doing now? They are consenting to every renunciation and never envisage for a second taking advantage of their victory to assume their responsibilities – they are even ready to adopt a new Auriol Constitution, one that is virtually the same. Equally, Bidault has only been put in office on the tacit understanding – but one known to everyone – including himself – that he won't govern, that he won't even attempt to govern. The evil is incurable because it's linked to the system . . . Not satisfied with having given the communists a quite disproportionate place in his government, he plays their game on every occasion, attending the so-called European congresses that they organize, being present at the ceremony in honour of that M. Ilya Ehrenburg*, yielding time after time to their pressures. And no one protests; no one! Not one Deputy stands up to point out that the State abdicated over the question of salaries and that, by ratifying the decisions of the interested parties, which it had the lunacy to unite together, it acquiesced in decisions that were all to its disadvantage and dragged it towards the abyss. And they allow that Ho Chi Minh to flout us on our very doorstep – while, little by little, our Empire disintegrates – when our only hope would be to profit from the difficulties by which fortunately all the other nations are beset to reorganize the Empire, pull ourselves together and achieve the stability that will be vital to us any day now if we are to survive."

I have had to give his speech in its broad outlines and forego reproducing the lyrical, emotional qualities to which I referred. At moments, it was France, herself, who was speaking, and this man who, after all, is no more than human, became the vehicle of something so great that one was completely overhelmed and amazed. Something so great and, at the same time, so comprehensive: impressive and comprehensive as a mountain, so self-assured, so wholly certain of the righteousness of the cause, using little light and shade but as compelling as some force of nature.

He went on:

"The State? That's what they all hold in abomination. If they've all been against me, all of them, always, it's not, believe me, because a single one of them has ever believed for a second in the so-called danger of dictatorship. No: it was the State that they saw reflected in me, and it was the State, personified by me, against which they fought. And, remember, they only attacked Pétain when he wanted to act for their own good. Not one Deputy, not a single one, opposed the armistice. The only grievance which those who attacked Pétain had against him was that he was threatening their parliamentary prerogatives, a matter of vast importance at that particular moment! But in as much as he believed (wrongly), but he did believe it – and so did they – that he represented the existing State, they could not tolerate him. Conversely, a number of worthy Frenchmen supported Pétain in the beginning from perfectly proper motives, because they hoped to ensure in defeat, thanks to him, the continuity of the State."

Then we worked hard for some time. And, suddenly, as he went on signing his letters (but mechanically, without paying any attention to what he was doing), he said:

"Well, then, what's to be done? What do you suggest? I've too much respect for France to present her with some kind of South American *pronunciamento*. So what can I do? War will come and we shall be nothing, count for nothing, disappear. The only hope was to rally the people round me, collect all the country's strength around me . . . But no, they've lopped off all the branches, even the last branch that could have saved them from plunging into the abyss."

After tea de Gaulle spent over an hour with Michel Debré in his office.

During a short stop at Troyes, leaning on the parapet of a bridge over a Seine still close to the original stream, which moved me because it was our very own Seine, I said to Michel Debré:

"We've just heard the epic words, 'L'Etat c'est moi', from the lips of a man, who has as much right to utter them as Louis XIV . . . Isn't General de Gaulle's indignant astonishment at the idea of his being willing to submit to the Constitution they're on the point of recommending to him exactly the same as the Roi Soleil's would have been if some madman had offered him the Presidency of a Constitutional Republic?"

Debré replied that de Gaulle was certainly much more of a Louis XIV than a Richelieu, but that, alas, he was living in a France that there had been no Richelieu to bequeath to him, a country impoverished in men (the best of them having been killed in 1914, though he, himself, had miraculously escaped the massacre) – and, tradition having gone by the board, with a younger generation that was unfitted to meet its destiny:

"Yes, Louis XIV . . . I mean, a man created to govern from a height. Whatever form the Constitution may take, his prestige, the force of tradition and his own personality mark him out – and no one but him – for the position. I begged him just now to think it over but, unfortunately, I found him completely set in his determination to refuse. I said to him: 'Be careful! You're in danger of missing the bus for good and all. Once the Constitution, whether good or bad, has been put to the vote and approved by the people, you will be either inside or outside the perimeter. And, if you're outside, only a national disaster will enable you to come back in again. From then on, there will be no opportunity of making speeches: apart from the 18th June, there will no longer be any place in public life for General de Gaulle. And the nation needs General de Gaulle!' "

Debré and I both think that the General will give in in the end, and may already have decided to give in. The impression he has given me for some weeks now is that of a man champing at the bit. His optimism before and after Bayeux has been superseded recently by an unaccustomed uneasiness: he has at last grasped that the train is about to leave and leave without him. I believe that he has too high a regard for France and himself not to decide to jump aboard at the last minute.

At lunch, de Gaulle had declared that, no matter what happened, there was never any breach of continuity in France – adding that it was no bad thing:

"When I decided that Laval's case should not be reopened, which would have meant repudiating Justice and leaving the way open for a lot of mud-slinging if Laval were to be saved from the firing squad, I received a tearful letter from Blum during the night . . ."

I replied that it showed a natural solidarity (I was thinking of my father and Béraud), and it was then that he said that it was all to France's good that things should be like that.

"What Bidault ought to have done within an hour of the English announcing their intention of administering the Ruhr as they thought fit," the General said to me on 12 July, "was to make a formal declaration that France was resuming full liberty of action in the Sarre."

I understood from Bidault's speech at Saint-Etienne last Sunday that this was the course he intended to take. They say that the General was not wholly unconnected with this decision. I pointed out to Debré that, however bad the constitutional machinery might be, such a man could affect the march of events merely by his presence, merely by the influence of his genius and by the prestige he conferred on his associates.

Wednesday, 7 August, 1946

As Mme. de Gaulle was in Paris, I lunched alone with the General and Claude Guy yesterday at Colombey. The first thing the General said to me was that he was by no means certain that the Constitution would be passed, since the communists were patently about to launch a campaign in favour of a 'no'. "And I'll make people vote against it, too," he said with a certain malice. And when, a little later, we suggested that there might be a last minute *volte-face* by the communists, he answered:

"Naturally. That's why I'm not so foolish as to declare my own position too soon. I shall only disclose it at the last minute: you can tell them so."

Despite the obvious irony, his last sentence did not fail to surprise me.

When I asked him for the explanation of the stand now taken by the French communists, who are officially in disagreement with the U.S.S.R. over the question of the Ruhr, a new and unexpected development, he replied:

"But it's in the U.S.S.R.'s interests to make the Germans believe that their only hope of any real recovery is by collaborating with them. 'Look at the unreasonable demands of the French!', they keep on saying. Demands which they are purposely making their French communists insist on, though you can be sure that these latter will stop advocating the internationalization of the Rhineland the moment they are given the order. And remember that, to them, internationalization means the presence of Russians on the Rhine. Naturally, that's not at all what I have in mind when I speak of inter-Allied control. You're going to see the U.S.S.R. presenting themselves more strongly every day as the champions of Germany. It wouldn't surprise me if they set up a German government in Berlin soon – which, of course, will not be satisfied with administering the Russian zone, but will claim to have a voice in the Western sectors as well. It is also significant that what the communists are denouncing, through their spokesman Thorez, is the threat to France from the Rhineland trusts and magnates: with the implication that the threat will disappear with the abolition of trusts. We're witnessing the first stages of an operation, of which the aims are plain enough even now."

Then, reverting once more to the war which he considers highly likely, General de Gaulle declared that there are clear signs of an imminent ultimatum from the U.S.A. to the U.S.S.R. on the subject of atomic control. A control to which Stalin could only agree if he renounced the present régime in Russia – a most improbable contingency, even if just possible. In any case, as soon as the Americans know that the Russians are close to success in manufacturing the bomb, they are bound to intervene.

Then, we again discussed the new Constitution. We had reached the stage of coffee, brandy and the cigar, of which the General is so fond. He and I were seated in deep armchairs on either side of the fireplace, with Claude a short distance away behind me.

"Now listen to me, Claude Mauriac: what's the real purpose of a Head of State? Certainly not to intervene in the country's affairs at every turn. On the contrary, his role should be discreet and, in appearance at least, self-effacing: he can give direction, certainly, if necessary, and impulse – but still self-effacingly. It's only in the event of a national crisis that he must intervene, since he is the only one answerable, the only one responsible for the welfare of the State. For him to achieve this, there are two vital prerogatives that the Constitution must accord him: that of dissolving the Assembly and that of forming a new government. Now the Assembly's proposed Constitution does not satisfy either of these requirements. Consequently, it's impossible for me, in all conscience, to accept the Presidency of the Republic."

I answered that it was precisely at a time of crisis that the letter of the Constitution carried the least weight, that dissolution, as the only way out, might well be desired by the parliamentarians themselves, and that it was far better for the man who felt himself responsible for the nation's wellbeing to be already working within the system, rather than have to intervene from outside it, where the chances of success would be infinitely smaller.

"Then it's a *coup d'état* that you're recommending?"

"Not at all, General, but in the event of a grave crisis a Head of State has a thousand ways of dealing with it open to him, the framework of the law becomes flexible and, in the name of the common good, he can always proclaim martial law."

"But that's just what the proposed Constitution doesn't give the President of the Republic the right to do."

"The radio . . ."

"The text of the preceding Constitution forbade me to use it – without permission. For you don't imagine that the clause was inserted because of Vincent Auriol, do you? The idea was to prevent General de Gaulle from speaking to the French people."

"But it would be easy enough for you to assume the right, whatever might be written into the Constitution, if the necessity arose. And, in any case, it would be even more difficult for you to go on the air, General, if you held no official position."

Guy then joined in and, after beating about the bush and apologizing for having recourse to such a precedent, ventured to cite the case of Marshal Pétain, who would have found it much more difficult to intervene in 1940 – against France's interests, admittedly, but the precedent was still valid – had he not been a member of Reynaud's Cabinet.

"You could go further and add that I couldn't have done what I did, either, at that period, if I hadn't been a member of the Cabinet; and you'd be quite right," de Gaulle broke in ironically, not above supplying his opponents with ammunition.

The truth is that he is equally attracted by the pros and cons – even though he pretends to confine himself to the cons – and, as Palewski said to me a short while ago on the telephone, "He never dialogues with anyone but himself." By bringing grist to our mill, he was really only supplying an argument to the side of him which agreed with us. And, while I tried to convince him that the welfare of the country demanded that he should place himself at the head of France without further delay, I was by no means certain that his own arguments, coming from a great man with the ability to see a long way ahead, were not more valid than mine. But I went on:

"The present situation can last for a very long time, since, fortunately, war is not inevitable. The State can continue to diminish for a very long time without anyone in France being aware of it. You can't deprive France, General, either on a national or international plane, of the enormous influence you can bring to bear. And, whatever difficulties or restrictions you may have to face, you have the qualities to deal with them."

He interrupted me again with his: "Then it's a *coup d'état* that you're recommending?"

And there we were, back again where we started.

For once, our long work session passed by without the General making any comments. But, as soon as it was over, he made me sit down and took up the subject again where we had broken off. The tête-à-tête enabled him to show a more affectionate confidence in me, which touched me. But there was not a second in which I was not acutely aware of the historical nature of the moments through which I was living.

He told me:

"These days, I often think of the Comte de Chambord: and think of the real reasons for his refusal.† Because that business of the white flag was only a pretext, of course. Well, I know his real reasons: he refused because he no longer had any confidence in France, knew that there was nothing to be made of France and preferred to see the monarchy dead once and for all rather than participate in its decline. The king could not accept the Treaty of Frankfurt. If the Comte de Chambord had signed it, he would have had to plan a counter to it immediately; otherwise, he could not have reigned. But the country did not want revenge and he sensed it: the country simply wasn't prepared to make the necessary effort."

How serious and sad General de Gaulle's expression was during this moment of despair for France's future! Staring blindly in front of him, he spoke his thoughts aloud to me, and went on to declare that, since the eighteenth century, our country had done nothing but slide downhill from her former power and greatness, that the resurgences during the Revolution and again in 1914 were only ephemeral and had cost the country the best part of her substance. He quoted me, as he had done once before at Marly, Voltaire's verses to Frederick II, which I am sorry not to have memorized, in which Voltaire described the French soldiery as being prompt in flight and skilled in pillage in such biting terms that they really hurt.

"Do you really want me to become what the Comte de Chambord refused to be?"

I replied that his own prestige was much higher – ("Yes, I know," he murmured. "The History of France will speak of me and Epinal's pictures will illustrate my story. But it's all over: one only exists as

† To accept the throne of France.

long as one can be of service.") – that there was no justification for his belief that his mission had ended and that, in my humble opinion, the Comte de Chambord's attitude, if motivated by the reasons he had just given, was far from admirable: that he had no right, no one ever had a right to despair of France and that, under his instigation, France would not refuse to make the necessary effort.

"But haven't I been blamed incessantly for pursuing a policy of greatness without having the resources to achieve it? In 1940, I was able to embark on my mission because I was convinced of two things. I was confident that I could rely on France, including the French who followed Pétain; and I was confident that I could rely on the Allies – by that, I mean that I knew that there were certain things that the Anglo-Saxons would never think of doing. As for the Russians, they were a long way away, and I was certain that they would never come to Paris. Today, I also have convictions, but now they are exactly the reverse. The French people, as a whole, have themselves abandoned any idea of independence; one can feel it, it's unmistakeably so, and there's nothing to be done about it . . . The Americans, as I know from reliable sources, have no intention of using France as a bridgehead. That means that the Russians will come here – and that they, themselves, will be in North Africa, which, this time, they won't give back to us. For France to count, for them to take France into their considerations, it's vital that France should exist, that she should have some minimum of reality, some modicum of substance . . ."

I cannot describe the sorrow on his face – or my own sorrow at hearing him, Charles de Gaulle, speak like that.

"And where's France today; what is she, I ask you? Where's her army? Where's her diplomatic service? She's nothing. France no longer exists. Is it over France's last days that you want me to preside?"

I replied that he was now more than ever the incarnation of the country, that the country saw itself personified in him and looked to him for its salvation, and that, in the event of a foreign occupation, he would be in a far better position to issue orders for resistance if he were Head of State. Whereas, if he had to start organizing things from Colombey . . . He concurred. Then he fell into a long silence, gazing out on the broad landscape of bleak woods and moors. Then with affection in his voice, reflected by his use of my Christian name in his first sentence, he said:

"How do you explain, Claude Maur . . . Claude, how do you explain that for so many years, France has been losing more and more of her greatness, and increasingly each year?"

I thought for a moment before answering:

"I think, General, that it springs from the fact that we have lost more and more of our material strength, when we were once the richest, most populous nation in the world."

He nodded, saying that this was precisely the reason why our decline was irremediable. Then I said – but, as I said it, felt that he embodied too deeply the France of the past to understand me – I said that, in an atomic age, it had become necessary to revise the traditional conception of greatness. That the world was faced with two alternatives: either to perish or to organize itself, and that the organization involved the abandonment of most of the privileges of sovereignty. And, while the hegemony of one country, probably the United States, would still exist, we should have to consent to the inevitable. That peace, a guaranteed peace, lasting and sure, would be no small compensation. That France's greatness would not be assailed because France would no longer have any army or colonies of the former kind. That a future of greatness would still be open to her, which the natural genius of our nation would certainly ensure.

He pretended to agree, but purely out of kindness. For, presently, he murmured:

"No, no, it's just as I said . . . believe me . . . it's just as I said . . ."

Meaning by that, that a nation cannot be great unless it is powerful.

If we had not been interrupted by the announcement that tea was ready, we should have gone on much longer.

He came with me to the station. We talked very little. At one moment, he asked me politely "what I was writing just now", and I gave him a vague answer. We had no common meeting-place in that field. I looked out at the austere countryside of forests, moors and hillsides – this fragment of eternal France – and I longed to say to General de Gaulle, a huge, mute shadow beside me: "Just look at her, this France, so splendidly laid out between her mountains and her seas, laid out for all time: look at her and tell me how she can possibly die . . ." But I held my peace. We parted at Bar-sur-Aube.

Tuesday, 27 August, 1946

On his way to the Ile de Sein, de Gaulle spent last night at his villa in Neuilly, to which he summoned me at 7.00 in the evening. I found him and Mme. de Gaulle installed in the small lodge, and entered the unpretentious ground-floor drawing-room, where they were sitting together. The General took me up to the villa, so that we should not be disturbed. He told me that his lease was up, as we walked along the resplendent, flowery path, and that he did not intend to renew it.

We went into the house, from which all the furniture had been removed. As we climbed the uncarpeted staircase leading up from the devastated hall, he asked me: "Well, what are people saying?", but, fortunately, we reached his study before there was any need for me to reply. I say fortunately, because I felt myself only present physically and quite incapable of making the slightest mental effort even for him.

M. Luizet, the Prefect of Police, was expected at any minute, so our session looked like being short. As he signed the letters, seated at the only table in the room, which was as empty as all the others, I looked out at the lawn and trees in the garden – detached from anything that might crop up between this stranger and me in the next few minutes. I had never seen him so tense. And quite extraordinarily short with me. What indignation when I had the pretension to ask him to sign a presentation book *below M. Gouin,* who had already written a few lines in it! What ill-tempered sarcasm when he showed me a letter, in which Teitgen, the Keeper of the Seals, had replied in official terms to something I had sent on to him ("You kindly drew my attention to . . ." he had had the impertinence to write to the General!) What bitterness when he showed me a pamphlet entitled, *The M.R.P. without De Gaulle*: "They seem to be managing very well!" And he remarked with reference to a violently critical anonymous letter, which he took the trouble to read to me from beginning to end, as he often does:

"I shall answer like Churchill: that it was the result of my inexperience."

He laughed each time, but bad-humouredly, coldly and hollowly. I watched the cars passing down the avenue beyond the garden and thought of other things.

"You know, it's all wrong," he said to me, forcibly, about the proposed Constitution, as though I were unaware that this was his opinion of it. "I'll tell them so in a few days' time. I'll tell them that I find it unacceptable. I'll tell them before it's too late, while amendments can still be made to it, but without the slightest hope."

When I asked him whether he were not afraid that, if amendments were made, the communists might not go back on their decision and vote 'no', he answered:

"What does it matter to me if they do? I should even prefer to have everyone against me again."

Bonneval came in to announce Luizet's arrival and we went down the huge staircase in that empty house, that empty, haunted palace, which might well have symbolized France.

"I've always gone from one setback to another . . ."

When I politely protested, he went on:

"It's quite true; I've always been on my own, with everyone against me. This just makes one more time. A further setback or two doesn't matter. I wanted to give France a motorized army before it was too late, and I failed; I wanted to take Reynaud with me to Algiers, and I failed; I wanted to bring the Empire into the war, and they fired at me in Dakar; I wanted to explain to the Allies that neither Darlan nor Giraud was the right man, and they wouldn't listen to me. And you don't call that having one setback after another? But I'm quite used to it by now, believe me . . ."

All the same, a short while before, he had said to me words that were not those of a man abandoning the struggle:

"I'm opposing the proposed Constitution because, unquestionably, it's the only attitude to take which offers any prospects in the future."

And that was de Gaulle as I saw him on a day when I had no very kindly feelings towards him.

Saturday, 14 September, 1946

It is rather late to describe with my usual precision my last visit to Colombey, which dates back to Wednesday 4 September. Actually, I went to Cannes by train on the following day, and stayed there for four days. I drove down to Colombey with Louis Vallon and Jacques Chaban-Delmas*, whom the General talked to separately and alone several times; so much so that I thought at one moment – and I must admit that I was delighted – that, for once, there would be nothing to record in my Diary. At the beginning of our work session, de Gaulle spoke of "the fine article which François Mauriac had just devoted to him", adding that he did not share its final optimism: parties would always be parties and the M.R.P. was not, never would be an exception to the rule.

When we had finished, he took Vallon, Chaban-Delmas, Guy, his nephew Cailliau (the youngest, I think) and me on a tour of the property. We were able to admire the improvements: the paths were now carefully laid out and edged, and a series of banks gave the garden the appearance of being well looked after. Only flowers were missing – they will be there next year – and creepers on the house. When we reached the end of the park, from which we could see, beyond a low wall, a broad landscape of woods and moors, with the foothills of the Langres plateau in the far distance, de Gaulle pointed to a small patch of field just on the other side of the wall, and told us:

"That's where I shall be buried. Then I shan't inconvenience anyone who's living in the house – and people can come on pilgrimage without being in the way."

Suddenly, Colombey took on new values in my eyes. The ground must be truly hallowed if he wished to lie in it. If he wished to lie in it, it no longer mattered that he had only settled down there a few years before. The property would remain de Gaulle's for ever.

Then we went back to the house and a long, long conference began, at which, apart from a few brief interruptions from Chaban-Delmas (and, at the very end, from his sister, Marie-Agnès, and myself) de Gaulle was the only one to speak. Mme. de Gaulle, seated on a small chair, was knitting in a corner of the room. M. Cailliau, the General's brother-in-law was there, too, with the face of a man burnt alive, calcinated, shrivelled, withered features, hollow cheeks and the lifeless hair that most survivors from deportation camps still have.

For long, long minutes, de Gaulle reverted to most of his customary themes (the impotence and noxiousness of the parties; their congenital opposition to the State; the slow degeneration of political and parliamentarian *mores* in proportion to France's loss of substance; his perpetual setbacks; the noxiousness of the proposed Constitution, etc.) As I was already well acquainted with the matter of his speech, I listened with renewed attention to the form in which he clothed it, being struck by the lyricism of his tone of voice, which became sharp, almost yapping in his moments of greatest indignation or irony, then changed in timbre and rhythm to become solemn and quite low.

"The last time I was in Paris, I sent for X . . . and Y . . . Well, do you suppose they defended the draft of the Constitution which they are backing? Not at all: both of them condemned it. 'Then, why the devil did you lend your name to it; why did you speak in favour of it in the Assembly?' I asked X . . . And do you know how he answered? That he was an advocate by profession and that it was an advocate's duty to defend any cause – even the worst – and see that it triumphed. 'And do you really imagine that it was in your capacity of advocate that your electors sent you to the Assembly?' I asked . . . No, there's nothing to be done, there never will be anything one can do, with men like that."

De Gaulle went on to tell us that he had put a number of 'sticky' questions to them, which they had been unable to answer and which proved the absurdity of the Constitution they had drawn up.

The first related to the decrees governing the allocations of the Legion of Honour, which, in their present form, must either be contrary to the Constitution or contrary to the provisions of the Order's rules. The second related to the case of a President of the Chamber being taken ill or being unavoidably absent at the time of dissolution. After that, there could only be unconstitutional governments:

"They would be just as indefensible as one established by Truman in Dakar or by Ho Chi Minh in Indochina or by Thorez in Paris. But they hadn't thought of that! It shows how seriously they tackled their job . . ."

He reverted, too, to the irresponsibility of ministers, who, in the present state of affairs, were only there *not* to govern; whose only purpose was to do nothing. He foretold, once again, the stampede that France would witness at the first signs of danger:

"You'll see them all disappear under the table as they did in 1940: within an hour, there won't be one of them left."

Then he mentioned the inevitable war, in which France would play no part other than that of helpless victim:

"I don't mind confessing – don't repeat it but, after all, there's no harm in telling *you* – it was by bluff that I was able, in 1940 and the following years, to make the Allies sufficiently apprehensive of France's vitality that they didn't dare to assail our sovereignty. By dint of saying, 'You'll see what you will see', I shook them. They said to themselves, well, maybe . . . But now they have seen – and you can be quite sure that, the next time, *they won't stand on ceremony* – that North Africa, in particular, will be taken from us."

Then he said that the most likely government would be that of Thorez, established in Paris under enemy protection. "If the whole thing has to be repeated," Chaban-Delmas declared, "treason will be so unambiguous, the road to salvation so clear . . ." I broke in there to say – and de Gaulle listened to me very attentively – that things would be less clear than they had been the time before: first, because the Russian troops would not officially be in Paris as enemies or occupiers, and probably not following a defeat; secondly, because, with France finding herself involved in a war that was none of her making, the French would choose, according to their affinities and beliefs, whichever of the two rival imperialisms they preferred; and as the General, himself, had declared that, if the U.S.A. won, we should lose our colonies, there was very little to choose between one side and the other; and finally, because members of the Front Populaire would side with the Russians in all good faith, without any thought of treason entering their heads: in any case, *a clear conscience* would not be the exclusive prerogative, this time, of the resisters in London. There was a communist mystique, whereas there had never been a Hitlerian mystique in France.

But de Gaulle replied that the anti-bolshevik mystique would serve the same purpose.

Last night, when I talked to Claude Guy on the telephone, he told me in that unnatural voice of his, which he puts on when he is speaking in a studied, official manner, weighing every word: "You can spread it around that the Epinal speech will be a very, very strong one. And even that the General intends to give his support to certain lists of candidates. I'll go into more detail when we meet, but there's no need to keep it under your hat; otherwise, I wouldn't be telling you about it over the telephone now."

Assisted by my brother Jean (just back from the Peace Conference, where I spent part of the day with him), I took it upon myself to draft an 'inspired' news-item, which he telephoned through to his Agency immediately. What a scoop! . . . All the papers featured it this morning in so far as their late receipt of the flash allowed. The following paragraphs have appeared everywhere on the front page (and were broadcast on the radio since 11.00 last night) just as I scribbled them down on a corner of the table:

GENERAL DE GAULLE WILL ADOPT DEFINITE POSITION IN ELECTORAL BATTLE.
The A.F.P. newsagency issued the following unofficial report at 9.30 last night:

> *It is confidently rumoured, in well-informed circles, that the Epinal speech will mark a decisive turning-point in the policy which General de Gaulle has pursued up till now.*
>
> *He is expected to announce his intention of supporting, in the forthcoming elections, a list of candidates in favour of the political line he advocated in his Bayeux speech.*

Jean has just telephoned me from the A.F.P. offices (10.50) to say that the news has come as a bombshell. President Vincent Auriol, who was celebrating his birthday yesterday evening at Senlis, was immediately informed by telephone. Considerable agitation is being manifested in political circles.

Saturday, 21 September, 1946
Malagar

On my last visit to Colombey, I found General de Gaulle more cheerful than I had ever seen him and, outwardly, quite calm: I mean

215

that he spoke with assumed indifference about the agitation which his more or less official intentions had aroused in the political world, while actually highly delighted at the turn events had taken. From time to time, in the course of our tranquil lunch, he repeated: "So there's quite a stir in Paris, eh?", in a voice of feigned unconcern that did not conceal his intense curiosity. And when I said: "It's odd to think, General, that it's from this peaceful country house that the storms have arisen, which have shaken the whole of France to the core," he replied, with that air of malice and irony, which he often adopts:

"And everyone imagines this to be a hotbed of intrigue, with conspirators rushing to and fro and goodness knows what else . . . Well, you can see for yourself what it's really like . . ."

What I saw, in fact, were gangs of workmen quietly working in the garden, where new gravel paths had sprung up giving it a distinct air of importance. I saw, too, the broad, austere landscape of the wild countryside. And a small, intimate party round the table, where the talk was of the weather. But when Mme. de Gaulle said: "In six months' time, everything will have calmed down and everyone will have forgotten about it", the General exclaimed:

"Don't you believe it! This is just the beginning of something very big . . ."

After lunch, his ritual cigar gave the General an opportunity to discuss at greater length, as it usually does, the events of the past week. He said that the Constitution might well be passed, but the important thing was that France should know that it would not work.

Thanks to the position he had adopted, the salvation-way to safety would be open and waiting the moment the necessity arose, whereas, if he had remained silent, the inevitable catastrophe would have had far more serious consequences. He confirmed that he would bring all his influence to bear in support of the candidature of men opposed to the unacceptable draft Constitution, no matter to which party they belonged, U.D.S.R. – P.R.L. – Gaullist Union, etc; but that, if the M.R.P. made up its mind to vote 'no', there would be no need of his intervention. I said that the A.F.P. report seemed to me to give the M.R.P. sufficient warning and that, to my mind, M. Capitant's activities were dangerous and liable to prove detrimental to the cause he wished to serve. He replied that he was only responsible for the report, which left me full of admiration for the subtlety and discretion with which an impulse emanating from Colombey had achieved by my publication of the report in question without anything definite being said to anyone:

"If the Constitution is passed," he said, "I've decided to spend the winter quietly down here, working. It'll be a good moment to take up my *Mémoires* again. But, if it's thrown out, I shall no doubt have to intervene very quickly."

Once again, he refused to admit that my strong criticisms of Capitant's movement were valid, insisting that he could not repudiate men who were fighting for his ideas; that, by joining in the electoral battle, the movement was playing the republican game and could not, in any way, be described as factious; that, nevertheless, he still regretted the use of the epithet 'Gaullist' and would make this clear in his Epinal speech; and, finally, that he did not lend his support to any one movement more than another and Capitant would receive no special favours.

Then he mentioned how exhausted he had been last January and how essential it had been for him to retire for a short while, not only to rest but even more to collect his thoughts and say his prayers. He had made a practice of these brief periods of retirement, which were indispensable if he were to maintain his full potential. He also said that there were only two forces in France, at the present moment, capable of governing the country: the communists and himself. And when I expressed doubts as to whether he could govern *without the communists* unless he formally broke with them and *disqualified* them in the eyes of the nation, he murmured:

"There's no doubt, that's what it will come to, sooner or later . . ."

He added that the communists were extremely annoyed by his having tricked them out of the promising position of opponents to an unworkable Constitution which they had been about to take up and had then had to discard when he adopted it.

When we went into his study to work, he picked up the manuscript of his Epinal speech (the one which bore on its front page in his own handwriting, as I noticed the other day, the title: *Speech of Serenity and Clarity*) and read me long passages from it, in which he referred to his attachment to democratic principles, his unflagging efforts towards the restoration of the Republic since June 1940, the fidelity with which he had fulfilled his promise to give the French people back their freedom to choose their institutions and representatives, which enable him to treat *with iron scorn* the accusations of seeking personal power, which had already begun to be directed against him during the epic days, in London. As he read, he glanced at me out of the corner of his eye when he wanted to stress passages, which he considered particularly important, and occasionally broke off, to add a few words of explanation (as, for example, "That's a dig at the communists,") but, for the most part, he confined himself to the silent but extremely explicit commentary furnished by the irony in his sparkling eyes or the malice in a smile that was more mocking than I had ever seen it.

Jacques Baumel, the U.D.S.R. Deputy, called on him in the evening, and it was with him, in his powerful American car, that I returned to Paris.

3 *October,* 1946
Paris

I was present on Sunday 29 September at the Epinal speech, in which the General disclosed in categorical terms, his opposition to the Constitution. When I got back to Paris next day, my father had already sent round to *Le Figaro* an article, which he must certainly have written conscientiously and after due reflection, but which had clearly been influenced by recent meetings he had had with influential members – and no mistake! – of the M.R.P. In short, the article, entitled *In Search of the Absolute,* while showing due deference to de Gaulle, plainly disowned him. Jean, alarmed by the manifestation of this attitude, anti-Gaullist for the first time, (whether its author intended it to be so or not) only managed to persuade him to delete the last sentence: "All things considered, I shall vote 'yes'." In the incredible hurly-burly of the Press, shaken by the puff of wind from Epinal as though it had been a tempest, Pierre Hervé, of *L'Humanité,* mockingly stressed how willing he would be to vote the same way as François Mauriac if he could only understand which way it was, (but how could he fail to?) Meanwhile, fervent Gaullists – such as Professor Pasteur-Vallery-Radot – expressed their grief, by telephone, over this 'desertion' . . . And what will de Gaulle think of it?

I saw him this morning at his Neuilly residence, where he is staying temporarily. Our work session reached its conclusion without him opening his mouth except to deal with specific details of the business in hand. But when we had finished, he offered me a cigarette and began:

"The quite disproportionate stir which the Epinal speech has aroused in the country proves how sick the régime is. It proves, too, that it knows this is so and is fighting against the fever. You wrote about Cocteau in a striking phrase – which is profound, too – that he cheats but cheats in hearts. That's just the diagnosis that poor Z deserves too. The fact is that in the present situation people must either be for Thorez or for de Gaulle, for there is no other choice – and Z, though playing hearts, is for Thorez."

Then I asked him nervously what he had thought of my father's article. He evaded the question with "What do you expect me to think of it?" accompanying it with a sweeping gesture, and passed on to the M.R.P. – (which I had facilitated by trying to explain the reality and vitality which a man like François Mauriac found in the party):

"But I haven't attacked the M.R.P.! It was the M.R.P., after winning largely thanks to me, that immediately betrayed me, through cowardice and weakness, when they only had to stand firm to carry off the prize. For, don't forget, the socialists didn't persist, they didn't waver after Bayeux; no, they didn't dare to. But because Bidault wished to remain in power at any price, the M.R.P. sacrificed their victory. He believes that you can haggle with the communists, he believes himself competent to engage in a battle of wits with them, whereas, in fact, apart from the communists and myself, there is no force in France at present capable of resisting the first flick of a dog's tail. You'll soon see how far they'll be seduced, from one concession to another. It's the Vichy business all over again. For Pétain did not like the Germans, I know that to my cost, having been well enough acquainted with him, I imagine. Laval, himself, did not like them. But the moment one abandons, in matters of that kind, the safe ground of total intransigence, believe me, one is lost. I'm perfectly content with my own position; perfectly certain that I can't fail. But I don't like it! I'm not looking for political disasters. I should much prefer, for the country's sake, that I was mistaken about the future. If all goes well, it won't be I who obstructs them. I shall keep silent. (Am I obstructing them at this moment, am I doing anything to prevent them from governing?) If nothing happens, I shall have pointed out to them the broad, theoretical basis of a good Constitution and that will be all to the good . . . But I'm sure they won't succeed. I'm perfectly sure I shall win . . . Moreover, the country is with me – you saw the crowds at Epinal. They may, perhaps, vote 'yes' out of obedience to their respective parties, but, in their heart of hearts, they are for me and will remain so, just as, in their heart of hearts, most of them who paid lip service to Vichy for ephemeral reasons of opportunism, were for me."

He went on to forecast the results of the referendum in round figures:

"Eight million: 'yes'; seven million: 'no'; nine million: abstentions. And in the face of imminent bankruptcy and war, what's a Constitution worth that's only accepted by a third of the country?"

His figures struck me as being on the optimistic side, but I did not say so, preferring to tackle him from another angle. It was not a question of *fundamentals* (on this point, I was sure that General de Gaulle was quite right; that either "the Russians would be in Paris and that would be the end of everything" – in the words he used this morning – or he would take over control himself and "deliver" – his own words again – "the Republic from the dual menace of fascism and communism"), but a question of method:

"Don't you think, General, that your speech could have been just as effective *without frightening people so much*? Couldn't you, for instance, have stressed the value of political parties, which you regard as necessary manifestations of the nation's leanings? Couldn't you have reassured the fervent democrats, which is what the vast majority of Frenchmen are?"

He replied that the time for half-measures was over: the country must understand the situation and make its choice.

I was struck this morning – and touched – by the particularly affectionate way that General de Gaulle confided in me, and especially by the fact that he bore me no ill-will over my father's defection, which is certainly more apparent than real. After I had left him, Claude Guy told me that the General had just 're-read' ('read' would doubtless be more correct), my *Cocteau,* and praised it highly to him, declaring that I was unquestionably an intelligent critic and showed great promise. I set it down here exactly as it was reported to me, without hiding the pleasure it gave me.

Overburdened by my work, which is all the more exhausting for being so varied, I was greatly relieved when de Gaulle informed me that he had given up the idea of cataloguing his *Speeches,* which I had scarcely embarked on and which had given me much difficulty, with an alarming three hundred pages still to go through.

Guy confirmed this morning that it was due to his intervention – but without his having to press the matter – that de Gaulle had written to the mayor of Epinal to express his categorical opposition to the members of the Gaullist League turning the Sunday of his speech to their own account.

Monday, 21 October, 1946

It has become all the more necessary to keep up my Diary faithfully as my memory grows more unreliable. The spiritual, intellectual and cultural enrichment, which I have pursued ever since I awoke to conscious life, and for which the research alone take up nearly all my *moral* life, accords badly without the account-book constituted by a well-kept Diary.

My 'return from vacation' was not like others had been, as, having only managed to snatch a few brief holidays (four days in Cannes and roughly the same in Malagar and Bayonne), I did not leave Paris during the summer. A number of matters, General de Gaulle's secretariat among them, occupied some hours and sometimes whole days of my liberty. My secretarial work would have taken up comparatively little time if it had not been for the journeys to Colombey which, rare as they were, (two a month on an average), always proved tiring, as I travelled to and from the same day by train or car, and often by both.

So I did have some contact with politics, which interest me to the extent of my interest in de Gaulle. It takes a strong reason like that. I do not gain the same profit from my position in the General's entourage as would anyone else in my place, since politics bore me and I always feel the time devoted to them is wasted. I follow them from a distance and strictly as an amateur, without enthusiasm or any genuine interest, always preferring reading, a walk, the joys of life, and of the intellect or even idleness to the greatest pleasures that they have to offer me. My friends, who are vicariously ambitious for me, would like me to make some effort in the political field. But I feel myself to be incapable of it, and the sight of those who have devoted their lives to it, and who know and like nothing whatever outside of it, is not one to make me change my mind.

My appetite for culture therefore remains my chief preoccupation, along with, of course, the old nostalgia for my own personal work, which I have never yet been able even to realize. For my books of criticism, like my *Malraux*, the final proofs of which I have just finished correcting, are not real *works*, and I attach no importance to them.

I saw Malraux, the other evening, at his house in the avenue Victor Hugo in Boulogne, after having sent him the proofs of my essay on him for his approval. He complimented me on it:

"It's the best thing you've ever done (despite it being the most disjointed of your books: but the writing is nearly always quite exceptional in its style). Julien Benda, who is your exact opposite, produces books which are admirably constructed, but from which the true flame is lacking. What I like in you, is that one is aware of your presence behind the very least sentence, aware that you, yourself, are almost wholly involved."

Thursday, 24 October, 1946

The General's predictions as to the results of the referendum have turned out correct – anyway, in regard to the ratios. There is considerable confusion among the M.R.P., whose members have abandoned it in large numbers and voted 'no'. And now the electoral struggle is in full swing . . . Furious accusations have been bandied about between the strictly obedient Gaullists and the M.R.P. Gaullists who have, moreover, been disowned by the General, in whom the outcasts (so they all told my father during a dinner at Francisque Gay's) are unanimous in recognizing a total lack of humanity. I found it difficult to make up my mind about this diagnosis – for while I am bound to admit de Gaulle's monolithic and ruthless character when 'principles' are at stake, I have often seen him big-hearted towards his fellow-men – always provided that the aforesaid principles are not involved. I have had to defend de Gaulle a lot, particularly at home, where my father, in that way of his of seeing things passionately from only one side and sweeping away every argument that might induce him to take a more balanced view (particularly that of remaining faithful to what he had thought the day before), strenuously espousing the M.R.P.'s cause and had adopted an attitude of absolute severity towards de Gaulle: throwing back at him the empty charge of treason; holding him responsible for the end of a great hope (a Christian party, owing no allegiance to any one class or to the forces of the right); and questioning his political sense and the timing of his main speeches, which would doubtless result in making the communists the largest party in the next Assembly. While I replied to these criticisms, I was nonetheless uneasy, myself, in regard to the direction in which de Gaulle was more and more clearly heading. Our last meeting at Colombey, Saturday 19 October, had not reassured me; far from it.

I had only just arrived (slightly earlier than usual, as the train had left Paris an hour earlier) when he took me into his study and immediately began a long monologue:

"All in all, the result of the referendum is good. The Constitution, with a third of the country endorsing it, is stillborn. No one believes it can work, starting with the parties, who, sooner or later, must give up. Mind you, I'm very pleased that the 'yes's won, all the same, because I should have been placed in a very difficult position if it had been the other way round. Now the parties will end up by dying, no doubt slowly, but indubitably – and, with them, the M.R.P., which has lost the people's confidence by their conduct in this affair and will never be taken seriously again; even if people continue to vote for them for a little time longer. They were in a very strong position; they only had to support me and then . . ."

I did not go on listening, being familiar with the tirade and too tired to force myself to concentrate. When I pulled myself together, I timidly asked a question about his participation in the electoral campaign:

"No, no, I shall let them shift for themselves. What part could I play

222

in it? Yet someone like Bardoux takes it into his head to make the preposterous suggestion that I stand as a candidate, myself . . . Can you envisage it? 'General de Gaulle requests leave to speak . . .' It would be ridiculous! And that wretched Z . . . If you want a laugh, read his last letter . . . I shan't answer it, naturally . . ."

I took the sheet of paper he handed me and rapidly ran through the clumsy expressions of affection and loyalty. In short, it said: – Now that the M.R.P. is campaigning for the revision of the constitution, your place, oh, my beloved General, lies in the Presidency of the Republic, and I beg of you to receive me so that we can settle the details of our common action . . .

"What I don't forgive him is not so much that he took an opposite view from mine, which, after all, he was entitled to do, as the fact that he had the impertinence to pretend that in voting 'yes' they were as fully in agreement with me as if they had followed my advice and voted 'no'."

And he went on to paint a portrait of Z, representing him so hypocritical and insincere, which doubtless had little relation to the truth.

It is this, in particular, that disturbs me about him. That he is right, in the absolute, on most points, seems to me unquestionable. But by the very fact of his always dwelling in the absolute, that it is from this viewpoint that he plans his manoeuvres (for he does manoeuvre), his essentially correct ideas suffer a distortion and tend to become false.

All day long, I listened to him, dilating on his usual themes; during lunch, while he smoked his cigar and at the bottom of the garden, where he came to join Claude Guy and me.

"We were talking about the Gaullist Union, General . . ."

"You can shut up about the Gaullist Union!"

After a long silence, he began speaking of the problem of the parties and the Resistance, abruptly resuming the conversation where he had broken it off an hour before. The three of us stood there for over half an hour, one foot on the stone bench, with the broad, autumnal landscape in front of us. On another little bench, to which he led me for a few moments before I left (Philippe de Gaulle was lingering and we made several false starts before getting away), he brought up the fickleness of the French, 'for whom he had truly done everything he could . . . but he couldn't snatch France back from disaster by the hairs of her head, at the last moment a second time . . .'; the alternating periods in our history of anarchy and respect for authority; and the loss of French substance, which made her salvation increasingly hazardous.

"God knows just how high France might have risen if the French had not been so ungovernable: with our intelligence, our wealth and our influence. For in the past, too, France failed to achieve her destiny. And now . . . now . . ."

Finally, he gave me a summary of what he would say in his next speech:

"I shall tell them, once more: I already warned you, you will have a government which isn't one, a parliament . . . etc."

What struck me as he developed each of his themes was that he was no longer *in touch* with the nation, in whose name he believed himself to be speaking; a hiatus had come into being, with the result that, while he was entirely in the right, he nonetheless was not entirely right.

Astonishing as it may sound, I must record it, since it is true: it was in a dream that the most likely explanation of this state of affairs came to me. Cut off for seven years from any direct contact with the French people from whom he is separated by his actions and his glory, de Gaulle only rejoins them now in a communion which, while remaining total in all essentials, keeps him apart when it comes to matters of detail (so important in practice) relating to what that people really feels and wants. To which, he would no doubt reply that it is only the fundamental communion that has any worth.

27 November, 1946
Paris

I was too busy during the last fortnight to report my last visit to Colombey (8 November) when I wanted to. But on the eve of going down there again and having finally finished my lectures for England, I am determined to record this outburst from General de Gaulle, which he vehemently called on me to testify to, as soon as we had gone into his study to work:

"But really, Mauriac, how can you explain it? How can you explain, after all I've said to them about the unacceptable Constitution, that they can be so imbecile, so base as to imagine that I am capable of the same imbecility and baseness; that I would stand as a candidate for the Presidency of the Republic?"

A little earlier, when someone asked him who, in his opinion, would be at the Elysée, he exclaimed:

"Auriol or Herriot or Ferdinand Lop or anyone; it's of no importance, in view of the lack of authority they'll have when they get there!"

11 *December,* 1946

Salient points of my last visit to Colombey (28 November) jotted down before I forget them. Drove down with Gaston Palewski. Curious accident (wheel almost cut through) which, at first, we thought was sabotage. "So you nearly killed yourselves?" – de Gaulle's words of welcome.

"In the present, and to be hoped temporary, decline of the State," de Gaulle said, "there are three vital points which must be defended at all costs: Germany, North Africa and Indochina. Fortunately, three triumvirs have been stationed there: Koenig, Leclerc and d'Argenlieu."

Implication: his own men. But as he identified himself with France, in his own mind this means: France's men; men who work hard for the cause of France.

At the beginning of our work session, he said:

"It was unpardonable of them not to have followed my advice in answering the question in the referendum. The marxists would have been so badly beaten – by seven million votes to thirteen – that we could have held the elections."

When I said: "But it's never too late for France . . .", he answered: "They're a people who has had enough."

1947

I spent the day yesterday at Colombey. Michelet, up till a fortnight ago Minister of War, brought me back in his car. From the adjoining room there drifted through to me snatches of his conversation with de Gaulle, which I could have followed in details if I had not a horror of being indiscreet, I had time to read the *Letter to a Class* 60 *Conscript,* written by Robert Brasillach in prison, which the General had asked me to procure for him: "Useless to answer that one," de Gaulle had said to me, as he picked up the book, when he was hunting for the latest presentation copies from authors to pass on to me. His laugh, as he said it, would have hurt me had I not known that he can conceal pity and even affection under a burst of laughter.

During one of my earlier visits to Colombey, after the General had said at lunch that, in his opinion N ought to be shot, someone observed that, while he certainly did not desire the death of anyone, it would be a surprising miscarriage of justice if N were saved when Brasillach who was much less guilty than he . . .: Brasillach had resigned from *Je Suis Partout* a year before; he had refused to flee to Germany; he had given himself up . . . and he had been executed.

"Exactly," de Gaulle replied. "N, that's to say, a nobody. Brasillach was quite another matter; the greater the honour, the greater the penalty."

To which I replied that, if he regarded capital punishment as an honour, there was no more to be said.

But the paradox was merely specious to a man like de Gaulle. He had been a reader of Brasillach, a former admirer of Brasillach. And he had raised the penalty to match the height of his disillusion. This did not prevent the refusal of a reprieve to Brasillach from remaining with him as a matter, if not for remorse – for no one can doubt that he made the decision with a clear conscience – at least for his regret. His laugh yesterday was charged with sadness.

I spent Saturday 18 January at Colombey. Two days before, M. Vincent Auriol had been elected President of the Republic; the morning papers reported that M. Ramadier had been entrusted with the task of trying to form the new government; and my father was justified in writing in that morning's *Figaro* that the third Republic was in remarkably good health; it was the Fourth, and the great hopes it had given rise to, that was dead.

I drove down with Gaston Palewski and M. Repesasé. The latter, who fought in the 1914-18 War alongside Captain de Gaulle – told us that his head and shoulders rose dangerously above the level of the trenches' parapets, but that nothing would induce him to bend down. A splendid symbol of a dedicated life. De Gaulle undoubtedly did right in rejecting our advice and refusing to be President of the Republic. If he had been in Vincent Auriol's place today, what else could he have done but call on M. Ramadier, too, and invest with his own glory a government, whose whole justification for existence would be in being presided over by the most reassuring figure the parties could find, in whose shadow to pursue their own private games?

I felt strangely moved at seeing the General again. No doubt because I had been thinking of him a lot during the last few days, when a so-called restored Republic was being established, from which one was more grievously conscious of his absence than ever. At lunch, the conversation turned towards the French and Germans, and de Gaulle said:

"The Germans keep on saying that they represent the masculine side of Europe and that we French have feminine characteristics. Actually, it's exactly the other way round: France is a man – an old man, admittedly – while Germany has all the defects and qualities of a woman: sincere in each of her successive lies, and just as authentically democratic today as she was Hitlerian yesterday."

We then turned to the journey to London made by Léon Blum, during the last few days that he remained in power. De Gaulle was sharply critical of this step:

"The English are extremely anxious to have us as allies. We want the alliance, too. But I've always said to them: before we can achieve the friendly understanding we both desire, there are certain outstanding matters between us that must be decided. It's a fact that your policy in regard to Germany conflicts with France's interests. It's a fact, in every part of our Empire, you are acting in a way that conflicts with

228

French interests. And the English have always been very annoyed. This cause for dissension has always embarrassed them. Bidault at least had enough good sense to leave the matter as it was. But Blum, during the few weeks he was in power, managed to destroy this longstanding attitude of ours, went to London and offered them everything they wanted, unconditionally, for nothing. And came back, triumphantly, with even less coal than we'd been promised before he made the journey. It was typical of him. Blum has never done anything – however well-meaning he may have been – that was not directly opposed to France's interests. When I, myself, was in London, it was certainly not with a view to preparing the way for France's submission."

Later, after he had signed innumerable acknowledgements of New Year wishes, he put down his pen for a moment and said to me in a tone of voice, of which the seriousness, both calm and heartbroken at the same time, moved me (he had never struck me as more objective or less concerned with his own interests in the matter under discussion):

"How do you explain it? Now, after six years – and what years! – a Head of State has finally returned to the Elysée. And he's a worthy man, a truly honourable man. A politician, of course, but with no meanness in him. But when he moves from Versailles to Paris, it's in an atmosphere of complete indifference: not a flag, not a cheer, not a hat raised, nothing: as silent as the sea . . ."

I mentioned France's disappointment, after expecting him and no one else. And when he had not answered the country's call, no one took any further interest in the matter. De Gaulle said:

"It's very serious . . . Even Doumergue, even Lebrun aroused some appearance of enthusiasm. Even take Pétain – when he came to Paris – even Pétain, with all his enormous faults, was welcomed with deep emotion: between France and himself, contact had not been lost in spite of everything."

I can confirm this last statement, for I cannot forget my own feelings on that day – all the more overwhelming for being wholly unexpected. The General went on:

"Today the current has been switched off. There's no longer any kind of contact between the country and the men who represent it . . ."

And he repeated:

"Nothing any more . . . the silence of the sea . . ."

Before resuming his signing, he added:

"Things can't go on much longer as they are, believe me . . ."

When we left, he walked with us to the car, as he usually does, and stayed outside with us for a long time, as there was a last-minute hitch. When the car finally started, he waved us a last goodbye. Claude Guy's face (he was returning to Paris, too) was contorted and he seemed to be having difficulty in holding back his tears. And it was in a tone of deep affection that he murmured: "He's a wonderful man . . ."

Sunday, 2 February, 1947

It was a discouraged de Gaulle, that I, equally discouraged, saw yesterday at Colombey, but he managed to give me back some of my confidence. My discouragement – like his – came from the mediocrity of present French political life, which seems so permanently established that one can see no possibility of a recovery, barring a national catastrophe, and no one would wish for that perilous redemption. I had come down by train with M. Bozel, de Gaulle's financial advisor, in the rue Saint-Dominique, and we were surprised, after leaving a snow-covered Paris to find the country only spotted here and there with white.

The difficult food situation in Paris, which is becoming a pressing problem, was the first topic in our conversation with the General and recurred as a leitmotif throughout the day: as usual, he asked very precise questions about the prices and form of foodstuffs which could be obtained. The visit paid by the Minister, Dupreux, to the Mouffetard district – where he seems to have been very coldly received – gave him a few opportunities to make ironical remarks, but otherwise, he was extremely serious in his examination of the many facets of the problem, which he declared insoluble under a party régime.

At lunch, the conversation turned to even graver matters, until we came to the future of the world. A discussion arose as to whether it was any consolation, as Mme. de Gaulle thought, to know, at least, that France was not the only country to be badly off and sickly. I advanced the idea that it would become less and less a matter of the fate of this or that nation, taken by itself. Sooner or later, as the result of political upheavals, the world would succeed in restoring order, and only the most powerful nations would have their say – the U.S.A. certainly, the U.S.S.R. possibly, and France indubitably not. De Gaulle, who had said nothing for some time, agreed with me and added that it was just this terrible certainty that distressed him so deeply.

However, he went on, the fact remained that both the U.S.A. and the U.S.S.R. were themselves going through a severe crisis. And from the misery of nations we proceeded to the misery of mankind. De Gaulle recited some lines of Péguy and I was struck by the way their thoughts ran on parallel lines – and by how admirably suited the General's voice to lend body and soul to the rhythm:

You have moulded them from this lowly stuff,
Feel no surprise that they are weak and hollow
You have moulded them from this lowly misery
Feel no surprise that they are destitute.

It would be impossible for me ever to forget that moment during a country meal when de Gaulle, on whose right I was sitting, hammered out those lines from *Prière pour nous autres charnels*.

He then mentioned a recent visit he had received from Churchill's son-in-law:

"I told him to remind his father-in-law of something which he had already known for a long time: that only an alliance between Great Britain and France could give Europe any hope for the future – but a real alliance, in which France would be respected, an *entente* between equals, without reservations. This would involve England in abandoning the hostile policy which she has adopted towards France for the last hundred and fifty years, in abandoning her attempt to outwit us. Then, indeed, salvation would be possible. Italy, Spain, Belgium, Holland and Germany would turn to us. But what hope is there of such a policy, when Churchill – backed up by the present British government – has only one idea; to put France and Germany on the same level in order to settle their differences all to Great Britain's advantage, which is the height of stupidity. By doing so, England is betraying Europe on the Rhine, just as she is betraying Christianity in the East."

And de Gaulle spoke in praise of the old, very sensible concept of a *European balance of power*.

With reference to Churchill, Bozel mentioned the military medal, which he had just received, and the resounding refusal it had met with from the General whom they wished to be associated with the honour (together with Stalin and Roosevelt). It was as we were leaving the dining-room, I happened to catch the General's expression, which was glowing with malice at the recollection of his letter of refusal to Léon Blum. He said: "One takes one's fun where one finds it." And he was certainly having fun.

It was, with the coffee and cigars, time for the long monologue, but for once there were a few exchanges. De Gaulle declared that the atomic bomb had saved us. The Russians would have already been in Paris, if the Americans had not possessed this weapon. It looked as though it would be quite a while before the Russians caught up, which should ensure peace for some time to come. He added that if the Americans left Asia (the Russians were already established, or trying to become so, in our Indochina under cover of Ho Chi Minh), it would be in order to fortify their position in Japan; that Japan, largely thanks to her Emperor – was playing an ingenious game, having now placed her hopes of resurrection in America; that the Emperor had been able to retain all his essential prerogatives; had his people well under control and was presiding, in complete collaboration with the U.S.A., over their recovery. Then we returned to France's present difficulties: de Gaulle couldn't have done better, he said, speaking of himself in the third person.

"No man is in a position to set France on her feet again while the means to do so – namely coal – are kept from him. Only, I amused the French with flags. I amused them with the Rhine. In short, I made them forget their miseries and they bore them patiently. Had I been able to remain in office, I should, of course, have been able to do better in certain ways, but the country's decline would have essentially remained the same. Only, I should have made it easier for them all to wait for better times."

At the beginning of our working session (which was divided in two), I cleared my conscience by telling the General that the French had been disappointed in him, from whom they had expected so much, and now in a sort of lover's quarrel were trying to forget him – and even believed they had forgotten him, paying homage to his past but no longer believing in his future. "Well, then, let them forget me!" he exclaimed grumpily. He was ablaze with pride, which he found it difficult to control and which was reflected in every inch of his rigid body. But, almost immediately, he relaxed; almost immediately, he stopped thinking of himself and only of France:

"The *Mémoires d'Outre Tombe* make fascinating reading, first because they are the work of a great mind, and secondly because of the lucidity, born of desperation, one finds in them. Châteaubriand knew that France had lost the secret of his power with the passing of the Ancien Régime – but he was aware that the Ancien Régime had vanished for ever. Whence comes the pathos of his attempts to give France a foreign policy, in spite of everything, when, as he was the first to realize, it was no longer possible."

It was snowing on the wild countryside. As de Gaulle went on signing the letters, which I handed to him mechanically, he said:

"So you would have liked to see me in Auriol's place? Seen me sign d'Argenlieu's recall, since I couldn't have done otherwise? You would have liked me to lend my name to this unstable system? Come to terms with it?"

I said, once again, that at least he would have been there, whereas now it was difficult to see how he could get back, short of a national catastrophe. I spoke, again, of the necessity to play the cards he had been dealt. But he said:

"Why do you want me to try and save a system that is bound to fail?"

Then, after a pause, he stopped signing and looked up at me, where I stood on his left:

"Don't think that I'm not distressed by it, I'm deeply distressed the whole time to see France in this situation."

And when, having misheard him, I said that the French were indeed distressed, he repeated:

"I said that it's I who am distressed; that I'm deeply distressed for France."

And suddenly – the great news:

"I'm going to attempt to form a political alignment – it's the only hope . . ."

I did not ask any questions and he seemed to be talking about something else when he went on:

"A consulship, in a country that is going downhill, isn't the same thing . . . Amusing them with flags . . . But one mustn't allow oneself to get discouraged: one must learn to see far ahead."

I watched the snow falling, thinking that he had just been talking about flags, in the same sense . . . He spoke of a *turning point,* of the day when he refused to carry out the reconciliation with Pétain that the Americans were demanding:

"If I had agreed to collaborate with the Noguès* and the Peyroutons, I should have been cut off from the whole French resistance – at least, from the most effective of them: the communists . . ."

Bonneval came in with Bozel, who had to go back soon. The rest of our work session was put off till later. I talked to Mme. de Gaulle. Bozel's piercing voice came to us from the nextdoor room. I could have listened to it if I had wanted to. Just over half an hour later, Bozel and Bonneval left by car for Paris and I was alone with the General again, as he signed more letters (I had brought him a suitcase-full!) but this time in silence. When he had finished, he got up and paced up and down the room. And there was this snatch of conversation, as I crouched on the floor, trying to cram the signed correspondence back in the suitcase:

"With the French today, one feels as if one were up against a mass of elusive gelatine."

"But gelatine, which is susceptible too, and doesn't want to be scooped up by any little spoon."

"Well, you know, it's like the pigs in the Chicago slaughterhouse,

233

that X was talking about: full of pride and reticence but emerging very satisfactorily in cans by the end of the process."

On this sally, we went and sat down in the adjoining drawing-room. The General went carefully through the Paris papers that I had brought him, while I exchanged a few scattered words with Mme. de Gaulle. Our task was to find a name for an enchanting angora kitten; it kept on jumping into the General's lap and was shoved away again politely each time. It was snowing outside, but had not begun to lie yet. The General commented on the day's news (the Minister of the Interior's visit to the Mouffetard market; the communists' attitude effectively torpedoing the five per cent experiment).

It was 3.30 and my train did not leave till 7.00. I would be with the General all that time. But at the moment, he had not yet finished with the papers. I opened the sixth volume of *Mémoires d'Outre Tombe,* which was lying on a nearby table, at random and read: "I might have been tempted by the role assigned to me: there was enough to flatter my vanity in the thought that I, an unknown and rejected servant of the Bourbons, should become the prop and stay of their race, should stretch out a hand, in their tombs, to Philippe Auguste, St. Louis, Charles V, Louis XII, Francois I, Henri IV and Louis XIV; and should protect with my modest renown the blood, the crown and the shades of so many great men; I alone against the faithless France and debased Europe."

I alone against the faithless France and debased Europe . . . How well I could see what attracted de Gaulle in those magnificent words! By now he had finished his reading and we embarked on a conversation that lasted several hours. First of all, he spoke of his projected political alignment. In about three weeks' time, he will go to Bordeaux to unveil a plaque commemorating Governor Eboué. It will be an opportunity to celebrate Eboué and pay him, for the first time, the homage he deserves. It will, above all, be an opportunity to speak of the Empire. Some three weeks later†, he will go to Bruneval to attend the ceremonies celebrating the memory of a British commando, which owed its whole success to the fact that the Resistance had prepared the way for it in advance from France.

"So all our networks will be present at the ceremony. It will be their day of remembrance. And it will be in that setting that I shall announce the birth of my group. What we must do is start from scratch, begin all over again . . ."

And he went on to sketch the broad outlines of his plan: a mass organization, which will not be employed, remaining more or less

† The order of the ceremonies was later reversed (20.2.47)

virtual, just so long as events do not require it to go into action; a very restricted nucleus of loyal, completely reliable and able men.

"It's a matter of being ready, should the communists take it into their heads to use force or seize power illegally. In that event, naturally, we should respond with fire and sword, but our task will probably be more pacific: to prepare for the next elections and put forward as candidates, in the most suitable conditions, as many of our men as possible; that's to say, Frenchmen determined to devote themselves to the cause of France. And then, my dear Claude Mauriac, you will be one of them; I shall sponsor you."

It was the first time that the General had alluded to the future which he has in store for me, which touched me. But politics are not my strong point and I told him so. I even went so far as to say they disgusted me. De Gaulle smiled, went into his study, came back with Volume 2 of André Rousseaux's *Péguy*, opened it and read out this admirable passage, the streets and rhythm of which could not have been better rendered by anyone:

"Politicians defend themselves, or believe they defend themselves by saying that, at least, they are practical and we are not. But it is here that they deceive themselves. And deceive us. We do not grant them even that. It is the mystics who are practical and the politicians who are not. It is we who are practical, we who *do something*, and they who are, not, they, who *do nothing*. It is we who amass fortunes and they who pillage them. It is we who build, we who lay foundations, and they who demolish them. It is we who nourish and they who are parasites. It is we who produce works and men, nations and races. It is they who bring them to ruin."

De Gaulle looked at me, his eyes sparkling, as though he had won a victory. I reminded him that, according to Péguy himself, all mystics inevitably degenerated into politicians. "I have never indulged in politics," de Gaulle replied, proudly. But, added:

"It's true that I had to resign from office, precisely in order to continue not indulging in them."

And I thought of what he had said to me at one of our last meetings: "The essential thing in politics" (this time he was speaking of politics in the best sense of the word) "is never to compromise our convictions, never try and be clever, never try to outsmart, never be calculating; that is our duty, and also a wise one, for the artful ones always end by being in the wrong." And a short while ago, the strongest argument he could bring to bear against the recent efficacy of the communists was: "that they lied systematically and that nothing durable had ever been seen based on lies." "It appears that mankind, that the exigencies of the human species have not changed in essentials since the beginnings of conscience." But I suddenly recollected that he had not said that with reference to human exigency for truth, but to the fundamental individualism of mankind.

Naturally, I did not accept without comment this plan for a political group, destined to affect so deeply, not only French political life but also the very nature of 'Gaullism'. Starting from scratch is certainly what it is. But, in playing this game, de Gaulle is putting his whole past at stake. Double or quits. And when I say quits . . . In short, I warned the General of the fascist construction which the communists will inevitably place on his movement and I begged him to furnish the least possible grounds for this accusation. I ventured to remind him of the *Croix de Feu,* which visibly annoyed him, though he kept his temper. I made it clear that I only referred to them in order to indicate what should be avoided at all costs. I spoke of the necessity not to offend the French in their democratic beliefs, to which they were fully entitled, since they had gone through all the various experiments. ("Not at all! No one, so far, has tried to do what I want to do!" de Gaulle exclaimed.) I begged him – with so much vehemence that I saw, myself, the absurdity of my: "What you should do is –" and laughed and asked his pardon – I begged him to play the cards available – as the communists are doing so successfully – and start with Parliament. The M.R.P. was deeply divided. A split was possible. Why not provoke it, so as to be sure of having reliable men in the Chamber from the beginning? Reliable? He laughed at my naïvety. Who had betrayed once would betray again – and he was off again on a long dissertation on the M.R.P.'s inexplicable attitude towards him. They had everything to gain by supporting him. Everything to lose by opposing him, as they could now see when they occupied none of the important state offices, to which they could have aspired. What was more, they knew the Constitution was a bad one.

"Be that as it may, the fact remains: I was beaten. The French people let their will be known very clearly. They wanted this Constitution. It's incredible, but it's true. I thought they would understand what was at stake and that it would be sufficient for my purposes to stress the importance of the institutions. But they weren't interested. They didn't understand. Don't forget that the referendum was my invention. It was I who forced it on them. The French people had to choose between greatness and degradation and they deliberately chose degradation. What could I do about it? The French people did not support me. Mind you, I could well have understood the radicals being against me. It would have been only normal. They have always been opposed to greatness. They have always preferred mediocrity. It wouldn't have offended me at all . . . But the M.R.P. How do you expect me to have the least confidence in people like that, who, apart from my brother-in-law, *all* voted in favour of a Constitution, which they regarded as disastrous? What's more, I shall never understand why. No, I've racked my brains, and I cannot understand."

X's visit to Neuilly came back to his mind. ("It's one of the charms of an advocate's profession to defend and win bad cases.") And he denounced the profoundly *displeasing* attitude which people like Poimeoeuf and Chevigné had adopted towards him, when he had believed he had every right to count on their support.

"The new Constitution has at least this in its favour; that it makes dissolution a normal expedient, which can easily be resorted to in case of necessity, much more easily than under the one of 1875; all that is required is a Cabinet decision – after a lapse of eighteen months, of course, not before. But I'm convinced that, with things as they are, eighteen months is the extreme limit. One thing's certain; the present Parliament won't last five years."

Even eighteen months seemed too long to him.

"Besides, in the present state of affairs, any one of the three big parties can make it quite impossible to govern if they want to. And one can always lend a helping hand . . ."

I shall have reported the substance of our conversations, once I have added:

Another reference to the *bluff*, by which he successfully led the Allies to believe, for four years, that France had lost none of her *greatness*:

A brief allusion to *his resistance*: "for there was only my resistance and that of my men . . ."

A nostalgic reference to the monarchic continuity: "the Monarchy was small when France was small. But it was there, preserving the essentials for a better future."

A criticism of marxism, based on the fact that he is not at all certain that industrialization will always exist: "the discovery of new forms of energy may reduce manpower to a minimum and make the conditions of our everyday life extraordinarily easy."

Thursday, 20 February, 1947

I did not carry away a very happy impression of yesterday's visit to Colombey. General de Gaulle only spoke to me again about his plan for a political alignment for twenty minutes just before lunch, when

I was alone with him in his study. He sounded unenthusiastic, not wholly convinced, almost resigned. It was not, it seemed to me, the right frame of mind in which to embark on such a venture, which strikes me as increasingly dangerous, the more I think of it. Time would be on de Gaulle's side if he could see his way to remain silent. Events, sooner or later, would lead to his recall. But I feel that he cannot resign himself to inaction any longer. So he intends to precipitate things – a step that appears to me particularly perilous, since he has never been less popular than he is at the present moment. Actually, it is not so much a question of non-popularity as of being forgotten, and in one whole sector of opinion, of unpopularity which, even if it does not dare to refer to him directly, is no less perceptible. I do not know what lassitude it was (for it was not timidity) that prevented me from bringing these matters to the fore in the course of my long day there yesterday, when I had ample opportunity to revive flagging conversation by this means. I regret it all the more because, from our conversation of 1st February, the General might well have gathered the impression that I was almost wholly in favour of his project. In the excitement of hearing such important news, and hearing it from his own lips, I had, in fact, completely shared his opinion of it. I meant to write to him, but the long draft, which I scribbled down yesterday evening in the train on the way home and copied out again this morning, does not satisfy me.

Here is the substance of what de Gaulle told me about the proposed Movement: it is not his intention to break windows, merely to set on foot an organization capable of immediately taking the place of declining parties in the event of their sudden collapse – and which, should this not occur, would enable him to pursue his aims, in the parliamentary field, by putting up candidates in elections.

I pointed out that his intervention would win much more support if it were to come at the time of some spectacular event, which furnished the country with manifest proof of the danger it was in. But he said:

"Why should such an event occur? Everything might well go on indefinitely as it is now, with a long drawn-out erosion of the State, imperceptible, from one day to the next, but making recovery more difficult each day. The degradation of the national energy and potential is such that I cannot wait any longer. Not that I wouldn't much have preferred to stay away from it all. Politics have never been less tempting than they are at the moment. But I consider that I haven't the right not to attempt the impossible in order to save the country. I may not succeed, but I must, at least, try. I can't abandon France in the state she's in now – even though she may be beyond recovery. We shall see . . ."

After a pause, he went on:

"Ah, it was easy enough to set up the Consulship in 1800!"

I shall not dwell at length on the conversations at table and after lunch between Mme. de Gaulle, Claude Guy and myself. The General spoke of the newspaper strike, of Ciano's diary (which I am reading at the moment), of a holiday he spent as a young man in the house of a worthy German priest and of German politics before and after Hitler. One thing does deserve to be set down: his mention of the fact, without parallel (for nothing of the kind was suggested at the time of the 1914 war) that, during the last war, every Allied nation had the good fortune to have the most remarkable of its sons at its head: Roosevelt, Churchill and Stalin were certainly the best men that their respective countries possessed. He did not mention his own name, but I expected he was thinking that France, too, had had the same good fortune. He also revealed, all through the day, an obsession with the atomic bomb, telling me, before lunch, that the Americans would end by dropping all the ones they had just to get rid of them and finish, once and for all, with this haunting nightmare. He went on to draw a dramatic picture of the world after an atomic war – a world without nations, returning, perhaps to barbarism.

He also spoke of his *Mémoires,* with which, as he told me, he had made good progress:

"I haven't pronounced any judgements since I'm both a judge and a party in the case. I've just stated what I did and why I did it. For example: it might have been better if I hadn't gone to Dakar, but the fact is that I went and with a definite object in view. So I've given my reasons for making the attempt: after that, History will be the judge."

In a temperature below ten degrees, we strolled for half an hour along the gravelled paths of the garden, which had never before seemed so small – bumping continually into the same small wall, hands thrust deep into our pockets, our necks well muffled up, both of us alone, he and I. Now, I must try and reconstruct the substance of his long monologue. I shall give it as I remember it, with the recollection of this or that bush, or a corner of the field bringing back the General's words uttered as I gazed at them with an absentminded eye.

"Ramadier, for whom I still have some respect, governs – or, rather, does not govern (but what else could he do?) with a lot of dignity. Nobody – including myself – could have done anything else – or, indeed, anything at all in those circumstances. Can you see me presiding over Ramadier's Cabinet seated between Bidault and Thorez? I shudder when I think of it. I shudder when I see myself at the Elysée during that four-hour strike of civil servants – police included! – which I could have done nothing to prevent, which I should have had to accept, me! Can you imagine that? I can't get used to the idea. I find it completely intolerable. I don't know what History will say, if there still is a History – for, with the atomic bomb, who can tell? (I often think about it, and ask myself a lot of questions.) I don't believe it will say that I was wrong, that I could have done other than I did since the Liberation. In all conscience, I don't believe I could. Perhaps we've embodied and lived through the last great page of France's history. It may only prove to be a springboard for even better ones – and it may prove to be the last. The French people did not support me. They gave up and foreigners are not mistaken. They recognize that France at last had a man of the required stature and that she had nothing more urgent to do than get rid of him. Even my enemies abroad have realized that France has turned down her great chance. Remember that the Republic in France was tolerated, not loved; that she never won the profound adherence of the masses. The popular acceptance of the Republic only came into being thanks to me. Thanks to me, the Republic could at last profit from the fundamental sentiment which it had always lacked. But it is the Republicans who have turned against me. And nobody mentions this in the Press, nobody!"

We had once again bumped into the low wall which separates the garden from the strip of ground where he wishes to be buried. The General pointed to the skyline beyond the black heath and said to me:

"Look at the solitude of this country in the dark, freezing winter. A time will come when the sun will cease to shine, when this land will gradually grow cold and become even more sombre than we see it now, when ice and darkness will ineluctably take possession of the world . . ."

"And then, General, even the best Constitution will make no difference . . ."

"Nothing will. That's what makes one philosophical, when one thinks of it. The atomic bomb, above all . . ."

Claude Guy came with me to Bar-sur-Aube. While we waited for my train, we strolled up and down outside the station. He told me that the General had gone back to Paris a second time and would be returning next day (today). According to him the operation looks like getting off to a bad start, since those responsible for the Bruneval gathering have been very casual about the preparations, and it may well be a flop. I confided my own fears to him and found he entirely shared them: cut off already from the working-classes, de Gaulle is in danger of widening the gap; he is furnishing his opponents with a most effective weapon: there is much more than his future at stake, there is his past, too, and the 18th June, itself, could be retrospectively spoilt.

20 February, 1947

"General,

"Since you did me the honour of confiding your plan to me, I have been giving it a lot of thought. If I venture today to let you know the conclusions to which I have come, it is not because I have any false idea of the value of my comments. It is only that I feel bound to correct the impression of wholehearted approval, with which our conversation of 1st February may have left you. In the excitement of hearing such important news and hearing it from your lips, General, I fell in with your views, all the more so, because your decision fulfilled my hopes and, at the same time, those of innumerable Frenchmen who find it hard to resign themselves to seeing France deprived of the help which you alone can give her in these difficult times.

"It is not, of course, in regard to this that my opinion has changed. But it does appear to me, on reflection, that such serious consequences can result from an operation of this kind that it is vital not to embark on it without having all the trump cards in one's hand. I am sure that this is your attitude, too. It is in the hope of adding, in my small way, to your information that I venture to write to you today what I wanted so much to tell you at our last meeting on 19th February.

"You know, General, how this step of yours will be interpreted by a large section of public opinion, into which interested advisors have systematically inculcated a distrust of your actions ever since the Liberation. When one remembers that, on 6th February last, a demonstration in Paris managed to collect a relatively large crowd to protest against fascism, of which not even the faintest shadow existed, one can well imagine how delighted the extreme left-wing parties will be to have an opportunity, at last, to brandish, with a certain appearance of reason, this bogey of dictatorship by the right, so convenient to those who are preparing a dictatorship of the left. One must not, therefore, conceal from oneself that the salutary impact of your initiative will be counterbalanced by a corresponding regrouping of your opponents. The operation, therefore, is double-edged and you stand to lose on one battlefield what you have won on the other.

"I only mention this point to place the remarks which follow in their right light. For the risk to be worth running, it is vital that the pros should outweigh the cons. There is no need to dwell on the pros: I entirely agree with your appreciation of the situation. The diagnosis is unquestionably correct; unquestionably efficacious the proposed remedy: the restoration of the State under the leadership of the man who, in fact, saved and represented France during the five years of her ordeal. What remains to be investigated are the conditions surrounding this resumption of control of the country's destinies. And it is here that the negative or even, in my opinion, the positively bad aspects of the proposed action intrude.

"On the con side, what do we actually see? An important section of the nation, the most dynamic and the most powerful, not only materially, but also – and this perhaps counts even more – on the plane of fellow-feeling: namely, the working-classes already alienated from you – there is no hiding the fact – not, of course, as a whole, but in all their elected representatives. If the foundation of a Movement, of which you will be the head, is not to widen the gap between you, it is essential that a powerful wave of sentiment should counteract the propaganda which the left-wing parties will certainly engineer with the aid of their considerable resources. *A priori*, the game is in their favour: they are made a present of the shadow of justification which they need to vindicate their existence and maintain the dynamism of their militants. And it is rather more than a shadow, whether one wishes to or not, that one is bringing into being: it is something that has the appearance of a genuine threat. For, while your intimate associates are well aware of the purity of your intentions, and while they know that it is you who are the true republican, and not those politicians who only denounce a class dictatorship with the idea of replacing it by a party one, there are, among the most well-meaning of your supporters, a large number of men, belonging to the extreme right, to whom fascism will seem to provide a solution. Courageous, sincere men, with a strong sense of duty, but, nonetheless, wellknown in their villages or districts as anti-communists of the blundering, stupid kind so often produced by anti-marxism. It is they and they alone, who, naturally, will assume the leadership of your Movement in their area, immediately giving it a reactionary flavour (in the worst sense of the word) and reviving on a local level the traditional hatreds. We have witnessed a dress rehearsal of this kind of thing in the case of the Gaullist Union, which, as one must never forget, General, did you so much harm, that is to say, did so much harm to France.

"The state of affairs, mentioned above, could only be averted if the wave of feeling aroused by your words were powerful enough to disintegrate, at least partially, or even conciliate this *spontaneous front populaire,* the existence of which in France is undeniable. This would undoubtedly have occurred at the time of the Liberation, had it been conceivable at that moment for you to have assumed the leadership of a party. But then you were representing France, General, and there could be no question of your favouring one category of Frenchmen more than another. On the other hand, after your resignation from the Government, such a move would have been quite possible and, up to a very few months ago, certainly successful. You preferred to try and win the constitutional battle and no doubt you were right. But the fact is that you lost and one does not lose a battle without leaving some of one's prestige behind on the battlefield. The French, as a whole, did not fully grasp your purpose; they did not become involved in the subtleties of a constitutional debate, of which the importance escaped them: they had, for some years, appointed you in their hearts as President of the Republic. When they saw that their beautiful dream was not to come true, they abandoned it, sadly and even with broken hearts, but they abandoned it. The truth is that, to the majority, I even believe to the great majority of the French people, you now stand for the past, a glorious past which they can never imagine once more becoming the present. So, while it appears that conditions have never been worse for attempting to create a Gaullist movement, it seems equally unquestionable that the country would again rally to your name on the first slightly dramatic occasion that brought home to them the dangers threatening their motherland. Slightly dramatic, but above all *spontaneous.* It is vital that events should force the issue, or at least seem to force the issue. The slightest suspicion that you, yourself, or your friends had engineered them would put the dishonest parties in a strong position to ruin the operation by arousing a distrust that would soon turn into hostility. Therefore, in my opinion, it is a question of awaiting this favourable moment, because it will certainly come. In a France, where men of worth are so scarce that a Doumergue could appear as a saviour, what power your name will carry when the moment comes! All the more so, because your silence will have become greater and the consciousness of your absence deeper and deeper.

"I make these comments for what they are worth. They are not necessarily incompatible with the creation of a Movement which could, indeed, be of great use in establishing a machine, which could be counted on when the moment comes. And it gives me another chance to stress the Gaullist Union's bad timing in embarking several months too early, without your consent and in considerable confusion, on an experiment, which it would have been so helpful to have been able to initiate today, without any unnecessary noise and with your acknowledged but discreet support, so as to encourage the faithful without alarming the enemy. It has become more difficult, after the spectacular failure of M. Capitant's movement, to start it up again. You are compelled, just because of this precedent and to avoid confusion, to put yourself even more in the foreground, despite the risk of providing your opponents with ammunition. But, after all, you have already decided to do so. I venture to hope, however, that the date has not been irrevocably fixed and that it is still possible to defer it, if the preparations have not been completed down to the very last detail. Because, in view of the risks I have mentioned, it is very important, should you feel you should nonetheless embark on the venture, that nothing whatever should be improvised. The least flaw in the mounting of the programme and the material organization of the movement will be exploited with all the more cunning because, in the event of your meeting with a setback, your enemies will be rid for ever of the danger you represent. The Xth of April will rob 18th June, not, of course, of its historical value in the past, but of its historical potential in the future. It is for you to judge, General, for I have no rudiment of information on the subject. But even if men of absolute loyalty, proved discretion and spotless reputation had meticulously organized the event (by ensuring solid bases from which it could be launched, so that from the very beginning, impressive numbers should hear your appeal and be able to respond to it), even if all these conditions were fulfilled, the sensational event (if sensational event there must be) would still take place in a period of debility without a spark of brilliance and an attitude towards yourself more indifferent – when not actually hostile – than it ever was before.

"I apologize, General, for this over-long letter. No doubt, I have abused to some extent the confidences you were pleased to make me. I beg you to regard my intervention as only another proof of my inalienable devotion.

Claude Mauriac."

Friday, 7 March, 1947

Having been told, as I got out of bed, that General de Gaulle was expecting me at 10.30 at the Hôtel La Pérouse, where he had spent the night, I was ushered yesterday at the appointed hour into a large room, though sad and bare, at the far end of which, the General was sitting forlornly in front of a small writing-desk, lost in thought. I had no idea where he stayed during his mysterious trips to Paris, of which, in the absence of newspapers (the strike is still on) there is a lot of talk in the capital's political circles. So it was here, behind the Majestic Hotel, which I could see from the window, at the corner of two deserted streets: in this relatively luxurious suite (at least another room and an inner anteroom) where Claude Guy's attentive hand (I assume) had placed some carnations in a vase and three bottles of apéritifs and liqueurs on a tray.

The General's welcome was icy and he signed all the letters without a word, looking so extraordinarily haughty that it was almost laughable. I thought for a moment that he had a grudge against me personally – for I had never known him so surly towards me – and I was wondering what I could have done to upset him when, at the conclusion of our work session, he began to talk to me about the situation with such overwhelming bitterness that it was obvious that I was not involved.

"Have you seen: they've got rid of d'Argenlieu? And sent in his place a deputy, for the sole reason, as they've admitted, that he is a deputy. So it's officially admitted that you have to be a deputy to fill the post of High Commissioner in Indochina, at a moment when it's vital to take all possible steps to retain Indochina. It's the end of the Empire, there's no changing the fact. We shall lose the whole Empire: they're giving it away, little by little, in shameful deals and bartering. What hope can one still cherish? This régime secretes shame and ignominy. It is its natural function. And no one dreams of protesting."

A glance at the empty pavement, where a solitary passerby turns the corner of the street.

"And the country accepts occupation by the parties with the same apathy as it displayed in accepting the German occupation. For it's the same thing. Exactly the same thing."

I told him of the death of Champetier de Ribes* which seemed to foreshadow, I added, that the communists would take over the Presidency of the Council of the Republic.

"There's no doubt about it. Which means, General, that the M.R.P. have lost everything, that they haven't a single important post in this Republic in which, at one time, they were the largest party: neither the Presidency of the Republic, nor the Presidency of the Chamber, nor the Presidency of the Council."

"Don't you believe it! They've got Bidault at the Foreign Office . . . To think that eight million French people voted M.R.P. for this sole purpose: to allow Bidault to remain at the Quai d'Orsay! And when the next elections come round, they'll do the same thing."

I spoke of possible splits, to which he replied with increasing bitterness:

"No, they're all alike. They are all built to betray. If only there was a grain of talent among them! A Poincaré, a Clemenceau, a Barthou, even a Briand had talent. There's a lot to be said against some of them, one could have a lot of reservations but still they had talent. But those others have nothing, absolutely nothing. Not a single word that's been uttered in the last two years is worth remembering. And that Anglo-French alliance is scandalous! The terms of it are appalling: once again, we are making pledges without getting anything in return. We are bound – they are not: just as it was after the other war. What's more, the existence of a Germany is officially recognized, before the treaty that will give a ruling on the matter, even before the Moscow conference. It's agreed that there is a Germany. We, ourselves, have declared as much in a diplomatic document, just when our thesis is that there should no longer be a unified Germany. And if only the English had given us something in exchange: but nothing. And to choose Dunkirk to sign the alliance – when one recalls what happened at Dunkirk – it's laughable! And Reynaud there! I have nothing against him, but, after all, it was he who betrayed the English – he who repudiated the Alliance. And Blum, who, at the moment of the disaster, hadn't a word to say. He may have protested in matters connected with parliament and politics, but he hadn't a word to say about France in June 1940. Not a single one! It seems to me that it's not thanks to Blum nor to Bidault that France has retained the friendship of the English, but to me. Isn't that so? When I think that Bidault had the cheek to send me a telegram from Dunkirk! It is always the same old story: trying to make the M.R.P. electors believe that the party leaders are on good terms with me. But if he dares make that telegram public he'll get a slap in the face in front of the whole world. I've prepared an answer that I'd like to let you see, an answer that . . . But he won't publish the telegram. He won't dare!"

We then spoke about B, whom the High Court has just sentenced to five years' hard labour. I thought it was too much. But the General did not agree with me: he considered him guilty.

As I left him, I gave him my *Malraux*, which has just come out. Guy told me that de Gaulle was delighted yesterday evening with his jaunt to Paris, but had a sleepless night. The only reason, according to Guy, for his ill-humour.

Sunday, 9 *March,* 1947

The other night, amidst the crowd at a very smart gathering (it was the opening of a bookshop, which Georges Poupet had managed to

246

persuade all his influential connections to attend) André Malraux honoured and delighted me by wedging me into a corner, and I was able to confide to him all my apprehensions concerning de Gaulle's plans. I saw him again yesterday evening for a long time at his villa in Boulogne, and he completely reassured me: the whole thing has been postponed, de Gaulle having given in to his and Soustelle's objurgations. (Soustelle and he are the only men, according to him, with whom de Gaulle does not only indulge in monologues – Guy counting as one of the family.) So the General will not speak of the proposed Movement at the Bruneval ceremonies. Malraux agreed with me about the danger of the General's impatience – but also saw the force of his argument: "How can I wait until France has ceased to exist before I try to save her?"

We paced up and down his studio for two hours and, for the first time, we occasionally exchanged ideas. I mean to say, that, as Malraux put questions to me, which I tried to answer – and I, myself, put some questions to him – his usual monologue was transformed into a dialogue. He had asked me to come in order to speak to me about my book on him and also about General de Gaulle's plans since, up till now, I have always taken a genuinely very humble view of my critical works – the only existing ones so far – I was surprised to find him attaching so much importance, not only to the book I had devoted to him, but also to all the others since my *Jouhandeau*, which is ten years old. I know that he has a direct interest in my last book, but I was still delighted to hear him speak about it as a work of some real merit, even outstanding, which should, he assured me, encourage me to persevere with my criticism, to which I had a very personal approach. When I asked him what practical effect such a study might have on the author to whom it was devoted, he conferred that it would not be negligible:

"Your book compels me to recognize what is the real substance in my works, and enables me to discard all the extraneous matter, to which I had, weakly, continued to attach some value. You know, there aren't many good critics; only eight or ten in the last twenty years. It isn't much."

17 *March*, 1947

When I got out of the car, which had come to meet me at the station, at Colombey, Claude Guy, just that moment back from Strasburg, where he had gone to make the initial arrangements for the General's next trip, was with de Gaulle; he left again at once for Paris. It was a gloomy lunch. I was thinking of matters other than the politics which are the General's only preoccupation: he envisages everything from that angle, even economic geography and history, of which he is also fond of talking. He said:

"I shall be very blunt again at Strasburg. But, I shall merely repeat again, as always, the same things, based on: 'I warned you.' The tone of the speech will be calm but categorical. Perhaps they'll understand me better this time? It's not too late: it's never too late."

During the first paces of the walk we took after lunch, both of us wandering aimlessly up and down the same narrow paths or strolling to and fro on the same rectangular patch of field, he asked me: "Don't you think I'm right to tell them what I think, in Strasburg?" I answered in the affirmative, but with the strict reservation that he should not yet announce the formation of the Movement. I thought that this had been settled – after Malraux had told me that there was no longer any question of his doing anything precipitate. But de Gaulle, looking both annoyed and surprised, asked me in a manner that left me no loophole: "Why not? Explain yourself!" He allowed me to speak for a long time, listening attentively to my reasons and interrupting me now and then with a few words, which, under the cloak of contradicting me, actually invited me to express my ideas more precisely.

So I told him what was troubling me, reluctantly and without choosing my words, but was careful not to conceal any of my apprehensions. Broadly speaking, I declared that, since it seemed certain that a word from him would be sufficient to electrify a large part of the country at any time, he must not make the mistake of uttering it too soon. After a magnificent start, the Movement might well become ragged and distorted if events that would justify it were long in coming. The extreme left would gain a vantage-ground from it, which it would exploit all the more easily because there was no altering the fact that, on a regional and local level, it would be men known for a long time to be strongly right-wing, who would from the *cadre* of the Gaullist Movement. In order to avoid reanimating the parties, by providing them with a justification for their existence, and running the risk of a setback, which would no doubt amount to a final defeat – for by becoming leader of a party, de Gaulle would cease to be a myth and even his past would be retrospectively misrepresented – it would be better to wait either for his return to power in response to a public demand (and time was more and more on his side), or the proximity of elections, not yet foreseeable in the immediate future, when he would be able to *take part in a campaign and play the game on a parliamentary level* with all the benefit of surprise and a favourable psychological climate. Let him, by all means, establish the *cadres* of the Movement

248

while he was waiting. But to give it official standing now, would, in my opinion, be premature.

De Gaulle listened carefully, without actual approval, but, equally, without raising any serious objections. I had the opportunity of replying to his statement that he could not look on at the disorganization of France indefinitely without trying to arrest it, by saying that I scarcely needed to remind him that a matter of six months or even two years more had not the slightest importance in history. He should not forget that his past, itself, was at stake and that if he failed (a semi-success being equivalent to a failure) it was the end of the de Gaulle myth, and consequently, of his possible role as saviour of the country. And I thought of what André Malraux had told me the other day: "Though one imagines that one hasn't made any impression on him, what one says influences him obscurely, and, it's happened more than once that he's paid attention, without acknowledging it – even to himself, perhaps of the use eventually made of it to save the country – to advice that's been given to him."

Meanwhile the shy young tips of the first crocuses were breaking through. A spring air was wafted over the countryside that was becoming brighter. Two fan-tailed pigeons, Mme. de Gaulle's latest acquisition, were hesitating on the threshold at their cote, not yet venturing to savour their newfound liberty.

We went back to work. I caught sight of the sheets of his Strasburg speech lying scattered on his desk and the first words, which I read stealthily, called on people to appreciate clearly the situation facing them. After we had finished, de Gaulle remained alone in his study till tea-time, no doubt working on his speech. Then, for about an hour and a half, he enjoyed himself by rewriting History for the benefit of Bonneval and myself. Supposing Pétain had won North Africa in November 1942 . . .

"I should have been extremely put out, because he would immediately have had everyone on his side; the Anglo-Saxons would have immediately left me in the lurch, as they did at the time of the Giraud affair, but to an even greater extent; a large part of the Resistance would have refused that kind of arrangement; the communists would have taken over control; then we should have had our own Tito; and the Germans would have come to a *sub rosa* understanding with the communists, agreeing to close their eyes to what was going on as long as it did not inconvenience them too much, and people would have been occupied by the civil war and not the national one."

De Gaulle spoke about the newsreels which he had seen in London, showing Pétain's triumphant progress through the free zone; at the time, they had affected him very much. He explained the reasons why the French people in the unoccupied area had trusted in Pétain; and reverted once again – and so did I – to the Parisians' attitude towards Pétain when he paid them a visit shortly before the Liberation, but exaggerated the warmth of their welcome, and I put the record right on this point. Then he said: "If Hitler had first attacked in the East . . . There's no doubt, he'd have quickly finished off the Russians and the Allies might have made peace . . ."

I was struck once again by the admiration, with which he spoke of the German people:

"You'll hear from them again in ten years . . . For this last time, they fought to the bitter end with extraordinary courage and stubbornness."

> *Sunday, 30 March, 1947*
> *Malagar*

The speech at Bruneval. Felt very excited and very anxious, but delighted all the same. My father suspicious. This time, de Gaulle has crossed the Rubicon. I shall stay with him to the end. Loyalty is the only faith I have left.

> *Saturday, 5 April, 1947*

On my return from Malagar, on the morning I was due to leave for Strasburg, Pierre Brisson was bent on seeing me. He spoke with great sincerity of his carnal love for democracy; and his obsessive hate for individual power. I tried to reassure him, citing how well I knew the General, but failed to convince him. He was not at all surprised when I told him that the last words of the Bruneval speech had also aroused my father's suspicions. I said that the lukewarm attitude on the part of *Le Figaro* would amount to hostility, and that the time for half-measures was past. It was up to him, if he wanted to, to string along, in the name of democracy, with the only antidemocratic party: the communists.

> *Sunday, 13 April, 1947*

I was in Strasburg last Sunday and Monday. I was present on the balcony of the Town Hall, from which de Gaulle spoke, at Monday's big speech. I shall never forget the huge crowd gathered on the Broglie and the rapture provoked by his own rapture, especially when enthusiastic 'calls' three times brought the General back on to the balcony. For the first time, I saw a crowd of that size all looking up at the spot where I was standing, myself, (between André Malraux and Jacques Soustelle): I had an astonishing impression of an immense assembly of deathmasks the faces at that distance, looking like white skulls with large black holes where the eyes should have been.

Our headquarters were at the Maison Rouge, but I slept in a nearby hotel, sharing Rémy's (Renaud Roulier's) room on the first night and staying on in it after he left.

A lively meal with the Pasteur Vallery-Radots, Louis Vallon, Gaston Palewski, Diomède Catroux, the Lavorelles, (Madeleine Carol), Harold King, etc. A dispute with Guy, who arrived exhausted at the restaurant Valentin on Sunday, at the end of a day that had gone slightly wrong, the crowd having failed to get into the Place Kléber. Conversation with André Malraux, on Monday before the official luncheon at the Town Hall. Shook the General's hand, just before he went down to the balcony on the first floor, when, with Malraux and Palewski, he was watching, unseen, the immense, patient crowd. Came back on Tuesday in Vallon's car with Patricia Guy and the Albert Olliviers whom I saw a lot of, too. Explored Alsace, where I had never been before. I went as often as I could to the Cathedral, where I attended High Mass on Sunday morning, and, that same evening the ceremony presided over by de Gaulle and Caffery*.

The day before yesterday, Friday, about 5.00, I went to Malraux's, where Guy and Bonneval were, too. I was immediately shown into the room where Malraux received me the first time I came to the house. A man was sitting at the low desk, on which I espied Malraux's passport: it was de Gaulle. The brightness of his face, and the cheerful serenity of his voice, did me a lot of good. The rage of the aroused Press, and the uneasiness of Pierre Brisson, whom I found even more wary after Strasburg than before, had influenced me in spite of myself, all the more so because I had always believed the formation of the Movement to be premature. But a few words from the General were enough to reassure me: such were his powers of persuasion, and the effect of which I had never felt so strongly before.

While he signed the letters I handed to him, he spoke, first, with considerable satisfaction of the time he had spent in Strasburg, and then referred with malicious pleasure to the commotion he had caused in the muddy pond:

"It would be amusing if it weren't the symptom of such tragic decay: it only takes a few words to send them into a panic! It proves the seriousness of the illness from which they are suffering . . ."

"But those few words weren't uttered by just anybody, General. How could they help being alarmed?"

"Mind you, it won't come to anything. They've quieted down already. Apart from the socialists, who have flown off the handle, as usual, like imbeciles, which will cost them several million votes – none of the parties has reacted. Even the communists have kept quiet. I have every reason to believe that the Left-Wing Conference will declare itself in agreement with the Strasburg speech which will prevent the M.R.P. from throwing out those of its members who join the Movement. They'll all be forced to show the same discretion, for the Movement stands for at least eight million votes, which they won't be anxious to lose."

I then observed that the only danger – but a grave one – lay in the formation of some kind of counter-movement of a Front Populaire type, but de Gaulle did not regard this as a possibility.

"What will affect France's domestic policy now is primarily circumstances abroad. A Front Populaire is no longer possible once socialists and communists are each dependent on a different *bloc*. That's why the S.F.I.O. passed the motion against me of which you're aware: so that the communists shouldn't get in ahead, and call on them to sign the joint declaration with themselves. But now that they're covered, they won't take any further steps, you can be quite sure!"

Once again, he repeated that, if the parties could deal with matters themselves, he would be the last person to stand in their way, that nothing would please him more, but that he did not believe they were capable of it. He reverted to the extreme difficulty of the situation and admitted that there was nothing to prove he could do much better, himself, but he had to make the attempt. He informed me that a communiqué, making the formation of the Movement official, would be published that same evening, and that each application for membership would be closely examined before being accepted: "I prefer to have fewer members rather than allow doubtful elements to be associated with us." Finally, he told me not to put 'Colombey-les-Deux-Eglises and the date' on the top of letters I gave him to sign, but only the date:

"You understand, one day I'm here, another I'm there: in a way, I've the gift of ubiquity . . ."

And, with a magnificent burst of laughter, he added:

"In fact, what you should put is: 'Somewhere in France, the . . .' "

When I came down again, the sheets of paper covered with the General's handwriting, which had been scattered all over André Malraux's desk when I arrived, had disappeared. They had been replaced by three sheets from a notebook, which Malraux and Guy asked me to read and give an opinion on. It was the text of the communiqué which the General had mentioned to me earlier, in three different drafts, and was not, after all, going to be published for another few days, despite what he told me. I chose two of them, which seemed to me equally good. Malraux was delighted: the one I had rejected was the General's, from which Claude Guy and himself had each drafted his own version (at his request).

André Malraux is now fully involved with de Gaulle. I told him: "Once again, you're sacrificing your own work . . ." But he said: "I work at night. I'll go on doing so as long as I have to." Then I went off to *Le Figaro* to try and reassure Pierre Brisson.

Friday, 18 April, 1947

I went to see de Gaulle in a new house in Paris yesterday – at the corner of the Avenue Mozart and the rue Georges Sand. After the Malraux villa, M. Vendroux's, the General's brother-in-law's small flat seemed even more cramped than it was. Guy was jammed into an ante-room, which was really just a dark corridor. Bonneval was seated in a corner of a bedroom where two beds took up all the space. And in what should, I suppose, be called the drawing-room, at a wretched table, was de Gaulle. He was morose, gloomy and irritable. I now know this aspect of his character and am no longer surprised when, instead of his usual amiability and courtesy, he displays a coldness only just short of rudeness. I informed him shortly of my vain efforts to persuade the staff of *Le Figaro* to bring a little more understanding to bear on his aims. (I shall return to that later.)

"There's nothing to be done! There they are again, more suspicious than ever: I give up! What's got into them?" de Gaulle asked me, looking up angrily.

"I can explain it all in two words, General, always the same two: personal power. It's impossible to shift them!"

The General did not deal with this main point – why should he, when he leaves the task to us, we who spend our time defending his aims and good faith? – but exclaimed instead:

"Well, what do they want? Would they rather watch France die? Do they want to see her finished? Are they deliberately turning their backs on salvation? For things are going to rack and ruin; the Empire is falling to pieces everywhere: and never has the international situation looked like becoming more embittered."

Referring to what took place yesterday at the Cabinet meeting (the communist ministers walking out to disassociate themselves from the measures taken against the Madécasse deputies responsible for the recent riots in Madagascar) I asked him if he did not think that the communists wanted to and would leave the government.

"But why should they, when it's generally accepted that they should be in power and in opposition at one and the same time? They'd be wrong to stand on ceremony. It's understood that there's to be no governing, that the government's there in order not to govern. It's a recognized fact. People have already stood for the communist deputies disassociating themselves from the government's policy in Indochina, while keeping their ministers in their posts, and everything will go on in the same way."

He then questioned me about the 'start' of the R.P.F.* Indirectly, without appearing to do so, asking the questions with an air of indifference, beneath which I sensed the extent to which they preoccupied him. Had I been to the headquarters? What was the atmosphere like there? and so on. I knew very little about it, did not dare say so, and gave him vague answers. He looked angrier and angrier and did not say another word, signing the letters I handed him in silence, glancing at them – or hardly so. There were a few passers-by in the Avenue Mozart. Young workmen profiting by their lunch-hour (it was between midday and 1.00) to warm themselves in the sun, sitting on a low wall, close to a large blue letter-box that I knew well. (The entrance to M. Vendroux's block of flats is from the rue Georges Sand; the flat is on a corner, on the mezzanine floor, just above a grocery.)

After we had finished, de Gaulle talked in the dark corridor in a flat, unfriendly voice, to Soustelle, whom he had summoned by telephone. Mme. de Gaulle, Guy and Bonneval studied a map in the bedroom, into which M. Vendroux entered for a moment. I imagined that the first days of the France Libre in London must have been very much like that.

Guy walked with me to my nearby rooms. I told him about my efforts to convert Brisson, and the luncheon arranged by Palewski at the Café de Paris, by the end of which P.B. seemed almost convinced. But on the same day (last Monday) the General's communiqué appeared, announcing the formation of the R.P.F. Brisson was once again disturbed by the 'personal tone' of the document. On the other hand, my father, who came back from Malagar on Tuesday night, was so much incensed against de Gaulle that he accused Le Figaro (discreet and reticent as it is) of excessive Gaullism. Who was astonished to find himself harshly upbraided on the telephone? It was Brisson. But they

* Realignment of the People of France.

were quick to explain and clear up their misunderstanding, becoming united in the same hostility. A hostility which, moreover, is general.

Claude Guy reminded me of our own apprehensions and the conversation we had outside the station at Bar-sur-Aube. All our fears had proved justified: the lack of preparation of the Movement's substructure; the untimeliness of its formation, inevitable compromises and the risk of it failing. We agreed about the sadness of it all. It is not pleasant having to defend all day to third parties an experiment, of which, in one's heart of heart, one disapproves. Not, of course, that we have any doubts about the General's republicanism, which seems to present the only chance of salvation for the parliamentary Republic. But we believe there has been a tactical and even a strategic error.

As far as I was concerned, it was with no enthusiasm that I joined the R.P.F. (which I certainly would not have done had I not been so closely linked with de Gaulle). It is distressing to find myself drawn into a camp, which is not the one I would have chosen. The truth is that the real French people – the militant, alive, dynamic and friendly part of them – are on the other side. A nostalgia all the more painful because I know enough about communist trickery not to yield to what would draw me into the communists' camp if I were willing to go. And because there is a bond of loyalty between that man and myself. And because I have such confidence in him that I hope, in spite of everything, that I am wrong. But his discouragement yesterday did nothing to reassure me.

Palewski, whom I met in the evening, treated my fears with an airiness that struck me as almost frivolous. He had seen de Gaulle in the afternoon and assured me that he had found him in good fettle and optimistic. According to him, the Movement has got off to a very good start. Gaston even talked about communist party cards being torn up ostentatiously, which seemed to me to display a deliberate blindness, which was extremely disturbing.

All this took place in a radiant Paris, where Spring has never been more beautiful.

Sunday, 27 April, 1947

General de Gaulle held a Press conference last Thursday at which he appeared more brilliant and persuasive than he has ever been. The irony with which he left matters to the 'objectivity' of the journalists seemed to be fully justified, judging by the next day's papers. *Combat*, from which the too pro-Gaullist Albert Ollivier had just been sacked, and *Le Figaro* were extremely guarded. So much for all the trouble he had taken to reassure them, at some length, on each of the precise points which had aroused their democratic uneasiness. I make no mention of the unfairness of the party newspapers, which was only to be expected.

The next day towards midday I met de Gaulle in the Avenue Mozart. When I mentioned my discouragement after reading the morning Press:

"There's definitely nothing to be done with those people, they have – there's no doubt about it – chosen mediocrity and servitude. Therefore, it's in spite of them and in opposition to them that we must try to arouse, to save the country. Believe me, it's June 1940 starting all over again; there's the same wilful blindness, the same abdication."

I had already spoken to him about the previous day's Press conference and brought up the subject several times; but he still asked me: "Were you there, yesterday?" And when I answered in the affirmative, went on:

"I didn't do badly, did I? So what is it they want? What's missing? What more does it take to make them understand? They see that there's virtually no government, that the Empire is disappearing, that war is imminent . . . But they're just resigned to it all. And people tell me that my intervention has come too soon!"

Then he added, spitefully:

"As for the M.R.P. I'll wring their necks! This time, I'll have no scruples. I'll take away their electors. This duplicity has gone on too long."

And as we parted, he said:

"The fact is that events control the issue, and they are not such as the régime can survive."

An eye-catching headline in *France-Dimanche*: CLAUDE MAURIAC AGAINST FRANCOIS, HIS FATHER (with reference to my Gaullist loyalty and his M.R.P.ism). But as he left the reception, given the day before yesterday at the Boeuf sur le Toit by the Table Ronde, he said to me:

"I'm like Louis XIV, making a point of being seen with his brother when rumour had it that they'd quarrelled."

And he burst out laughing. It certainly will not be politics that set us at loggerheads!

Thursday, 1 May, 1947

Yesterday, de Gaulle was smiling and relaxed when I saw him again in M. Vendroux's rue Georges Sand flat. The last time I was there, a diplomatic corps car was waiting outside the front door and I heard

23. Colombey les deux Eglises.

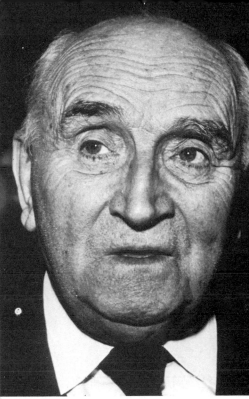

Above, left to right:
24. Rear Admiral Thierry D'Argenlieu.

25. Professor Raymond Aron.

26. Albert Camus.

27. Paul Claudel.

Below, left to right:
28. Léon Blum and Alfred Duff Cooper.

29. Henry Bordeaux.

30. General Corniglion-Molinier.

31. (Right) *Admiral Darlan.*

32. (Far right) *Jacques Duclos (third from left).*

33. (Below) *Daladier (centre).*

34. (Below right) *Capitaine Guy (third from right).*

35. (Right) *Ilya Ehrenburg.*

36. (Below) *André Gide.*

37. (Left) *Philippe Henriot.*

38. (Below) *Edouard Herriot talking to Jules Moch.*

39. (Right) *Paul Léautaud.*

40. (Far right) *René Mayer with Vincent Auriol and the members of the January 1953 Cabinet.*

41. (Right) *Charles Maurras.*

42. (Far right) *Jean Monnet.*

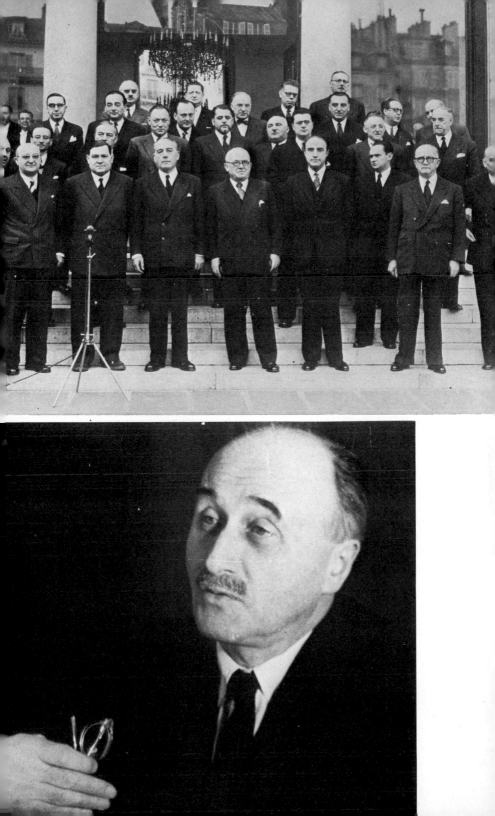

43. (Above) *Jean Paulhan.*

44. (Above right) *André Philip (left) and Robert Schumann.*

45. (Right) *Gaston Palewski.*

46. (Far right) *André Pinay (right) and Edgar Faure.*

Above, left to right:
47. *Paul Ramadier (second from left).*

48. *Jean-Paul Sartre.*

49. *Maurice Schumann.*

50. (Right) *Jules Romains and his wife Lyse Dreyfus.*

51. (Far right) *Maurice Thorez (right) and Laurent Casanova.*

52. (Above left) *General Weygand with Reynaud (third from left) and Pétain.*

53. (Above) *General Strike, August 1953.*

Below, left to right:
54. M. Tillon.

55. Paul Valery.

56. Virulent left-wing anti-Eisenhower campaign.

TWO OF THE
MOST MEMORABLE
MOMENTS
57. (Left) *the
reception given
Eisenhower and
de Gaulle.*

58. (Below) *My
father receiving
from the General
the Grand Cross
of the Legion
of Honour.*

the General, in the next room, saying good-bye to someone ahead of me – whose Anglo-Saxon accent I could not identify – with an "Au revoir, your Excellency . . ." This time it was the honourable M. Capitant, whose place I took.

A moment before I walked in, a messenger sent by Philippe Barrès had told me that at the conclusion of the morning's Cabinet meeting, Minister Ramadier had virtually handed in his resignation, after the communist ministers had declared their solidarity with the Renault strikers. This was a face-saving measure, for the strike had been decided on not only in spite of them but against their advice. I passed the news on to de Gaulle, who with that air of indifference he often assumed when he is deeply interested, made various prognostications on the turns the crisis might take. He went on then:

"In any case, there won't be any real solution, because the situation is insoluble. The whole problem for the party men lies in trying to remain in office. Don't believe they've any other motives. Only events take over command and they'll do so more and more. I suggested a solution, but naturally the parties did not want it because it threatened their exploitation of power. But as time goes by, not only does the situation become more difficult to solve, but it also becomes more and more unlikely that it can be solved in a way that will save what could have been saved of the parties. I mean to say that one could have dealt gently with them, but I don't see how they can be spared today. In any way the French people are beginning to understand. The communists are becoming more and more out of favour with the greater part of the country, which regards them with suspicion, as though they were a foreign body, or, anyway, something different and impossible to assimilate. The attitude adopted at last by the U.S.A. towards the U.S.S.R., this resolute, defensive decision to resist and refuse, has been of considerable help. In the realm of domestic affairs, I put forward a solution; I offered the French something solid to hang on to. There had been nothing solid before; no one knew what to do; there was only darkness ahead. Now everything's clear, and even those who don't yet support me will rally round me sooner or later, naturally, compulsorily – I'm speaking of the huge masses, who are on the side of France. Yes, I'm completely certain, they'll all end by joining. And the parties won't be able to do anything about it, you'll see them planning and scheming to find some makeshift solution, *to save themselves from de Gaulle,* but events will have the upper hand . . . Paul Claudel came to see me this morning . . ."

(I remembered seeing the old man lost in the crowd at the Press conference, the other day; Paul Claudel, who could not reach de Gaulle, and for whom Jean Schlumberger, André Rousseaux, Pasteur Vallery-Radot and I provided the guard-of honour, to which he was entitled.)

"He blamed me for not having taken up a stronger position against the U.S.S.R., and for going to Moscow. 'But *cher maître,*' I said to him (de Gaulle's voice rose as if he were still talking to a deaf man), 'you're forgetting that at that time America was a long way from making up her mind, that it was the period when M. Roosevelt believed he could get round Stalin, when he took the trouble to go to Yalta and Teheran. How could I adopt a firm attitude in those circumstances? Now, fortunately, everything has changed . . .' Apart from that, I found Claudel very clear-headed. He summed up the international situation with a cogency that very much impressed me."

With reference to a treatise on his government, sent him by a Professor V, he altered the letter of acknowledgement that I had drafted for him, finding it too warm, and said:

"Though there are one or two good passages, it's teeming with errors – even material ones, ones of fact. Moreover, the gentleman belongs to that ineffectual breed, so often found among historians; who imagine that one can do what one wants when one is in power, whereas one does what one can. It's only after taking into consideration whether the elements with which one had to deal, at a particular moment in particular circumstances were favourable or, more especially, unfavourable, that it's possible to try to form a clear judgement."

And he quoted in German a few sentences from Goethe's *Faust.* When I confessed that I did not understand the language, he translated: "Mephistopheles says: 'Concentrate on the words and you will find yourself on the surest path to the temple of certainty.' To which the reply is: 'Yet, the words must always contain an idea.' " De Gaulle commented:

"They, too, concentrate on the words alone, but action is never born of words!"

De Gaulle went on signing for several moments in silence, then, his face lit up by a smile, he searched for something in one of the files – "It's very amusing, you'll see," – and handed me an article in *Picture Post,* which I had already seen – there had been a lot of talk about it during the last week – with three pages of photographs, showing Hitler and de Gaulle face to face, an ingenious but scurrilous piece of work. The General laughed wholeheartedly. I told him that they could have done the same montage trick, with the same poses and crowds, with Churchill.

"Of course," he exclaimed, "and with Roosevelt, too. And, now I come to think of it, Thorez is speaking tomorrow in the Place de la

Concorde: I'm sure they could easily dig out photographs of Mussolini. Those two fat men . . . Think what they could make of it!"

Then, becoming serious:

"The truth is, that all the dollars we borrow from America deprives England of them; that she knows it, just as she knows that the dollars will assist us in our recovery, and that France's recovery is what the British Empire fears most. And so – they will always systematically do everything in their power to encourage anything that may perpetuate our cowardice and weakness. That's why I've always distrusted the English. I've always known that France had a no more determined adversary. We can, of course, fight a war together against a common enemy, but we mustn't expect anything further."

When he had finished signing his letters, he ran quickly through his last batch of mail before handing it over to me, his good humour reflected in his comments. *"This is what you must do, General . . . There's another V for you!"* His face lit up with childish pleasure as he read a sentence written by an embittered woman correspondent. "You don't receive me because I'm not M. Ramadier!" (an allusion to a recent visit which the President of the Council paid to Colombey).

His final words were optimistic and very similar to the ones he had used at the beginning of our conversation:

"On the whole, things aren't going too badly."

"Perhaps that's rather overstating it, General."

"Not at all! I'm much less pessimistic than I was this time a year ago. A year ago, the United States hadn't made their minds up. One might well have feared the worst. Since then, in a more or less distant future, salvation has become a possibility."

Sunday, 11 May, 1947

As the General only came to Paris on Thursday evening for a family gathering, so he told me, and strictly incognito (because he did not want his presence to be linked with the ministerial crisis)† I went down to Colombey yesterday. After re-reading a book on surrealism in the train, I was far from being in a Gaullist frame of mind and was preoccupied with matters other than the success of the R.P.F., about which the General questioned me. His questions were precise (What about the organization of such and such a headquarters? What about the

---

† Crisis is too big a word: it was only a matter of a reshuffle, M. Ramadier having been authorised by the National Council of the S.F.I.O. to proceed with the replacement of communist ministers.

secretariat at the rue Taitbout? Did Vallon go to his office regularly?) and I gave vague replies, having never been in any of the R.P.F. offices.

"I've been waiting to see how the Movement was going," he said to me. "Now I've come to the conclusion that it's well worth my while to take a more direct interest in its development. My move to Paris, which I've now decided on, will make things easier. On the other hand, I intend to go round the big cities and speak there – in Lille, for instance – only to the members. This will compel the waverers and the half-hearted ones to give proof of their loyalty."

He said this with an impish expression, smiling.

When I arrived, he had glanced through the morning papers and tossed them aside almost immediately, saying: "Nothing of importance there!" (After lunch he took a much closer look at them.)

"There's no one of any quality in that cabinet of theirs – he declared – no one! Those, like René Mayer, who have some talent, have refused to join it, and they're quite right. There's no one. No Blum, and, naturally, no Thorez – who's an opponent of course, but still, amounts to something. In short, it scarcely exists. And inflation is inevitable, by July at the latest. And then the parties, in order to avoid shouldering the whole responsibility on their own, will beg the communists to come back. Which they well know, and are merely waiting for it, to happen."

And he went on to explain what the communists had wanted to do and what they were now failing to achieve.

"At the time of the Liberation, their aim was to seize power, not by force, certainly, but nonetheless, effectively. This I did not allow them to do. So then they relied on the proletarization of an increasing number of Frenchmen – which would serve to decrease the number of those fundamentally opposed to communism. In these circumstances they believe that force of circumstances must naturally and inevitably put them in power. But they've failed to reckon with one detail: the international situation. In the present state of affairs, there's no possibility of France becoming communist." He added:

"Only a short while ago, the communist party absorbed everyone's attention. Whatever happened people would wonder: what are the communists going to do? But a wholly unexpected change has occurred and the question everyone's asking now – including the communists, themselves – is: what is the R.P.F. going to do?"

André Malraux had said exactly the same thing, a few days ago, at a luncheon, to which I was invited with my brother Jean, at the Pasteur Vallery-Radots (where all the guests were Gaullists: Soustelle, Rémy, Palewski, Vallon). I wondered which of them – Maulraux or the General – was the first to advance the proposition; the correctness of which may not appear to have been demonstrated, up till now, quite as conclusively as they assert.

"The truth is that everyone's scared to death," de Gaulle continued, "the M.R.P., most of all, naturally. But the socialists, too. Blum thinks of nothing else, which explains his whole attitude."

This, too, is by no means certain, but I was not in a mood to argue. I was struck more than ever by the self-confidence of the man. By the sublime naïvety of genius. But with de Gaulle, as Jean Cocteau said about Victor Hugo, it's a case of General de Gaulle taking himself for General de Gaulle.

"What Blum can't forgive me for, what makes him hate me so deeply, without daring to admit it, is that I've succeeded in becoming what he'd envisaged becoming himself, one day: the man to whom the nation will owe its salvation. I've always thought that one musn't confuse self-seeking with ambition. The self-seeker is always thinking of the position he will occupy; he overlooks essentials. Ambition is quite another matter and, to do Blum justice, contrary to the great majority of politicians today, he is an ambitious man in the good sense of the word."

I quoted from memory the passage in his *Vers l'Armée de Métier*, in which he already spoke of 'the hard core of ambition that sustains the real man of action'.

"Not that it should arouse a passion for rank and honours, which is – yes, certainly, nothing but self-seeking, but, the hope of playing a great part in great events", he went on with what he had been saying, without making any comment.

"That's the reason, too, for Reynaud's attitude towards me. We're on good terms, of course, but how could he avoid having a grudge against me after throwing away the cards he held?"

Then he mentioned Churchill's reception, when he arrived at Le Bourget on the previous day to receive the military medal on the second anniversary of victory.

"First of all, it's doubtful whether he should have accepted the decoration . . . But that's not the point. In spite of his rudeness, Churchill is undoubtedly one of the grand old men of History. But he comes to Paris for a ceremony of this kind, and there's no one to receive him. Not the smallest guard-of-honour! Not even the Prefect; let alone the Military Governor or any members of the government. No – just a lot of stooges! I tell you, this is the age of meanness; France has never seen such a triumph of meanness! Mind you, if I went to London it would be just the same thing. And that's exactly why I shall take good care not to go there!"

He confirmed the fact that he had refused Vincent Auriol's invitation to the dinner being given that evening at the Elysée in Churchill's honour, adding:

"Make no mistake about it: we're in the middle of another Weimar. Except that the Stresemanns and the Brunings were on a wholly different level from our present rulers."

He signed the five hundred or so letters I had brought with me, and composed, from a draft I had prepared for him, a brief tribute to go at the top of a presentation book: then he wrote a letter that he asked me to deliver that same evening to Palewski. (The latter read it aloud in front of me: it expressed de Gaulle's deep regrets to Mr. Churchill at being unable to attend – for reasons which in no way affected the high regard in which he held him – the Elysée dinner.)

While he was working, I drifted discreetly away and stood a short distance behind him, looking at the wall, where he had hung Rommel's ultimatum at Bir-Hakeim, a collection of France Libre insignia on an immense velvet V, and a collection of swords. Then I gazed out of the window at the broad landscape, its wildness softened by the approach of summer. I forgot about de Gaulle until his reflection as he bent over his desk, which I caught in a pane of the library window, suddenly brought him back to me somehow retrospectively, as though I were recalling him from memory.

Wednesday, 21 May, 1947

On the Thursday of Ascension Day (15 May) de Gaulle spoke in Bordeaux about the Union Française in front of an immense crowd. I was there, having arrived the evening before with Jean and my father, who had decided to come at the last moment, lured by the stay at Malagar, which we had promised him as a reward. Though the crowd was probably even larger than the one in Strasburg, the atmosphere seemed to me much less friendly. I was in the narrow street, when de Gaulle, bad-humouredly and ignoring the officials who were present, paid a hasty tribute to the Bordelais childhood of the future governor, Eboué. I had to run to get to the Places des Quinconces in time and take my place on the platform. Though the foundations for an exhibition obstructed the promenade, an enormous crowd had managed to collect all over the place, as far as the eye could see, on the quays and in the side streets of the Quinconces. I was upset by the behaviour of those on the official platform, who made it unpleasantly clear that the detestable and unfortunately eternal extreme right had, willy-nilly, managed to monopolize de Gaulle. My father felt even more strongly about it than I did, which was only to be expected in view of his distrust of the R.P.F. It was curious, to say the least of it, to hear Malraux defending the General's Movement against charges of fascism and begging him, Mauriac, to join the left wing of the Movement where he was so badly needed. When one thinks of Malraux's and my father's backgrounds, one cannot help pondering on the unexpected directions into which men's destinies lead them.

And that same evening, it was summery in Malagar despite the cold weather. Meadows buzzing with crickets, flowers in full bloom, the last calls from the cuckoos (which I could not forgive myself for having missed), the song of the oriole, walks, and my *André Breton* which I can work on again at last in tranquillity and delight. And the silence of the evenings by the open fire. My father said that we had caught Malagar asleep and it had not yet realized that we were there.

"All the same, the density of the silence is rather trying. Not to mention that, when one's alone, it's full of the dead, here, they're all around one."

I came back to Paris on Monday night and saw de Gaulle the next day, that is to say, yesterday evening, at the Hôtel La Pérouse. His new room does not look out only on the Place Jean Giradoux, but is on the corner of the rue la Pérouse, on the second floor. It was late, and neither of us felt like talking. He asked me if I had been in Bordeaux and spoke to me of the blunders of the mayor "who will feel it when it comes to the elections"; of the alarm in the parties, when they saw all their members at Bordeaux joining him; of the communists' bluster in talking a lot and finally doing nothing; and of the impolicy of their attacks on him in the Press, which were excellent propaganda for the Movement. When I said that the constant threat he represents to the Government had at least the advantage, where they were concerned, of inducing a new sort of awareness of the situation, born of their fear, and that, thanks to him, things were not going too badly, he answered:

"Yes, but they've given in on salaries, and they won't pull out of that."

Saturday, 31 May, 1947

When I saw de Gaulle at the Hôtel La Pérouse on Thursday morning, he criticized the tone of the letters, replying to those he had received, which I gave him to sign, for being too affable:

"I don't have to thank people for joining the Movement. Above all, don't give them the impression that they're doing me a favour, when, on the contrary, it's they who ought to be grateful to me."

263

He added:

"What does this phrase mean: 'At this time, when the splendid welcome given to the Rassemblement du Peuple Français . . .'? Either the French people reassemble or they don't, in any case they can't welcome themselves!"

Then he said:

"The government has just given in on gas and electricity. Tomorrow it'll be the miners. And the day after that, the civil servants will demand and obtain increases in salary. Therefore inflation is inevitable. What strikes me is the extent to which the parties are losing their importance; the communists have been peppered in the wing, the socialists are losing ground, and, as for the M.R.P., nobody even mentions them any more: whatever problems arise, they are only conspicuous by their absence. It all strikes me as very curious. Don't you agree?"

I agreed politely, but unenthusiastically. The heat in the room was overpowering. De Gaulle was one of the least of my preoccupations at that moment, and it was I, rather than he, who let the conversation drop. Then I left.

Monday, 9 June, 1947

I saw de Gaulle very briefly last Friday, 6 June, at the Hôtel La Pérouse. Throughout my visit, his egocentricity was at its height:

"The socialists have betrayed me: now they're betraying each other . . . All this wouldn't have happened to them if they'd remained loyal to me; their troubles spring from the fact that they all thought they could do without me."

('They' here did not mean only the socialists.)

"I should be only too happy if they could, but look what's happened!"

When I replied that M. Ramadier was still one of the best Presidents of the Council we had had for a long time, he mentioned again – in the same words as before – the respect he had for him when he was Minister of Food. "I've nothing against him. In fact, I'd go so far as to say . . ." etc.

We spoke a little about the Hungarian situation (the U.S.S.R. had just gained control of the country through leaders they had forced on her) but mostly about Abd-el-Krim's escape.

"When I arrived in Brazzaville, I found him there – head of the Moroccan nationalists. A remarkable man, with many good qualities, but dangerous. I immediately put him under my protection – with every consideration, of course, but he was, in fact, my prisoner and all the efforts of the English to get him over to England were in vain. So far, so good. But when I resign, the first thing they do is to let him go. With the result that he's now in Cairo. The same thing happened with the Grand Mufti, whom I had such difficulty in taking prisoner and whom they let escape almost before I'd gone. And now they want to fetch Abd-el-Krim to the Reunion and bring him via Egypt, where he has only to slip off the boat. And no one attacks Bidault. That he took steps to repatriate Abd-el-Krim was bad enough, but, still, there may have been some reason for that. But do you imagine for a moment that they'll have him watched on the voyage? Certainly not! That's Moulet's responsibility, who doesn't give a damn, and Bidault doesn't bother to see to things himself. The result is: this meeting of the Arab League, in Egypt, so full of menace for us . . ."

Thursday, 12 June, 1947

I saw de Gaulle this morning at the Hôtel La Pérouse. The greater part of our signing session took place without a word. Then suddenly his lips moved as though he were about to speak, but nothing emerged and I thought he must have bitten back some criticisim of my work. Not at all: when he finally did speak it was to observe that the R.P.F. was getting off to a slow but steady start. (That might be so, but I could not help thinking of what Bonneval had just told me: that the General had wanted to organize an R.P.F. meeting at Lille, where he had been told that there were 50,000 members; but when Guy went down there, he discovered that there were barely 5,000. Fury from the General who bawled out Soustelle and decided to deal with national affairs in his speech of 29 June.)

The railway strike ended this morning, "but at what a price," de Gaulle said to me as I was packing up my files before leaving.

"Ramadier only stood firm, verbally. Moreover, he was the only one to put up a fight. Nobody supported him. Blum, with arrant cowardice, wrote about Lend-lease, or I don't know what else, in *Le Populaire*. As for that famous Parliament, which claimed to be sovereign and weaved garlands for itself, it took great care not to intervene. All it could do was to applaud Ramadier, but as for assuming any kind of responsibility . . . In short – it abdicated. Inflation is now inevitable. What's more, it's been admitted by the government, whose insolvency is as obvious as that of the Chamber. Tomorrow it'll be the civil servants who ask for a rise, and they'll be quite right; and the day after, it'll be the railwaymen again, because the prices will have become so high that today's victory won't have done them any good. And so it'll go on until we reach daily readjustments. The régime is ruined. The only question that remains is whether France will perish before it does. The sole chance for the régime lay in the Blum experiment, but it legislated for the decline in prices before taking action in any of the fields which could have made it possible."

He declared that the present régime had shown itself incapable of intervening in any of the three vital problems:

1. The low level of production. Blum had not increased the number of working hours.

2. The insufficiency of imports. Blum had not built up our credit abroad.

3. The excessive domestic expenditure. Blum had not decreased the number of civil servants.

I have given the bare outlines and summarized a lot, because he developed his theme at length, explaining that the régime, prisoner of its own demagogy, could do nothing in any of these fields, nor return, in so far as it was possible, to individual liberty and initiative, the indispensable conditions for economic recovery.

"In short, they will go hurtling down the slope faster and faster, and drag us with them . . ."

Then he proceeded to deride the M.R.P., who were never in evidence, scoffed at X's articles and talked of a 'colossal swindle'.

"And they're perfectly happy as they are. Completely unmoved! Who raised his voice to ask Bidault to account for the farcical disaster over Abd-el-Krim?"

I looked at his head, getting slightly bald, and the well-furnished little hotel room with its English print above the low desk. (It was the same one as the week before.) And, meanwhile, he went on, with repressed emotion:

"I despise them more than I can tell. I can't say I hate them. One can hate Hitler or Stalin. One can't hate nullity. They're such miserable puppets! How can I feel any hostility towards an X, a Y or a Z? But I despise them from the bottom of my heart; that, yes! If only they had stuck to me! I was their only hope, the régime's only chance. . ."

And his last words were murmured with such transparent sincerity, that I was moved:

"If we have to return to power, it will be a heavy ordeal . . ."

Monday, 7 July, 1947

It has been a long time since I saw de Gaulle. An abcess in my throat caused me to postpone our next meeting, which finally only took place

266

on 4 July at the Hôtel La Pérouse. I did not wait for him to question me about the R.P.F. rally at the 'Vel d'Hiv' (on the evening of 2 July) before bringing the subject up. (Particularly as, having missed his Lille speech on 29 June, I had not a very clear conscience – but he knew I had been ill and asked me with great solicitude about my abscess.) I told him how contentious I had found Jean Nocher, how unpleasant Thorez, but, on the other hand, how surprised I had been by the brilliant performance of Gaston Palewski, who controlled the gathering of 30,000 people with great skill and apparent ease. He had suddenly been transfigured; dominating and thinner, too, with the sharp profile of a conductor of crowds. The General who had listened to me, smiling, and seemed plainly amused by my account, murmured, with an air of surprise:

"Yes, that's what everybody's been telling me about Palewski's speech!"

I then described Malraux's admirable contribution, which began as usual on a rhythm that everyone found difficult to understand (even myself, and I'm used to his style) but gradually found the right cadence as a torrent finds its bed. And it then became a great, prophetic voice, which kept the electrified audience breathless, the voice of a magus, a poet, a religious leader.

Having arrived at the Vel d'Hiv with reservations, which the mediocrity of the first speakers and the facile arguments they employed, only too fully justified, I left with the impression that the R.P.F. did represent something completely new and possibly even great. Was it not surprising, for a start, that, without de Gaulle, it had been able to fill the Palais des Sports, only two and a half months after it had been formed? The General asked me what sort of crowd had been there. I decided that I could not give him a better idea than by saying: "It was exactly like a Métro crowd."

We spoke very little. He made a brief reference to the failure of the U.S.S.R. – England – France conference, which had met in Paris in connection with the American aid-to-Europe plan, saying that the Russian rudeness had surprised him, that he had not expected such an unsubtle attitude. But I let the conversation drop.

He also asked me if I had heard about the offices we were going to get on the rue de Solférino. (I certainly had! The flat in question had been promised to my sister, Luce Le Ray. She had to give it up when she heard that de Gaulle wanted it! She, who has been hunting for somewhere to live with her two kids, plus the one due to be born at any minute, ever since the Liberation!)

"You'll have your office there next to mine, like Guy and Bonneval. It'll be much more convenient."

What an upleasant surprise! It was so agreeable *not* to have an office. If it had been anyone but de Gaulle, I should not have agreed, for now that I could earn a living from journalism, I had sworn to myself that I would never again accept such slavery.

I forgot to say that de Gaulle spoke to me with the greatest contempt of the 'plot against the Republic', recently highlighted, if not actually invented, by the struggling government:

"Under any régime there are always inoffensive imbeciles who plot. The government knows it and keeps an eye on them; if necessary it discreetly puts them somewhere where they can't do any harm. But all this publicity, all this yelling is ridiculous. One can well see what they're after, but who'll be taken in by them? As for O, he's a madman. Naturally, he has nothing to do with this business. But as he's been slanging the men in power pretty sharply and has done one or two rather foolish things into the bargain . . ."

Sunday, 13 July, 1947

I saw de Gaulle on Thursday morning, 10 July, at the Hôtel la Pérouse, under the print of *La Petite Thérèse,* as on former occasions. We did not talk much during the signature session. He merely expressed once again his contempt for the M.R.P. in connection with the Minister of War, Coste-Floret, whose letter relating to the 'plot' I had described as 'blunt and courageous'. But not enough so, according to the General. He should have attacked those who smeared the French army, beginning with the Minister for the Interior, Depreux. "Those people make me vomit!"

As I collected my things, he got up and asked me:

"So the civil servants are going on strike tonight?" And when I said that I knew nothing about it, he went on:

"Anyway, it doesn't really matter. Everybody knows, everybody's quite convinced that the government will end by giving in to them . . . That's a dead certainty . . ."

His tone was mild. But it soon became more serious, though he did not raise his voice. His voice was muffled as he said to me, while I clasped my briefcase bulging with papers to my chest (and pivoted round, while he strode up and down, so as not to turn my back to him):

"What is unbelievable is the irresponsibility of the newspapers. Instead of preparing public opinion for the catastophe that is looming ahead, they are lulling it to sleep. But the facts are there; the race towards the abyss has started. Our currency is going to collapse and after the harvest there'll be ruin and hunger; yes, hunger, for, naturally, the peasants won't be willing to part with their goods. The demands of the salaried class will become almost daily affairs for the same categories of workers. What will happen? What's already happening now: the printing of more bank-notes, which means final ruin, and misery. And the Chamber – something that's never happened before – hasn't passed the budget. How could it make any kind of estimates?"

When I mentioned a possible hope, American aid, he said:

"But that's only more bluff! Certainly, if the country was showing signs of pulling itself together, it would be a valuable contribution towards her recovery. But in the present state of affairs, it would be as much use as a poultice on a wooden leg, I assure you! To begin with, don't forget that France isn't the only country waiting for a loan from the United States; there's also Great Britain, Portugal, Italy, Germany, Austria, Switzerland, Holland, Belgium, Scandinavia, Greece and Turkey. And secondly, you mustn't close your eyes to the fact, that, in the best possible hypothesis – I mean if too much time doesn't elapse before Europe presents her plan to America and Congress accepts it (which I think it will in the end) – even in that hypothesis, we shall receive fewer dollars than we've been granted up till now. In fact, we shan't get more than 350 million dollars a year when we were getting a thousand million; and, over and above that, our exports and our gold exports have dropped to nil because we're asking too much for them. As for our gold reserve, it's become so small since Schuman last totted it, that we're only left with just enough still to be able to say that we have some gold. Finally, all the currency of our nationals abroad has been spent."

And with precise figures to support him (I envy him his memory), he proved to me that the American credit that we shall receive will be just enough to pay for the corn we shall need.

"The fact is that there's no longer any Government or any State. We witness, for instance, the inevitable spectacle of the representatives of the management and those of the C.G.T. meeting together to take decisions which it's understood the Government will have to put up with. In short, two feudal barons deal with problems directly affecting the whole of France over the head of the King of France. There's no reason why other feudal barons shouldn't one day succeed in dictating to the country her foreign policy. There are still people driving about in beautiful cars (ministerial ones) but there's no more State. And, mind you, everybody knows it, even if they aren't prepared to admit it. Ramadier, himself, solemnly announced to the country, if the Blum experiment fails, he said, it will mean the end of money and the end of the régime. On these two points he was certainly right! He even added – but there he exaggerated, for France will outlast the Republic; she will bury *their* Republic – the end of France. They took no steps to make the Blum experiment succeed: they merely lowered prices by ten per cent as though this artificial decision would of itself produce a real reduction. So the experiment failed: they recognize that. But the régime will never admit itself defeated until there's misery and bloodshed. At the moment the régime is working willingly against the welfare of the country, but it prefers to aggravate the disaster rather than admit defeat. My speeches? All I expect from them is that they'll arrange a date for me later. You think the government will call me back? They certainly won't! First, because they will know I wouldn't come and, secondly, because it's a matter of life and death for the régime. Those responsible for this régime will pay dearly for their mistakes and they know it. And, mark you, when one sees them alone, *there's not a single one of them* who doesn't admit that the régime is totally incapable of saving the country. But when they're together, they close the ranks."

He spoke with a kind of suppressed emotion, gravely, without anger, but in the ominous, weary tone of a prophet, to whom people persistently refuse to listen. His pessimism did not become really profound till the moment when he muttered, by way of parenthesis:

"Unless the French are no longer able to pull themselves together . . . There are nations that die. Yes, it has happened before now . . ."

But his discouragement was only momentary. It was in a completely different tone of voice that he declared, a little later, that, when speaking of France's welfare Ramadier had gone much too far in linking the country's fate with the Blum experiment!

When I gave my father a rough summary of the General's words, he appeared provoked by them. He thought such pessimism exaggerated:

"Besides, it's normal for de Gaulle always to be several degrees more defeatist than anyone else."

Friday, 18 *July,* 1947

De Gaulle showed such affectionate graciousness towards me yesterday, that I was deeply touched. Not that he said anything particularly kind, but his manner was trusting and friendly, though we did not talk much. But the way in which he told me he had listened to me the other evening on the radio and the attention he gave to my opinions, after asking for them, on Jean Nocher's merit as a speaker or the prize that should be awarded to Pierre Jean Jouve's poetry, could not fail to move me. While he was signing the letters, he soliloquized several times, but too low for me to hear. In any case, he was not addressing me, but allowing certain words, by an association of ideas, lead him into a train of thought I could not follow. For instance, correcting the mis-spelling of the word *Gambetta* in an address, he exclaimed (in the tone of voice we employ when we are imitating him) "Gambetta! Gambetta!"

But when we had finished, it was certainly to me that he muttered – still in the same low voice:

"The situation isn't too good, is it? There's more and more talk of war, eh? And of course we're heading for war. When? No one knows, but things have become so entangled that there's no other way out. It's not the first time I've said war was coming."

"And what a war!" We both uttered these words simultaneously. There was a pause; then, in little above a whisper, looking deeply discouraged and tired, he added:

"And we're going into it with men who've grown soft . . . My morale is very low . . . I've no confidence . . ."

Before we parted, he declared that the government had given in to the civil servants (under the threat of a general strike) since it had granted them almost everything they had asked for, selling the thousands of millions of francs so granted against future receipts which would never materialize. And, by way of conclusion, he resorted to his customary phrase:

"All that isn't really serious . . ."

For, there we are, back again to recognizing war as a possibility or, rather, as a probability. After the euphoria of the Liberation, little by little, we have suffered one disillusionment after another until, little by little, we have reached our lowest ebb. Admittedly, we are not yet going through the anguish of the years 1938-39. But, perhaps, this is only because we have endured so much that we are no longer capable of anguish.

Saturday, 27 September, 1947

On my return from my holiday, I saw de Gaulle twice: the first time in the Hôtel La Pérouse on Sunday 31 August, and, the second, in our new offices at 5 rue de Solférino, on the day when he first started working there (17 September). There is nothing of note to record about these meetings, as we did not talk much. In between times, the General travelled a lot and made an increasing number of speeches: Brittany, the Basque country, Lyons.

Last Thursday, 25 September, the simultaneous absence of two A.D.C.s led to my standing in for them for a few hours. Consequently, it became my duty to watch from the window looking out on the rue Dumont-d'Urville for the arrival of the small grey Citroën from Colombey, rush to the door, see if the coast were clear – I mean, free from prying idlers – bring in the General and Mme. de Gaulle by the hotel's staff-entrance, keep them waiting in the corridor while I made certain that the hall was empty and there were no ambushes on the way to the lift, conduct the travellers to Suite 24 on the second floor and arrange the afternoon's interviews.

The General made me stay for lunch. The meal, at which I was the only guest, sitting between him and his wife, was served upstairs in the suite by a head-waiter, whom de Gaulle introduced to me as a militant member of R.P.F., and who triumphantly exhibited a number of subscription books at 5.000 francs the ticket of which he had already sold several. The General shook him warmly by the hand and I followed suit.

One of the first things the General asked me was whether I had yet got the Banque de France's weekly balance-sheet, which actually appears on a Thursday. He was waiting for it as if it had been the temperature-chart of a beloved patient. Then followed the usual tirade against the menace of inflation, which could only be arrested by a government free from daily control by the parties.

"Even I was unable to govern once my ministers were delegated to the government by their respective parties. My only mistake, if I made one, was in failing to resign earlier. Dictatorship? But if I had turned myself into a dictator, I should have antagonized the United States, whose support France needed more than ever at that particular moment. I wanted the left bank of the Rhine, Tende and Brigue. To achieve this, the most important thing to do was to humour the United States. Also vital interests of the country were involved. Régimes pass, but France remains, and it was of France that I had to think."

I mentioned a recent, rather astute article by Stibio on the difficulties encountered by the R.P.F., but de Gaulle said:

"Stibio belongs to the breed of the eternally discontented. His criticism is facile and completely unconstructive. The R.P.F. consists of mediocre individuals? How could it be otherwise in a country that has completely sunk into mediocrity? However, the fact still remains that the only fire and influence left in France today are to be found in two sectors, and in those two sectors only: the communist party and the

272

R.P.F. And the communist party's influence is on the decline. It is now attacked from all sides and from the front, which was unheard of after the Liberation. As you rightly say, because of its role in the Resistance, but even more so because the nation was obsessed by the hope, by the need for unity. It was an attitude which had nothing base in it: it was possible then to nourish a hope of rallying the bewildered French, of integrating them into the bosom of the nation, and to achieve that, no trouble seemed too great. But, in the end, one had to admit that it could not be done. So something else has to be found."

And suddenly he reverted to the past in a way that took me by surprise. I had always suspected that, in his heart of hearts, he had not wished Marshal Pétain to go to North Africa. But there was no doubting his sincerity when he said to me with utmost gravity:

"Pétain lost everything by failing to avail himself of excellent opportunities. How much easier everything would have been if he had decided to go to Algiers. The parties, already so badly discredited, would not have recovered, since they would have gone on wrangling in occupied France, while the true France would have assembled, complete, in her North Africa, freed once and for all from her antiquated political practices. You were speaking just now about Rémy Roure's* bitter article, which appeared the other evening on 'my entourage'. But Roure belongs to that generation, which has lived so long in the world of electoral chicanery, that any idea of the traditional political game ceasing to exist altogether, leaves it completely lost. And yet, it is the only way out."

De Gaulle agreed when I said – to keep the conversation going, for I well know what he thought – that a catastrophe would have to occur before the parties acknowledged their defeat:

"Yes, naturally; and we shall have that catastrophe, there's no doubt about it. I'm told that Vincent Auriol will send for me one of these mornings. But I'm quite certain that he won't; that he knows I wouldn't accept his – their – conditions. Only the catastrophe may come in quite a different form to that of 1940. It may, for instance, come in the shape of a France in which everything has ceased to function; in which any kind of action has become impossible at every level."

I raised the objection that the C.G.T. would still exist and might prevent him from governing, even if the communists had resigned. He replied:

"First of all, no one knows – not even the C.G.T. itself – to what extent, at the time, its troops would obey certain orders. And, secondly, once the C.G.T. became political, it would lose all reality and all semblance of power at the same time as the parties."

We spoke, too, for a long time about the war psychosis which has recently arisen in France, as a result of an increasingly alarmist press. The Minister of National Defence, if *France-Dimanche is* to be believed, is even forecasting war before Christmas.

"Of course there'll be a war. It's impossible to see what other alternative is open to the world. But I've no reason to think it will be in the immediate future. As the diplomat said to the novice: 'Above all, never give a date!' "

This was a phrase ascribed to Léon Noël in this week's *Carrefour*. De Gaulle, without quoting the reference, said that he had just seen the excellent remark recalled in that magazine.

Mme. de Gaulle broke in timidly to raise the possibility of parachutists being dropped round Colombey at the very start of the conflict. De Gaulle smiled:

"Certainly, it would be unfortunate for me. But it wouldn't affect the outcome of the war. Certainly, Coste-Fleuret and de Lattre aren't the men to stop the Russians occupying France, but the Russians won't be any better off for that."

After Mme. de Gaulle suggested that with humanity having had more than enough of war, men might refuse to go, the General exclaimed:

"But men always go. You tell them there's no more bread and they do without bread. You send them into battle and they go. It has always been so, and never have poor human wills and poor human resources counted for so little as they do today. But, having said that, I do believe, in fact, that it will be some time yet before world opinion accepts the idea of war being inevitable, without which acceptance war is not possible."

He then spoke of the Russians:

"They invented nothing in the course of a war in which their independence was at stake – neither radar nor jet aircraft, nothing – and they are so behindhand in the atomic field that we have nothing to fear. Moreover, even if they possessed the secret of the bomb, they probably would not be able to make it. The construction of a single bomb requires such a complete aggregration of apparatus, such precision in the manufacture, that one is justified in thinking that the Russians are incapable of producing it. And they are desperately short of material. Their rolling-stock, just to confine oneself to railways, is on its last legs and they can't replace it. Whereas the U.S.A., if they devote their talents and the powerful resources at their disposal to war preparations, can completely revolutionize present methods of warfare in under two years and perfect instruments of destruction, beside which those they have today are mere toys."

He also declared that he could well understand the U.S.A.'s distrust of Western Europe.

"You see, it's beyond the average American to grasp how France can be in need of corn and England of coal, and I don't blame them. We have the corn but we don't know how to apportion it. I know that this year's harvest, as you rightly remind me, was exceptionally bad. But we had too much corn the year before. We should have done as Pharaoh did: stored some away."

I saw him again next day at the rue de Solférino – where I now have an office close to his – to get him to sign his letters. He spoke of nothing but matters connected with our work. But he did tell me:

"You know, this time, we've succeeded: the R.P.F. is really on its way. I've received reliable evidence of it from too many quarters to harbour any doubts. And, as you say, events will ensure its success."

Thursday, 16 October, 1947

Since the Vincennes rally, which was a triumph, and the one in Algiers, at which I was also present, having flown there in Admiral Ortoli's plane, I had not seen General de Gaulle alone (at the Algiers reception, given by General de Vitrolles in an atmosphere reminiscent in its simplicity, I was told, of the real Algiers days, we had exchanged three words). This morning, our working session in the rue de Solférino, took place in two parts. Strike of buses and Métro. Imminence of municipal elections. Exaggerated claims by the communists. The R.P.F.'s progress. Signs of disruption in the M.R.P. Such were the surrounding circumstances. But de Gaulle was very pessimistic, seeming to attach no importance to the elements in the present occurrences, which served directly as propaganda for the R.P.F. (the unpopularity of the strikes, the application for membership by the editor of *L'Aube*, etc.) He sees further ahead. He thinks of France.

"Cracks are beginning to appear," he said to me. "The parties are disintegrating more and more. We are witnessing the start of the ultimate convulsions. And, naturally, they all want de Gaulle – even the socialists, not to mention the Rassemblement des Gauches and the P.R.L., but joining them, as before, in a system that maintains them in their prerogatives. But one experience of that is enough."

He murmured these last words under his breath and I could only just hear them. He went on, his teeth clenched, in so low a voice that I lost part of his monologue.

"We have never fallen as low as this. And we are approaching the ordeal in the shoddiest (*sic*) atmosphere. And without resources. It's easy enough to carry out great policies with great resources. But in our present state?"

Returning home on my old bicycle, resurrected because of the strike, I thought sorrowfully of the civil war that might well be inevitable but, in any case, so abominable, since our 'enemies' will be men of integrity, alas! – mistaken and confused but believing that they, too, are sacrificing themselves for France. I spoke about it sadly to my father at dinner: he had come back yesterday (with maman) from Malagar. I have neither the time nor the inclination to write this Diary. I saw Malraux, the other day, in his office in the Boulevard des Capucines, opposite the Café de la Paix. We talked for a long time. When he complimented me on the extracts from my *André Breton*, which appeared in the *Nef* (and which caused quite a stir among certain surrealists, who were angered by my sentence: 'A Christian would have said just the same.') I told him that I had had enough of working so much on other people's writings.

"It's probably the last time," he said.

I had the same feeling.

Friday, 28 November, 1947

Yesterday was the fourth time I saw de Gaulle since my last entry. Despite the importance of the events that have occurred in the meantime (the shattering victory of the R.P.F. in the municipal elections, the worsening of the social and political crisis in the way, alas, foreseen by the General a long time ago: we are on the eve of a complete interruption of the life of the country as a result of the strikes; on the eve, too, of the definitive fall of the franc; and perhaps of a communist insurrection) I have not considered it necessary to write this Diary, my meetings with de Gaulle having been very short, due to his heavy programme when he comes to Paris, and entirely devoted to work. We are again in a state of appalling anxiety, close to that experience during the worst days of the Occupation: the other night, neither my father nor Brisson slept at home and there are a great number of people who, fearing the worst, consider it unwise that they should do so these days. Strikes of railways workers, miners and postal workers are more or less widespread, and sufficient to paralyze the country, despite a partial reaction by the trade unions against the communist political aims.

Yesterday, at the end of our working session in the rue de Solférino,

General de Gaulle said a few words to me for the first time after a long lapse – and I shall not easily forget them. I shall record them verbatim, for they are graven on my memory and, besides, I jotted them down immediately afterwards.

When he had asked me what I thought of the situation and I had summed up in a few words the anxiety everyone was experiencing, he said:

"It's heartbreaking, you know, and it'll cost dear."

It was really France, facing me, *heartbroken* and suffering.

"The astonishing thing is," he continued "that the perpetrators of this régime could have expected anything else to happen. It was all, alas, only too foreseeable and now look at that wretched Blum, still motivated by a single preoccupation: the hate he bears me, that hate which is the only thing that still unites 'them'! As for Robert Schuman, who, following Ramadier's resignation, has just formed a ministry after Blum's failure, I used to know him very well; we were under-secretaries of State together in Reynaud's ministry. He's as much fitted to hold out against events of the gravity of those which he is now facing, as I am to be Pope! And this time the franc is done for!"

He fell silent, thinking of other even more precious riches which may be lost, too, and waved one goodbye with a discouraged gesture.

Friday, 28 November, 1947

General Leclerc has been killed in an air-crash. The gravity of the crisis is for an instant forgotten. There is genuine sadness.

Saturday-Sunday

Debate in the Chamber, lasting thirty-six consecutive hours as a result of communist obstruction, Schuman manages to get his bill through. (80,000 reservists to be put at the disposal of the Minister of Home affairs. Defence of right to work. Sanctions against sabotage.)

Monday, 1 December, 1947

First electricity cuts. Paris plunged into darkness. Less water and gas. No Métro.

Tuesday

The Métro working again, the power stations having been recaptured from the strikers. Great victory for the Schuman government.

Wednesday

One more act of sabotage, but this one caused twenty deaths in Arras. The General in Paris. I did not see him.

Thursday, 4 December

Several electricity cuts. The General leaves. Riots in the country. The first two deaths in Valence. Another one in Saint-Omer. Several local supply cuts.

Friday, 5

No water when we woke up. The Métro stopped during the morning, but started again in the early afternoon.

Friday, 19 December, 1947

I saw the General for the first time on 12 December. He was more friendly towards me than I can ever remember him. After enquiring with genuine solicitude and urbanity about *Le Passage du Malin,* which, to put it mildly, has not exactly had a smashing success, the General drew my attention to the fact that he had given up smoking – which I already knew. He was chewing some jujubes, looking very pleased with himself, but failing to conceal from me how much he was really suffering from the abrupt deprivation. I saw him again yesterday. This time not a moment was wasted on friendliness. After we had finished, I rode in the security squad's car, which followed his Citroën to the Hôtel La Pérouse, where he was lunching. No one recognized him. It was very moving to drive up the Champs Elysées behind him and catch a glimpse of him, in his felt hat, through the rear window of his car.

1948

Friday, 9 January, 1948

Just before New Year the General came into our offices to give us his good wishes, which, once again, threw my secretaries into ecstasy. After that, I saw him for a few minutes while he signed some letters in the presence of Gaston Palewski, who was wishing him a Happy New Year.

Later – on Sunday 4 – came his speech in Saint-Etienne, which was disappointing, but delivered to an enormous crowd, under a spring sky. Stupid, juvenile shouts of 'De Gaulle in power!' dismayed me and I was unable to conceal, even before the speech, how dissatisfied I felt with the R.P.F.'s policy, during a luncheon with Mrs. Perkins, Mme. Vallon, Patricia Guy and Albert Ollivier whom I visibly shocked by my outspokenness. My loyalty to de Gaulle himself, and the confidence I have in him, fortunately enable me to stick it, but I have painful moments when I feel completely in harmony with the Third Force.

The Third Force, whose Manifesto my father publicly signed a few days ago and of which de Gaulle, without, of course, making any allusion to my father's membership of it, said to me yesterday, with such a weight of contempt in his voice that I was immediately swept away, overcome by his conviction, after losing my own:

"That lamentable Third Force – it's Vichy all over again! Like Vichy, those gentlemen are against the enemy and against the war – at one and the same time. They don't want to be in the enemy's camp, that's to say the communist camp, but they don't want to go to war, that's to say join me, either. And like Vichy, it'll all end in the High Court. Not that there's much danger for them in that, admittedly, as you can judge from the previous example."

Coming back to the Third Force, he spoke of the socialist party's failure (not a single socialist municipal councillor in the proportional elections in towns like Saint-Etienne and Lyons), which, according to him, explained Blum's fury:

"He's lost his head – look at his recent articles about me, which, naturally, I shan't answer. All that wouldn't have happened, if they'd joined me. They won't recover from failing to do so."

279

Referring to the Bollaert-Bao Daï meetings, which took place in *Switzerland,* he expressed his disgust, in a burst of anger:

"In Switzerland! In Switzerland! It's past understanding!"

He had begun our conversation by reading me the invitation from M. X . . . Mayor of Colmar, 'an M.R.P. whom I got elected,' stressing the point that his attendance was desired along with that of a number of others, not mentioned by name. In short, the implication was that he would be thrown in with other officials. He read me his reply, which he asked me to have typed: "Therefore, I think it better to postpone my visit to a time when I can make it in different circumstances." He observed: "Which means: when you will no longer be mayor."

With regard to the R.P.F., de Gaulle repeatedly expressed how tired he was of the quarrels, which are setting the leaders, everywhere, at each other's throats.

"I'm fed up with all their croaking!"

The General, whom I saw again this morning (it was the second time he had summoned me outside of our regular meetings, a new factor which will compel me to be more assiduously in attendance between Tuesdays and Fridays, the days when he is in Paris) told me of a postscript he was adding in his own handwriting to a letter to Monseigneur Hincki, a postscript relating to his refusal of the Colmar invitation: "The programme which Mr. X . . . sent me strikes me as entirely inadequate both in fact and intention." He added:

"That'll lead to a lot of palaver in Colmar! I know those Alsations . . . But what a fool that mayor is! Typical of the M.R.P. Typical of the Third Force, too, that fear of offending people, that cowardice. All he had to write was: 'I invite you to come and celebrate the liberation of Colmar. Enclosed is the proposed programme, which I should be grateful if you would approve.'"

Thursday, 15 January, 1948

I saw the General at 12.15, after his last morning interview. He began unwrapping a piece of chewing-gum and apologized for chewing it in front of me to allay his desire to smoke. There were a lot of letters to sign. He talked a good deal, but only of insignificant matters. However, he did say:

"It's the lack of responsibility in everyone's attitude towards what's going on here that's so striking." (With reference to a headline in *La Bataille,* which was launching a violent attack on the Sultan of Morocco.)

A little later, he said:

"The régime will snatch at the smallest straw that seems to offer it some faint hope of survival. Look how they refuse to face the truth! They'll grab any nonentity, even K . . . , himself, if necessary."

He said this with tranquil irony, devoid of malice, and exhibited it again when Pompéi came to tell him, while I was there, of some parliamentary manoeuvre that was being carried out, which should, according to him, do Reynaud some good. De Gaulle said that he would find a deputy to give him further details on the subject but he made a gesture that as good as said "For what the matter's worth . . . ." He informed me that he had decided to speak at Marseilles, where the communists would be staggered by a crowd even larger than the one at Saint-Etienne. He also mentioned the Film *Monsieur Vincent,* which he went to see yesterday in a small cinema, and in which he greatly admired Pierre Fresnay's performance.

29 *January,* 1948
5 *rue de Solférino, Paris*

A copy of *Le Monde* was lying on the desk, and I deciphered its main headline: A Drastic Remedy.

Standing up, very tall, the General was reading a document, as he chewed gum. Presently, he said:

"I hope for your sake that you haven't any 5.000 franc notes?"

For no one was talking about anything else, since this morning's step in withdrawing these notes from circulation, when no one expected such a move, being preoccupied with the devaluation on its way and the plan for allowing gold to return to its value on the free market. I reassured the General and spoke of the latent bankruptcy imminent if the small holders of the notes were not reimbursed.

De Gaulle muttered: "It's not my fault!", as though denying that he were involved with France in the present happenings and, for once, disassociating himself from France. The Schuman Government bears the whole responsibility. When I remarked that he would have a large majority that afternoon, the General declared:

"It's by no means certain! I myself consider there's a good chance of the Government falling, and that he may want it to, to take advantage of it by falling towards the left."

And he read me two vehement protests from Paul Reynaud and Edouard Daladier* in *Le Monde*:

"Anyway, the middle group certainly won't vote for a law like that."

He told me that the peasants would be the main victims. But what about those living on their savings? And the workers?

"The pity is that René Mayer got involved in this business," the General added. "He was absolutely determined to be a minister. You may well talk about waiting: he couldn't wait another minute . . ."

I saw Pleven in the evening when he came out of the General's office. According to him, feelings were running high in the Chamber. He had no very clear idea of which way the vote would go.

30 January, 1948

The bill was amended but approved. There has been a suitable apology from the Mayor of Colmar and the General will now be going there.

Thursday, 19 *February,* 1948

With reference to an article of my father's on Malraux which appeared in *Le Figaro,* the General began by saying:

"What an excellent article by François Mauriac this morning!" and followed it up with a long lecture on the relationship between literature and action, which contained striking observations such as "Racine would not have been so great without Louis XIV – or Chateaubriand without Napoleon, whom, basically, he was very fond of." And now my father had put Malraux in the light reflected from de Gaulle. De Gaulle added that it was not so much Boulanger that Barrès had liked, as Boulangisme.

Thursday, 26 *February,* 1948

I had my first talk with the General in a long time. I mean to say that I talked a little myself, too, and not merely to acquiesce. He questioned me about the events in Prague, where the communists have just seized control, and I expressed my surprise that Benès should have given in. I added that he had not made any kind of public appearance since his capitulation, which might mean that he had not agreed to anything and that they had dispensed with him. The General admitted that this theory could not be ruled out. In his opinion, however, Benès surrendered because his only thought was for Czechoslovakia's welfare and he believed he should stay no matter the cost, to save what there was to be saved. (What about Pétain, then? It was a question I thought wiser not to put to de Gaulle.) "In any case, it's the end of their independence," the General murmured, sadly. He was surprised by the lack of reaction from other countries, especially from the U.S.A., which could have taken some kind of action, being the only one with other means than vague expressions of sympathy. He then disclosed that the next communist camp would be in Italy and that this one, too, would be achieved with an appearance of legality.

"There won't be any outright majority after the next elections, and that will make it easy for them."

I did not pay very close attention to his detailed technical explanations, but waited to ask:

" What about France?"

"In France, they'd already have brought off their *coup* if I hadn't been there. But my presence prevents the Third Force from capitulating. And then, thanks to what we've done, thanks to the Resistance, the French haven't acquired a defeat complex, as the Italians have. The French have a deep-rooted conviction that they were not defeated, that to some degree they participated in the Victory. Therefore, they are better shielded against despair – and also, further developed politically than the nations of Central Europe."

(What I should convey is his underlying thought, unexpressed but implicit and sometimes transparent, that France's victory was virtual, born of a bluff that little by little was translated into a reality, but spiritual rather than material.)

"What's so incredible," he continued, "is the country's cowardly laxity when it can well see that the present government is incapable of dealing with the situation, knows that the régime, itself, is out-of-date and, yet, stubbornly refuses to acknowledge it. What's even more incredible is that it's displayed by men, who are far from being imbeciles, like Blum, for instance."

He dwelt for some time on Léon Blum's lack of integrity, which it had taken him a long time to detect but which was now apparent to him, beyond the slightest doubt.

"Do you want proof of it? He's just written in *Le Populaire* that my resignation came as a complete surprise to him. Well, I summoned him to the rue Saint-Dominique shortly before the elections and told him my intentions. I said to him: 'My intention is to go, to resign from office in order to safeguard the future. In the present state of affairs I consider you the most suitable choice to succeed me.' He refused, after advising me to stay on in the government; he refused, as he has always done when he has seen no personal advantage in accepting, for you know how delighted he is to accept when he regards the circumstances as propitious, though he contrives to give the impression that he does so reluctantly. Then he said to me: 'I advise you to choose Gouin; he's the one most like Attlee.' So, you can see that he was well aware of my intentions, and had lied about it."

De Gaulle, who has aged lately, looked incredibly youthful again in the alacrity with which he spoke of Léon Blum. There is little point in recording my part in the conversation, when I defended Blum, since I did so with no great warmth, having come to the conclusion that de Gaulle was basically right. Finally, I said:

"From my own personal enquiries, I gather that the communists are up to something."

"Yes, they're going to make a nuisance of themselves, we can certainly count on that."

2 April, 1948

The few words that the General said to me yesterday confirmed the impression I had formed, derived as much from the course of events as from de Gaulle's silence during our last few work sessions. The fact is that his prognoses have for once proved incorrect, anyway for the time being. The steps that Schuman has taken have succeeded, not in solving the crisis (is there any solution?) but in putting a brake on rising prices and getting the public to recognize that there was a possibility of averting the financial catastrophe and therefore no necessity to have recourse to the R.P.F. This has delighted a large number of people for, though de Gaulle remains popular and continues to enjoy an immense prestige even among his opponents, his Movement still arouses very strong distrust.

De Gaulle, with whom I had hardly exchanged three words unrelated to the business in hand during our recent meetings (which explains this Diary's silence) asked me yesterday, point-blank:

"Well, so we are on the decline?"

I replied that, at any rate, we were not on the ascent, and that Schuman had at least managed to restore some kind of confidence after the recent near-panic. He agreed with good grace and not with the ill-humour and ironic implications which I suspected he would have displayed a few weeks before when this setback could already be foreseen (a setback for him, but what does it matter if it is a success for France? What did it matter if de Gaulle is not in power, if his menacing presence in the wings serves to call them to order and induces our leaders to find the courage that they lack to act in the interest of France?) – (And no doubt he kept silent during our last interviews in order to avoid recognizing the *fait accompli*.)

"Yes, you're quite right," de Gaulle replied, "but the real threat comes from outside the country. Everything will be settled abroad."

And certainly there is acute tension, between the U.S.A. and the U.S.S.R. as is particularly apparent just now in Berlin.

"The Russians are in the process of throwing the Allies out of Berlin. And after that, you can be certain they'll chase them out of Vienna."

That was what de Gaulle said but, from the latest news, it looks as if the Americans have no intention of allowing it to happen. However that may be, there is nothing but talk of war all over the world, especially in the U.S.A. But the French do not believe it, probably because they are in the greatest danger and an inhibitive reflex has already come into action.

The General told me that the professional groups in the R.P.F. are functioning better and better on a national level (in labour and agricultural affairs). Then he disclosed that, in view of his approaching trip to Marseilles, he had instructed the municipal councillors there to draw in their horns but that, after the R.P.F. congress, it would be quite otherwise, as it would in Tours and Reims where he would also see to it that new elections were held – as a result of which the M.R.P. and S.F.I.O. would be heavily defeated.

Then he spoke about my father's *Journal*, which he had received the day before and, in reference to Mme. de Noailles, asked me which of the writers between 1920-40 would, in my opinion, live. This was precisely the topic of two interesting discussions I had with my father (during a walk in the Bois de Villeron and in his library in Paris), some of the fruits of which can be found in *Le Figaro* article I typed for him this morning.

Tuesday, 13 April, 1948

I spent Sunday with Jacques Soustelle at Colombey, to which I had not returned for almost a year. I found the property embellished by the spring, almost smiling, instead of wearing that air of austere grandeur with which it had always met me before. Hyacinths, narcissi, periwinkles and jonquils brightened up the orchard where almost all old fruit trees have been replaced by cherry and plum trees, fruiting as late as possible, because, according to the General, they have frosts in May in that part of the country. One of the two fantails having been eaten by a buzzard, the General had returned the other one to its breeder. The cedar had been killed by a frost and replaced by another one in the same spot, which the General showed us, pointing out that it had been nipped by a frost, too: if it does not recover, he does not intend to plant a third.

Mme. de Gaulle, whom I saw for the first time since little Anne's death, was smiling, quiet, and busy with domestic duties: her way of going about things was so much like maman's that I was touched

285

(for instance, when she was looking through her cupboard for a piece of linen that might go inside a cradle, for she is about to become a grandmother).

I happened to catch sight of a photograph of de Gaulle taken about four years ago, (when I first met him) and was struck by how much he has aged, and how low his spirits seemed to be!

But he spoke quite briskly and good-humouredly to Jacques Soustelle, while I was there, devoting most of the conversation to R.P.F. personnel matters. He discussed the most minor details connected with the organization, knew everyone by name who had been appointed or was up for appointment to various posts, and had much more the air of a politician than of the statesman I usually recognize in him. The fact is that his main preoccupation is no longer the State but the Movement; or, more precisely, the Movement as a means of gaining access to the State.

Naturally, the Marseilles congress frequently cropped up. He asked me again if I were going – but in a tone of voice that clearly showed he assumed I would be going (as Soustelle had already done that morning and Pasteur Vallery-Radot yesterday) which virtually made it impossible for me not to go. Actually, I am not unwilling to go – but I am daunted by the expense involved, just now when I am so hard-up. The communists are talking of obstructive tactics and attempts to break the meeting up, and, apparently, have distributed a large number of whistles. But de Gaulle said:

"I'm certain they won't do anything. They'd lose too many votes. There may be a few isolated spots where they'll whistle: I don't say that's impossible; But it won't be more than that, I'm quite sure."

Soustelle thought the same. We were having lunch: calf's head, beautifully cooked and delicious. The conversation turned to some wonderful dresses, which Mme. X . . . was supposed to have ordered and took on a satirical flavour. De Gaulle and Soustelle outdid each other in their comments and we all laughed a lot, quite unreservedly. The General frequently glanced towards me seeking signs that I was enjoying his sallies. He finally put an end to our mild diversions with his ritual:

"Anyway, none of that's important!" . . . and went on to more serious matters, in particular the need to incorporate Algerian Muslims into the Movement. He mentioned the Dakar conferences at which ministers were discussing French sovereignty with private individuals representing powerful American interests, solely for the benefit of their own party:

"That's what happens under a party régime. There's no fragment of the State that they aren't prepared to sacrifice to ensure their survival."

He cited an illustrated magazine:

"On the first page, pictures of Italians shouting 'Vive la France' in reference to Trieste. It's only the Americans who can be fooled by that. We're too old a people – the Italians and us – we know each other too well to be taken in to the smallest degree by the Trieste demonstrations – provoked by self-interest and certainly not sentiment. Then I ran through the rest of the magazine and found photographs of M. Caffery, opening this, being received by such and such a town, visiting some exhibition or other. It only took me two minutes to grasp the reason: *it was signed*."

And this is the man, whom the communists declare to be sold on American imperialism!

Towards evening, as we strolled up and down the narrow, gravelled garden-paths, he said to us:

"It's frightening, the way American pressure is developing. If ever that young country, by force of circumstances, becomes master of the world, one daren't imagine to what lengths her imperialism will go. We must certainly keep a close eye on them."

I said that, nonetheless, France might still have a future, even though economically dependent on the U.S.A., whereas it would be inconceivable in the event of a Soviet victory. But de Gaulle looked sceptical:

"What I said doesn't prevent me from preferring the Americans at the moment, naturally . . ."

After a brief pause, he added in a gloomy, discouraged voice:

"No, you see, what changes the whole situation, is the atom bomb. No problem presents the same facet since the atom bomb. I even begin to wonder whether it's worth trying to do anything nowadays. No action one takes has any meaning any more, nor has any humane project. The conception of individual nations has lost all significance. What does *France* stand for now?"

(The France which owes everything to him, which for years has been his sole preoccupation, his only reason for living – and which suddenly is slipping out of his grasp, making his efforts on her behalf futile, and destroying all the hopes of a man born too late into a world that has become too old.)

"Besides, marxism itself is obsolete; there's no place for communism in a world of which the very existence is threatened."

Soustelle said that humanity was in need of a new mystique, or rather, a new legend. But de Gaulle observed that, from all appearances the new legend would only emerge after the disaster had occurred, when there would be nothing left of our civilization.

A thrush lay dead on the path ahead of us. De Gaulle picked it up carefully and threw it on a refuse heap behind a low wall.

"Poor creature . . ."

His compassion was so geniune that it surprised me. He said:

"I've three speeches to make at Marseilles, and I haven't yet started on the most important of them, the Sunday one. You can't imagine what a torture these speeches are for me. I find them harder and harder to write, and that's the literal truth . . ." (Bonneval told me a little while before that the General works best between midnight and 3.00.) ". . . Harder to write and they take me much longer. For three reasons. First, because I'm no longer inspired by what's going on. Secondly, because I'm getting older. And, finally, because I must admit it means repeating the same thing over and over again, and the thing is becoming tedious."

A little later, Soustelle asked:

"General, how do you explain England's failure to make a firm stand on the Berlin issue?"

"For the simple reason that they're socialists, that's to say, the kind of people who are prepared to give in on everything *and who don't want to fight.*"

"And what about Claude Bourdet's views on the need for European neutrality?"

"A neutrality which would lead to being occupied by the Russians and bombed by the Americans! The truth is that those people *are thoroughly scared.*"

He added, with sad irony, a moment later:

"And I must admit they've good reason to be!"

We were just getting into the car, when Malraux rang up to give Soustelle details of the communists' grenade-throwing last night, in which some of the militant members of the R.P.F. in Epernay were injured. The General wrote them a letter, wishing them a speedy recovery, and asked us to deliver it.

So we went by way of Epernay on our return to Paris. The electoral campaign there was at its peak (they were voting next day to replace the retiring municipal Council). The staff at the R.P.F. headquarters excited but friendly, and I was struck by the fact that they were all working-class. Not a bourgeois among them. A communist cell must be composed of much the same people. The wounded – none of them seriously – had been taken to the hospital in Reims. We entrusted the General's letter to a responsible native and went on to Paris.

288

Thursday, 22 April, 1948

I shall always remember the final session of the R.P.F. congress in Marseilles at the Palais Chanot on Saturday 17, when Malraux spoke, followed by de Gaulle, both of them admirably, but particularly the former, who was *greater* than I had ever heard him, in the way he combined political enthusiasm with classic poetry (what images! what style!) to bewitch the crowd with verbal spells, the effect of which was doubled by the emotion with which he delivered them.

I shall pass over the other proceedings at the congress, which were of no particular interest, and even the General's speech from a landing-stage moored in the Old Harbour (it was less effective than either, less to the point and less warmly received than usual, revealing for the first time signs of fatigue on the part of the speaker and a certain alienation on the part of his loyal supporters).

And it was then that I experienced, for the first time in my life, such a strong irresistible longing to write a novel – or, rather, my novel, the one that has been more or less in my mind for the last fifteen years but for which I had not yet found the theme (or the right way to set about it). I now feel that I have discovered the substance and the form of it, that I can achieve something really good and original, something wide enough in its scope – but when shall I ever find time for it? I should have to retire to the country by myself for two months. But my film reviews, my work for the General and so many other commitments prevent the realization of my dream. . .

But how heady it is, when I am just on thirty-four, to feel younger than ever before, each day more in control of my physical and intellectual resources, always taking a step forward. If, so far, I have not produced anything worthwhile, it is less due to lack of ability than to lack of confidence. I have at last achieved the necessary self-assurance and feel that my ambition, which certainly does not lie in the political field, is justifiable. But de Gaulle, to whom I became less attached the closer he got to returning to power, is growing dearer to me again, now that, contrary to his predictions, his success seems more open to doubt, anyway for the moment. He had foreseen everything, except that the Schuman government might be able to hold on, and, if it continues to do so, it will certainly be due to the threat that the R.P.F.'s influence presents to the political parties, just as it was due to General de Gaulle's influence that the communists are losing strength, an influence that he did not require to exert on his supporters, naturally, but on the timorous and cowardly. France's whole story continues to be the work of de

Gaulle since his departure from the rue Saint-Dominique – at least all that is best in it. But that, perhaps, does not entirely fall in with his plans and certainly not with those of his entourage. I seem to discern the first signs of discouragement among his supporters, which only serves to enhance my own loyalty to him. In short, I no longer think of leaving him. I, who dreamt of nothing else when his triumph seemed close.

I am due to spend today with him standing in for the absent A.D.C.s. And what I should have looked on, only a few days ago, as another drudgery, today seems an infinitely sweet duty.

26 April, 1948

So I replaced the A.D.C.s on Thursday and Friday, leaving the General to wait in the Hôtel La Pérouse's small service corridor while I made certain the coast was clear and then going up in the lift with him and Mme. de Gaulle. I lunched with them in their modest suite (No. 26).

"I didn't see you in Marseilles."

"I was there, General. I was there, lost in the crowd."

We exchanged impressions of the Congress. De Gaulle thanked me for drawing his attention to the fact that Nocher's comments over the microphone before and after he made his speech had distracted, by their vulgarity, from the grandeur of the occasion. Then he went on:

"Have you seen the papers? All of them, the whole lot of them, omitted any reference to what I said about the partnership between capital and labour. They took good care to. A lie, by omission, but a lie just the same. The truth is that we have a programme just when the parties are accusing us of not having one. We are, in fact, alone in having a programme. We have one and they haven't! The capital levy, naturally, wasn't in their manifesto, but they brought it in just the same. And, apart from the capital levy, what have they achieved?"

De Gaulle questioned me again on the alleged fall in prices and expressed his conviction that the government would soon find itself again facing insoluble problems. At the moment it was living on certain Treasury funds borrowed against the expected yield from taxes and the capital levies. But this was an operation that could not be repeated.

"Their whole attitude is founded on the fear of losing the parts they've secured. You may say it was always like that and you'd be right. But it was never acknowledged before and now it's an admitted fact."

He went back to the capital – labour partnership, in which employees would be entitled to a share in the profits. He declared that the plan had never before been tried out and that, in his opinion, it was the only way to give the workers the due rewards they were demanding and avoid a disastrous class-war. Mme. de Gaulle asked a number of questions and then we discussed the means by which the plan could be put into execution. Then he said:

"The communists have been defeated in Italy. And I'm convinced that the existence of the R.P.F. has played some part in de Gasperi's* success in the elections. It's partly due to us that Europe is beginning to recover."

A rather rash statement, perhaps.

"The only solution to the present situation is to make a strategic treaty with the U.S.A. and, once a powerful united Western *bloc* has been formed, face up to Russia and present her with peace terms: first of which would be her withdrawal from the whole of eastern Europe. It might mean war, for you're right in saying that their régime would not survive acceptance of the peace terms and they might prefer to try the alternative. Well, in that case, there'll be war. A war to save oppressed Europe."

We reverted to the Marseilles Congress and the large numbers of police scattered unnecessarily pretty well all over the town.

"I said to the mayor: 'Don't expect any thanks from me. That large police turnout was quite unnecessary and you know it as well as I do.' Nobody was fooled by it. The government was merely trying to make people believe in a non-existent danger. If the communists chose to hold a rally in another part of the town at the same time as us, I saw no harm in it. They only showed their separation from the rest of the country, which the country is already well aware of."

At 2.30, I got into the back of the Citroën with him and we were driven, via the Avenue Marceau, Place de L'Alma and the embankment, to the rue de Solférino. Whenever we were stopped by the lights, de Gaulle hid his face behind his hand. But no one paid any attention to us. He spoke to me about the beauty of Paris.

He saw people all through the afternoon, and rang for me several times to give him a quick yes or no. Soustelle, Vallon, Malraux . . .

Malraux said to me:

"I'd very much like to know what he thought of my speech, because, naturally, he didn't mention it and won't mention it. And it's better that way: that's how it should be. No, I didn't submit it to him in advance, because I hadn't written it down. Five lines of notes and a few 'old records', lifted from other speeches and improved. 'What do you intend to say to them?' he asked me. 'Well, General, how would it be if I called on them to join in a new crusade?' He glanced at me sideways out of the corner of his eye, in the way he does, and just said: 'Try it, try it. See what happens.' "

At 8.20 we left again in the Citroën. Opposite the Esplanade des Invalides (on the quay) he drew my attention to the beauty of the red sky, in the East, in this tranquil, vernal Paris. Then he said:

"But all that is out of keeping with the world as it is today. In New York, they're building four air-raid shelters that can each hold 100,000 people. There's the housing problem solved!"

With a certain pride, he informed me that the R.P.F. Municipal Council had just authorized the necessary expenditure for the erection of blocks of flats, which would house 30,000 tenants, and went on to speak of the high cost of building.

As we passed *Le Figaro* offices where enormous placards announced the publication of Churchill's war memoirs, he asked me to get him a copy. I told him that Churchill's memoirs in book-form only went as far as 1939, and promised to produce them next day.

I took him back to his hotel, and he released me for the rest of the evening.

I returned next morning at 10.00, and we made the same trip in the car. On our way down the Champs Elysées, he asked me a number of questions on newspaper circulations, and the effect that a rise in prices would have on them, etc. There is nothing very absorbing in all that, and I have only recorded it out of conscientiousness.

Friday, 14 May, 1948

There is nothing to record since my last entry, apart from de Gaulle's visit to the new room in the Legion of Honour Museum, devoted to France Libre, a visit which I had great difficulty in persuading the General to make at the request of the Grand Chancellor, Bloch-Dassault. It took place on 28 April and was of no great interest. Bloch-Dassault showed him the portraits of his principal lieutenants (Leclerc, Larminat, d'Argenlieu, etc.) surrounding his own, and asked him whether anyone had been forgotten. De Gaulle replied:

"These ones should unquestionably be here. But there may well be others."

And, a moment or so later, he mentioned General Giraud with copious praise, but just a shade ironically – though you would have had to know de Gaulle well to perceive it.

"It's true that he had no success in Algiers, but one mustn't forget his escape and his high standard of behaviour."

I saw the General this morning. Very pleasant and considerate. Too much so. He was obviously feeling guilty about something which concerned me. I should have guessed from his first words what it was, which were to announce that Georges Pompidou was going to take over as his Chief of Staff:

"Naturally, that won't affect your duties in any way, but I was anxious to tell you the news, myself."

I acquiesced in silence, largely through indifference. And also because I could see no reason why I should mind: I have none of the qualifications required to fill such a position, which demands a wide knowledge of the political world. And my ambition, if I have any, does not lie in this field. The manner in which I accepted the news must have surprised the General, who was, no doubt, expecting recriminations, for in the middle of our work, he suddenly asked me:

"There's nothing on your mind, Claude Mauriac? Nothing you want to ask? You're quite satisfied?"

I told him that I was perfectly happy in my present job, rather rashly perhaps, since I had been presented with an opportunity to reserve myself a possible way of retreat. But, actually, I am no longer anxious to get away and my modest position suits me better and better, first and foremost because it enables me to be close to de Gaulle.

And we talked of something else. Or, rather, he talked to me, something he has not done for a long time now. But I sensed that he wanted to be nice to me and show some consideration, when I doubtless had a certain amount of reason to be annoyed with him. We spoke of the levity again displayed by the Paris newspapers on the occasion of Stalin's macchiavellian disclosure of the secret talks that had been going on between the U.S.A. and the U.S.S.R., news that had been treated by all the leader-writers with wholly unjustifiable outbursts of enthusiasm.

"All that is unimportant. World affairs are being run by men of frightening mediocrity just at the moment when it's in the greatest danger. Truman, at best, is just another Ramadier. Wallace understands nothing whatsoever. As for us, we don't count any more. And it won't be that wretched X . . . nor Y . . . , that flunkey of the English, nor Z . . . (as weak as the others) who'll manage to make anyone listen to us. Stalin and Molotov are far the stronger. And, in addition, they have the enormous advantage of not having to rely on the support of public opinion. But this failure to take the situation seriously may well end up in the dropping of atom bombs. The war will come, though no one wants it, and the whole irresponsible affair which no one will have treated sufficiently seriously in time, will be settled by atom bombs.

Do you know that story of Octave Mirbeau's? Have I told it to you before?"

In fact, he had, but I said no, although I had not forgotten its point.

"Well, it takes place in Belgium, a funny country, where a certain man commits a funny crime and is brought before a funny tribunal. None of it's taken seriously. And, then he's condemned to death, but in a funny way, and no one attaches any importance to it, not even the condemned man himself, up to the moment when he finds himself, to his great surprise, in front of the scaffold. 'You're not really going to guillotine me?' he exclaims. But, yes, they are! They cut off his head in a light-hearted way with a funny guillotine! Well, that's the funny story that our light-headed planet is liable to find itself living through . . ."

He laughed, delighted with his analogy. Then, in connection with the election of an M.R.P. mayor, thanks to the communist vote, which I brought up to get the conversation going again, he said:

"Make no mistake, they're going to revive the Popular Front. The communists will be brought back into the government. Did you see Blum's appalling article this morning in *Le Populaire*, in which he writes that we must come to terms with the Soviets *at any price*? Have you been following the M.R.P. congress? I'm not speaking so much of their wickedness (*sic*) as of the utter emptiness of their discussions."

I said:

"And things look like going on as they are for a long time!"

He threw out his arms in a broad gesture:

"It's really not my fault!"

When I added that there might be some hope in October if the elections to the Republican Council reflected the results of the municipal poll, he answered:

"No, the only hope now lies in the cantonal elections, where the electorate, at least, will have a direct say."

When he got up to see me to the door (a new and quite unprecedented mark of attention, for, ordinarily, he only gets up) he said:

"It's a painful business, the death of the parties. And I shall do nothing to ease it, they can count on that."

I observed timidly that, in a manner of speaking, his own presence was of some service to the parties, since their fear of him compelled them to make an effort to stick together, which, as far as the government was concerned, had undeniably proved effective. But de Gaulle retorted vehemently:

"Not the parties! France! It's the country I serve, in the way you said. And that's all that counts in the end: the country."

Friday, 21 May, 1948

The last time I saw him, the General said: "One knows exactly what it means, that 'no negative anti-communism' that the M.R.P. congress passed." And this morning, he added:

"If it weren't for the Marshall Plan and their fear of having American aid refused them, you can be quite certain that they'd bring the communists back into the government without further delay. The M.R.P. are really outrageous. The more I think of them the more infamous I find their false pretences and the more abominable everything they do. The régime is vanishing into thin air."

Thursday, 3 June, 1948

"So what do you think of the situation?"

"That there seems no reason for it to change."

"Yes, until the next invasion, it'll stay the same. They're perfectly happy as long as they remain in office."

"And they've just given in on Germany."

"As they have on everything else. This government is incapable of doing anything but give in on every issue, without exception. There may be some people who are satisfied with the present régime. But I'm certainly not one of them!"

All the same, he looked relaxed and cheerful.

Tuesday, 20 July, 1948

At the Maison de la Mutualité, yesterday, at 3.00 in the afternoon, General de Gaulle opened the first session of the National Council of the R.P.F. I had never heard him speak in public as intimately and movingly. With a skilful moderation of his own, well-designed, no doubt, to produce the required effect. Nevertheless, this did not prevent me from being immediately won over and far more deeply touched than I had expected.

"Never before, in my life, let me tell you, have I felt the call of duty so intensely. We must take France under our protection to guide her in the right direction, but she must support us of her own free will, otherwise everything we do will be fictitious. This is the Movement's inviolable task."

And, again, as always happens when I am in direct contact with de Gaulle, all my doubts, reservations, and, in particular, my detachment from public affairs, which has always been my strength and my weakness, were swept away in a flash.

At 5.30 I was ushered into his room at the Hôtel La Pérouse where he was having tea with Diomède Catroux, who had come back with him from the Mutualité a quarter of an hour earlier to ask him for the script of his speech, in order to give it to the Press. De Gaulle offered me tea, very kindly and courteously. Before the three of us sat down at the table, he quickly signed all the letters I had brought him, without glancing over a single one of them. We spoke of the government's perilous position, and Diomède Catroux, with the General nodding agreement, was saying that, in his opinion, it would somehow contrive to prolong its existence until the October elections, when Georges Pompidou was shown in, straight from the Chamber. "I'm beginning to think that Schuman is about to resign," he announced, and went on to enumerate the various party alliances which might result from it. To which de Gaulle observed with irony:

"I'm not interested in how they group themselves: they won't solve their difficulties whatever they do."

He also spoke (after his ritual comment: "In any case, none of that matters") of the imminent war, which would be fought by people who were wholly unprepared for it, wanted no part of it and were in fact, irresponsible children. And I was reminded of what Bénouville* had just told me, on his return from the States: that the unpreparedness of the American forces was quite terrifying. Just at the moment when the Berlin crisis had reached its most dangerous peak and a trial of strength between the Allies and the U.S.S.R. might have catastrophic results.

I forgot to note down that the General's first words to me were: "I quoted your father, a moment ago." And I had to confess that I had not identified 'the famous author' whose words he had quoted: "We are heading towards an unknown sea."

Schuman resigned tonight.

Speaking in Colmar a few days later, de Gaulle said: "We have had enough of this system, which consists of perpetually mixing the ones with the others, always the same others with the same ones."

Wednesday, 4 August, 1948
Paris

The A.D.C.s being 'worn to a frazzle' after the two trips East and West, de Gaulle asked me to stand in for them today and tomorrow. Therefore I was there to receive him when he reached the Hôtel La Pérouse at 1.00. Admiral and Mme. Ortoli had been invited to lunch and there were five of us at table, as Mme. de Gaulle was there, too.

The meal began more or less in silence as the Ortolis were intimidated, but the ice gradually melted. Mme. Ortoli spoke of her farming problems which de Gaulle seemed to treat with a certain scepticism. Presently we moved on to more serious topics. "Stalin has won the game," the General said, with regard to the talks now taking place in Moscow, but I only listened with half an ear to his ensuing discourse and am not sure that I took it in well enough to record it here. Internal matters, of immediate concern, interest me much more, and we proceeded to discuss them. De Gaulle asked a question (which turned out to be his main preoccupation throughout his stay): "Has the country any confidence in Marie's new ministry and in Paul Reynaud's financial policies (as yet, undisclosed)?"

Mme. Ortoli replied that, judging by the Press, it was clear that no such confidence existed, but de Gaulle exclaimed:

"There, you're wrong! It's the Press that makes any pretence of having confidence. They're always the same: it's Vichy all over again."

I said:

"It's quite true, General, that from reading the Press one would never have guessed what a reception you got from the crowds on your last two trips."

"But the Vichy press took just as little notice of Bir-Hakeim!"

The reply cut like a whiplash, despite his surface good humour and the twinkle in his eye. (A little earlier he had said to me: "In the Charentes, in Alsace, I sensed something quite new in the crowd's warmth; a rejection of the present régime by the French, which did not exist to such an extent a few months ago."

Ortoli then said that Monsieur X had telephoned him to ask him a straightforward question. 'I'm told that you wore uniform when you attended the various ceremonies that took place during General de Gaulle's tour of the Upper-Rhine. Is it true?' "I said it was." Ortoli added. He looked very put out. I then witnessed the remarkable spectacle of a General giving his superior officer a lesson in discipline. Not as remarkable as all that perhaps, when I thought back to 18 June

297

and his broadcast appeal a few days later, when it was a question of persuading the Empire territories to join the Resistance: "If necessary, I shall appeal to the people," (against the Governors):

"But, my dear friend, you should have sent him packing! Told him that you'd considered it the right thing to do, and if he disapproved, you couldn't care less! If three or four of you spoke to him in that way, they wouldn't dare take the matter further, because they're a timid lot. The whole of France knows it! And that's what I've been saying, all through my tour, from West to East: 'Look around you; it's you who are France!' But where are the official representatives? They alone are missing: from now on, we are entitled to ask: where does legitimacy lie?"

And when Ortoli remarked that Monsieur X wanted to keep in with the régime and de Gaulle at one and the same time, the General retorted contemptuously:

"But I don't give a damn about Monsieur X. You can tell him so. You can tell him that I recognize him for what he is: a minor politician, like all the others, and that any respect I have for him is extremely relative!"

A silence followed. Then, in front of the head-waiter, which disturbed me slightly, he went on:

"I've decided now to treat them to a roll of drums (*sic*). People keep on telling me: 'This one or that one is not as badly disposed towards you as all that.' As if I cared in the least what the Maries and the Meyers think of me. I don't believe, no, I truthfully don't believe that Reynaud can succeed. He'll end by making concessions, by agreeing to half-measures like René Mayer. And, from then on, failure is certain. What's more, we've seen Reynaud at work when faced with extremely difficult problems; the whole country's seen him. We already know how ineffective he is, despite his undoubted ability. Instead of coming to decisions in the light of Space, Geography and History, he comes to them in the perspective of Blum, Herriot, in short: on a parliamentary level. And that's why he missed the bus in 1940."

When Ortoli remarked that it was a pity that Paul Reynaud had not held back and waited for the General's future government, the General exclaimed (still in front of the head-waiter):

"That's what I had someone tell him. But he replied he was already too far committed to Marie. In short, always the parliamentary angle, which has blinded him once again to the real facts of the problem."

This did not stop de Gaulle, when we reached the coffee stage, from asking me once more (and it would not be the last time):

"Well, do people have confidence in Reynaud?"

Pierre de Gaulle arrived and I made myself scarce until it came time to leave for the rue de Solférino. I was alone with the General in the back seat of the car. He spoke to me again about Reynaud's experiment, which is the problem that really concerns him most:

"The régime being what it is, it's impossible for him to succeed."

I spent the rest of the day showing in the various people who had appointments with him, the most notable being M. Brugère*, followed by the delegates from the Gaullist middle-group, led by Soustelle and Giacobbi. Georges Pompidou told me later that the General had been much pleasanter to them than was expected. At 8.00, when we left the rue de Solférino, in the car, de Gaulle said to me:

"It's deliquescence, one can sense it everywhere. But they're losing this poor country precious minutes! It's tragic! And with the complicity of the Press. It's Vichy, all over again: the country betrayed by its élite."

Thursday, 5 August, 1948

In the car, as we drove through the Place de l'Alma, the General said:

"It's becoming more and more unspeakable, this sickening pettiness on all sides."

"And yet you're here, General."

"If I hadn't been, France would already have fallen completely into the hands of America, there's no question about that."

There was a pause. Then, as we drove along the Quai d'Orsay he added:

"Marie, Reynaud. Not a word to say that's in the least inspiring, not a word. I preferred Schuman or even Ramadier. But they won't dare to postpone the elections to the General Council and to the Republican Council."

At 1.00, as we were leaving the rue de Solférino, in the car:

"Everything's at sixes and sevens. They won't be able to extricate themselves. Reynaud's plans? You may say that we don't know them yet, but Reynaud, himself, doesn't know them. Reynaud, himself, I can assure you, has no idea what he means to do."

We were driving up the Champs Elysées as he made these somewhat unfair remarks.

Lunch, in the small suite (No. 24) in the Hôtel La Pérouse, at which I sat between him and Mme. de Gaulle, was a taciturn affair. We spoke of Pierre Bourdan*. The General considered it overdoing things to give him a state funeral, an honour which, in his opinion, should be granted very rarely:

"In any case, they won't give me a state funeral. I've said I'm opposed to it."

He said again, about Pierre Bourdan: "He wasn't with us (in London)", though he paid tribute to his ability:

"What he said was intelligent and clear, all the more so, because one never felt that he was overstating the facts."

It was an uneventful day, taken up with unimportant interviews. ("One always sees far too many people," he said to me, smiling, when we were in the car, after I had remarked that there had been no need for him to receive most of that day's visitors.)

But towards 6.00, he summoned me with an imperious ring of the bell. I found him with Soustelle, whom I had shown in a short while before. Looking furious, the General was brandishing a copy of *Le Monde* and, after pointing out an article on the last page on 'France Libre's accounts', he said, obviously in the last stages of exasperation, though he managed to control it:

"Find out *who*, in the Express newsagency, wrote this article, and send him to me. I want to know *who* it is. If it's M.Ollivier, I want to see him at once. Or if it's M. Pia or M. Catroux, he's the one I want to see, but right away . . ."

Twenty minutes later, Pascal Pia and Diomède Catroux, looking none too comfortable, were in my office, where Pompidou, Bozel, and a moment before, Palewski (whom I had just shown in to the General), pointed out to them sharply the untimeliness of the clumsy article. Silence would have been the best answer, but Pia and Catroux, on the contrary, defended their point of view, claiming that what they had written had nipped the affair in the bud. Then I announced their arrival to the General, who did not keep them long. I do not know exactly what he said to them, for they were reticent when they emerged, but it is not hard to guess. What de Gaulle no doubt found intolerable was their failure to consult him on such an important matter. Georges Pompidou rightly remarked to me that de Gaulle's entourage embraces an extraordinary combination of complete submissiveness and in-dividual displays of initiative, which commit him, without his knowledge and against his will, on matters of vital importance.

17, 18, 19, 20 *August*, 1948

My departure to Venice was delayed by two days because I had to stand in for the General's A.D.C.s. The leitmotiv of his monologues (each time he had a predominating idea, to which he returns over and over again in almost exactly the same words) was:

"If, as now seems certain, the Assembly puts off the October cantonal elections, you'll find that there'll be no more elections in France, none at all, as is the position throughout Europe at the present time. It means the end of democracy in its present form."

On the morning of Wednesday 18, in the car, he remarked, with reference to the government and the régime: "The game's over." With reference to X, who had nothing better to suggest than that General Giraud should accompany him on his approaching visit to Corsica: "What an imbecile!"

During lunch, we had an odd conversation about the Olympic Games, which disclosed an unexpected interest in them on his part. He even spoke of Cerdan, and his chances of becoming world champion, with a precision that showed he knew what he was talking about. He regretted that French victories in the Olympic Games (with the exception of Mlle. Ostermayer, "who, in parentheses, is a member of the R.P.F.") had never been won in the real realm of sport: athletics.

"The elections? You can be quite certain they won't hold them, and never will again. When one has once backed away from universal suffrage, it's finished with; one doesn't dare risk it again."

He spoke, too, of the U.S.S.R.'s systematic expansion into Asia:
"We shan't offer any resistance."

Thursday, 19
In the car, on our way back, in the morning.

"There will never be any more elections. Moreover, the position's the same all over Europe. We're heading for a free-for-all, where everyone grabs what they can."

He repeated the same remark, word for word, to his brother-in-law, Jacques Vendroux, during lunch:

"No, there'll be no more elections in this country. I'm completely convinced of it. One has to face the fact. Ever since the National Assembly resigned – in 1940 – there has been no democracy in France. An effort was made to set the machine in motion again – it was I who made it – but it didn't work; the spring had broken. During the Occupation, there were people in France who did not want to get embroiled with the Germans – they followed Pétain – and people who refused to accept the Armistice and its consequences – they followed de Gaulle. But no one supported the régime. No one mentioned it. No one thought of it. Anyhow, as long as the danger was there . . ."

All the same, de Gaulle thinks that the elections to the Republican Council will be held, but that they will be the last.

"We shall get about a hundred members of the R.P.F. elected. Not more than that, because I only want candidates who are for *us*, reliable men and not the cunning sort, who snatch at the first opportunity to betray us!"

As we have just witnessed in the Assembly, when the members of the Gaullist middle-group defected on an important vote.

Jacques Vendroux spoke of a forthcoming project: the creation of a sort of middle-group inside the existing middle-group. "They're only awaiting a sign," he said of the loyal Gaullist deputies. According to him, Capitant and Giacobbi are opposed to the project. The General and he had a long discussion on the subject. The other topics were of only passing interest and I shall not record them.

In the car, on our way back to the rue de Solférino, de Gaulle observed:

"Reynaud's lost here and now. The revenue's dropped."

I found it difficult to understand since it had, in fact, risen during the first few days after Reynaud's scheme came into operation.

"The price of gold is rising. The deliveries at La Vellette are very limited. He's been there for a month and what's he done?"

When I said that we should hear what his plans were that evening in the broadcast that had been announced, the General answered:

"He won't say anything. It'll just be a lecture."

During the day, he showed me on a map the itinerary of the visit he intends to make to the area round Paris in September.

"At the inauguration of the Avenue du General-Leclerc (Avenue d'Orléans), I shall come by way of Antony, Bourg-la-Reine and Montrouge, following the same route that I took at the time of the Liberation when I came to Paris from Rambouillet. In that way, we'll show them we're at home everywhere!"

Friday, 20
Morning, in the car . . .

But I was forgetting the most important thing: the drive up the Champs Elysées, by the side of a thoughtful de Gaulle, on the evening of 19 August, a beautiful evening, four years after his return to a Paris in the process of liberating herself. The indifference of the passers-by, their self-absorption seemed to pain him. And I felt that he, who takes so much trouble not to be recognized, who insists on travelling in the most modest Citroëns in order to pass unnoticed, would have been happy at that moment if a cheer had arisen from that inattentive crowd.

Ten minutes later, having left him for a few hours, the tart, shrill voice of Paul Reynaud, audible the whole way down the pavement, plunged me dizzily back eight years in time, for we have not heard that voice of catastrophe since June 1940. How ridiculous to think that, four years after the Liberation, it is to this man that the nation appeals for help in her hour of danger, in him that she puts her trust. But her confidence is a pretence.

That evening, I was kept very late at the Hôtel La Pérouse. There were two important visitors, who must not be allowed to run into each other: Maurice Schuman (that was something new!) and then General Juin, the French Resident in Morocco. I showed them in, one after the other, and did not get away till 1.00 in the morning.

Now back to Friday 20, morning, in the car.

"Reynaud could only talk of the peril we're in. On the other hand, he's virtually nothing to say about any possible remedies. . ."

In his office, he made me alter a letter to a foreign diplomat, whom I had made him address as: 'Monsieur l'Ambassadeur'. When I said that I thought he kept 'Mon cher Ambassadeur' solely for French ambassadors, he made this splendid remark:

"No, not at all. I'm always France!"

During lunch, at midday, I said that, in my opinion, Reynaud had been particularly anxious to get himself out of bond, break the spell, and become a minister but that, once he had achieved it, he would see to it that he 'fell', so as to be in a position either to head the government at some future date or, more probably, to become Minister of Finance in the General's Cabinet. De Gaulle gave me a piercing look, obviously interested by this diagnosis. After a brief silence, he said:

"No, he isn't good enough, and I'll tell you why. First of all, in his speech yesterday, there was no mention of the anniversary of the Liberation, an omission it's hard to forgive. I shan't forget it. And then he said that France had never been in such danger. That's enough to make anyone laugh! June 1940, our frontiers penetrated, the whole population on the roads, then the armistice and our fleet scuttled because the country wasn't prepared to fight; those were the worst hours that France ever had to face, not the present difficulties with the C.G.T."

He laughed sourly and went on:

"There are four men who want to be de Gaulle's Minister of Finance: Pleven, for a start, naturally; Giacobbi, Mayer and Reynaud. (I am not quite certain that I have remembered the two middle names correctly.)

I said it was a pity that U.N.O. was meeting in Paris just when governmental crises were looming up. De Gaulle burst out laughing, and said, arrogantly:

"So much the worse for U.N.O.! They shouldn't have betrayed the real France: de Gaulle."

He passed on to the demonstrations expected to occur in the vicinity of Paris in September:

"The annoying thing is that I shall have to make a speech. I can't avoid it. I thought of getting a tower built in the Ile de la Cité: then they'd be able to see me from everywhere when I spoke to the country. What do you think about it?"

He seemed delighted with the idea, which seemed to me pure whimsy. I explained why in discreet terms. As I spoke, I noticed how astonishingly furrowed his face was. How he has aged in four years . . .

8 September, 1948

The day after I got back to Paris. Since the fall of Marie's government (I was in Venice for the Film Festival) it has been a time of crisis . . . a new Schuman government – overthrown two days later . . . then Queuille's* government. De Gaulle, the clairvoyant . . .

Tuesday, 22 September, 1948

I have just spent two days at Colombey in order to organize the secretariat necessitated by the stream of letters in connection with the so-called stamp campaign. (Around 300,000 have come in in the first five days.)

I arrived at Bar-sur-Aube on Sunday evening and was hard at work early next morning helping the cameraman sent by the newsreels (Gaumont-Métro and Pathé-Journal): thirteen sacks, that Monday morning, filmed as they were unloaded from the mail-van; the staging of a pseudo-secretariat (the real one not being organized yet); etc. The General arrived back in the evening from his long tour in the South-East, marked by gory incidents in Grenoble.

I saw him almost at once at the house. He had never appeared so cheerful and in such good form. He enquired about the number of letters that had already come in and then informed Bonneval and me of his astounding decision: we could take three weeks if necessary but we were to count the stamps! As there were often several in the one letter, we should have to open them all. Would it take us long? We were free to bring down all our secretaries from Paris. And we would carry out a test there and then. De Gaulle made Bonneval and me sit down, gave each of us a paper knife and a packet of letters and took out his stop-watch. At the end of five minutes – during which he had been unsparing with his advice – the score was thirty letters for Bonneval and twenty for me. The General confirmed, after I had drawn his attention to it, my lack of aptitude.

"But, after a little practice, you should both manage fifty letters every five minutes . . ."

I left the house, mortified, with the prospect of spending several weeks at Colombey, and furious at being landed with a task so unworthy of my talents – if I have any. Bonneval tried very kindly to console me, explaining that it was because de Gaulle trusted us that he had given us the job: for it meant recovering his personal mail from the avalanche. The real point was that Colombey was a private place in which only a private secretary was entitled to set foot, etc.

I went back to spend the night at Bar-sur-Aube (Hôtel du Commerce) and at 9.00 next morning was at work with Bonneval in the big reception room at the Town Hall. The result of our exhausting labour was that by 11.30, Bonneval had opened 1,300 letters – or rather counted 1,300 stamps – myself 900, and our assistant (a policeman) 700.

A counter-order fortunately arrived from the General, who, on learning that five more sacks had been delivered (about 70,000 letters), had realized that we should not be able to cope. He had called in Fouchet, who would bring the whole with him to the rue de Solférino and take charge of opening the mail.

So I returned to Paris yesterday evening after having lunched with the General and Mme. de Gaulle.

Before the meal, the General listened to the 1.00 news, striding up and down between the drawing-room door and his desk at the far end of the adjoining room, the door to which had been left open. I had never seen him walking to and fro like that, particularly at such a pace. He put on an air of unconcern and even an ironic smile, but I could feel that he was preoccupied and tense.

What news was there? The arrival at Orly of the mortal remains of the U.N.O. mediator, Count Bernadotte, assassinated in Palestine at the same time as Col. Serot, who was killed by mistake according to the Jewish terrorists. When the newsreader recalled that this was the fifth French officer to meet his death in Palestine, de Gaulle nodded:

"That's quite true. When you come to think of it, it's only the French who are dying out there!"

The solemn opening session of the General Assembly of the United

Nations at the Palais de Chaillot. De Gaulle made occasional scathing comments:

"Don't you think that all this smacks of the end of a world?"

I said that it was a pity, as U.N.O. was a splendid endeavour. But the General takes little interest in projects that are out of touch with reality. A feminine voice then announced that a debate would take place that afternoon in the National Assembly on the occurrences at Grenoble.

De Gaulle pretended to attach no importance to it. According to him, the whole thing would be forgotten within ten days. Mme. de Gaulle broke in, from the small desk where she was writing letters, to say that if the cantonal elections took place (as now seems possible after the communist *volte-face* of yesterday), the R.P.F. would lose votes as a direct result of the fights in Grenoble. De Gaulle did not think so, but he did not reply when I said:

"It's a serious matter, General, the first deaths since the Liberation . . ."

After a long silence he said:

"There is, in fact, only one death, that of the communist member. For, though the R.P.F. may not be in a very good condition, he's still alive."

According to him (and I think he is right), the greater part of the responsibility lies with the communists, who had been alloted another part of the town for their meeting and should not have been in the square where de Gaulle was speaking (moreover, they arrived after he had left and only ran into the R.P.F. security squad – a very small group of men waiting to receive his congratulations) – and even more with the police: there were some C.R.S.* present but one refrained from allowing them to take action:

"The State still possesses its implements but no longer has sufficient conscientiousness to use them: there isn't any more State."

I used the word 'tactical' to qualify the attitude adopted by the M.R.P. who appear to be in favour of the cantonal elections in the Republican Council (so as not to alienate the electorate) and against them in the Assembly.

"Nothing of the sort," de Gaulle thundered. "It's ignominy pure and simple!"

He used the same word in referring to the socialists and then branded his one-time friend X . . . with it (to the great distress of his wife).

"He's slipping towards ignominy, he's already sunk deep into ignominy. It's the same old story: one starts by making a mistake, then one persists in it because of public opinion and finally one's covered in ignominy."

He shocks me profoundly by his scorn for everyone who does not share his opinions. I shall never grow reconciled to an intransigence of thought that never entertains the slightest doubt of its own correctness. Yet I know that here lies his strength. But I, myself, have the weakness of trying to be just, even and above all to my political enemies, if I have any – and it would be difficult for me to have them: I often feel myself to be far closer to the communists than to members of the R.P.F., and I have to think of the Russian concentration camps and of Eastern Europe, terrorized and gagged, before reaction sets in. That does not, however, mean that I approve of the R.P.F.'s methods, though they may be the only possible ones; merely that I run up against my eternal inhibition towards the injustices that are perpetrated in the name of justice.

"One feels as though one were back in 1940: there is the same deliquescence, the same capitulation."

De Gaulle's voice broke my train of thought. It was profoundly sad. And like that, how close to my heart, as it dwelt on the *insoluble* problem of salaries. His enemies believe that he is more and more delighted as things grow worse for France, since the R.P.F. benefits by it. But he never thinks of anything but France, and, to him, the R.P.F. represents France's only hope.

I ran through the pile of newspapers he had just been reading and came across the headline in *Franc-Tireur*: CLEMENCEAU WOULD HAVE STUCK YOU IN GAOL, GENERAL! *And since you demand the 'dissolution' with so much arrogance, how about starting by dissolving your civil war troops?* Embarrassed, I covered *Franc-Tireur* with another paper, but it was *L'Humanité*. De Gaulle, who was standing behind me in front of the fire (he is sensitive to the cold and had informed us, several times, that summer was over) had seen me reading. But it was about Cerdan and his world championship fight in America that evening that he spoke. He said that our champion's chances are not much fancied. He had been seen about too much with American beauties. It augurs badly. He is very much afraid he will lose. He discussed the matter very seriously. French boxing is another aspect of France.

With reference to *Franc-Tireur*, he asked us, smilingly, if we had found any of the satirical stamps *cause toujours* in favour of a counter-referendum which that paper had offered its readers, in his mail. We told him the truth: thirty to forty in about 3,000 letters. "Yes, there'll be about a thousand in all," he commented sarcastically. He predicted that there would be a million R.P.F. ones, not more!

But that is already very good, at fifty francs a time. He was enraptured by the campaign: "No one's ever seen anything like it!" He was looking delighted and made me run through the scenes again that had been filmed: the postman falling off his bicycle because of the weight of the sacks, and so on. His eyes were sparkling with malice. He was drinking whey.

I had a long wait at Bar-sur-Aube station. Mulhouse station was blocked by a strike and the train was two hours late. There was an atmosphere of discontent. I twice heard workmen grumbling about the lack of relation between their pay and the cost of living:

"Some of the postmen here get 9,000 francs a month. The pension-deductions come to 250 francs a day. That leaves them 1,500 francs. How can anyone live on that?"

And, truly, how can they? . . . There are grave days ahead.

Tuesday, 28 September, 1948

I took a step today that had been in my mind for some time: I suggested to the General that my presence in his secretariat might no longer be serving any very useful purpose. He agreed so amiably that I could only accept when he immediately offered to find me another post for "in fact, I could be put to better use than I had been, now that the secretariat I had organized was running smoothly". My secret wish was to leave him and return to private life, to which I feel myself better suited. But I knew that it was out of the question. The most it would achieve would be to make it easier for me, once I ceased to be in direct contact with the General, to resign from the R.P.F. as soon as I felt out of sympathy with its policy. But there is no hope of that at the moment! De Gaulle, who was seeing Malraux immediately after me, said that he would discuss with him where and how to employ me, for he was certain that I should be more at home in some kind of intellectual work closely associated with him.

I saw Malraux after he had left de Gaulle:

"When the General spoke to me about you, I said to him: 'Claude Mauriac should be in a director's job and not under anyone's orders. So the matter requires close consideration. What seems to me best would be to put him in charge of all intellectual questions and liaison with intellectuals.'" And that left me delighted.

The fact is that I took advantage of a moment that seemed to me propitious and took the plunge, as I might have done twenty times in the last few months – or never ventured to do. After he had signed the letters, de Gaulle asked me, as usual, what I thought of the situation.

I said that it was becoming increasingly confused, both inside and outside the country. As regards our domestic difficulties, I could see no way out of them unless elections were held:

"But it's precisely elections that they won't hear of at any price!" the General exclaimed. "What Auriol wants to do now, what he intends to do, is clear as day: to appeal to the communists and invite them to join the government. And his only reason for that, make no mistake about it, is to ensure that he remains in office and does not have to leave the Elysée. 'By all means!' the communists will say. 'Particularly as it was we who put you there!' As for the Western Powers' appeal to the Security Council on the Berlin issue that only means they've given in. One's given in from the moment one agrees to embark on thorny questions of procedure . . ."

He also said:

"Inside the country, everything's sliding away, everything's dissolving into ignominy."

After that there was a long silence. Obviously, it was up to me to say something, no matter what. But I did not feel the slightest inclination to revive our conversation. It was then that I made up my mind to ask him if I might speak to him on a personal matter and prove that I was of no further use working in his private secretariat; that Xavier de Beaulaincourt was now well qualified to replace me, thereby saving my salary, since I very well know that his available budget was limited.

Friday, 1 October, 1948

I saw de Gaulle again yesterday. He asked me how far the question of my collaboration with Malraux had got. The aforesaid Malraux, whom I saw this morning on the conclusion of the Press conference held by de Gaulle in the rue François-ler, gave me a rendezvous for Monday and told me that I should be taking up my new appointment at once.

Thursday, 28 October, 1948

It was the second time I saw de Gaulle since leaving his secretariat. The second time that I sat down in an armchair facing his desk, 'like a grown-up'. But yesterday the conversation was not confined to my work. He asked me his ritual question about the situation and what I thought of it. The miners' strike has now lasted over three weeks. The government, after letting it go its own way, has now stiffened its attitude. Men have been killed on two occasions. And, on order from the Kominform*, the nation's industrial activities seem likely to be brought to a halt in a number of new fields. What could I tell him that he did not know already? I stammered out a few vague remarks (half-heartedly, without imagination or inspiration). Then there was a long silence; so long, that I told myself sadly that he would terminate the interview, convinced that I was excessively stupid. But no: he had merely been taking advantage of the silence to reflect, and this is what emerged from his meditation:

"You're quite right, the Republican Council elections, whatever comes of them, won't bring in their train the great change of attitude which might save us. So, what will? What hope have we got? This poor country is dying, every Frenchman can see that she's dying, slowly and surely. And instead of a trend towards unity, what do we see? A movement, more and more pronounced, towards dispersion and division . . ."

I do not think I have ever seen him so pessimistic, particularly in regard to his own powers as a 'uniter', about which he has never, up till now, whatever the circumstances, betrayed the slightest signs of harbouring any doubt. I remembered his quiet confidence when the R.P.F. was first formed and how, I, myself, had thought: 'You're deluding yourself about your powers . . .' Yet it was at the very moment when the Movement had developed to an extent that astonished me, at the very moment when Frenchmen were attracted to it in greater and greater numbers (so it seemed to me), leaving aside the fanatics of the Third Force and the communists, it was at this moment that he allowed himself to become discouraged. I confided to him my own, more optimistic view of things. He made a pretence of agreeing with me. He made the pretence, and I was suddenly no longer so confident. In my heart of hearts, it was I who agreed with him.

1949

Thursday, 17 *March,* 1949

I regret not having made any notes about the two interviews I had with de Gaulle immediately after the publication of Nos. 1 and 2 of *Liberté de l'Esprit.* He seemed to be extremely pleased and he, who never pays any kind of compliment, came close to congratulating me after the first number. He treated the attacks on me, which even came from inside the R.P.F., with sarcasm (the same attitude he displayed, I am told, when General de Bénouville and Pasteur Vallery-Radot spoke against Max-Pol Fouchet's article at the Executive Committee). As for the small note devoted to Jean Nocher (. . . "Where Companions are concerned, we insist that our right be recognized to prefer M. Max-Pol Fouchet to M. Jean Nocher") the General laughed and said: "All the same, don't break too many windows!"

I saw General de Gaulle from 11.00 to midday at the Hôtel La Pérouse. His first words, which were in distinct contrast, despite his measured tone, with the cheerful appreciation he had shown when he had welcomed me on the two previous occasions, were:

"Liberty of the mind? That's all very well, but one's never entirely free. Your work is integrated into that of the R.P.F. therefore it's essential that there should be a certain cohesion between the positions you adopt and those of the Movement. That being so, Max-Pol Fouchet's article took a line that was hardly acceptable and it was a mistake to publish it. The same applies to the reference to Jean Nocher."

He said all this nervously and embarrassed, as though it were a lesson he had learnt by heart. I was convinced that he had said it against his will, at the express wish of his entourage. He seemed relieved when he had finished and was free to resume our normal conversation ·

"Admittedly, to have turned down Max-Pol Fouchet's work would have compromised our venture from the start. Publishing it was the lesser of two evils," etc.

Then he went on:

"Your review once more poses the absorbing problem of the relationship between thought and action. There must be a lot to say on the subject, plain truths that no one knows any more, and if you expose them in *Liberté de l'Esprit* I'm sure it'll arouse very interesting controversy. Liberty of thought must certainly be safeguarded and exercised, but only on condition that it doesn't undermine, in its name, the national strength which generates it. It's unquestionably true that intellectuals like those on *Combat,* under the pretext of liberty of thought, are now jeopardizing its very existence."

The General went on to quote, once again, the passage from *Faust,* of which he's so fond (he gave it to me first in German and then translated it: "In the beginning was the word. No, replies Mephistopheles, in the beginning was action.")

I mentioned the article that Raymond Aron* had sent me for the third number on the Atlantic Pact, and gave him the gist of it in a few words, because I was afraid that it might go against his policy and that of the R.P.F. It contained some very sharp criticism of Etienne Gilson's two articles, in which he accused the Americans of wanting to buy French blood with their dollars. It censured the Atlantic Pact for not having given the French any guarantees on the time or place of American intervention in the event of a Russian invasion of Western Europe.

"But it's obvious that it's M. Gilson who's right," the General exclaimed. "You must understand this: that America is essentially an isolationist country for the simple reason that she's an island. She has never felt any solidarity with Europe, from which she's separated – one can't dispute that – by a wide stretch of water. In the 1914 war, as in that of 1940, it was certainly not because Paris was threatened or occupied that the Americans came in. And, if London had been occupied in 1940, she certainly would have deplored it, just as she would deplore it if Paris were occupied, this time by the Soviet armies, but it wouldn't be to liberate London or Paris that America would go to war. She would choose her moment and take her time. In the same way, in the Atlantic Pact, they have taken good care not to say when or where American armies will intervene. The crux of the matter is that with their present weapons, the Americans regard it as unnecessary to come out here, since they can wage war, relatively calmly, without leaving their own country, by means of their Flying Fortresses, rockets and so on. If Paris and France were occupied by the Russians, it would undoubtedly strike them as an extremely regrettable occurrence but not one that, in itself, would justify an American landing. The whole situation would obviously alter if Europe, that's to say France, were strong enough to slow down the Russian advance or halt it, or, who knows, advance themselves. Then the Americans might judge it worthwhile to send their divisions to the point occupied. The error that the Queuilles, the Arons and the gentlemen on *Le Figaro* are committing lies in making us believe that the Atlantic Pact is all that's needed, and that the French can now sleep peacefully in their beds."

As I was leaving, I told the General briefly that I had been present at the meeting which Louis Vallon had held at Villeneuve-Saint-Georges, a communist stronghold, where none of the political parties, up till then, had been able to obtain a hearing. At this news, the General displayed considerable optimism about the result of the cantonal elections, which start on 20 March.

"They'll see – we're more alive than ever."

Tuesday, 22 March, 1949

Following our conversation on 17 March, I sent Raymond Aron's article on the Atlantic Pact to the General today for his opinion.

After a summons from the General to come round at 7.00, I was certain that he would raise the strongest objections to the publication of the article just now in its present form. So I was astonished by the words with which the General greeted me:

"Well, it's not bad at all, that article you sent me."

The fact is that the General seems to have greatly modified his opinion of the Atlantic Pact in the last few days.

When he announced that he would explain to me the real crux of the matter, I told myself that he had no doubt forgotten that he had already disclosed his point of view to me at some length and that I was about to hear more or less the same speech. But it was nothing of the sort.

"It's certain – and Raymond Aron was right to stress the point – that the Pact, even without any definite commitments, is of a kind to give Stalin food for thought. I don't say it ensures that he'll leave us alone, but at least he now knows that, if he occupies Western Europe, it'll mean war. And we might reasonably suppose that, if such a pact had existed in 1939, Hitler would not have embarked on his Polish venture. Obviously, it would have been better if Aron had emphasized the fact that a strong France would make the chances of war even smaller. It's to the interest of Queuille and his crew to make us believe that the Pact, as it now stands, is all that's required. This does not alter the fact that such a Pact is better than no Pact at all, and that's where Raymond Aron did very well to point out the weakness of Gilson's arguments. Formerly, there was a concept, that was never written into any treaty, called *balance*, which at that time meant *European balance*.

313

All the nations had a tacit understanding that no single one of them should obtain excessive power to the detriment of the others. It was in the name of European balance that Europe made war, in turn, on Louis XIV, the French Revolution and Napoleon. Bismarck's great strength in 1870, lay in his ability to hide from England and Russia that the European balance was being threatened. It was thanks to this concept, that the small countries like Holland, Belgium etc., were assured of their existence. The Atlantic Pact is nothing else but an official recognition of the same concept. It, too, is concerned with the maintenance of the European balance."

As I was leaving, de Gaulle said to me:

"Now you know how I view the matter. Naturally, you are free to publish the article or not, but I would not like Raymond Aron to think that I disapprove of the line he has taken."

No diary for 1950 has been found.

1951

France-Soir announced yesterday that I would be standing as a candidate in the Landes in the elections. It was news to me two days ago, still highly unlikely and I do not know whether to hope my adoption is confirmed or not. I am astonished that such an unimportant, uncertain and recent project should have reached the ears so quickly of a woman-reporter, whom I have never met.

This morning, when I looked in at the rue de Solférino with no particular object in view, Bonneval told me that the General had wanted to see me when I was away at Cannes. Twenty minutes later, he received me. It had been months and months and months since I had seen him – and I had even avoided occasions when I might have seen him. I feel so impoverished and lacking in talent when confronted by this man, in whose eyes I do not stand for anything! I had the same feeling again today when he was questioning me about *Liberté de l'Esprit* and making, with great politeness and equal lassitude, a show of being interested in my answers.

When I had finished, de Gaulle made a few remarks about the forthcoming elections. I asked him whether he thought they would be held on 10 June instead of in October.

"Yes. Though certainly not for my sake. But they're so afraid!"

He made a brief reference to the M.R.P. and their fundamental 'hypocrisy'.

"We must crush them. I hope the least possible number survive . . ."

Then he indicated, still very politely, and with the same air of boredom, that it was time for me to leave.

Outside his office, I ran into Georges Pompidou, who asked me: "Well, did he speak to you about a possible candidature? Not in the Landes, but in the second sector in Paris?" I told him that de Gaulle had not said a word about it. Pompidou was astounded, for the General had discussed the matter with him and added that he would speak to me about it. Whatever happens, I do not feel any inclination to take part in active politics in this way. The worst in me (idleness) is as

315

much against the idea as the best in me (a certain intellectual honesty and a taste for liberty of existence and action).

Tuesday, 22 May, 1951

I sent a letter round to the rue de Solférino, informing General de Gaulle of my engagement to Marie-Claude Mante.

Monday, 11 June, 1951

There is an optimistic attitude in the rue de Solférino towards the result of next Sunday's elections. Government circles and Pierre Brisson, a dogged opponent of the R.P.F., are, according to my father, displaying a similar confidence. They predict 111 seats for the Gaullists, who are expecting 160, in the metropolis – and 180 with the Union Française. In the rue de Solférino, they think that the affiliations, the great hope of the governmental coalition, will only affect the results in five or six of the electoral districts.

Sunday, 17 June, 1951

I voted in the morning and lunched with my father, who is thrilled by my *Conversations with André Gide*. He had even forgotten the dinner, to which Gide came, in the Avenue Théophile Gautier, and Maman did not remember it either.

My father told me:

"Your diary is a test, which has led me to discover something that astounds me: we forget everything, absolutely everything, about our past. I thought for instance, that I remembered my childhood, but now I feel that it, like the rest of my life, has completely vanished!"

I dined with Marie-Claude at Saint-Germain-des-Prés. We went to see the election results outside *Ce Soir* and then, in the Place de l'Opéra, outside *L'Aube*. But it was too early to draw any conclusions from these partial results (in both senses of the word).

After that, we went to *Le Figaro* offices, mingling with the crowd outside for a long time before going in. Pierre Brisson's worried expression reassured me. My father said, amusingly, that the length of his nose would be the best barometer tonight as to the fortunes or misfortunes of the R.P.F.

In the reception rooms on the first floor, there was a fashionable empty-headed crowd of guests. Drinks and sandwiches were being handed round. Pierre Brisson came in from time to time with the latest results. The R.P.F. and the communists were heading the polls in Paris. The M.R.P. were sweeping everything before them in Alsace.

In the rue de Solférino, I saw at once by Louis Vallon's expression (though he got in, himself) that things were going badly for the R.P.F. I stayed with Georges Pompidou and other friends to listen to the broadcast results and those coming through by telephone.

Monday, 18 June, 1951

The results were discouraging as far as we were concerned: about 110 deputies. It will be a little more, with those of the Union Française, but still a long way short of the expected 180. The R.P.F., from the point of view of numbers, will be the leading party, but it is just a party, like any other, and it was not to amuse himself by playing petty parliamentary games that de Gaulle risked (and lost) the battle. The new Chamber appears to be able to be governed without the support of the R.P.F. It is very disappointing (though I have an inner feeling that the electorate may have been wise and that all may be for the best, the way things are now).

Friday, 22 June, 1951

General de Gaulle held a Press conference at the Palais d'Orsay. It was sparkling, but there is nothing worth reporting about the events or of those present.

Monday, 6 December, 1951

I received the following letter:
"My dear Claude,
I should very much like to submit an article to you for *Liberté*. But (1) I am afraid that it may strike you as rather shocking, and (2) it is too long and needs cutting. Would you care to come and see me one morning about 11.00, read it and tell me what you think of it?

With kind regards (and many thanks for your *Gide*),
Jean Paulhan"

Friday, 7 December, 1951
24 Quai de Béthune, Paris

I arrived at the rue des Arènes about 11.00 and found Jean Paulhan in his bedroom, where he was recovering from a bout of flu. His window looked out on a formal French garden, copied, he told me, from La

Fontaines (in Nimes?). These little houses were occupied by sewermen. The biggest one, over there, by the head sewerman. One could see them leaving every morning about 7.30 in their big boots, and so on ... Then, after asking me where I lived, he broke in with: "Do you fish? It's supposed to be the best corner of Paris ..." All that in his usual style, about which nobody has ever discovered whether it is acquired or innate.

He gave me his manuscript and sat down at his desk, protected from a draught from the window by a high screen, which left him in partial darkness, restful to his eyes. I began reading, slightly perturbed from the very beginning by the indeed *shocking* nature of the article on the excesses of Justice after the Liberation – in as much as the truth is, alas! only too often shocking. I could scarcely see those pages appearing in a review sponsored by de Gaulle who, though he had disapproved of the excesses, had perhaps not done all he should to prevent them. Or, if not de Gaulle, his government. I fully realize that it was far less easy for him to intervene than is generally supposed and that he had already achieved something of a miracle in disarming the militia when he, himself, was disarmed. I can see him now when, shortly after the Liberation, he told me the news with a smile, which I recall was one of immense *satisfaction* (satisfaction at a duty accomplished – and a difficult duty). Also, in viewing the question from the abstract field of what he called the *grammar of ideas,* Paulhan had not presented the *problem in its true light.* I told him so. He replied that his theme was the one I had just read and, in the circumstances, he was under no obligation to deal with another one. I added that treason did exist, that, after all, there was an absolute in treason.

"Agreed!" he retorted. "In my opinion, Brasillach thoroughly deserved the death penalty."

His opinion was not shared by me. But that was not the point. I said, "The possible treason of the communists does not wipe away the actual treason of the collaborators. It merely makes two treasons."

He agreed to this and that there was an absolute in treason – in the sense I meant, for I am certain that we thoroughly understood each other: on a plane more of sentiment than reason, but were we not on the territory of the sentimental and passionate? His mistake was to talk of the grammar of ideas in a context where ideas did not represent abstractions but very carnal reactions.

All the same, I should very much like to publish his article, though I do not think I can because of de Gaulle, to whom I am morally (and materially) committed. I asked for permission to think it over for a few days and obtain some authoritative advice. He agreed on condition that I only showed his article to the few people that I felt bound to consult. I suspected that he would have liked to have the General's opinion. In any case, he told me, *Liberté de l'Esprit* was the only review in which he considered his article could decently and honourably appear. If I do not like it, he will publish it as a brochure in the *Editions de Minuit*.

Before allowing me to leave, Paulhan showed me his paintings, stacked in the ground-floor drawing-room: one of the earliest Braque's (he says: *the* earliest), in which, as he pointed out to me in comparing it with a recent still-life by the same artist, the whole of Braque's talent can be discovered already (and it was true): some Klees, two Chiricos and, naturally, a lot of Dubuffets, mostly portraits, "which he had come into after the horrified models had turned them down". Paulhan said modestly, in front of an extravagant figure: "This one is supposed to be me." And there was one of Artaud, equally misshapen, but with a resemblance. I confessed to Jean Paulhan (but without any shame) that I had never liked that kind of crude 'art'. His high opinion of Dubuffet astonished me (as does, on another level, the importance Malraux sees in Miró). Paulhan granted me Miró, but, without arguing about it, stuck to his opinion of Dubuffet. When I told him that I liked his way of not hanging the paintings, but leaving them like that, unframed, one against the other, he confessed that the disorder was not deliberate. His wife was ill and he had not the courage to start tidying them up and arranging them. In a corner of the room, lay bowls, with which he plays matches in nearby parks on Sundays with his friends, Jouhandeau* among them. He invited me to join them.

Saturday, 8 December, 1951

When I woke up, I was given an urgent letter from Paulhan about the advantages of publishing his article:
"My dear Claude,
I have given my little article a lot of thought during the last year. I certainly believe it to be true. But I also believe it could be efficacious: nothing stands in the way of French reconciliation so much as a certain pharasaical satisfaction displayed by the Resisters of which Vercors* furnishes the most striking example (and which I have properly tried to denounce). I should be very glad if the General would look at the question from this angle, too.
                    Affectionately, Jean P . . ."
It clearly expresses his hope that General de Gaulle will give his opinion of the article, which he will do, as Georges Pompidou gave it

to him yesterday and he took it down to Colombey. I forwarded Paulhan's letter to him, so that he can have another standard by which to judge it. Georges Pompidou, in reply to my criticism of the article, said:

"Yes, but one can't turn down a contribution from Paulhan just like that. The General will decide . . ."

All the same, there is not much hope, in my opinion.

Tuesday, 11 December, 1951

General de Gaulle wants to see Paulhan – in order to tell him, according to Georges Pompidou, that he has allowed himself to be deceived in regard to the numbers of the condemned (or the victims of summary trials): and also to try to make him understand the difference between legality and legitimacy by quoting a number of historical examples, Isabeau of Bavaria among them.

"What's good in the General," Georges said to me, "is that, though he has no juridical culture, he has a very extensive historical one . . ."

In short, de Gaulle does not want the article to appear in *Liberté de l'Esprit*. And I, in my heart of hearts, am very much relieved, despite the disappointment of losing such an important contributor. At a time when my review is about to enter its fourth year, I should have disliked seeing the first breach in the certain unity of outlook that, up till now, has made our small irreplaceable team so consistent. We modestly occupy, but beyond all question (and less and less obscurely) a position that is unique to us in French letters.

I shall have to refer to it in the editorial that it has fallen on me to write, due to the lack of an article worthy of taking first place, in our January number. Our embarking on the fourth year of our existence, in any case, makes such an editorial desirable.

Monday, 17 December, 1951

That same Thursday, I received Jean Paulhan in the rue de Solférino and had to keep him waiting before de Gaulle received him. In reply to his question, I told him that I did not know what the General had thought of his article. Then, half-ironically, half-seriously (but more seriously than he was aware of, no doubt) Jean Paulhan said, in his blank voice: "It's very moving to be the young author who doesn't know whether he'll be received or not, or whether his contribution will be accepted or not." Our conversation was without interest, and his usual paradoxes left me cold (it is a long time now since this particular style ceased to bowl me over). Saint-Martin was (after Sade) the greatest prose writer of the eighteenth century, etc. He also sang the praises of Amiel, whose journal he tried, so he said, to get published in full by Gaston Gallimard. But as this would form (I do not remember the exact number any more) seventeen (I think) volumes of *La Pléiade*, Gaston did not think it practicable, etc.

When I showed him in (after he had walked past Pierre de Gaulle, who did not recognize him) I caught a glimpse of the office through the half-open door, as I often do, and saw de Gaulle standing up, ready to welcome the visitor and throwing a glance, both indifferent and curious, at those in the next room. I always get the feeling that his eyes have stayed on me for a second. I left without waiting any longer. But the next day I received the following letter from Paulhan:

Friday

"My dear Claude,
De Gaulle talked to me at length, with great friendliness and common sense. It seemed to me that he agreed with me on the composition of the jury. As for the rest, he thought that I should have stressed more precisely the difference between 'a legal government and a legitimate one.' 'What difference?' 'The one that establishes the Declaration of Rights by its appeal to insurrection.' Finally, the figure of 500,000 for the victims seemed to him exaggerated.

"I did not have the feeling that he wanted my article, even corrected (and I am going to correct it) for *Liberté de l'Esprit*. He spoke to me after that of Pétain, Maurras and several other matters. I was somewhat struck by his sort of calm benevolence, by his serene kindness. (I wanted to ask him whether he would be able to bear, without too much impatience, the existence of a parliamentary group in R.P.F. but I was afraid of being indiscreet.)

Yours with friendship
Jean Paulhan"

Friday, 21 December, 1951

I have just come from a Press conference held by General de Gaulle. He has rarely been so brilliant. A little too caustic, perhaps, a little over-emphatic when he attacked, but soaring over the present with the sense of History, the sense of France, that render him so different from the politicians of our times, with striking intelligence and ease. One cannot, however, help regretting that he does not make some concession to what he condemns, if only to try and save what can still be saved in the great disaster that looms ahead, to which he would reply, once again, that it would mean throwing away one of France's best cards and giving in to impotence, since the present system forbids any action to be taken by anyone, no matter what post he holds.

1952

"General de Gaulle

"I wish my funeral to take place at Colombey-les-deux-Eglises. If I die elsewhere, my body shall be transported to my home without any public ceremony whatever.

"My grave shall be the one where my daughter Anne already lies at rest and where one day my wife will lie. Inscription: 'Charles de Gaulle (1890 . . .)', nothing else.

"The ceremony shall be arranged by my son, my daughter, my son-in-law and my daughter-in-law, assisted by my staff, in such a manner as to make it extremely simple. I do not want a national funeral. No president, no ministers, no committees, no organized bodies. Only the French armed forces may participate officially, as such, but their participation shall be of very modest dimensions, without music, fanfares or bugle calls.

"No speech shall be made, either in church or elsewhere. No funeral oration in Parliament. No seats shall be reserved during the ceremony except for my family, my Companion Members of the Order of the Liberation for the Municipal Council of Colombey.

"The men and women of France and other countries of the world may, if they so wish, honour my memory by accompanying my body to its last resting-place, but I wish it to be conducted there in silence.

"I refuse in advance every distinction, promotion, dignity, citation or decoration, whether French or foreign. If any one of the aforesaid should be conferred on me, it would be in violation of my last wishes.

Charles de Gaulle"

Thursday, January 17, 1952
24, Quai de Béthune, Paris

There he was, frail, extraordinarily young, and pale, with his quick, nervous walk and his conspiratorial air. André Malraux had asked me to meet him at the Ambassade du Champagne in the rue de la Paix, a resort that must be familiar to him, as I have been there once already with him and Arthur Koestler. So we met there at the appointed hour, having both been, with out running into each other, at the Manet exhibition, which is only on for three days at the Orangerie, with the Manets from the Louvre added to those in the recent exhibition by the German museums. We spoke first about the exhibition, or rather, about the disappointing crowd of idle, and, to all appearances, unappreciative women attending it. I told Malraux that it was no doubt these same beautiful or elderly ladies, who had pounced upon the de luxe edition of *Voix du Silence* and exhausted it within a few days of its appearance. He agreed about that but said the (relatively) cheap edition was coming out shortly and would find its first real public. After a few observations about painting (on his favourite theme: that no painting now is beyond the pale; to which he added that an *inspired* collector today could only manifest his genius by making a collection of *anonymous* paintings of all periods), Malraux asked me what I thought of the notices of my *Conversations avec André Gide*. And, from his tone of voice, and his close attention, I gathered that he had wanted to meet me after such a long lapse of time in order to talk to me about my book.

I was surprised to see with what interest he had read it and what an *effect* it had had on him. For the first time since we have known each other, Malraux spoke to me in this completely different manner, as equal to equal and with a new respect, which was very gratifying. It was a reward I had not hoped for.

"It seems to me that homosexuality certainly played some part in André Gide's relationship with you. Don't misunderstand me: I don't think he expected any response from you. Right! But the mere fact that he was a homosexual made the nature of the interest that he took in you fundamentally different from that which another man, who did not share his known propensities, would have felt. When you and I are with a woman, we feel no urge to desire her explicitly, nor do we feel at the back of our minds that our attitude towards her should be any different from our attitude towards a man, or, say, the cloakroom woman. Gide had the same attitude towards you: he was not looking for any response from you, even in the distant future. Right! But without being in the least interested in this way, he took an interest in you. Now with Martin du Gard*, his attitude was quite different."

"Martin du Gard? But wasn't his secret that he was ashamed of his homosexuality? Hence the expurgated diary, the brevity of which disappointed me?"

"Not at all," Malraux replied. "He was very much interested in women, even the less reputable ones. But that's another matter. Let's get things clear about the disappointment you said you felt when you read *Notes sur André Gide*. The strength of your *Journal* is its breadth; the continuity in time and agglomeration of details, all of great interest and recorded from life. We never doubt for a moment that the words you put into Gide's mouth are the ones he actually uttered. And the portrait you draw of him (probably without having deliberately intended to do so) emerges in his relationship with the painter who, in the case of the portrait, is as important as the model. As you know, in a novel, the most elaborate description of a face never succeeds in making us visualize it, whereas one only has to mention the expression for the reader to see it as clearly as the author. You've been able to see the expressions and make them seen. Your testimony is the most alive of them all; and it (I knew Gide well enough to say so) bears the closest resemblance.†

"Martin du Gard's is valuable for the sharpness of the outline. It's a working drawing, while you, to quote Barrè's phrase about the Goncourts, you put in the colour. His attitude towards Gide is one of enquiry and incomprehension. His searchlight reveals an enigma, but it still remains one for him. And for us. Though the enigma emerges along different lines in your book, it is the same enigma. You report, with all the ardour of youth, remarks that are not, in themselves, very original. Nevertheless, you succeed in conveying the wonder you experienced in hearing them: you make the reader share your admiration. The odd thing is that these remarks are, at one and the same time, very empty and very striking, without one being able to determine what it is that gives them their stamp of poverty and what their stamp of richness. This is Gide's enigma, which one comes across not only in your book and in Martin du Gard's, but also in the tributes paid to him in the *Nouvelle Revue Française*. Saint-John Perse*, who is no fool, racks his brains to recall anything of importance that Gide said to him over a period of many years. And he ends by recalling one solitary thing, though a vital one."

It so happened that I had not read Saint-John Perse's contribution to the tributes in question. It also so happened that I had one of those moments of absent-mindedness, a price paid for too much concentration, which very occasionally make me stop listening to Malraux. I am unable to record the uniquely vital declaration that Gide made to Saint-John Perse. However I pulled myself together and heard Malraux saying (or perhaps it was his final question that woke me up and com-

† I have since read this declaration of Malraux's to Julien Green, dated 1951, with reference to an article of his on Gide which appeared in *La Table Ronde*: "It is the only true portrait that has been done of him." (J. Green. Diary VI, page 101.) Admittedly, the publication date of my *Conversations avec André Gide* is 15 January, 1952.

pelled me to recall the sentences preceding it before they were erased):

"So I wonder where the real problem of Gide lies, what is at the root of his enigma, what is the source of the discrepancy between the importance of his work and the insignificance, not of the man himself, naturally, but of most of his utterances. A shattering difference. Did you know Valéry?"

"Very well and not at all. I mean to say, that he was a friend of my father's and I often met him after my adolescence – but, as I always remained an adolescent in his eyes, I never had the honour of a serious conversation with him."

"Well, Valéry was always M. Teste. So – I'm simplifying, but roughly speaking – Martin du Gard could never understand how it was that Gide was so unlike Ménalque. Mind you, Gide never said anything stupid, which is very remarkable, in itself. And he was quite right when he blamed Barrès for never being able to say quite simply: 'This joint it good,' when in fact the joint was good. There was quite a lot of window-dressing about Gide, but his simplicity towards simple things was not assumed."

There had been no one around us for some time now. The barman and the cloakroom woman, who had served as a simile a short while before, were growing impatient. They must have been surprised by that slender individual, whose swift breathless conversation was punctuated with raucous wheezing. André Malraux finally realized that it was time for lunch and took me to an expensive, nearby restaurant, the Chatham in the rue Daunou.

On the way and while we were sitting down at our table, he spoke again of my book. No, he had not read the one that the notorious 'Victor' had written as a reply to the *Journal*. He had too much respect for Gide to descend to this level, to have anything whatever to do with such an unworthy piece of work. I agreed, but added that there had, at least, been one interesting passage in the book: the one picturing Gide, fascinated and fascinating standing behind a young gardener, who did not dare to try and escape from the grasp that terrible look had on his back.

"That's a side of Gide that I find hard to understand," Malraux answered. "I found some traces in your book and also in Martin du Gard's of what I had experienced myself. 'He's on the prowl,' your father said, somewhere in your book. And that's just what it was. When we were in Berlin, where we hadn't gone for fun, since we were there to deliver our letter about Dimitrov* to Hitler, we stayed at a hotel where everything – in particular, the large number of page-boys who were clearly there for no other purpose – where everything was dedicated to homosexuality. And this is what happened . . ."

What happened, I shall never know. Because the phenomenon, which I have already mentioned, occurred once again. It was as though a burst dam had swept away my attention. When I came back to myself, or, rather to him, it was to hear him say (for this, I did not allow to escape me):

"Whenever I read a diary, I always ask myself: would this account *hold* one, if it were concerned with Tartempion? If not, its value, if any, is purely documentary. If yes, then it is in the category of a work of art. Now, your book does *hold* one, even if one has no knowledge of the characters you bring on to the stage. What Cocteau said remains just as brilliant even if one doesn't know who Cocteau is; and the story of the unusual friendship that existed between Gide and you, both in its development and its decline, has an interest of its own."

We just had time to order, very quickly, two underdone Chateaubriands, and (with rather more care) a good bottle of Bordeaux, before he went on:

"In the same way, your pages on the Jouhandeau's dinner are first-class. Your good angel must have arranged that evening, where everything was designed to show Gide off at his best. It is certain privileged encounters like that which lift your *Journal* up to the highest romantic level. Everyone knows that he has every chance of going down to posterity if he keeps a diary but, in practice, idleness always wins the day. We hear a lot about X or Y's diary, and when it appears one finds that, like Schwob's, it consists of fifteen pages. Apart from Martin du Gard's, Léautaud's* and, possibly, our friend Claude Guy's, I doubt if any diaries exist at the moment, which have been kept seriously and continuously."

With reference to Claude Guy's notes on de Gaulle, which he and I have been allowed to see, Malraux embarked on an interesting digression about the General.

"De Gaulle, you see, there is a man who doesn't deceive, and one is constantly being made aware, always to one's great admiration, that what he says never fails to tally with what he's done. He, too, never says anything stupid which is rare in an army man! You say that he knows nothing about the plastic arts and, certainly, he's no artist. But he talks far better than Gide about History! Even if there had been no 18 June, what de Gaulle says would still retain its value: his incomparable way of surveying History, his outlook on institutions, men and events."

I interrupted Malraux to observe how inconceivable his action on

18 June appeared (and all the more admirable) when one knew the respect the General had for institutions and the State hierarchies. But Malraux exclaimed:

"You're forgetting the *defeat*, the collapse of the State, in fact. It was from anger, from indignation that he 'disobeyed', as Gide called it. You remember the Algiers dinner – and the only interesting question that Gide put to de Gaulle, when he asked him how he could bring himself to disobey. Now to de Gaulle, the situation having been what we know it to have been, the question was entirely without meaning. It was completely idiotic, a reaction which is only comprehensible to those, like you and me, who know him well – one which throws a revealing light on his personality."

I lack my former enthusiasm and feel incapable of rendering the style and rhythm of this conversation, carried on, as always with Malraux, at breakneck speed, with unexpected digressions, obscure ellipses, scarcely decipherable anecdotes and vague allusions to men whose names I did not even know, and to books I had never heard of. Or else, I again became inattentive and it is from great stretches of darkness that I call to mind a few enigmatic sentences. There was a moment when I was absorbed in studying Malraux's sensitive well-manicured hand as it lay on the tablecloth, a hand I was surprised to find so wise and somehow familiar – and, which brought me the realization that this remarkable man (the only one in de Gaulle's entourage today who impresses me) was approachable.

But his voice broke in on my thoughts:

"Surprisingly enough, you knew Gide better than I did, you knew him very well, whereas, in view of the relationship I had with him at the time of the publication of his complete works, one would have expected it to be the other way round. You say I dumbfounded him but there was a lot of irony in his 'he's too intelligent for me.' The N.R.F.* is an institution in which promises are never kept. When I undertook the handling of his complete works and the volumes began to come out one after the other, well, then, yes, Gide was dumbfounded. But to tell you the truth, he didn't like, never had liked what I wrote: whom did he like, in fact, among his contemporaries? Michaux*, Giono*, (but only his very first books) and Jouhandeau (because he liked him as a person). In short, he scarcely read anyone writing today, merely keeping in touch with what was going on and occasionally selecting a book solely because he was interested in the author. But, basically, he was no fool: what he scornfully referred to as Claudel's Spanish baroque, certainly did not cause him to underestimate the old man, and you can be quite sure that he realized that Jouhandeau was just Jouhandeau. And if he sailed for the Congo, it wasn't Jouhandeau he read, but Bossuet*. Great artists in every period and every form of art run each other down, and their mutual condemnations, if they don't give them proper thought, may temporarily delude them. But, basically, they're conscious of being among their equals. You may remember what Renoir said about Monet: 'Why does he go on painting?' And do you know why old Gallimard, our Gaston's father, only has Monets? Simply because Monet advised him to sell the ten Van Goghs he'd bought, assuring him that they weren't worth anything! But if he had considered the matter conscientiously and alone, he'd undoubtedly have come to a different conclusion."†

We passed on to *L'Homme Revolté*. Malraux appreciated what I had just written in *La Table Ronde* about Albert Camus' unforgivable omission of any kind of mention of him in a book of that kind on that particular subject:

"You're the only one who's written that. But within the next five years at most, you'll be blamed for not having gone even further. In five years time, your reference to me, and, in general, most of your criticism of *L'Homme Revolté*, will have *become public property*.

He embarked on a long discourse, to which I paid no great attention, on the thesis that Etiemble* had just produced on Rimbaud (but I have been dealing with this theme of the unwarranted deification of certain authors from Sade to Roussel, by way of Lautréamont and Rimbaud for two years now in my *La Table Ronde* contributions). I brought up the extraordinary *stand* that Malraux himself held, so impregnable that he can do whatever he wishes, without his reputation being assailed – as for instance, belong to a party, which everyone whose judgement matters to us considers reactionary, the R.P.F. But he replied, with a simplicity that made his genuine sadness all the more apparent:

"I seem to be the only one who has always been unaware of the position you're so certain I hold, which you say everyone's certain I hold. Oh, how impossible it is to size oneself up! Every day's post brings the same form of deception; (leaving aside the crank letters, which go straight into the wastepaper basket), it consists either of exaggerated compliments, which are all *beside the point*, or equally extravagant insults, which are also off-target. I'm, as all true artists are, like Lawrence, who had then already been aircraftsman Shaw for ten years, when he exclaimed: 'If only I could hear what strangers think of the *Seven Pillars*, instead of friends and critics! If only I could hide

† I am not sure that I have remembered the names correctly, except for Van Gogh's.

in the chimney when strangers are talking about my book among themselves!' Your disappointment, which you just mentioned, when you're in the company of critics, your recent cancellation of your subscription to the *Argus* ('No, I never take cheese, thank you'), your indifference to whatever they write about your *Gide,* must spring from the same feeling of total lack of communication, total solitude and ignorance."

André Malraux had never confided in me so unreservedly. When he expressed surprise that Gide, once he had become famous, had never seemed to experience that kind of misgiving, I replied that the N.R.F., church of which he was high-priest, had served to reassure him of his position. Malraux said:

"You're absolutely right! The sect saves from solitude. Breton*, sitting in his café, surrounded by his little court of disciples, must feel much more certain of his importance than Paul Claudel, in the depths of his true solitude."

At one moment – I can no longer remember in what context – the names of Gustave Thibon* and François Mauriac somehow came up together in the conversation. When I said: "I don't trust that fellow!" Malraux's eye lit up, as he asked: "Which one?" with an air of expectancy. But he was disappointed: I was not referring to my father; he would have been delighted if I had been on distant terms with him.

I must record one more conversation which Malraux started at the end of lunch, on the theme: "There are no more light-weights. The breed has died out. Name just one of them at the rue de Solférino. Pascal Pia was an excellent one but there are none of them left, etc." Then he commented on the disappearance of *La Voie Royale,* from 'By The Same Author' of *Les Voix du Silence*: the book struck him as rather childish; he hopes one day to write the novel, that has been at the back of his mind for so long, on the King of Laos; Perken's walk to his death will be integrated into it. Finally, he informed me that he was about to embark on a long novel, a sequel to *La Lutte avec L'Ange,* if I understood him right.

The time for parting had arrived. We left the restaurant and walked past Cartier, the jewellers. Then, the distance between us re-established, we both shook hands clumsily and coldly. And, once more, we shall not meet again for several months. In all probability, an occasion like this will never be repeated. Unless I write another worthwhile book.

Friday, 22 February, 1952

I went to the Town Hall in Vincennes, where the National Council of the R.P.F. is housed, to see which way the wind was blowing. A wind which no longer blows anywhere, Raymond Aron informed Albert Ollivier and me in a corner of the corridor. His alert, lucid mind led him to make a serious of indisputable deductions, as always – but he himself finished up by admitting that reality is often lacking in logic and can upset the best-founded predictions. He went on to give us his conclusions on foreign as well as domestic policies, open the door to possible solutions, even though plain reasoning and a straightforward examination of the facts do not present any. I shall pass over foreign policy – since Raymond Aron merely paraphrased the article, *In Search of a Strategy*, which he had sent me for the next number of *Liberté de l'Esprit*. But about domestic policy, he said:

"As far as domestic affairs are concerned, things are going far worse than they say or even know. For months now, I have been playing Cassandra, and am astonished that what hits one in the eye still apparently remains invisible. If Edgar Faure had been a genius, he probably couldn't have done much more. Since the 17 June elections, the R.P.F. has lost the game. It's no longer strong enough to act as a counterbalance, no one's afraid of it any more – the Third Force has disintegrated in the same proportion as it has ceased to be afraid of it. We needed 150 deputies at the lowest. And we should have had them if we'd played our cards properly. I can remember how astonished I was when the R.P.F. refused any alliances. It was Soustelle who didn't want them; he thought they wouldn't cooperate – which shows how little he understands the French. I was certain they would! Moreover, the R.P.F. could only pursue a policy, which would be against the interests of her only conceivable allies: the independents (discontinuance of the *forfeit* in taxes, etc.) The papers are kicking up a fuss because we're suddenly buying gold instead of stocks, but the problem remains the same, it's just an episode, the situation, where the franc's concerned, was just as serious yesterday. No, it's impossible to see any solution. However, our opponents are so weak, that an accident, the last hope left us, can always occur."

In the same way, Raymond Aron saw no logical outcome to 'the cold war', and consequently did not put forward any solutions, but still retained some hope that 'the hot war' might be averted by some unforeseeable event. "History always finds a way out . . ." But at what price?

Saturday, 23 February, 1952

Passed the early afternoon at the Avenue Théophile Gautier. In the evening, not without some difficulty, I took my grandmother Mante-Rostand to the Vel d'Hiv', where she was determined to hear de Gaulle. I had to park the car at the exit during the afternoon, fetch the old lady and her nurse in a taxi and clear a hazardous path for her through the crowd obstructing the entrance. After that, all went well – except for our disappointment at finding de Gaulle looking so old. And it is only too true, alas, that he has changed a lot. His speech, which did not contain anything new (but was none the less important for that in this world of the deaf, to whom one must continue shouting the same words), was delivered in a flat, gloomy voice, without any spirit. He had learnt it by heart, as usual, but, a very rare occurrence, he forgot, if I followed the written copy which I had been given correctly, a whole paragraph – and one of the most important. Before him, there were a number of ineffectual speeches – apart from Malraux's, which was uneven, but, at times, in his best style. Chance put me next to Roger Nimier, sombre, strange and charming. His presence saved my evening.

Friday, 7 March, 1952

Events took a dramatic turn in the National Assembly yesterday. Pinay, the Independent, whom everyone expected to be beaten, was voted into office by 324 against 206, after twenty-seven R.P.F. deputies had defected. *Le Figaro* quoted the neat retort by my friend Louis Vallon to someone who shouted out: "What'll the General have to say?" "He believes in plastic surgery!"

I went round to see what the atmosphere was like in the rue de Solférino towards midday. Gaston Palewski and Christian Fouchet, all in black, passed by like sad phantoms with Georges Pompidou.

As for my father's attitude, what no one can understand (and quite naturally), is that his disappointment after the high hopes raised by the Liberation has driven him to the *sidelines*. He writes as little as possible about politics in his leading articles.

I cannot remember whether I have already recorded it, but I recall that at the last meeting of the National Council of the R.P.F. at Vincennes, Raymond Aron and Albert Ollivier foresaw, while I was there, the possibility, if not the probability, of a number of the Movement's deputies defecting. And now it has happened. It was one way out of the present political deadlock – but clearly, not the one we wanted.

Saturday, 8 March, 1952

I looked in at the rue de Solférino this morning. Everything there seemed to be in the greatest disorder. Pinay has formed his government – but that, it appears, is of minor importance. The problem to be faced is what the General should do about the twenty-seven dissidents. Apparently, he is absolutely furious and determined to let some of them know what he thinks of them in no uncertain terms – a decision approved by Malraux and Vallon, but one which most of his entourage are trying to persuade him to abandon. A letter from Palewski was already on the way, last night, to Colombey, where the General will be staying until his Press conference on Monday. "And, naturally," someone present said, "he'll lock himself up and refuse to see anybody." This Press conference of his is a disaster, leaving us no time to keep him quiet or give him the time to think things over. And as it is part of his nature to be contrary, the more one tries to make him change his mind, the more he digs his heels in. Apparently, Billotte has declared that he will see him on Monday, "whether he likes it or not". But it will not make any difference.

I said that from the point of view of morality and even, in the long run of practical politics, I should be inclined to agree with the General's intransigence, subject to his being rather more diplomatic in expressing his contempt.

"But that'll mean the disintegration of the parliamentary group," people told me, "make no mistake about it: if we expel a number of deputies, seventy others will go too – from pure solidarity – which will create a centre-right majority."

Guichard*, who was there, broke in:

"The other day, when I assured the General that Soustelle had saved the situation, he laughed in my face: 'You don't really believe that there's a majority in the parliamentary group in favour of Pinay's appointment!' He wouldn't believe it. And yet it was true. I had no doubts about it then, and everybody realizes it now."

I said that a centre-right majority would be better for the country than no majority at all, though it was obviously discouraging if after working for five years to achieve a Gaullist parliamentary group, to see it deprived of any practical effectiveness. But there was no harm in cutting oneself off from the right and remaining the nation's conscience. It would pay in the long run.

"That may be so," Guichard retorted, "but, in that case, we shouldn't have become associated with men whom we know to be on the right."

Someone else exclaimed:

"The truth is that since his resignation, de Gaulle has become a man of half-measures. Yesterday, in choosing parliamentary action, but refusing to be in Parliament: today, by expelling a few deputies, at the risk of losing seventy. The majority principle should operate: there was – one may regret it but it's nonetheless a fact – there was a majority in the R.P.F. group which considered that the Gaullists could not refuse their votes to a man whose first objective was to save the franc – leaving themselves free, if necessary, at a later date, to help in bringing him down."

We only found one piece of news to console us: Bergasse proposed a toast yesterday to the integrity of the parliamentary group. It is all very sad and ridiculous. It is not enough, in politics, to be in the right. Events have to prove one right. It would have taken very little for de Gaulle to have had a majority in Parliament that would have enabled him to embark on his plans for saving the country. Events decided otherwise.

Monday, 10 March, 1952

I looked in at the rue de l'Université before going on to the Palais d'Orsay, where the Press conference was to be held. I saw Georges Pompidou, who was afraid that de Gaulle would be exasperated by too many questions and would end up with an outburst. Photographers pursued him from Colombey to Paris, which put him in the sort of humour one could expect. A dense crowd of journalists had gathered in the big reception-room with its gold ceiling. Claude Guy told me that if they had come hoping for sensations, they were likely to get them, judging by what de Gaulle had just said to him . . .

Then the General appeared and, in a total silence, began with a statement on the general situation. His tone was disillusioned, slightly ironical, but strikingly serious. After pointing out the extent to which the situation had deteriorated since his last Press conference, he laid himself open, as they say, to questions – which were, to start with, though not actually irrelevant, merely devoted to problems quite other than the one everybody had in mind, as though no one dared to tackle the President of the R.P.F. – or, more probably, as though they were deferring the pleasure for a time in order to savour it all the more. Well, their hopes of reactions and sensations were disappointed.

What about the dissidents? "It's true that some deputies, the other day, took it upon themselves to dissolve the cohesion that is desirable.

But I must confess that in the light of present-day events – what is going on and what we may expect as a result – I am not, myself, hypnotized by what took place in the semicircle regarding that particular matter."

What would happen to the rebels? "Sir, that's a domestic matter which is solely the Movement's concern, and I have no intention of dealing with it in public, here." This was certainly the best reply he could have given.

Tuesday, 18 March, 1952

I saw Raymond Aron, who said:

"I've lost all interest. I've had enough of explaining to people what must inevitably happen, and meeting with no other response than their further entrenchment in positions which I have shown to be untenable. Yes, I've had enough of playing on a certainty, all by myself. And what for? The world doesn't need me. It'll get along all right on its own!"

We spoke of *Liberté de l'Espirt,* and I mentioned my fears for the R.P.F.'s future. He answered:

"It's obvious that it'll split up. The General is to blame. He's only interested in strategy and neglects tactics. It's impossible to say 'no' the whole time, particularly in the parliamentary field. Sooner or later the deputies are bound to have had enough of such a negative attitude. We've seen it and we shall see even more of it. De Gaulle got off on the wrong foot from the very beginning – and Malraux encourages him in his mistakes by saying: 'You've a very strong position in the country, your reputation there carries great weight, and you can only retain it by keeping it unsullied, whatever the cost, in other words by refusing to make any concessions.' I find this all wrong: de Gaulle's reputation has already suffered. And it's wrong, too, to imagine that the worse things get, the closer the General's hour will come. That's what de Gaulle believes and he also believes that he's the only one who can resolve the deadlock. But in fact, things can go very badly, get worse and worse, without his having an opportunity to intervene."

He added:

"As I said, one can't go on and on saying 'no'. Sometimes one must say 'no', and sometimes 'yes': one must follow the game . . ."

And he went off, looking grieved, pale and furtive, with stooping shoulders – haloed by the ineffectual light of the spirit.

Thursday, 5 June, 1952

Yesterday, at the rue de Solférino, I went down the stairs with André Malraux, whom I had just run into there, and who was on his way, with Soustelle, Guy and some others, to a meeting, presided over by de Gaulle. Malraux remarked, with a lyrical irony that was not always comprehensible, due to his ellipses, on the Press that provoked his speech at the final session of the Congress for the Liberty of Culture (I was present at it last Friday). Suddenly a stir and a distant murmur told me that the General was coming down. I bolted and had already reached the hall-door, when the General's powerful voice called me back. I returned to the foot of the stairs, where he was waiting for me. We shook hands and he said:

"Well, at long last, shall I manage to see you one of these days?"

I replied, awkwardly, that I had just been with Bonneval and had an appointment with him next day – and rushed off. (Bonneval had actually told me that the General had asked him whether I were still alive and said he wanted to see me.) I found him looking calm, untroubled and much younger yesterday. And it was the same relaxed man who welcomed me today, with that slightly starchy affability and great courtesy which he always displays. I gathered from his opening sentences that he had nothing in particular to say to me, and that he had only wanted, from pure friendliness, not to lose all contact with one of his staunch supporters. He began by 'repeating his congratulations on my marriage', and went on to speak of the Ile Saint-Louis, 'where he had always dreamt of living, a dream which would never be fulfilled', and to ask me whether I found it disappointing. Then he passed on to *Liberté de l'Esprit*. Yesterday, when I heard he wanted to see me, I had imagined that he would corroborate the financial difficulties, which Pompidou often mentions to me, and announce the review's death. But his smile, at the foot of the stairs, had reassured me. And indeed, all that he said about *Liberté de l'Esprit* today, confirmed that any question of its disappearance had never even crossed his mind – though there was no suggestion of increasing the subsidy (100.000 francs a month), which has become so inadequate that I no longer get paid (which I did not venture to tell him).

After enquiring about *Liberté de l'Esprit's* financial situation and suggesting certain ways of improving its circulation (he gave me, for example, the name of a number of intellectual militants whom he met during his last tour in the South), he asked me the ritual question, which had cropped up at all our previous interviews:

"Well, what do you think of the situation?"

I replied that my views were doubtless much the same as his and that, while, of course, the future of the Movement was not endangered, thought it might be otherwise for France, it was discouraging to fail when so close to port, at the very moment when power seemed within our grasp, due to the hasty action of a few dissidents.

"Are you so sure of that?" he answered with a tinge of irony in his voice. "I feel, personally, that, in any case 'they' would have managed to put off the evil day, found some other means of doing it, and, that the result would have been the same. Or, which would have been worse, 'they' might have called us in, in order to compromise us along with themselves and see that we drowned at the same time as they did."

I thought, without saying so, that the General, who has more than once referred to this snare, would have taken good care not to fall into it. Alluding to the success of the loan launched by Pinay (but on terms that put the whole future in pawn) and to his cleverness in taking advantage of the recent communist demonstrations to arrest Jacques Duclos and start proceedings against the communists (a hardening in the attitude towards them which, unfortunately, does not seem to be matched by the Americans) I said that the relative and temporary success of this 'experiment' would, for the time being, put the country which, at the same time rejoices (or is disquieted, according to circumstances) by our dissensions, off the scent.

De Gaulle replied, preceding the name of the President of the Council with a *Monsieur,* which marks the deference, which, at least in appearance, he displays from time to time, towards this or that privileged member of the government:

"It's only too certain that Mr. Pinay has cleared the consciences of all those people who have abdicated and surrendered. 'You see,' they'll say, 'the loan has succeeded, the C.G.T. has been rendered powerless, and pay has been frozen.' And these apparent results will allow them to think of other things, and avoid thinking, in particular, of the external danger. As for the few dissidents, they will leave."

"But they're still there, and people don't understand it . . ."

"They'll go very soon now. And in such circumstances that everyone will understand that they were given every opportunity to stay; that it was they who wanted to leave us . . ."

Speaking of the failure of the general strike called for the day before by the communists in protest against the arrest of Jacques Duclos, I said that I was not as pleased as most people were because I saw it as one more proof of the lassitude of a country which is not prepared to make the slightest effort one way or another. The General's expression lit up sombrely:

"You're quite right: France is dead. Only, you look around; you'll see the others aren't much better. England is very hard hit, in her very substance."

"She's at least been capable of making the sacrifices necessary to safeguard her security. She has an airforce."

"You're right, she has an airforce."

"And a navy."

"No, her navy is very much diminished. But you're right; their main effort has been directed towards an airforce. They've got planes."

I then said that the disappointment with our domestic politics would amount to nothing, if it were not for this one real danger, but a shattering one, of external politics. De Gaulle, naturally, agreed.

"There, too, there, above all, the French only think of surrender. Sooner or later, there'll be a President of the Council who'll hand over the nation's finances to the Americans, in the same way that they've just handed over her army. 'They' have only one idea: to make France an American protectorate, a protectorate, moreover, which is not protected."

We then talked of the coming American presidential elections. I expressed my anxiety in the event (a possible one) of Taft (who advocates abandoning Europe) beating Eisenhower.

"Taft could conceivably be elected," the General said. "All the same, I believe Eisenhower will win."

When I exclaimed: "Let's hope so!", he nodded, but unenthusiastically, and made a gesture of doubt:

"Yes, of course. Though all those fine words of Eisenhower's, unaccompanied by any effective guarantee, which give Europeans the illusion that they're defended and have no need to defend themselves, may be the worst of all."

Then there came a "Voila!", which made me understand that the conversation had ended. I got up. De Gaulle saw me to the door where, after the obligatory mutual civilities, we separated.

A few moments later, I ran into Georges Pompidou in the street.

Saturday, 5 July, 1952

He was so much out of his element among the crowd of delegates surrounding him that at first I had difficulty in recognizing him. But it was definitely he, de Gaulle, dressed formally amidst the militants in short sleeves, who, at the moment when I arrived, were listening with polite patience to the deputy, Prélot, a 'conciliator', who, I was told, was trying to save a situation which, in my opinion, his clumsiness ended by making far worse. We were, on an exhausting day, in the Town Hall in Saint-Maur, at the enlarged Council of the R.P.F. which had met to decide the fate of the 'dissidents', in relation to a paper on parliamentary discipline.

I was standing in a corner, looking down on the skull of Edmond Barrachin*, a virtual dissident, whose convinced monosyllables were approving the words of the new speaker, Legendre* – or responding (for the pure pleasure of it, since no one could hear him and he was not trying to make himself heard) to the interruptions of the angry militants.

Suddenly de Gaulle, stood up, quelled the uproar with a gesture, and said (I wrote down his words immediately: they were spoken with all his pride and grandeur):

"My companions, I beg of you. You can see what this is turning into. Kindly behave as I do, I who am saying nothing."

But he was doing a lot of thinking, I felt sure, confronted by sharp criticism from Legendre, who spoke directly to him and did not hesitate to reveal for the militants' edification, secrets of what had gone on at a certain meeting of the Directors. From below came an approving murmur, and Barrachin's voice: "It's quite true, we never knew that: they never told us. That's exactly what happened." Then Barrachin went up to the rostrum, himself (much abler than his predecessors), followed by General Billotte, (so little worth listening to that the hall began to empty) and Léon Noël, at last, a representative of the loyalists. The embittered militants no longer had to interrupt with their shouts of "Vive de Gaulle", which were idiotic but moving: they listened, now blissfully. For the first time de Gaulle's expression softened to a smile.

Then it was Malraux's turn: he started off, as usual, at a hundred miles an hour, carrying the whole audience with him with one sentence: "Our opponents – for I say it quite clearly – our opponents – say . . ." There was a thunder of applause. Barrachin, his arms crossed, shook his head. At the end of the evening, in the corridors, I was told later, he displayed great courage in face of the militants' insults. But I was no longer there, having gone to join my wife and my son, after hearing the short, surprisingly moderate speech, which nonetheless allowed one to divine the scars underneath, from a tranquil de Gaulle, who, if not confident, was anyway almost indifferent.

Sunday, 6 *July,* 1952

Having had too much to do to make enquiries, I only heard, when I reached Saint-Maur in the afternoon, of the resignation, last night, of four or five of the 'dissidents' – 'heroes' of the day, who had found themselves in the minority (Barrachin, Legendre, etc.)

After yesterday's exciting session, the debates seemed dreary. Capitant's speech went on for ever. I met Malraux for a moment in the lobby. When I congratulated him on his speech the day before, he said:

"I only wanted the militants to hear a voice between Léon Noël – who spoke very well indeed – and the General – which responded to their demands. For, in the end, the mystique is more important to them than the tactics. I wanted to prevent the General from speaking in the guise of the accused defending himself. The aggressive attitude I adopted was designed to allow him to appear, no longer as a defendant, but as a peacemaker, and speak calmly. People have blamed me for my aggressiveness (Christian Fouchet in particular), but I was right, believe me."

Malraux added:

"However, none of that would have happened if the General had expelled a few of the dissidents' leaders at the time of his Press conference. There are certain laws in politics, of which this one, proved by Lenin as well as by Mussolini, was deliberately broken, despite my objurgations: one must never allow a dissident movement to spread. One must immediately strike at its head, as swiftly and harshly as possible."

Applause told us that Capitant had finished. Malraux broke off and murmured. "It's the General's turn!" and rushed off. I did the same, finding a more modest place, standing up.

De Gaulle ended the session with a magnificent speech:

"I call on you to witness, my companions, that our enlarged national council, contrary to the predictions of our opponents, some of whom, it appears, were among us, has not ended with a debit balance sheet, but quite the contrary . . ."

Tuesday, 8 *July,* 1952

. . . Yes, but twenty-six members of the R.P.F. group in the National Assembly have today announced their resignation.

Thursday, 27 November, 1952

When I arrived at André Malraux's house in Boulogne, he was showing Francis Jeanson the photographs he was going to give him to illustrate Gaétan Picon's *Malraux par lui-même,* which will appear in the *Editions du Seuil.* (I have done the same thing with the same Jeanson, whom I have to see again tomorrow on this matter, for it was I who was asked to do *Proust par lui-même,* which I wrote blissfully, this summer in June, July and August.)

He said:

"That was during the Spanish war: my shot-up plane. I was in the front turret."

There was a discreet murmur of admiration from Francis Jeanson, and Malraux went on:

"And there am I in the cemetery in . . . (I can no longer remember whereabouts it was in the Far East): no point in putting it in the caption, but I was the first European to come to those parts. This is the municipal Council in Linares – the real one – and this is the one in the film *Espoir.* I don't know if Claude knows . . ."

I was, in fact, surprised: the expressions and attitudes in the council-room were exactly reproduced in the film. I felt naïvely proud that Malraux implied an intimacy between him and myself (non-existent, in fact) in front of Francis Jeanson, the editor of the *Temps Modernes,* one of whose articles was the cause of the quarrel between Sartre and Camus, which was a sensation at the end of last summer.

I listened absentmindedly – and discreetly – from my armchair. The words 'side-splitting', 'buffoon' came constantly to Malraux's lips, whether he was showing a photograph of himself, as Minister of Information, signing an agreement with Clémentis* (condemned to death in Prague only today, with other communists, following an iniquitous trial); or revealing on the back of a photograph of himself, published by an American paper a cat – the same cat that always accompanies his signature when he is writing to intimate friends.

"A lot of ministers should look more like that, Information or otherwise," he said jokingly, showing a snapshot in which he was extremely photogenic.

When he had finished with the photographs, he launched into improvisations, part of which I failed to grasp, in connection with *Baudelaire par lui-même* by Pascal Pia, for whom he again expressed his admiration and friendship. The usual rapidity of his speech and the customary ellipses added to the obscurity of this theses: I felt humili-

341

ated, as I reflected sadly once again on the inadequacy of my culture (largely due to an increasingly poor memory). But this is something that suddenly did come through to me:

"If one re-reads them, supposing they are letters to Jeanne Duval – not even supposing because they actually were letters – some of Baudelaire's poems suddenly become clearer. The fringe of obscurity that made them so mysterious – vanishes. It seems as though Baudelaire understood what deliberate suppression of one of the elements, essential for comprehension, added in the way of enhancement, depth and even meaning. Just as Apollinaire must have known that he was renewing and deepening the language merely by omitting punctuation."

While Jeanson was still there, he asked me:

"Do you think I should include a photograph of myself with the General in the book? Or do you think he would object?"

I said that I thought it would be best to have a snapshot taken at the time of Liberation, in which they were alone together.

"I've only been taken alone with de Gaulle at R.P.F. meetings, where I look rather too much like an *Eminence Grise*."

Francis Jeanson left. Malraux showed me the pages from his *Introduction au premier musée imaginaire de la sculpture mondiale*, intended for *Liberté de l'Esprit*. The contribution requires illustrations, which have to appear on the page opposite the text referring to them, which will make my work more difficult. What is more, it will be the first time that my review has contained photographs.

Malraux took the opportunity to explain the broad lines of his *Introduction* thesis:

"You realize that, if I'm right, marxism will be dealt a blow to the heart. And I shall once more be bringing grist to the Catholic mill, as well."

He gave a little wry smile as he told me this; and his eyes lit up, as though the matter were one that directly concerned me, as though he were supplying an adversary with arms in all good faith, while showing him at the same time that he was not deceived by the temporary conformity of their ideas.

Malraux leafed through the large set of proofs of his *Introduction*:

"It's the enormous extent of the documents that I've collected that will produce the most effect . . ."

And he went on to say that, while he had never underrated it, he had been astonished to find that there was no sculpture in the world that approached the beauty of the David of Chartres; added that, when I looked at the illustrations in his book, I would see that there had been no great sculptors since Michelangelo; and drew my attention to the new dimensions displayed in this 'musée imaginaire' by the sumerian, precolombian, negro and other sculptures.

I told him that, in my opinion, the photography had modified the difficulties he had to face, raising quite simple works to the level of masterpieces, purely by lighting and the skill of the photographer. He agreed, adding to the qualities I had mentioned, the details in the sculptures taken in close-up, the carefully chosen and sometimes faked surroundings, etc.

"But, increasingly, the various arts will come to be known, for the most part, through photographs. Records, of course, do not dispense with the need to hear live music. But that must not blind us to the fact that the transmutation achieved by photography, of which you spoke and which unquestionably occurs, raises a different problem, and a grave one, since it is from the aspect presented in the photograph that all works of art from now on will be known to the masses."

We would have gone on like this for a long time, but I had to take charge of the setting-up of his pages of *Liberté de l'Esprit*. So I took my leave.

1953

Wednesday, 7 January, 1953
Paris

The Pinay ministry resigned over a fortnight ago. After the foreseen defeat (but which was an unforeseen success) of Soustelle and then of Bidault (once more allied with the Gaullists, which is odd when one remembers the mutual anathemas exchanged at one time), René Mayer was accepted by the Assembly yesterday, thanks to the support of the R.P.F., which now will have a place in the régime, to the great displeasure of a number of people – beginning, no doubt, with the General, outflanked by his own troops, and remaining in the background as the only way of preventing the Movement from splitting up. I am weak enough to feel relieved. So many years in opposition have been hard to take even for the editor of a modest review . . . On the other hand, have I ever wanted the R.P.F. to triumph by a crushing defeat of the other parties? I am too democratic at heart to regret what would, after all, have been a form of totalitarianism: I see guarantees of wisdom in the equilibrium between opposing forces. There still remains the risk of death run by our country, when all the dissensions leave her so powerless. But now that the R.P.F. have emerged from 'systematic opposition', they may have a chance of assisting in her recovery. It may be all to the good that events have prevented them from taking charge of the Republic's destiny on their own.

Thursday, 19 February, 1953

Lunch yesterday at the Hôtel La Pérouse. Marie-Claude had never seen General de Gaulle. She was touched by his small eye, half-closed as a result of the operation he has recently undergone.

The Daniel-Rops* and Mme. Henri Focillon* were there, too. The conversation was without interest, consisting for the most part of polite chit-chat. Twice, for a few minutes during lunch and again during coffee, the General had quick conversations with Rops. I had to talk to Mme. Focillon and could not overhear. Such snatches as I caught seemed to suggest that de Gaulle's comments were much the same as

345

usual, with the same references to the key-positions he has assumed once and for all: "But I couldn't . . . my ministers themselves . . ."

At one moment, de Gaulle addressed me, saying, with an air of malicious pleasure: "So there's no more Press . . . They've deserved it!" I said that some papers were still coming out (hinting at *Le Figaro*, in particular). I made two contributions to the conversation, without flattery, but in a way that was likely to give pleasure to de Gaulle. It was also because I owe him – and him alone – this sense of the State which makes me say, for the first time, in reference to the newsreel shots, generally regarded as ridiculous, of Vincent Auriol bestowing the cardinal's biretta on the nuncio Roncalli, by virtue of an old prerogative of the French Head of State:

"Though it was laughable from one angle, it was also very moving and had a certain grandeur as a living reflection of our country's magnificent past."

The second time I spoke, it was in reference to the headline in that morning's *Figaro*, which had given me cold shivers: *Strasbourg calm, but ready to revolt, awaits Paris decisions.*

"What are they doing to the Republic, one and indivisible?"

(It was a question of the reaction, understandable but wholly improper in the form that the Alsatians had adopted, to the sentences imposed on their fellow-countrymen in Bordeaux at the so-called Oradour trial – very badly conducted at the outset and one in which it would obviously have been better not to mingle French and Germans. The convicted Alsatians had just been pardoned, no doubt the only solution after getting off to such a bad start.)

At my words, "one and indivisible", the General's eye lit up in a way which I took to signify wholehearted approval and friendly connivance.

In reference to the Oradour trial and to the war in Indochina, he said, with the same air of malicious satisfaction:

"They're both problems that the régime is stuck with . . . and, being what it is, it won't be able to solve them . . ."

Apart from this tinge of bitterness, he remained as great and magnificent as ever, even in his silences. No doubt in order to show Daniel-Rops that he had read his latest book, he questioned him about Saint Bernard and observed:

"All the same, I wonder whether he was really fond of mankind, whether he had a heart, as they call it today . . ."

It was an unexpected question to come from the lips of a man who is accused, quite wrongly though, of lacking human sympathy. Daniel-Rops replied that, despite what the Abélard affair might lead people to believe (but that had been a matter in which principles were involved), Saint Bernard had had a heart, as his love for his brother proved.

"Yes, but it was *his* brother," de Gaulle broke in, with a mocking intonation that he seemed to apply to the remark without reason. Then he added, more seriously, (no doubt thinking of his own ruthlessness on occasions which did not permit him to show clemency, occasions when principles were likewise involved):

"I did not say that as a reproach ... Quite the contrary ..."

And he repeated, in a lower voice: "Quite the contrary ..."

The conversation turned to the adaptation of *The Power and the Glory* for the theatre and the uneasiness we had all felt at seeing and hearing the beginning of the Mass on the stage. Then the General said, looking towards his wife:

"At the end of *L'Aiglon,* too ..."

Marie-Claude made a small gesture and uttered a couple of words which revealed how little she cared for *L'Aiglon.* I am afraid that this faint expression of her feelings did not escape the General, who knows many passages from Rostand's plays by heart and who really regards being a relation of Rostand's as a matter of some importance. Earlier, during lunch, I had heard him whisper to Mme. Focillon:

"She's Rostand's great-niece, you know ..."

Art is a closed book to him: I am, for instance, always astonished that, spending several days a week, for so many years, in this small suite in the Hôtel la Pérouse (which I found unchanged), he can bear the sight of that horrible painting, in the purest chromo style, which depicts a vaporous shepherdess among her unsubstantial sheep. He does not see the ghastliness of it. But to return to Rostand, what he likes in him is the bard of French epic, the poet of France.

When we were leaving he asked me to come and see him:

"I've some things to tell you ..."

But he is going on a semi-official visit to Africa and I am off to Montevideo. It will have to be put off till we get back.

During the evening, I was taken ill and felt worse and worse. I shook hands with the René Clair* when they arrived and then had to rush back to my bedroom. Nausea, heartburn, stabbing pains in the kidneys and vomiting. About 10.00, when I was beginning to recover, Yvonne de Bonneval rang up.

"Aren't you ill? Gaston is in bed, feeling awful. And the General isn't much better, himself."

A vol-au-vent was responsible for this collective poisoning.

Friday, 20 February, 1953

Yes, he gave me a sense of State – and that is no small thing. But at the price of such repudiations, which have been causing me obscure pain for some years now. I am sincere in my political Gaullism. But if chance had not brought me into close relationship with Charles de Gaulle after the Liberation, should I ever have been a Gaullist in the political sense of the word? Certainly not a member of the R.P.F. in any event. I only bore with the R.P.F. (with difficulty) because it had at its head a man whom I trusted and admired. My political position, spontaneously, is quite different. Jean-Paul Sartre and Claude Bourdet look on me as the enemy, whereas to me, in all essentials, they are brothers. An article by the latter in *L'Observateur* on the Rosenberg affair filled me with acute nostalgia because I felt such physical and spiritual solidarity with it.

Man's grandeur lies in this protestation, in which the sense of State no longer has any meaning. General de Gaulle's grandeur lies elsewhere. He has chosen his path and sacrifices everything that does not conform to it. Not I.

Thursday, 2 April, 1953

"We are speaking of a country that is sinking lower and lower. And I do not see what I can do to shake her out of her torpor."

That is what General de Gaulle said to me this afternoon on his return from Africa, where he was received officially everywhere he went and also, it appears, triumphantly. He had sent for me after learning (from whom?) that I was intending to give up *Liberté de l'Esprit*, since my present financial situation makes it impossible for me to devote so much time to a benevolent undertaking.

The General assured me, very kindly, that he fully understood my position and had no objections to offer, quite the contrary, if I kept to my decision. A copy of *Hommes et Idées d'aujourd'hui*, published on my return from South America, lay on his desk. His compliments (so rare, coming from him) embarrassed me by their extravagance.

"You're rising higher . . . Yes, unquestionably . . . Your success is more marked every day," etc.

What is more, he really seemed to believe it.

We spoke about the peace offensive, recently launched by the U.S.S.R.:

"It had already begun before Stalin's death, which merely served

348

THE OTHER DE GAULLE

as an opportunity to give it the full treatment. It's designed by the Russians to increase the crisis looming ahead: if orders for armaments drop off, stagnation spreads . . . No, the Americans aren't fooled by it. But, in these conditions, they can't avoid relaxing some of the pressure. Do I think that, after Korea, peace or at least relative calm will spread to Indochina? It's possible, even probable. But we can't accede to Ho Chi Minh's demands to achieve it . . ."

A few more kind words followed. He again expressed his regret that, in the present state of affairs, it was impossible to do more for *Liberté de l'Esprit* financially, and then came the sign to leave: as usual, he had the great courtesy to wish me *au revoir,* which never takes place without his escorting me to the door.

Monday, 4 *May,* 1953
Paris

Georges Pompidou asked me this morning (with tacit reference to the results of the municipal elections, which turned out to be even more disastrous than the R.P.F. expected):

"What would you do in the General's place?"

"I should carry on harder than ever. One should never lie down under a defeat . . . Besides, we all know how quickly the political climate can change. In a few months' time, or a year or two, perhaps the situation can turn our way."

"I entirely agree with you. But the General doesn't seem to think so. You ought to write to him . . ."

When I replied that I would not have the presumption to try and give advice to de Gaulle, Pompidou insisted that I should let him know my reasons – or, rather, *his* reasons – for thinking he should not throw his hand in. I shall do nothing of the kind, naturally. But such a suggestion, coming from his Chief of Staff, seems to be a symptom of the confusion in which de Gaulle finds himself. The defeat is, unquestionably, a shattering one. And it will be very difficult to recover the lost ground. All the same, will M. Pinay's reputation, as the new man of destiny, survive a second test? And does not de Gaulle, in his own person, still carry such weight, that if he throws it into the scales at the right moment . . .?

Thursday, 7 *May,* 1953

De Gaulle has viewed the R.P.F. defeat from the parliamentary angle and instructed his deputies and senators that 'until further notice, whatever they may feel called on to do within the framework of the régime shall be done without involving the Movement and on their own responsibility'. His curt tone (and no mistake!) which must have wounded a number of those in question, is the inevitable reaction from a man of his stature, never more admirable in thought and utterance. The General's decision will have important repercussions both in Parliament and in the Movement, itself, of which a reorganization has been announced.

Le Monde is perfect: "No one – whether opponent, friend or mere looker-on, can remain unmoved by General de Gaulle's declaration. Written in blunt, noble language, it consists of two parts. The first is a return to the past. A man who has never been willing to despair of his country, either in war or peace, acknowledges his defeat. He compels us, at the same time, to recognize that this defeat is to some extent our own." Jacques Fauvet, whose signature is at the foot of the article, goes on to say that if General de Gaulle's defeat is also that of the whole French people, the Movement's defeat is mainly his own, a point that is open to discussion but doubtless partly true.

Friday, 8 May, 1953

Combat takes the same line: "Whatever opinion each of us harbours about General de Gaulle, it is impossible not to acknowledge the simplicity and, let us use the word, grandeur, with which he has accepted his defeat." (Jean Fabiani)

Yesterday, I wanted to find out how my old friends in the rue de Solférino were taking things. The house, which I had always seen so full of life, was completely empty, apart from the concierge and a few secretaries. It gave the impression of a sinking ship, which the rats had abandoned. A wholly wrong impression, for, whatever happens, de Gaulle can count on the loyalty of a number of ardent supporters – and of mine.

Saturday, 9 May, 1953

My father read me the article he had just written for *Le Figaro* on de Gaulle. He seemed very astonished when I told him that the tribute was not of a kind that I could approve of, but he immediately said, without my asking him to, that he would make the necessary amendments and corrections. There is no doubt that he genuinely wanted to pay a tribute to de Gaulle, bearing in mind the hostility he has always felt towards the R.P.F. I went out and bought him *Le Rassemblement*,

350

so that he could at least glance through the General's declaration – which he had not read.

Wednesday, 13 May, 1953

Under the heading 'Conclusion', my father's article has appeared in *Le Figaro*, very much improved (in his assessment of de Gaulle) in particular, by the insertion of a question from the General's declaration and a number of phrases implicitly testifying to his sincerity: as, for example: "a new party, *which he believed to be a realignment*". My father asked my mother to telephone me to find out my opinion of the article, which, despite the alterations, certainly does not move me to any great enthusiasm.

Friday, 15 May, 1953

Pompidou tells me that there is considerable bitterness among those of the deputies most loyal to de Gaulle, because of the miraculous way he has managed to emerge from the defeat without loss. It is certainly true that Press reaction to his last decision (both dangerous and debatable), has been, as far as he is concerned, better than the most optimistic predictions could have led him to expect. Proof of the enormous prestige he still retains throughout the country. Louis Vallon is alone in being satisfied with the General's present position and that is because, as he admits himself, he is without ambition and can watch what is happening with the amused eye of a looker-on. But the others, all the others, who had counted on being ministers – and counted on it for so long! Georges Pompidou cannot see himself leaving the General. He cannot desert him in defeat after having remained at his side in the hope of success. The tone of voice, in which he told me this, had the ring of truth.

Wednesday, 21 October, 1953

"I warn you, in case you're on bad terms: I'm expecting André Breton at 6.00."

Malraux said that to me as soon as I arrived. He added that he had not seen Breton for twenty years, except for brief greetings when they ran into each other at picture exhibitions. He was coming to see him about the row that had been going on since his visit to some prehistoric grottos or other, when he rubbed his sleeve against one of the drawings and expressed doubts about its antiquity. This led to arguments, scuffles and threatened court proceedings:

351

" . . . Which I'm going to try and stop, because when these things start, you never know where they'll end."

I have never been able to be natural with this man, with his deluge of words, whom I find so remarkable, but whose line of thought I have difficulty in following and who constantly refers to facts, which he assumes to be universally known, of which I am entirely ignorant. He launched into a long discourse on the problems, as yet unsolved, presented by the prehistoric drawings: I did not listen carefully, though I was particularly attentive to appear attentive.

When he passed on to my last book (*Hommes et Idées d'aujourd'hui*), I scarcely listened any more carefully. Largely, because I have always been embarrassed by compliments and am inclined to believe them insincere.

"I have a feeling that you work the same way as I do: that you rewrote the whole thing – redid it from beginning to end. That's what leads to real progress," etc.

It so happens that I had not rewritten anything, that I never rewrite anything, either from laziness or lack of time; but I was convinced of the excellence of the method recommended by Malraux and regretful that I had not pursued it. However, I was obliged to keep this to myself, for it would have been impossible to confide it to him.

It was time to come to more serious matters, and I asked him:

"How about the General? Do you know what steps he's taking?"

"With the R.P.F. in such a mess."

"There's not much he can do . . . But the truth is that he's getting old."

"And knows it."

"I was struck by the photograph in the last number of *Rassemblement*, taken during his trip to Africa, which shows him being acclaimed by the local population, in some town or other in Madagascar. That thick neck . . . that heavy face . . . Yes, he's certainly aged!"

"Don't get the idea, though, that he looks older than he is. He's merely beginning to look his age. He did so for the first time when History withdrew from him. He then became as he always would have been if History hadn't raised him above himself. And now he's like all the men of his generation. An old man. It's sad."

Now, all I needed to do was leave the conversation to Malraux. I hung on to every word:

"Ah, he's no longer the man that History swept along with her, the one who said to me, in his inimitable voice, with that gesture of the arms which is so uniquely his: 'Those poor communists!' and that at a time when they were at the height of their power here. So then, I thought: 'All's well. He's still assuming his role.' My admiration for the man has remained complete. He is, whatever one says, he is Philopoemen. He fights against gods. His *Mémoires* (which occupy and preoccupy him so much just now) seem likely to present him in his proper light, and so much the better. You and I don't care a straw about his present defeat. It's a pity for France. But we aren't involved personally, like those on the hunt for ministerial appointments. In my opinion, it's a lamentable idea to have joint sittings of the R.P.F. To say what? To do what? A pseudo-revolutionary speech from Capitant? Another, more moderate one, from Pierre de Gaulle? With the General as the referee? But with nothing achieved at the end of it all. The truth is that, for more than a year, where the R.P.F. has been concerned, de Gaulle has merely *been putting up a pretence.* Should I attend the sessions? It's a question that I'm asking myself. I'd prefer not to make a fool of myself on the platform. But, on the other hand, I don't want to give the impression of disassociating myself from the General. It would hurt him, at this particular moment; it wouldn't be right if I seemed to be deserting him."

I asked him about the *Mémoires*. Had he read them?

"He's read me some passages from them, selected by him, which is quite a different matter. But what he read me had great quality. A little too literary perhaps in the most classic meaning of the word and the style. But what is slightly too Retz about it is compensated for by the fascinating actuality of the subject . . . His chapter on Pétain is masterly. He considers him a very great man, who, at a certain date, and entirely because of his age, changed. The moment of this fundamental change of personality occurred long before June 1940. Everybody thought they had called back the man of Verdun and it was a wholly different person who came on the scene."

"He told me this a long time ago."

"You must read the chapter for yourself. Beginning with: 'Too proud to be vain', and ending with 'Old age degrades'. You can see the viewpoint he has adopted. And how preoccupied he is with the menace of old age."

Malraux said that if de Gaulle had stood for parliament, he would have agreed to stand himself. Without him, he would no doubt have found himself in opposition to de Gaulle after two months.

"And there's nothing more idiotic than Gaullism without de Gaulle . . ."

After that, we spoke of practical matters in connection with the editing and publication of the *Mémoires*, and then came to André Breton, whom I preferred not to wait for, in order to avoid what could have been an embarrassing scene. (He sends me his books, but with dedications for the most part stressing the issues on which we disagree.) Malraux said:

"His position is a difficult one. He was always addicted to bistrots and a man for whom conversation was liable to sap his production powers. Now that Aragon and the others have been replaced by a number of young men from Saint-Germain des Prés, the stimulation can't be the same. And laziness must have got the upper hand, from which his former wives preserved him, by compelling him to work. He must be well aware that once the new post-Liberation flame was extinguished (one had been so deprived that no matter what intellectual nourishment was welcome), surrealism was dead. That it can't be taken seriously any longer. These are things that you sense. And the leader is the first to sense them. In the same way, de Gaulle knows that all the life has gone out of the R.P.F. That the R.P.F., too, can no longer be taken seriously. And that's why, even if he still pretends to be joining in the game, he is no longer taken in by it. And the same with poor Breton . . ."

I left. Outside, I peered into the distance of the misty avenue, hoping to see André Breton's rather heavy figure emerge from it. But in vain. I should have liked to have been present, invisibly, at his meeting with André Malraux.

Thursday, 12 November, 1953

An impressive Press conference held by General de Gaulle on, or, rather, against the plan for a European army. In spite of the R.P.F.'s defeat, his prestige has never been greater. It was France, threatened in her body and soul, once again reared up in front of us, to resist the forces seeking to destroy her, great France, who, without this man (for there is no one left but him) would no longer have a voice. Malraux was there, standing up, like a mysterious archangel.

1954

from General de Gaulle's Press conference: *7 April,* 1954

Q.   *This year, official ceremonies will be held to celebrate the tenth anniversary of the Liberation. What part do you intend to play in them?*
A.   *The Liberation took place and that was what counted, wasn't it? Now there are the anniversaries. These belong to everybody. I've been told that this year they will be celebrated in the presence and under the presidency of strictest officialdom. I have no objection. But how can I then take part in it, I, who have no official position?*

However, outside the ceremonies thus planned, I think it is my duty to take part publicly in the remembrance of our miseries and our glories. This is how I shall do it:

On Sunday 9 *May, the date of the day following the victory to which I had the honour of leading France, the State and the Armies, as well as the birthday of Joan of Arc, I shall go to the Arc de Triomphe. I have never been there since* 11 *November* 1945. *I shall arrive alone, without a procession at* 4.00 *in the afternoon. Under the vault, I shall be alone in saluting the Unknown Soldier. And, then, I will leave alone.*

I ask the people to be there to show that they remember what was done to save France's independence and that they intend to maintain it. I ask the ex-servicemen of the two wars, and of Indochina, to surround the monument. The Paris garrison will be responsible for the honours and the bugle calls. The glorious Paris police will maintain order, clear the approaches and direct the traffic. All of us, whoever we may be, who are present, will not utter a single word or raise any kind of cheer. The soul of the country will hover above the communion of this immense silence.

May the French Press help to see that this ceremony is invested in the eyes of the country and of the world, with the character of national unity and will!

Friday, 23 *April,* 1954

As I was in Cannes, I could not be present at General de Gaulle's Press conference on April 7. It was, I believe, the first I have missed (much to my regret!) since the Liberation. With what admiration (and emotion) I read the next day, under the palms of La Croisette, such extracts as the Press chose to publish. Something stirs physically within me at the name of de Gaulle – and it is not affection for a man: if it is a matter of sensibility, it is France alone that is involved in it, today's France, mocked, sick and ashamed.

One passage in the General's conference affected me in a more subtle manner, because, while I could appreciate the grandeur of his attitude, I could well see how it might shock, and what was outrageous and possibly even abnormal about it. Knowing de Gaulle as I do, his arrogant words could not surprise me – and I could only admire them. But I was dimly afraid that they might have appeared ridiculous to the profane, I mean to those who had not fathomed the mystery of the man. I learnt of the reaction of the journalists present from my father, who for the first time in many years had attended the General's Press conference. And attended in a spirit of sympathy – which is explained by the R.P.F.'s defeat, the fact that de Gaulle was not compromised by it and the unexpected fluctuations of a policy, which tends to bring the General back into favour again with men of the left, now that they have nothing to fear from him. (It is only when he is powerless that they venture to extol the powers of his genius.) My father was also moved by that conference, as his *Note-Book* testifies. As he always commits himself wholeheartedly, once de Gaulle had become sacred to him again, he admired him again in totality. The sentences relating to his solitary presence at the Arc de Triomphe, on 9 May, profited from this prejudice in his favour, and passed muster with the others. But not with the ears, mind and heart of François Mauriac alone, who said to me:

"When de Gaulle announced that he would arrive alone beneath the vault of the Arc de Triomphe, remain there alone and leave alone, I glanced towards the hospital to see whether the male-nurses were not on their way . . . But at the moment I noticed the rapt expression on the faces of all the journalists present and saw, with relief, that not one of them, not a single one, had flinched. Not the vestige of a smile anywhere. Those representatives of all the parties, those sharks who aren't easily fooled, listened seriously, even with gravity, to these words, of which they only caught the grandeur, yes, the grandeur and the beauty . . ."

At the beginning, he had announced, to me, triumphantly

"You know, I went to hear de Gaulle and found him marvellous!"

And I had replied (without trying to conceal my bitterness):

"Yes, and it's high time!"

But he remarked:

"Well, what could you expect, I hated the R.P.F."

I had made no retort. He had had so many reasons (which I had secretly shared), for hating the R.P.F. But the result was there to see: France in a dizzy spin, and de Gaulle unemployed.

Sunday, 9 May, 1954

As we made our way very early towards the Place de l'Etoile, Jules Roy said to me, with reference to de Gaulle, in that vibrant, intense tone of voice he often uses:

"It's fortunate he's here. There's no one else. At least, we have him to lean on and the assurance his presence brings. The man of France. But also of Destiny. He makes this rendezvous with us and it falls, as though haphazardly, on the day following such a disastrous event for the country, like the fall of Dien-Bien-Phu. But, this is no coincidence: it's a sign and a stimulus."

I had seats on the terrace of the Arc de Triomphe. All the leaders of the former Gaullist demonstrations and the R.P.F. were there. It was both moving and a little sad. At the appointed hour, exactly 4.00, all traffic disappeared from the Champs Elysées and the Place de l'Etoile. And de Gaulle appeared in the distance, level with the Avenue George V, standing up in an open car. The car was approaching very quickly, followed by the acclaim of the crowd. Distance made the General look as slender and young as he had in the glorious days, ten years before. It was the same remarkable man in the same uniform. And it was easy to pretend to oneself that it was also the same France that had come, unanimously, to acclaim him.

He got out of the car. I had a close view of him, in his slightly older guise of today. I recognized that smile of his, official and intimate at one and the same time. He reviewed a detachment of Republican Guards, and bowed in front of the tomb. The military band played the *Marseillaise* and a beautiful moment occurred (but a short one, for our immediate neighbours began to sing, too, and then we could only hear them): from the Champs Elysées and the edges of the square, arose the vast, deep singing of the crowd, as it accompanied the brass. Then came the last post on the bugles and the shouting and cheering stopped instantly: in the even deeper silence that followed, the only sounds to be heard were the cries of the swallows, high up in the sky (they returned on Friday) and the usual fluttering of the disturbed pigeons.

Standing up in his car, de Gaulle drove round the Place de l'Etoile (after following his customary practice of shaking hands with various members of the crowd) and disappeared into the distance down the Avenue de la Grande Armée, leaving bursts of cheering in his wake. Emotion kept Jules Roy and myself silent. Then we became caught up in embryonic demonstrations, swiftly quelled by one of the most impressive police operations that I have ever seen in Paris. There were a few isolated cries of "De Gaulle to power!" and "Pleven to resign!" It was sad that it had all happened so quickly: de Gaulle had only been present for a quarter of an hour. An hour later, the last demonstrators were dispersing, swallowed up by the passive Sunday crowd.

The Eternal France

The presentation of the Grand Cross to my father by General de Gaulle had to be postponed twice. The first time, at the end of last year, because of Pierre de Gaulle's death; the second time, because the new date chosen came right in the middle of the Algerian insurrection.

All the family cars were lined up this morning, a little before 1.00, along the Avenue Marigny, where a policeman, no doubt accustomed to this kind of wait, allowed us to park in spite of it being forbidden. My parents and Jean were in the first car, we in the second, Alain (whom I was seeing for the first time in his general's uniform), Luce and Françoise le Ray in the third, and lastly my uncle and aunt, the Roger Gay-Lussacs.

We means not only Marie-Claude and myself, but also the eight-year-old Gérard, invited to the presentation but not to lunch. He was so happy, and we so proud for his sake, that the ceremony, which had not fired us with much enthusiasm, suddenly enchanted us: it gave my father pleasure to have me there and my son's presence delighted me.

We were received by Courcel and Brouillet; met a number of eminent people in the salon, among them General Catroux, Grand Chancellor of the Legion of Honour; and watched the arrival of the Henri Troyats. We were lined up near the door through which the General would enter – the family first: my father, mother, Gérard . . . Gérard, who blushed scarlet and seemed about to retreat, which I had to stop, when a gentleman-usher announced "General de Gaulle, President of the Republic and Mme. de Gaulle."

He came in, smiling and debonair, greeted my parents with a few kind words and shook Gérard warmly by the hand, as he said: "I'm very happy to meet you," which my small boy, himself, did not find probable, but, nevertheless, did not take as a mere polite formula. If it were one, the General invested it with great spontaneity and friendliness, as he did the whole ceremony and lunch that succeeded it, giving no impression of carrying out just another duty, among many, a tiresome responsibility attached to his office, but, rather, one of entertaining a family of whom he was very fond.

He had greeted me by my Christian name when he shook my hand, and I immediately felt at my ease, as though all those many, many years had not rolled by since the days when I used to see him often. His presence seemed so natural to me that I allowed several minutes to pass before I looked at him. When I did, it was almost unconsciously: imposed on my blurred memories of him as he had been during our period of (relative) intimacy, were the pictures of him I saw daily on television or in newsreels, so that there was no hiatus in our relationship (anyway as far as I was concerned) and I did not notice that he had grown older: on the contrary, I felt as though I had never left him. And I again became conscious (without any surprise) of that physical radiance of his that, when you are with him, makes you bound to him, body and soul. A few days before, there had been the disappointment of his so-called *tour des popotes*† in Algeria, and the extraordinary conversations he had held there (reported by the only journalist present, my brother Jean); there had been this political error (or so it seems in the light of today), in addressing speeches to officers, of which the least one can say is that they seemed to be wholly inconsistent with all his liberal policies, depriving him in one go and quite unnecessarily of the adherence of the French masses, unanimous since the events in January, without winning him a single friend more from among the extremists. And this very morning, we had learnt that he had refused to unite the Chambers for motives that could not have been more legitimate, fundamentally, but were close to illegality in the methods employed. But now, all was swept aside: nothing remained than this almost-physical, sentimental attachment, which I recognized and judged as such, but without being able to blame myself for yielding to it, despite the knowledge of its dangers.

Meanwhile, the ceremony went on, quietly, facing a French window opening on the garden, with the muffled hum of Paris in the distance. Colonel Bonneval fussed round my father, adorning him with the broad red ribbon, and trying somehow or other to secure the star, which the General had pinned on even more clumsily. My father, standing very straight, almost seemed small as he faced de Gaulle, who said in a loud voice:

"François Mauriac, we raise you to the dignity of the Grand Cross of the Legion of Honour" adding, in an undertone, (and I am sure I

---

† *Tour des popotes* is military slang for going round the troops to find out the state of their morale: theoretically, eating soup with them.

am quoting this verbatim): "It is an honour that France is doing to herself."

After that, my father was relieved of his glorious trappings and drinks were served. Even more than I looked at de Gaulle, I looked at my son looking at de Gaulle: at Gérard, so charming (anyway, his parents had the normal weakness to find him so), certainly shy, but not behaving any less naturally as a result and not refusing – very much the opposite – to take a canapé from the tray proffered him by one of the waiters.

I remained on one side, making no attempt to hear what de Gaulle was saying to my father, maman, or Henri Troyat, but watching the time when I should have to take Gérard back to the car, while determined to let him stay as long as possible in this Palace de l'Elysée, where his presence was so unbelievable.

There came a moment, however, when I found myself and Gérard beside the General and my father. The latter mentioned that Edmond Rostand's sister, Juliette Mante, was the little boy's great-grandmother. And the General said:

"I had great affection and respect for Mme. Mante-Rostand. She was a woman of great generosity, as I well remember."

He said more than that and with more 'feeling', but I cannot remember his exact words.

When, later on, I asked Gérard what had struck him most in what the General had said to him, he answered at once: "When he said he was very fond of Mout and often saw her", which was an even less exact version than mine; but I am glad that the memory of this great day will remain linked in his mind with that of his great-grandmother Rostand, whom he mentions now and then and who, when he paid her a visit at Valmante or in the rue du Bac, made such a strong impression on him that, in spite of his young age (he was four years old when she died) he will no doubt remember it all his life.

It gives me pleasure to think that this Diary will remain as a testimony to such an important event in his childhood and to his great-grandmother. He has already a sense of family and a proper pride in it. I do not find anything wrong or ridiculous about it; it is another frail but comforting little barrier against death.

Meanwhile, I had a feeling that we were about to go into lunch and that it was time for Gérard to leave. He said goodbye to Mme. de Gaulle and then the General, very shyly, but with the unaffectedness of his age and the appropriate niceties. Before giving him a kiss, de Gaulle made him a short speech, to which he, himself, obviously attached some importance. For, for him, too, it was a little barrier, a

361

minute bulwark against death. Not against oblivion (which will not come as far as he is concerned, until the moment which, we hope, may be distant, when our civilization is destroyed), but against physical death. Thanks to this small boy who, as he said, "would still be young in the year 2000 and who would remember all his life the day when his grandfather had received the highest decoration that existed in France", a living man would still then be there to bear witness to the living General, and say to young men, who would not believe their ears: "De Gaulle, yes, I saw him, I shook his hand, he spoke to me and even kissed me."

I accompanied Gérard through the sumptuous rooms, under the sympathetic eyes of the ushers, and saw him into my father's car. I just got back to the salon in time, as they were going in to the dining-room. It was an intimate family lunch. I sat some way from the General. Now and then, but not often, I tried to hear what he was saying. For instance, in reference to Khrushchev's forthcoming visit to France, which had been postponed for a few days (which is why we were there: there is a big gap in de Gaulle's timetable); he declared, good-humouredly that "the people's welcome will be what it should be: correct but nothing more". And he asked Catroux how far the plans for the restoration of the Napoleon on the Colonne Vendôme had gone. And he also asked my father: what uniform should he wear; the one chosen for him by Louis Philippe or that of the *petit caporal*?

Nothing of this has any great interest. But suddenly, as our eyes chanced to meet, he smiled at me, and made a wide gesture of friendship, that no one noticed except myself. And, between us, there was one of those brief but meaningful wordless dialogues, like those we try to put into our books, when this admirer of Edmond Rostand suddenly became a hero out of Nathalie Sarraute.

And Marie-Claude was to say to me later:

"What I like about de Gaulle is his wonderful *reserve*."

She did not need to say more: I knew exactly what she meant. For it is true that, in him, as in every man, but to a greater degree (either because his character appears richer, or because we pay more attention to what such a great man reveals, formally or silently) there are several levels of expression. For instance:

– What he says loudly;

– What he mutters, but with the intention of being heard;

– What he does not say, but which his expression reveals;

– Finally, lower still but perceptible, other mysterious, shrouded mutterings.

There was some of all that in the smile and in the gesture with his hand that he addressed to me, by no means unobtrusively in front of everyone, but which I alone saw and understood.

When the champagne was served, he briefly proposed a toast to François Mauriac, saying it was high time that he received the decoration for very shortly it would seem incomprehensible to everyone that he had not had it. My father, naturally, replied that the honour, for him, lay less in the decoration than in the fact that he had received it from the hands of de Gaulle.

After that, there were a few words that were almost too familiar from my mother and father, the General rose and we returned to the salon. Again, I remained well away from the group formed by de Gaulle, François Mauriac and Henri Troyat. My son was no longer there and the scene did not hold the same interest for me. The real ceremony, that of the torch passed on by de Gaulle to a small boy, had ended long before.

When I took leave of the General, he said to me as he always does whenever we happen to meet:

"I never see you."

And, as always, I replied that I did not want to disturb him. And, as always, he retorted that I did not disturb him, adding that 'at the level at which he was now, he had all the time in the world, since he had very little to do'. I smiled, as was expected of me. I promised to call on him, particularly as my mother said, on coming up to us: "The General was complaining at lunch that he never sees you any more." And that was the end.

Sunday, 12 June, 1966
Goupillieres

Last Thursday, 9 June, Marie-Claude and I were invited to lunch at the Elysée. Having arrived on time, we thought we must be early; the Cabinet meeting had only just broken up. So we were sitting quietly in our car, parked in the courtyard, where there were no others, apart from those of the departing ministers, when a colonel made urgent signs to me from the top of the steps. All the guests, except us, had already arrived. As we came in, the introductions had already started. Had I known the timetable, which I received next day, I should have been in a panic: 1.10, 1.12, 1.14 . . . Every detail had been worked out to within a minute or two!

I was awed and embarrassed, and wondered what I was doing there at this luncheon given to Baron Jaspar, the Belgian Ambassador, whom I did not know, on the occasion of his relinquishing his post. The

General spoke to me for a moment just before we went into lunch, asking me how *La Conversation* had done. I was touched that he had remembered the title, and he went on to pay me compliments on my writing in front of Vice-Chancellor Roche.

I was awed, but not at all surprised to be there, feeling as though I were there every day: looking at the General, in this room, then at lunch, and seeing him as though I had not stopped seeing him more than twenty years ago. And, indeed, not a week, almost not a day, passes without our seeing him on our television screen. But it was less this that was responsible for my feeling than a more intimate and direct familiarity. Time, stationary, peaceful and profound, took up again at the point where it had left us, the time of my existence close to General de Gaulle; an existence that had suffered no interruption and which I resumed as though I had never left him for more than a few hours.

There were many ministers and eminent persons present. I was at one end of the table, Marie-Claude at the other, and we smiled at each other from afar, in this Murat salon, where the really intimate lunches do not take place – they are given in the private apartments – but the meals at which the guests are relatively few. Today, twenty-eight of us sat down to lunch: Couve de Murville, back last night from Brussels where a crucial conference had been held: Joxe, Palewski, Alphand, whom I only discovered at the last minute, and Baumgartner.

Only two days before, the General had been present at the Alpine manoeuvres; yesterday evening, there had been an important dinner; he had just come from a Cabinet meeting. All that might not amount to very much, but, at the same time, he is pursuing, all on his own, a policy of independence in his relations towards the United States, which alarms a number of people, is approved by the majority of them, and requires constant vigilance and self-control. Yet he is relaxed, hale and hearty. "When I think," Marie-Claude said to me as we left, "that people dare talk of his age!" At the end of the frugal and rapid meal, he made a speech, as always beautifully turned and perfectly phrased.

In the garden, where we had coffee under the trees, in front of the wide lawn, hollowed out into its unusual, attractive concave shape, he gathered around him the more important guests, then got up and left that circle of chairs for another, where he sat among the ladies next to Marie-Claude: meanwhile, I was standing up, listening to Bruno de Leusse telling me how magnificent Couve de Murville had been once again in Brussels; serene, imperturbable, and achieving, without raising his voice, the insertion of a small adjective, which resulted in the conference having to recognize a Europe stretching from the Atlantic to the Urals. "They'll notice the consequences in three months' time and swear they'll see to it that they aren't taken in by that clever devil again."

Somebody spoke to me about *Dîner en ville*. Somebody else, a little later, about *Le Déjeuner au Salon Murat*. People got up, members of the General's household staff made meaningful gestures and it was the cue for Bruno de Leusse and myself; there was no question of disobeying it and a moment later I was sitting close to de Gaulle, only separated from him by Alphand, who suddenly noticed me and said hello, when I had not seen him either till then. Baron Jaspar was on the General's left. De Gaulle did his duty by me, did what he thought was his duty by me by paying me further compliments on my books, which threw me into confusion.

"Mme. Jaspar was telling me just now how much she admired you..."

Some questions about films followed, to which I replied. Then fortunately, Baron Jaspar put an end to the ritual, trite conversation by returning to one of the subjects he had raised in responding to the General's toast during lunch:

"Don't you think, General, that Valéry was wrong, that there are lessons to be learnt from History, that they can serve some purpose?"

De Gaulle answered in a few words, of which the banality was proportionately compensated for by the fact that he is de Gaulle, that everything he says carries weight, and also because, beneath his least important utterances, there are always latent meanings, a whole context that, while unexpressed, is nonetheless there. (It had occurred to me during the Ambassador's speech, and it occurred to me again, now, that, on 18 June, de Gaulle could not have found any historical precedent to refer to.) In any case, de Gaulle answered in a somewhat professorial tone of voice, but less tritely than it appears:

"Yes, I know, Paul Valéry wrote that, and believed it was so. He said that the lessons of History were useless. It was his opinion, but it's not mine."

Then, Baron Jaspar, alluding to the heroic London period, said that de Gaulle had prevented him from accompanying him to Dakar and that he still regretted it. De Gaulle did not reply at first, his usual practice when asked an indiscreet question or when a subject is broached that he wishes to avoid. There was a silence. Perhaps he was merely musing on the past, suddenly made present, when he undertook the ill-fated expedition to Dakar. Then, with irony in his expression and voice ("the man is full of humour", Marie-Claude was to remark to me later) he replied, verbatim:

"It was just as well for you . . . For me, too, for that matter."

He made a pause between the two sentences. The second one appeared to mean: 'It would have been just as well if I hadn't gone either.'

It was time for us to get up and go. Two daisies, their stems crushed, lay where his feet had been a few seconds before: I picked them, knowing I would be made fun of (as I was by Gérard, with his sweet, limpid laughter); I laughed at myself, I still picked them.

A relic, Nathalie will say. Anyway, a memento.

Just as when we arrived, he had a kindly word of welcome during the formal introductions, so now there was a brief sentence of farewell, but his goodbye was less conventional; it lasted and was spun out, while some minister or other waited behind us.

"You really must come and see me one day."

I said that I did not want to intrude, and Marie-Claude added that I was always afraid of disturbing him. He said:

"You should know that we have great affection for you. And admiration."

The royal 'we' impressed me. I disregarded the obligatory admiration; but I believed in the affection, and was overjoyed. Marie-Claude burst out, spontaneously:

"He does, too, General: you're the passion of his life."

He did not answer. Perhaps she had gone a little too far, and it was not a thing to say to the President of the Republic; nevertheless, I think he was touched and did not want to show it. We took leave of him, happy and overwhelmed.

Thursday, 12 *November,* 1970

Catch this headline in *Le Figaro* as Marie-Claude, Nathalie and I reach the Rond-Point: *L'Adieu.* A wave of grief sweeps over me. Run into Luce, Sophie and Alain le Ray in the crowd. Progress slowly up the Champs Elysées, where once I drove beside him in his car. Rain coming down torrentially. Not a man, not a woman, not a child leaves the immense, silent procession. Here, indeed, is his old, beloved country! The rain on the faces mixes with the tears.

Tuesday, 10 *November,* 1970

Stunned, then deeply distressed, by the death of General de Gaulle, of which we hear, belatedly, this morning. I scarcely have time to become conscious of my grief, the violence of which surprises me, before Jean-François Brisson asks me to write an article in little over an hour and telephone it through to *Le Figaro*. "Does one ask a man to write an article on the day of his father's death? No one dared do it on 1st September, and yet this morning . . . I had two fathers. Their destinies were linked. I am an old orphan of fifty-six. I must write, despite my tears . . ."

Monday, 18 May, 1970

It is true that at this period the only entries in my Diary refer to my meetings with General de Gaulle, either in Paris or Colombey. Another volume of *Temps Immobile*, dedicated to eternal France. *At the Elysée, Friday, 12 February*, 1960. My turn comes. The General calls me by my Christian name, which touches me, and says to me (as always: "Delighted to see you, Claude . . . We don't often see you, nowadays . . ." And I reply, as always (on the rare occasions when I meet him): "It's because I don't like to disturb you, General." And he says, as always, but with a little more insistence than usual, it seems to me: "You wouldn't disturb me if you came to see me one of these days." He appeared to mean it. I called on him, I talked with him without any sense of wonder, happy to see him looking so well, but finding it quite natural to be physically in his presence and not consciously aware of the difference between the direct impact of television and reality.

Wednesday, 2 September, 1959

De Gaulle and Eisenhower standing up in their car, drive up and then down the decorated Champs Elysées, among the acclaim of the crowd. Eisenhower looking in better shape than I had expected and emanating an undeniable atmosphere of charm. De Gaulle, seen as he remains in my memory – distant, inaccessible, for whom my feelings have remained unchanged and in which affection plays such a great part. Have seen my brother Jean in the crowd (he has just been with de Gaulle in Algiers): very thin and suddenly a different man, a man whom habit had before prevent me from seeing. On his face, which *I no longer recognize*, I find features that belong not only to him, but to our mother, which moves me deeply.

Sunday, 9 May, 1954

And de Gaulle appeared in the distance, standing in his open car, level with the Avenue George V. The car was moving fast, at the same rhythm as the rumour of the crowd. Distance helped to make the

General appear as young and slender as in the glorious days of ten
years past.

Thursday, 19 August 1948

This drive down the Champs Elysées with a de Gaulle wrapped in
thought, on a beautiful evening, four years after his entry into Paris
in the process of being liberated. The indifference of the passers-by,
their absence appears to hurt him. And he who is so keen not to be
recognized, refusing to move except in the most modest of Citroëns in
order to remain unnoticed, I feel he would have been happy now if a
cheer had emerged from this inattentive crowd.

Thursday, 26 April, 1948

As we pass in front of the *Figaro* he asks me to buy him a copy of
Churchill's *Memoirs*.

Friday, 19 December 1947

Nobody recognizes him. The emotion of driving up the Champs Elysées
behind de Gaulle and catching sight of him in his soft hat, through the
back window of his car.

Tuesday, 15 May, 1945

That man whose sleeve in khaki cloth on which two stars were glisten-
ing, fascinated me; he was the same man I had seen on Victory Day, at
the Arc de Triomphe, pressed in by the crowd which was acclaiming
him, and whose face was lit up by a joy he could not suppress;
the same man who, a few moments ago, had addressed a victorious
France from the rostrum of the Senate.

Monday, 13 November, 1944

Churchill, Eden, de Gaulle. And the enthusiasm of the crowd when
the General and the British Prime Minister, surrounded by mounted
Republican Guards, drive down the triumphant avenue.

Saturday, 26 August, 1944

In front of me – the Champs Elysées! Ah! It is the sea!

NOTES

p. 19, 23   ANTONESCU . . . Fascist Marshal of Rumania, who had just been arrested by King Michael (23 August). Turned over to the Russians, he was condemned to death by them in 1946.

p. 19, 29   AUBOYNEAU . . . Philippe Auboyneau joined de Gaulle in 1940. Commander of the Free French Fleet in the Pacific, and Naval Minister in the Government in exile in 1942.

p. 20, 5   ROBERT VICTOR . . . he had been charged with special duties earlier on in the Algerian Cabinet.

p. 20, 6   PHILIPPE HENRIOT . . . having been the Vichy Minister of Information, he was tried and condemned to death by the National Resistance Council on 28 June 1944.

p. 20, 8   COURCEL . . . Geoffroy de Courcel was the General's aide-de-camp.

p. 20, 29   ANDRÉ ROUSSIN . . . dramatist and friend of the author.

p. 20, 32   JIRI MUCHA . . . Czech journalist, son of the painter Alphonse Mucha.

p. 21, 4   M. BILLOUX . . . François Billoux. Deputy of the Communist Party and Minister of State in the National Liberation Committee 1944.

p. 21, 14   PAUL VALÉRY . . . poet, dramatist and diplomat. Member of the French Academy.

p. 21, 15   CLAUDE GALLIMARD . . . son of Raymond Gallimard, and subsequently head of the famous publishing company.

p. 22, 8   B.C.R.A. . . . Central Information for Action Office.

p. 23, 23   GEORGES DUHAMEL . . . writer, Permanent Secretary from 1942–46 of the French Academy.

p. 29, 7   GEORGES IZARD . . . member of the Resistance in France.

p. 29, 17   S.F.I.O. . . . French branch of the International Labour Organisation.

p. 31, 30   DEBÛ-BRIDEL . . . Jacques Debû-Bridel, a writer and journalist. Prominent member of the Resistance and the National Resistance Committee 1940–43, and member of the Consultative Assembly 1944–45.

p. 31, 31   JEAN PAULHAN . . . was a prominent member of the Resistance and a writer who resigned in 1946 from the National Committee of Writers because of Communist domination. Member of the French Academy.

p. 32, 25   COLONEL CORNIGLION-MOLINIER . . . subsequently General Edouard Corniglion-Molinier, he was Commander of the Free French Air Force with the British in 1942, and Commander of the Atlantic Air Force in 1943.

p. 33, 40   ADMIRAL MUSELIER . . . Emile Muselier, Commander in Chief of Marine and Air Free France until 1942. Chief of Police, Civil and Military, in Algiers in 1943, and in Paris 1944.

p. 34, 8   GENERAL GIRAUD . . . Henri Giraud, Commander in Chief of the French Army in North Africa.

p. 35, 4   JEAN PRÉVOST . . . killed in Vercors by the Germans. A militant Resistance fighter, he had been a journalist/author and a critic of acumen and intelligence.

p. 35, 18   D'ASTIER DE LA VIGERIE . . . Raoul d'Astier de la Vigerie was the organiser of the Resistance for the southern area, and founder of the publication *Libération.*

p. 35, 18   ANDRÉ PHILIP . . . Minister of the Interior from 1942–44.

p. 36, 42   F.T.P. . . . Free Fighters and Partisans.

p. 39, 29   PAUL CLAUDEL . . . poet, author, diplomat. Member of the French Academy.

p. 41, 11   GENERAL CATROUX . . . Georges Catroux was Chief of the Reserve Corps, and subsequently Ambassador of France to Moscow.

p. 41, 13   DE LATTRE DE TASSIGNY . . . Jean de Lattre de Tassigny, much beloved General of the French Armies, and posthumously given the rank of Marshal.

p. 45, 33   MARCEL CACHIN . . . Communist politician, and first French Communist senator in 1935.

p. 51, 10   EMILE ROCHE . . . economist, politician, journalist, he was editor of *La Republique* from 1929–39. President of the Radical Socialist Movement in 1932, and Cabinet Minister in 1935.

p. 53, 24   TIXIER . . . Adrien Tixier. Socialist and Minister of the Interior in 1944. He was wounded during the War, and died in 1946.

p. 57, 30   C.N.R. . . . National Resistance Council.

p. 59, 13   THIERRY MAULNIER . . . political writer and playwright.

p. 60, 28   BURIN DES ROZIERS . . . Etienne Burin des Roziers was Secretary General to the President of the Republic, and subsequently French Ambassador in the United States.

p. 64, 9   JOUVE . . . Gérard Jouve was Director of the radio station in Brazzaville, and head of the organisation to assist the Free French in Constantinople.

p. 65, 28   BROUILLET . . . René Brouillet was chief adjutant of the Cabinet when de Gaulle was President of the Provisional

Government from August 1944–January 1946. Subsequently ambassadorial adviser and Cabinet member.

p. 67, 37   PAUL CHACK . . . had been a writer on the newspaper *Aujourd'hui*, and the Chairman of the Committee for Anti Bolshevik Action.

p. 67, 37   BÉRAUD . . . Henri Béraud had been a Resistance writer and journalist, but was blacklisted in September 1944 for his association with Vichy.

p. 68, 33   TEITGEN . . . Pierre Henri Teitgen was a member of several Gaullist governments.

p. 77, 29   THOREZ . . . Maurice Thorez went to Moscow in 1943 to take part in the dissolution of the Third Internationale. He took up his post as Secretary General of the Communist Party in 1945. Elected as Deputy and Minister of State later the same year.

p. 85, 10   HENRY BORDEAUX . . . writer of domestic tragedies, he had been a member of the Academy since 1919.

p. 85, 12   DUC DE LA FORCE . . . was born 1878 and was a famous historian and member of the Academy.

p. 85, 13   MADELIN . . . Louis Madelin was an expert on the French Revolution and the Empire, and also represented Vosges from 1924–28.

p. 89, 26   M.L.N. . . . National Liberation Movement.

p. 91, 14   JOXE . . . Louis Joxe. Historian and Chief of the Centre of the Study of Foreign Affairs, he became Secretary General of the National Liberation Movement 1942–44. He held the same post in the Provisional Government until 1946.

p. 92, 27   GENERAL FRÈRE . . . Albert Frère. Head of the Seventh Army. After the occupation of France in 1940 he firmly resisted the German demands and openly encouraged his military colleagues to be prepared at all times to take up arms against the occupiers. In 1942 he created the organisation for Resistance within the army itself, and secretly kept in touch with the French Government in London and Algeria. Arrested in 1943, he was deported to Struthof.

p. 93, 26   BRIAND . . . Aristide Briand died in 1932 aged 70. Had been 22 times a Minister in the Government, 15 of which he was Foreign Minister. Co-author in 1928 of Kellog-Briand Pact. Dedicated pacifist and brilliant orator.

p. 96, 16   MENTHON . . . François de Menthon. He amalgamated his organisation for the Movement of Pre-Resistance with that of Combat, and was Commissioner of Justice for the Committee for the Liberation of France 1943–44. Minister for Justice the same year, and for National Economy in 1946.

p. 96, 23 GILLOT ... Auguste Gillot. Member of the Front Nationals in 1941, Communist delegate to the National Council for Resistance in 1943, President of same Council in 1944. Mayor of Saint-Denis in the same year, and member of the Central Committee of the French Communist Party in 1945.

p. 96, 32 COUVE DE MURVILLE ... Jacques Couve de Murville. At the beginning of his illustrious political career he had been a member of the French Committee for National Liberation since 1943, and French delegate to the Consultant Council for Italian Affairs in 1944.

p. 97, 16 MONNET ... Jean Monnet. On the committee for the furnishing of arms and encouragement for the reconstruction of the French Committee for National Liberation in Algiers.

p. 98, 29 ANDRÉ HAURIOU ... Vice President of the Consultative Assembly in Algiers from 1943–44, and in Paris as a delegate.

p. 100, 2 JACQUES DUCLOS ... for 33 years until 1964 Secretary of the Communist Party. At this time delegate to the Consultative Assembly.

p. 100, 10 C.G.T. ... General Workers Union.

p. 102, 28 VINCENT AURIOL ... this forceful politician had only begun his career two years earlier in Algiers.

p. 107, 25 R.P. PHILIPP ... Father Philipp was a powerful Resistance leader.

p. 109, 3 R.P. CARRIÈRE ... Father Anselme Carrière was one of the heroes of the Resistance movement in the Middle East.

p. 111, 16 LOUIS VALLON ... having been a delegate to the Consultative Assembly in Algiers, he was a member of de Gaulle's Cabinet until 1946.

p. 116, 3 GENERAL DENTZ ... his crime was that on Vichy orders he permitted German squadrons to land in French occupied Syria. He also used those forces under his command against the French and British armies. His sentence was commuted to life imprisonment.

p. 118, 7 JEAN LUCHAIRE ... despite the fact that he had been a Resistance writer, the editor of Les Nouveaux Temps, at the time of writing, under suspicion of having been in contact with the enemy, he was a doomed man. Finally tried in 1946, he was sentenced to death.

p. 125, 35 WEYGAND . . . General Maxime Weygand had been Governor of Algiers in 1941. He was arrested by the Germans in 1942 and imprisoned in Germany until 1945.

p. 127, 3 GENERAL HÉRING . . . Pierre Héring just before the fall of France reassembled a military force which he named the Army of Paris. He took up a position beyond the capital, but because of orders from above, he abandoned his stand.

p. 131, 3 PEYROUTON . . . Bernard-Marcel Peyrouton was Governor General of Algeria in 1943, and before that Minister for the Interior.

p. 131, 4 JACQUES CHEVALIER . . . Minister in the Vichy Government from 1940–41.

p. 131, 5 BOUTHILLIER . . . Yves Bouthillier. Another member of the Vichy Government.

p. 135, 1 LEBRUN . . . Albert Lebrun, 1871–1950. First elected President of France in 1932, he was still President at the fall in June of 1939. Deposed in favour of Pétain. Rather than dwell in the Vichy capital, he retired to Vizelle, and was subsequently arrested by the Germans and imprisoned in Bavaria. The last President of the Third Republic, he returned after the War and lived in retirement.

p. 141, 2 M.R.P. . . . Popular Republican Movement.

p. 142, 5 U.D.S.R. . . . Social Democratic Union.

p. 143, 23 JULES MOCH . . . since 1942 he had been closely connected with de Gaulle, and from this time on was always prominent in French politics.

p. 155, 33 D.G.E.R. . . . Information Service attached to the Prime Minister's cabinet.

p. 163, 36 GENERAL BILLOTTE . . . Pierre Billotte had been Military Assistant to de Gaulle and Secretary to the Committee of National Defence from 1942–44. Commanding ten divisions of infantry, he campaigned from 1944–45 and then was nominated head of the military delegation to the United Nations until 1950.

p. 168, 7 A.F.A.T. . . . Women's Auxiliary for the Army.

p. 172, 25 JULES ROMAINS . . . born Louis Farigoule, author of *Jean Christophe*, a novel roughly based on the life of Beethoven which won him international fame. Spent the War years in the United States and Mexico. Died in 1972.

p. 176, 1 BYRNES – BEVIN – MOLOTOV – BIDAULT . . . James Byrnes, American Secretary of State; Ernest Bevin, British Foreign

Secretary; Molotov, Russian Foreign Minister; Georges Bidault, French Minister of Foreign Affairs.

p. 180, 4 HENRI MULLER... publisher.

p. 186, 31 P.R.L.... Republican Liberty Party.

p. 192, 36 FRENAY... Henri Frenay. Became a member of the French Liberation Committee in November 1943. Charged with the task of looking after prisoners, deportees and refugees. He continued in this work, given the title of Minister, in the Provisional Government.

p. 193, 31 MR BARUCH... Bernard Baruch was the American financier, philanthropist and consultant on affairs of State.

p. 196, 32 CAPITANT . . . René Capitant, loyal Gaullist, Minister of Education in the Provisional Government.

p. 201, 10 MICHEL DEBRÉ . . . during the War had participated in the Resistance in many different ways. His first political post was in Angers from 1944–45 to work with de Gaulle himself, and at the time of writing he was about to prepare the arrangements concerning the Sarre Basin. He later became Secretary for German and Austrian Affairs, establishing himself as a politician of the first rank.

p. 202, 35 ILYA EHRENBURG . . . the Russian foreign correspondent turned novelist. First came to international note with his account of the Fall of Paris, and won the Stalin Prize in 1949.

p. 212, 21 JACQUES CHABAN-DELMAS... at this time he was an Inspector of Finances, but had been very active in the Resistance. He rose quickly from 1946 as a member of the National Assembly, and was Mayor of Bordeaux in 1947, a post which he still held in 1972. From Minister of State, National Defence, he became Premier. Forced out of that position by a series of rumours and scandals.

p. 233, 24 NOGUÈS . . . General Charles Noguès was French Resident General in Morocco from 1939–43, when he moved to Lisbon. From 1945 he gave himself up to the French authorities. Two years later he was sentenced to 20 years hard labour for disloyal conduct.

p. 245, 29 CHAMPETIER DE RIBES . . . recently Secretary of State for Foreign Affairs.

p. 251, 23 CAFFERY... Jefferson Caffery was first accredited to the *de facto* French authorities in 1944, and was subsequently named Ambassador to France by the U.S. Government. Transferred in 1949 to Egypt.

p. 254, 13 R.P.F. . . . Union of the French People.

p. 273, 21 RÉMY ROURE . . . editor in chief of the newspaper *Le Monde* from 1945–52. He had been co-publisher of the bulletin of Fighting France. Arrested by the Germans he was imprisoned in Auschwitz and then Buchenwald.

p. 281, 35 EDOUARD DALADIER . . . several times Premier and Foreign Minister of France before the War.

p. 288, 23 CLAUDE BOURDET . . . During the Occupation he was a member of the Committee of the National Resistance and in 1944 was arrested by the Gestapo and imprisoned at Oranienburg and Buchenwald. Vice President of the Consultative Assembly in 1945, he became Director General of French Rediffusion. Returned to journalism on *Le Combat* 1947–50 and *l'Observateur.*

p. 291, 8 DE GASPERI . . . Alcide de Gasperi. Soon after the Proclamation of the Italian Republic, which he himself fostered, he became Prime Minister and maintained this post until 1953. He always aligned himself with the allies in the Peace Treaty.

p. 296, 24 BÉNOUVILLE . . . Pierre de Bénouville. Having organised the Concerted Action for Resistance in 1942, he reformed it as the National Liberation Movement. It was under his direction that the Algerian operations of the Free French Forces of the Interior were so successful in 1944.

p. 299, 7 BRUGÈRE . . . Raymond Brugère, formerly Secretary General in the Ministry of Foreign Affairs, and subsequently Ambassador.

p. 299, 37 PIERRE BOURDAN . . . in previous Governments he had held the post of Minister responsible for young artists and writers.

p. 304, 17 QUEUILLE . . . Henri Queuille. Prominent radical socialist politician who held various governmental posts from 1948 on.

p. 306, 28 C.R.S. . . . Rural Motorised Police.

p. 309, 36 KOMINFORM . . . was the central office for information set up in Warsaw the previous year, which supposedly gave directives throughout the world. Extremely unpopular, it was dissolved in 1956.

p. 312, 12 RAYMOND ARON . . . editor for *La France Libre* from 1940–44 in London.

p. 319, 26 JOUHANDEAU . . . Marcel Jouhandeau, until his death in the summer of 1972, had always been a prolific, highly personal and very controversial writer.

p. 319, 33 VERCORS . . . pseudonym used by Jean Bruller for his works

376

of fiction (*Silence of the Sea*; *By These Signs You Shall Know Them*). He was also a publisher, designer and engraver of note.

p. 324, 37 MARTIN DU GARD . . . Roger Martin du Gard. Highly acclaimed writer whose successes were prominent features of the between-the-Wars literary scene. Best known for his epochal novel *The Thibauts*.

p. 325, 28 SAINT-JOHN PERSE . . . Alexis Léger used this pseudonym for his poetry, which merited him the Nobel Prize in 1960.

p. 326, 40 DIMITROV . . . Georges Dimitrov was a prominent Bulgarian politician who, because of his left wing politics, was condemned to death and reprieved several times. Leader of the Peasant and Workers Union, because of his anti-Communist policy he fled his country in 1945. Later became President of the Bulgarian Refugee Committee in Washington.

p. 327, 27 LÉAUTAUD . . . Paul Léautaud. Until 1940 he was in charge of the *Mercure de France*. He had just published interviews with Robert Mallet, and this was greatly admired for its vivid language and brilliant portrayal of people and conversations.

p. 328, 31 N.R.F. . . . New French Revue.

p. 328, 35 MICHAUX . . . Henri Michaux was a talented painter/poet. Highly travelled in Far East and South America, he was enormously influenced by the Surrealist Movement in his art.

p. 328, 36 GIONO . . . Jean Giono has been respected for his tender novels in which there are great evocations of time, space and simple earthiness.

p. 329, 2 BOSSUET . . . Jacques Bossuet, 1664–1743. A philanthropist.

p. 329, 21 ETIEMBLE . . . René Etiemble, novelist and literary critic on *Temps Modernes* from 1946–52, was Professor of French Literature and Language at the University of Montpellier.

p. 330, 13 BRETON . . . André Breton. One of the founders of the Surrealist Movement, he was poet, writer, and painter. But because of his politics he was banished and spent the War years in the United States.

p. 330, 18 GUSTAVE THIBON . . . scholastic essayist who devoted his life to literature and philosophy. He was awarded the literature prize by the Academy in 1964.

p. 333, 28 GUICHARD . . . Olivier Guichard. Until July 1972 he was Minister of Education, since which time he has been Minister of Territorial Planning and Housing.

377

p. 339, 8   EDMOND BARRACHIN . . . Vice President of the parliamentary group of the R.P.F., and also for the Republican Social Action Group.

p. 339, 9   LEGENDRE . . . Jean Legendre, journalist, and one-time magistrate, also representative for L'Oise 1946–58 in the Assembly.

p. 341, 27   CLÉMENTIS . . . Vladimir Clémentis, lawyer and politician. He had been Under Secretary of State in 1945, and Minister of Foreign Affairs three years later in Czechoslovakia. Relieved of his post in 1950, he was arrested in 1951 and was hanged at the same time as Slansky.

p. 345, 24   DANIEL-ROPS . . . Henri Daniel-Rops. Religious historian, renowned for his *Jesus in his Own Time.*

p. 345, 24   MADAME HENRI FOCILLON . . . widow of the art historian.

p. 347, 34   RENÉ CLAIR . . . the film director, was also a writer and member of the French Academy.